D1527938

PSYCHOANALYSIS

and

PSYCHOTHERAPY

PSYCHOANALYSIS

and

PSYCHOTHERAPY

Selected Papers
of Frieda Fromm-Reichmann

Edited by

DEXTER M. BULLARD

Foreword by

EDITH V. WEIGERT

THE UNIVERSITY OF CHICAGO PRESS

CHICAGO & LONDON

THE UNIVERSITY OF CHICAGO COMMITTEE
ON PUBLICATIONS IN BIOLOGY AND MEDICINE

EMMET B. BAY · LOWELL T. COGGESHALL
LESTER R. DRAGSTEDT · PETER P. H. DE BRUYN
THOMAS PARK · WILLIAM H. TALIAFERRO

THE UNIVERSITY OF CHICAGO PRESS, CHICAGO 60637

The University of Chicago Press, Ltd., London

International Standard Book Number: 0-226-26595-1 (clothbound)
Library of Congress Catalog Card Number: 59-10746

FOREWORD

Frieda Fromm-Reichmann was a born psychotherapist. Her younger sister remembers a scene from their childhood in which Frieda threw herself between a threatening dog and the little sister with the words, "You don't need to be afraid!" This protective attitude toward the helpless younger one became characteristic of her relation to her patients in later life. Even as a child she knew that she wanted to be a doctor. The study of medicine was still a startlingly new and bold enterprise for a girl at the turn of the century in Koenigsberg, East Prussia, where she grew up, but her parents supported her aspirations. A kind and understanding father—he was a banker—and an energetically progressive mother helped her to traverse the unbeaten path which led to her graduation in medicine in 1914.

During World War I she took care of brain-injured soldiers as a member of the staff of Kurt Goldstein, who later also immigrated to the United States. Under his leadership she gained a solid foundation in the physiology and pathology of brain function. She acquired insights into the "catastrophic reactions" of brain-injured patients that prepared her for an understanding of psychotic panic states.

During the early 1920's Frieda became more and more interested in psychiatry and psychotherapy. She worked with I. H. Schultz at Weisser Hirsch, his sanitarium near Dresden, well known for its relaxation therapy called "autogenous training." Later on she became a visiting physician at Kraepelin's psychiatric clinic in Munich. Her discovery of Freud's writings led to a turning point in her professional career, for here she found many of her burning questions answered. The new understanding of transference phenomena, in particular, clarified aspects of the doctor-patient relationship that had puzzled her. After completing her psychoanalytic training she practiced in Heidelberg, establishing a private psychoanalytic sanitarium there; and, together with Erich Fromm, she founded the Psychoanalytic Training Institute of Southwest Germany.

Georg Groddeck, an original thinker and an ingenious therapist, played a stimulating role in the group of Heidelberg psychoanalysts to which Frieda Fromm-Reichmann belonged. The discoveries of Freud—who had taken over from Groddeck the term "id"—in turn had stimulated Groddeck's own understanding of symbolic communication, and Groddeck now boldly tackled the psychoanalytic treatment of somatic diseases with impressive results.

Adapted from a memorial paper by Dr. Edith V. Weigert published in *Psychiatry: Journal for the Study of Interpersonal Processes*, Vol. XXI, No. 1 (February, 1958). Copyright 1958 by The William Alanson White Psychiatric Foundation, Inc.

When Germany was overrun by National Socialism, Frieda Fromm-Reichmann was endangered by the persecution of the Jews and had to leave her homeland. Her first temporary refuge was in Alsace-Lorraine, which she chose because it enabled her to complete the psychoanalyses of some of her German patients. After another temporary stay, in Palestine, she immigrated to the United States. New horizons extended to encourage her professional development. While skepticism and prejudice had prevailed against psychoanalysis in Germany not only in the lay public but also among her psychiatric colleagues, she encountered a warm welcome in this country.

Wide opportunities to test psychoanalytic treatment of functional psychoses were offered to her by Dexter Bullard, himself a psychoanalyst, at Chestnut Lodge, his sanitarium in Rockville, Maryland. There, in an atmosphere of open-minded, enthusiastic understanding, her ingenuity blossomed, and she achieved, in the course of the years, surprising results in the treatment of psychoses.

At Chestnut Lodge, Frieda Fromm-Reichmann became a close friend of Harry Stack Sullivan, whose brilliant mind and deep understanding of schizophrenic thought processes stimulated her own ingenuity. She was able to respond to his sometimes irritating sensitivities with never-failing tact. If there was any competitive envy between these two congenial and yet very different friends, it was transcended by Frieda's forever youthful capacity for hero worship.

The four outstanding teachers in her life—Sigmund Freud, Kurt Goldstein, Georg Groddeck, and Harry Stack Sullivan—suggest the wide range of human potentialities which Frieda's mind was able to encompass. She remained receptive to all creative ideas in her field. She welcomed the modern development of ego analysis, initiated by Heinz Hartmann, Ernst Kris, and Rudolph M. Loewenstein, which stresses the integrative aspects of ego functions; it agreed with her own growing understanding of the integrative processes of the total personality.

Freud had considered the functional psychoses and narcissistic neuroses—in contrast to the transference neuroses—as inaccessible as yet to psychoanalytic method, although he expressed the hope that it might become possible to tackle them in the future. Frieda Fromm-Reichmann's research into disintegration and reintegration in schizophrenia threw new light on the study of schizophrenic as well as manic-depressive psychoses, borderline diseases, and typical psychoneuroses.

Frieda Fromm-Reichmann called her therapy of psychotic patients "psychoanalytically oriented psychotherapy," since she was aware that the quantitative and qualitative differences between the dynamics of psychotic and neurotic patients made some modifications of classical psychoanalysis necessary. In later years she stated, however, that these modifications were not so great as had at first been estimated. Her gradual evolution of thought is reflected in this book in the papers of Part III, "On Schizophrenia."

The center of Frieda's technique with psychotic patients was not so much interpretation as it was communication of understanding. Primarily, this understanding was directed less toward the content of the patient's productions than toward the phenomenon of his resistance. She worked, in particular, to elucidate all those defenses that had delayed and distorted his ego development, while protecting his acute sensitivity from experiencing massive anxieties. Frieda used to point out to her students that the schizophrenic overrates his hostility and the power and effectiveness of his destructive fantasies with which he tries to defend himself in his desperate isolation. His arrest at, or regression to, the narcissistic level makes it sometimes impossible for him to distinguish between thought and action, fantasy and reality. His system of defenses, however, increases his isolation and his guilt feelings.

Frieda Fromm-Reichmann's technique with schizophrenic patients was mainly directed toward the alleviation of these intense anxieties and guilt feelings. In the process of alleviation she rejected oversolicitude, however, and she avoided verbal reassurances, since the distrustful patient would regard such reassurances as bribery and exploitation of his intense dependency needs. Thus the reassurances would mobilize his anxieties and his defenses against closeness. She respected the schizophrenic's vigilant caution against such intrusion. She was even reluctant to offer interpretations herself and preferred to listen, without theoretical prejudice, to the schizophrenic patient, who is more surprisingly original and removed from conventional lines of thought than the neurotic. She was ready to learn from her patient, and if he was able to arrive at interpretations himself, this was so much the better for the fortification of his weak self-esteem. She never insisted that any single interpretation was the correct one; the complex and cryptic communications of the schizophrenic permit multiple facets of interpretation which have to be timed according to the patient's ability to assimilate them.

Toward the termination of treatment she usually reviewed the history of the illness with the patient and discussed the findings of analysis, thereby helping him to establish continuity between the morbid and the healthy periods of his life. Through her respectful understanding she was able to win the patient for a collaborative teamwork that put him back on his feet and formed a bridge between him and those sectors of reality from which he had withdrawn. At last, together, they could remove the scaffolding of highly ambivalent transference by which the teamwork of reconstruction had been aided or, at times, disturbed.

Frieda Fromm-Reichmann's technique in the treatment of psychotics was particularly characterized by the high degree of awareness which she demanded from herself and from her students in the observation of countertransference. While she considered mild degrees of anxiety on the part of the therapist a stimulus for empathic understanding, she was convinced that the relatively unanxious therapist could achieve the greatest amount of collaboration with his patient, since his lack of anxiety would be helpful in dissolving the patient's fear of his own unbearable malevolence. She was fully aware of the anxiety which the psychotic patient can arouse in the therapist; for instance, the delay of therapeutic progress can painfully attack the therapist's narcissism, as can the patient's potential or actual assaultiveness, inaccessible loneliness, or suspicion that the therapist might exploit any progress as his own success. When anxieties in the analyst become great enough to mobilize defenses, inhibiting his alertness, and produce the need for compensation through positive or negative countertransference, she advised her students to seek help through discussions with colleagues or through such available technical help as the assistance of an administrator in the treatment situation. This doctor-patient relationship and its demands on the doctor constitute the main topic of Section II.

It seems to me that Frieda Fromm-Reichmann's success was based not only on her knowledge and experience but also on the exceptional character qualities which she brought to her challenging experiments. Frieda was courageous. That does not mean that she was free from anxieties. She was highly sensitive—otherwise she could not have accompanied her patients so fully into the depths of despair, into the horrors of loneliness, into the frantic impulses of destructive rage. But she did not flinch. She was all there with the patient. I am inclined to assume that such courage on the part of the therapist, transcending the anxieties in the interpersonal situation, is an important factor in tuning down the patient's anxieties. Frieda Fromm-Reichmann recognized the extravagant passions of psychotic transference. More than that, she detected the frequent inclination of the psychiatrist to escape into defensive counter-transference whenever the onslaught of the patient's despair becomes too much for him. But Frieda did not escape into professional toughness or indifference, into psychiatric pompousness, into sentimental conspiracy with the patient's infantilism, or into moral exhortations which would further burden the patient with crushing guilt feelings. She faced the patient firmly, with the presence of her whole personality—simple and straightforward, without pretense and without grandiose ambitions—brushing aside the barriers of conventionality. She remained fully open, with a broad attention not narrowed down by preconceived ideas, to what lies beyond transference and countertransference in the realistic interpersonal relation between doctor and patient.

And sooner or later the schizophrenic patient realized that he was no longer alone, that here was a human being who understood, who did not turn away in estrangement or disgust. This rare moment of discovery—unpredictable and unforeseen, like a gift of grace—sometimes became a turning point in the patient's life. The gates of human fellowship were opened, and thereby the slow way to recovery was opened also. When the patient remained distrustful, suspicious, encapsulated, Frieda was able to wait. When the highly sensitive patient showed signs of having been hurt by verbal communication—or more often by nonverbal communication—she was sincerely able to apologize. Her courage enabled her also to respect the recalcitrant patient and his limits of understanding. Even though a patient was deeply deteriorated, she could envisage the potentialities of integration of his total personality. I shall not forget the radiant joy with which Frieda once returned from the wedding of a patient whom she had helped to emerge from a severe schizophrenic illness as a whole, creative personality with liberated gifts of artistic self-expression.

Older and younger colleagues rallied around Frieda Fromm-Reichmann at Chestnut Lodge, in the psychoanalytic and psychiatric societies, in the Washington School of Psychiatry, in the William Alanson White Institute in New York, and in the recently founded Academy of Psychoanalysis. She was able to evoke in the younger generation enthusiasm and an eagerness to emulate her. She was a most generous teacher and friend of her younger colleagues. To supervision she gave her full presence, grasping with alertness the total situation, in all its complexities, which the student presented. She was able to put her finger on the gaps and evasions, the sore spots, in the doctor-patient relation. Her criticisms seldom hurt, because they were usually so startlingly true and so adequate to the needs of both the doctor and his patient. Frieda did not lose herself in theoretical argumentations. She was, above all, a very practical clinician, able to grasp the interpersonal situation and to see, in the course of the therapy, the points at which the dissociative processes might be bridged and the patient's self-acceptance re-established.

Frieda Fromm-Reichmann has laid down some of her ideas in her book, *Principles of Intensive Psychotherapy*.[1] Here again, the reader catches the spirit of courage, devotion, and integrity which characterized her relations to all the mentally handicapped. Among her research projects she worked on topics concerned with the function of intuition and the problem of loneliness. A first draft of her paper "On Loneliness" is the final chapter of this book. It is characteristic of her research work that her integrity did not permit her to use any formulations that had not really become her own through experience. She generally avoided the technical

[1] Chicago: University of Chicago Press, 1950.

lingo that might foster intellectual labeling devoid of integrating experience.

In 1952 Frieda Fromm-Reichmann received the Adolf Meyer Award for contributions to the understanding of neurosis. In 1955 she gave the Academic Lecture to the American Psychiatric Association, Paper 15 of the present volume. During 1955–56 she was a Fellow at the Center for Advanced Study in the Behavioral Sciences in Stanford, California, where she enjoyed the life on the "magic mountain" of interdisciplinary exchange and gained new allies and friends. While she was there, she studied, in particular, the nonverbal aspects of communication, and she returned with joy and gratitude from this stimulating experience. She was invited to give a lecture at the Second International Congress for Psychiatry in Zurich, Switzerland, in September, 1957. Her paper "Basic Problems in the Psychotherapy of Schizophrenia" was read at the Congress after her death. It is reprinted here as Paper 16.

Deep shadows fell across her rich life. The fate of Israel, where her sisters and many of the friends of her youth live in political and economic danger, weighed heavily on her mind. She did her best to relieve their hardships. Frieda missed a family life. No one could watch her play with children, or with her dog, without knowing how deprived she felt by not having had a child of her own.

There were hours when this courageous woman became deeply discouraged. She knew well what her disturbed patients talked about—more than that, she knew what they were silent about. An inherited impairment of hearing threatened her in her most vital interest—listening to people. It limited her participation in group discussion. When Frieda became discouraged, she did not want anybody to know about it, for she did not like to burden her friends. It was therefore difficult to be helpful to her. Since so many patients and students depended on her, she felt obliged to keep up a good front even when she felt lonely and distressed.

When she was struck by a virus infection early in 1957, she felt an exhaustion which touched off in her some premonitions of death. She faced the shadows of the ultimate farewell with the same courage with which she had faced all human tragedy. Her fundamental uprightness seems to me to be best characterized by Paul Tillich's phrase "the courage to be." This courage to be, this uprightness in having existed, has a perennial ring. Transcending death, it leaves us the image of Frieda Fromm-Reichmann which, in its intense aliveness, we will never forget.

EDITH WEIGERT

CHEVY CHASE, MARYLAND

EDITOR'S PREFACE

Early in 1935 Dr. Frieda Fromm-Reichmann saw the handwriting on the wall in Germany and decided to come to this country. In July of that year she came to Chestnut Lodge, at first as a summer replacement during the vacation period. Because of her previous work with psychotic patients in her own institution in Heidelberg, she felt at home working with schizophrenic patients in this country. Many times she commented that, while cultural differences between Europe and the United States made the analysis of neurotic patients difficult for her in the beginning, the thinking of schizophrenic patients seemed almost identical in the two cultures.

What was originally intended as a two months' association at the Lodge lengthened into twenty-two years. Then, on April 28, 1957, it was suddenly terminated; Frieda Fromm-Reichmann had died from an acute coronary thrombosis at the age of 67 in her home at Chestnut Lodge.

In the circle of her friends the wish arose to preserve and concentrate Frieda Fromm-Reichmann's thoughts and ideas, which were spread out in many scientific papers. Dr. Otto A. Will, Jr., one of her outstanding former students, initiated the idea of this book of selected papers and did the preparatory work. It represents her papers written in the United States but does not include the many papers she wrote in Germany between 1914 and 1931. A bibliography of these German papers is included here (pp. 337–39). We are grateful to Dr. Will for his enthusiastic efforts on behalf of this publication. Funds for preparing the manuscript were supplied by the Washington Psychoanalytic Society through its committee consisting of Dr. T. Douglas Noble, Dr. Otto A. Will, Jr., and Dr. Edith V. Weigert, chairman.

Some people influence others by the force of their personalities and the contagion of their enthusiasms. Others, less socially amiable and gregarious, present their work for consideration and evaluation through the medium of the printed word. Frieda Fromm-Reichmann combined in felicitous proportions both these attributes. Her intuitive skill was the envy of many and was equalled by few of her colleagues. Yet her message came through to all in both the spoken and the written word.

Those who for the first time saw her tiny figure mount the platform, lower the microphone to her four feet, ten inches, and look out from the podium were in for a pleasant experience as she charmingly and surely captivated her audience. The mobility of her features, her smiles, her frowns, her mimicry, her mixture of humor and seriousness, were all part of a superb showmanship. Behind this showmanship, however, was the solid, painstaking work that had gone on with her patients perhaps for months, perhaps for several years, and that she drew on for her lively presentations.

She knew that the normal in the patient was of paramount importance, and she appealed to this aspect of the personality over and over again in her therapeutic work.

She also knew that there was really nothing abnormal about the abnormal, and that what seemed so might be made logically understandable as the historical development of a bit of psychopathology was elucidated.

She knew and conveyed to others her belief, founded on many years of careful and astute observation, that patients never make mistakes about matters of vital importance to themselves. She sensed that they are correct in their assessment of the basic attitudes of persons significant to them, and she was not misled in evaluating the hidden meanings of the infinite variety of ways schizophrenic patients express themselves.

Her ability to convey the essence of her philosophy through her writings will, I believe, lead to these papers being read and reread for many years to come.

It is a pleasure and a privilege to have been her friend and colleague.

DEXTER M. BULLARD

CHESTNUT LODGE
ROCKVILLE, MARYLAND

TABLE OF CONTENTS

IV. ON MANIC-DEPRESSIVE PSYCHOSIS

V. ON GENERAL PSYCHIATRIC PROBLEMS

VI. EPILOGUE

I

On the Philosophy of the Problem

(1)

REMARKS ON THE PHILOSOPHY
OF MENTAL DISORDER

Several years ago a South American woman in her early thirties, whom I shall call Margherita, was under treatment with me for a serious mental disorder. She had been suffering for eight years from schizophrenia, catatonic type, and had part of the time been in a catatonic stupor, that is, mute and practically without motion; there had been no voluntary food intake or elimination. At other periods she was assaultive and given to self-mutilation, and she had made several suicidal attempts.

This young woman had been for four years at several mental hospitals in her South American home state, and then another four years under intensive psychotherapy with me at the Chestnut Lodge Sanitarium, until she reached, at last, a state of full recovery and personality maturation. In our therapeutic interviews, she had gained insight into the dynamics of her previous mental disorder, and she had become sufficiently aware of her interpersonal relationships to be able to handle them. She returned to her native country and has lived there successfully since then without needing any psychiatric help.

During the last two years of her treatment and hospitalization she had started to write some poetry and poetic prose, partly in English, partly in Spanish. Since her productions seemed to show remarkable talent, I sent them to a well-known poet and art critic in order to make sure that this was not just a nice pastime for an otherwise not too articulate schizophrenic person but an expression of artistic creativeness which deserved encouragement. The critic confirmed my initial impression; and thereafter the woman's productivity was encouraged for therapeutic reasons. It seemed important in the process of this recovery of a schizoid personality to have her find valid means of artistic expression, all the more so since I did not consider it the goal of the treatment for the young woman to learn to lead a conventional life with the standard means of social adjustment used by the average so-called healthy citizen in this culture.

Presented before the Society on the Study of Personality, the Academy of Medicine in New York, May 1, 1946.

Reprinted from *Psychiatry: Journal of the Biology and Pathology of Interpersonal Relations*, Vol. IX, No. 4 (November, 1949). Copyright by The William Alanson White Psychiatric Foundation, Inc.

Since then Margherita has published a considerable number of poems in various English and Spanish art magazines, has won several poetry contests, and is now assembling her works for publication in book form.

Shortly before this woman's projected dismissal from Chestnut Lodge Sanitarium was put into effect, she went one day to the municipal hospital whose job it is to decide whether a mental patient needs hospitalization or not; there she complained of being kept at the sanitarium against her will. Upon her return, she reported these events to me, and I asked myself what could have moved the young woman to complain on the eve of her dismissal about being kept at the sanitarium against her will. At first, I did not find the answer. Suddenly it dawned upon me, and I asked her why she was afraid to get really well, the connotation being the following: The patient went to see a psychiatrist who did not know the history of her illness and treatment, shortly before her psychotherapist considered her ready to leave the hospital—that is, at the time when she was still considered to be in need of treatment as an outpatient by the psychiatrist who had known her for a long time. This could only mean that she was afraid to go through the last psychotherapeutic phase with her own psychotherapist. When I questioned her about this, the patient broke into spontaneous, healthy tears and said, "Are you surprised at my being afraid; how could I help it? Remember, I have been in mental hospitals for eight years. All my friends and relatives have been living their lives during these years, and I could not participate. How do you expect me ever to catch up with them?"

My serious answer was, "That is true; however, you have gathered during these years a tremendous amount of human experience, having had the opportunity to observe practically all types of emotional experience in your fellow patients and in yourself. And what are these emotional experiences of the mentally disturbed other than human experiences of the kind we all go through, seen as if under a magnifying glass?"

This I said not for the sake of reassurance, for which a schizoid personality such as Margherita would not "go" anyhow. I said it because of my belief that it was actually so and in the spirit of putting something into words which Margherita would realize immediately, once this knowledge was recalled to her awareness. Upon hearing me, Margherita stopped crying and said, "You mean to say it is just a matter of the courage to look at life from the other side of the fence?"

I have started with this account from the treatment history of this former mental patient because it contains in brief what I have to say about the philosophy of mental disorder; and I want to elaborate on four points which follow from this account:

1. Serious mental disturbance—psychosis—can potentially be treated successfully by a collaborative effort between the mentally disturbed person and

the psychiatrist as participant observer, with modified psychoanalysis—dynamically oriented intensive psychotherapy—even after many years' duration.

2. A person can emerge from a severe mental disorder as an artist of rank. His previous liabilities in terms of his pathogenic, history, the expression of his subsequent mental disorder—that is, symptomatology—or his inner responses to either of them can be converted into assets.

3. The emotionally and mentally disturbed reactions which Margherita and her hospitalized fellow patients showed are different in degree only, and not in kind, from the emotional and mental experiences and modes of expression of so-called healthy people.

4. Special sensitiveness, alertness, and consideration for the past and present suffering of the mentally disturbed are required from the psychiatrist who wants to understand what these people have to convey. How do the special sensitiveness, alertness, and considerateness, which the psychiatrist has to develop in his dealings with the mentally hurt and disturbed, influence interpersonal contacts with the emotionally healthy?

Let me elaborate first on my third point, that the emotional and mental experiences and modes of expression of mentally disturbed and of not disturbed people differ only in quantity and not in quality. This fact is well known to any psychiatrist who experiences it as a participant-observer while doing modern, intensive psychotherapy with his patients. In addition, I would like to prove this point by discussing two sets of facts: first, the common denominator in physical symptoms, mental symptoms, and modes of emotional expression in the healthy and, second, the similarity between the mental productions of the psychotics while they are awake and the mental productions of the so-called healthy while they are asleep, that is, in their dreams.

Every general practitioner knows that many physical symptoms are not only the expression of the patient's disease but also an expression of the tendency in the physical organism toward regaining health.

Take, for example, a patient who suffers from cardiac disease. He may rush up a flight of stairs and almost faint as he reaches the top, the fainting being an expression of his cardiac disease as well as a warning signal not to enter into the serious danger of repeating this effort. Now think of a patient who wounds himself with an infected article. A wall of white blood cells—pus—will be built up around the wound. There will be local pain and inflammation; yet at the same time this wall of white blood cells, which constitutes the symptomatology of a local inflammation, will serve as a protection against the spreading of the infection, thus preventing a local infection from turning into a generalized one. A third and last example: a patient is suffering from bronchitis; among other signs he will show the symptom of coughing. At the same time, the coughing helps toward discharge of mucous substance, thereby freeing the bronchi from this mucous substance and facilitating the clearing-up of the bronchitic process.

The same holds true for processes of mental illness. Its symptoms, too, both express the illness and show the mentally disturbed person's tendency toward mental health, that is, toward adjustive success in his relationships with other people.

For example, a patient may suffer from compulsive hand-washing; that is, he feels he has to wash his hands each time he touches an object or a person which may contaminate him. Such hand-washing may take place any number of times, say from five to twenty or more times a day, and come to interfere seriously with the smooth-running maintenance of the patient's relationships with other people, all the more so since his hands will soon look red and chapped, thus leading him to hide them, if not himself, from other people. Should this person, however, resist his compulsion, then his fear of being contaminated, which he tries to counteract with the compulsive hand-washing, would become so severe that that in turn would interfere even more with healthy interpersonal adjustments than does the compulsive hand-washing. The compulsion is thus an expression of a mental disturbance but also an attempt to alleviate it.

Again, a patient has withdrawn his interest from the outward world; he is aloof, detached, and uncommunicative; he shows the symptoms of a schizophrenic disturbance. But this symptomatology may be this person's way of avoiding the danger of "another rebuke," as one patient put it.[1] The patient shows withdrawal of interest, aloofness, and detachment, which are signs of his schizophrenic disturbance, as a means of protecting himself from additional fear and potential hostility, which might be aroused against the person who evokes the fear and against the people in his previous life who have done so before.

As another example, consider a patient who shows a negativistic attitude as a sign of mental disturbance; that is, he may not feel like doing anything that is suggested to him just because it has been suggested, or he may be driven to do the opposite. Such behavior constitutes, indeed, a serious disturbance in the patient's contacts with other people. Yet, at the same time, the patient may show this because he has given up hope of ever getting attention from his fellow men in any other way. Hence his negativistic behavior also constitutes an attempt at maintaining or re-establishing interpersonal contacts, an attempt in the direction toward mental health.[2]

Think now of an obsessional patient who shows the symptoms of obscure power actions and all types of magic performances which interfere with the healthy setup of human interrelationships. I think, for example,

1. Frieda Fromm-Reichmann, "A Preliminary Note on the Emotional Significance of Stereotypes in Schizophrenics," *Bull. Forest Sanitarium*, I, 17–21.

2. Harry Stack Sullivan, "Conceptions of Modern Psychiatry," *Psychiatry*, III (1940), 1–117, see esp. p. 39.

of a patient who made it her job to stand for many an hour on many consecutive days at the corner of the street where I was living, in order to secure the secret satisfaction of finding out, in spite of me, what coat I was wearing. Another one hoped to exert magic power over me after having succeeded in finding out what toilet water I used and then using the same kind herself.

What time- and energy-consuming, obscure, and magic attempts at exerting power over another person! What an interference with the establishment of healthy human relationships! Yet again these signs of severe interpersonal difficulties serve at the same time to hide a lifelong insecurity and constitute an attempt at remedying this insecurity. In other words, they are an attempt at maintaining what is left of the obsessional person's self-esteem or at re-establishing it. This, however, means an attempt at maintaining or re-establishing relationships with other people, because one can respect others only to the extent that one respects oneself. Or, to put it differently, one can love others only to the extent that one loves oneself.[3]

The Bible expresses the same idea in "Love thy neighbor as thyself," meaning that you cannot love him more than you love yourself. Let us forget about the masochistic interpretation of this biblical quotation by which this statement is supposed to mean that one should love one's fellow men more than oneself; such interpretation is an outgrowth of the present masochistic and unwise culture. It has nothing to do with the original concept, in which a decent self-love and a reasonable self-respect are considered to be the roots of decent and healthy human relationships.

The symptomatology of the obsessional is, therefore, just like the symptomatology in the three other examples of mental symptom formation, not only an expression of mental disorder but also an expression of an attempt at re-establishing mental equilibrium in terms of maintaining and re-establishing valid interpersonal relationships.

Let us ask now: Does this statement about the two-sided motivation of emotional expression in the mentally disturbed sound familiar to many persons, because they are aware of the same two-sided motivation in their own interpersonal adjustive processes?

What happens, for example, when one feels angry? The anger stands first for itself, as an unpleasant interference with one's smooth-running contacts with other people. However, frequently enough it stands at the same time as a self-deceiving mask of anxiety, anger being the only emotional discharge from anxious tension to which a person may dare to give vent. Direct display of anxiety in our culture goes with an alleged loss of prestige in the eyes of other people and with a loss of self-esteem. Thus it creates a more severe disturbance in interpersonal relationships than does the release of anger. Hence conversion of anxiety into anger

3. *Ibid.*; see also Erich Fromm, "Selfishness and Self-Love," *Psychiatry*, II (1939), 507–23.

represents successful interpersonal adjustment, and anger expresses both an unpleasant interpersonal experience and an attempt to avoid the more unpleasant interpersonal experience of anxiety.

Consider, now, the people, known to all of us, who are given to boasting and bragging, thus showing a picture of pseudo-euphoria, seemingly characterized by a disproportion between their self-appreciation and the appreciation of their accomplishments by their fellow men. Frequently this seeming euphoria is nothing but a deceiving mask for a person's low self-esteem. Where there is low self-esteem, there is, as said before, low esteem of others and fear of low appreciation by other people. Both feelings constitute, of course, a serious interference with a healthy interpersonal adjustment, so that a mild megalomania, as described above, is not only the sign of a disturbance in one's relationship with oneself and with others but also an expression of an adjustive attempt in maintaining a satisfactory relationship with oneself and with one's fellow men.

From these examples, one can see that many emotional experiences and modes of expression in healthy people have in common with the symptoms of the mentally ill and of the mentally handicapped the fact that both may be understood as an expression of disrupted interpersonal contacts as well as the expression of the human mind's tending toward maintenance or re-establishment of mental health in terms of security and satisfaction in one's interpersonal adjustments.

Hence it follows that my thesis is correct, that the difference between the emotional experiences and modes of expression of the mentally healthy and the mentally disturbed is one of quantity and not of quality. As Sullivan puts it: "In most general terms, we are all much more simply human than otherwise, be we happy and successful, contented and detached, miserable and mentally disordered or whatever."[4]

Another proof that this statement is correct—surprising though it may seem to some people—is the similarity of the mental processes of the so-called healthy while asleep, known as "dreams," and the mental processes of the mentally disturbed. There are hallucinations, illusions, and delusions in both. There is disturbance in logical thinking or expression, change in concepts of time and space. There are displacements, condensations, and distortions in feeling regarding the persons toward whom the process is directed. Frequently there is the expression in pictures, images, and allusions instead of in words, in both dream productions and the productions of the mentally disturbed.[5]

Sullivan and the Austrian psychoanalysts Silberer and Tausk have

4. Sullivan, *op. cit.*

5. C. G. Jung, *The Psychology of Dementia Praecox* (New York: Nervous and Mental Disease Pub. Co., 1936), see esp. pp. 10–11, 21, 82, 83; Sigmund Freud, *Basic Writings* ("Modern Library" ed.), see section on "Dream Interpretations"; see also Sullivan, op. cit., pp. 33 ff.

studied the changes in mental operations which people undergo under utter fatigue and while gradually falling asleep. They show the same similarity to the operations of the mentally disturbed in the making as the dream processes ultimately do. Silberer describes, among other examples, the following illustrative conversion of thought processes into imagery:[6]

While falling asleep, he was pondering about a complex philosophical problem, the correct solution and formulation of which seemed to offer insurmountable difficulties. Following this, he saw himself at one bank of a stream, knowing that he should cross that stream but feeling that there were insurmountable difficulties in doing so because he could not see any bridge. This way of expressing thought processes in pictures, as all persons experience it while falling asleep and while dreaming, is exactly of a piece with the dynamics of many mental processes in the mentally ill. This means that every so-called healthy person goes in his dreams through a transitory psychotic state, of a piece with the condition that the mentally disturbed undergoes persistently while awake until he regains mental health.

If one is given to teleological thinking, one can believe that the transitory psychotic state undergone by everyone while dreaming may serve as a safeguard against mental illness. In this connection the words of the German philosopher Nietzsche should be remembered: "The man who does not lose his mind over certain things has no mind to lose."

To illustrate how serious modern psychotherapists are in their concept of the similarity between the dynamics of dream processes and mental processes in the mentally disturbed, I may mention in passing that the recital of dreams in psychotics, especially schizophrenics, is discouraged for the purposes of psychotherapy. It is felt that the experiences which they communicate from their waking life have so much of a dreamlike character that the reproduction of their mental experiences while asleep will only add to their state of disturbance and not contribute to therapeutically valid insight.

So much for the suggestion that the differences between the mentally healthy and the mentally disturbed are of degree and not of kind, of which the double proof may be seen in the similarity in the dynamics of the symptoms of the mentally disturbed and the types of emotional experience and modes of expression in the mentally stable and in the similarity between dream processes and psychotic productions. Both show the same two-sided motivation, and they are different only in intensity, not in principle.

Now as to my second statement, that a person can emerge from serious

6. Sullivan, *op. cit.*, p. 72; Herbert Silberer, *Der Traum—Einführung in die Traum-Psychologie* (Stuttgart, 1919); Victor Tausk, "Zwei homosexuelle Träume," *Internat. Ztschr. Psychoanal.*, II (1914), 36–39 (no English translation of Tausk is available).

mental disturbance of many years' duration as a creative artist. In elaborating this, I shall not comment on the complex problem of the psychology of artistic creativeness, which is outside my field and beyond the scope of this paper. I want only to discuss the possibility of the conversion of a person's mental liabilities into various types of assets, among them poetic creativeness, as in the case of the girl Margherita. She grew up in utter loneliness in a family group in which there was bareness of any understanding of the values which mattered to her and where she was forced to accept her family's values. This utter loneliness and isolation made, first, for the development of her mental illness, yet ultimately also for her ability to express her lonely strivings in poetic language.

This is one way of converting the liabilities of a traumatic life-history with subsequent mental disturbance into a creative asset.

A second possibility is that a person may be able to turn the skills and powers, whose development was forced upon him in counteracting his difficulties in living, and the mental symptomatology derived from it toward a creative end.

Consider, for example, a factory worker, Mary, the unwanted eldest daughter of an alcoholic father who used all his earnings to buy liquor and of a chronically overworked mother who had to earn the living for the entire family, which included five younger siblings who had come a year apart. It was Mary's job, from her third year, to take care of the babies, and she learned early to protect them as best she could from what she herself had suffered: the assaultiveness of an alcoholic father, the irritability of an overworked mother against her unwanted children, and the physically and emotionally unhealthy atmosphere of unsanitary, overcrowded, and noisy quarters. When she was sixteen, Mary escaped this atmosphere by getting married to an alcoholic husband. Because of the sensitiveness and skills she had acquired in her own childhood, she was able to protect her own children from what she and her siblings had suffered until her little family ran so completely out of money, as a result of her alcoholic husband's losing his job, that they had to let her nagging in-laws, whom her husband had previously maintained, live with them in their small apartment. The repetition of life in inescapably noisy, overcrowded quarters, where she could no longer protect her babies from facing the results of their alcoholic father's and their now overworked mother's ill moods—that is, the pressure from the repetition of her own thwarting childhood experiences—led to a schizophrenic break. A skilful psychiatric social worker succeeded in finding out from Mary the reasons for her breakdown. She secured separate living quarters for Mary's in-laws; temporarily a separate bedroom for Mary; and, guided by Mary's ability to express her longing for privacy and quiet, a special job in the factory where Mary had worked before—precision work, which had to be done in a separate room by a skilled worker who did not mind being by herself. This work was disliked by the other workers because of the solitude which went with it. With Mary's pathological hypersensitivity to crowds, this was just what she wanted, and she recovered from her schizophrenic breakdown while doing it; that is, she became one of the many schizoid persons who succeed in turning their symptomatology into a creative asset. Her work was also a valuable contribution to the war effort of her country.

Another way in which mentally incapacitated people may be able to turn their difficulties into assets is by "sublimation." These people may succeed in unwittingly solving their difficulties in living by combining their anxiety-provoking, socially inacceptable tendencies—such as one finds as reason for, and as outcome of, any mental disorder—with socially acceptable techniques of living which the culture provides.[7] Thus they succeed in turning their mental liabilities into assets.

To illustrate—John, the oldest son of happily married parents who gave him their undivided love, was faced at the age of three with the arrival of a brother with whom he had to share the parental love. His parents had neglected to prepare him adequately. Subsequently, he found himself hating a darling little brother who deprived him of part of the parental attention and hating kind and understanding parents who made him share their love with the little brother. From this utterly painful childhood experience which repeated itself time and again in subsequent years according to John's interpretation of life-events, he learned that it was necessary to stay away from people, lest one might find oneself loving them or being loved by them, only to head for subsequent disappointments from which one would come to hate these same people. Having great artistic abilities, he studied sculpturing and used his talent to model people who frightened him with the threat of mutual closeness. Thus the possibility of human intimacy was turned each time into an impersonal artistic experience. In other words, John succeeded in turning his socially inacceptable fear of getting into undesirable love-hatred entanglements with people into creative accomplishments which are appreciated in the culture.

Other creative people who are hindered by their mental difficulties in getting what they want from life may be able to make an asset of their unfulfilled longing for the unattainable. They may feel so keenly that they are unable to get what seems desirable to them that they try to counteract grief or sickness over the lack by creative expression of that which they cannot live. These are then the people whose lives are so strikingly in contrast to their teachings or other spiritual performances or creations. If not many of them, at least some of them, are able to give spiritual life to the vision of what their actual lives should be like, not in spite of, but because of, their inability to live it. Too handicapped to live what they want, yet sensitized and pushed by their ever so strong, yet unfulfilled, longing, they are specifically equipped and called upon to give creative expression and to erect a spiritual monument, as it were, to their ardent desires which have to remain unsatisfied in actuality. In so doing, they may also safeguard against additional difficulties in living by

7. Sullivan, *op cit.*, pp. 61 ff.

which they are threatened because of the constant pressure of their unfulfilled desires.

This possibility of turning liabilities into assets is another example of the two-sided motivation of human modes of expression.

Cultural history furnishes an immortal example of the functioning of this mechanism in the life and work of the philosopher Arthur Schopenhauer. He led the life of an isolated, haughty, paranoid, megalomanic hater and cynic. He looked down upon his father, and he hated his mother, who, being the inspiring muse and the spiritual center of a salon for the famous writers and artists of her time, showed no sign of furthering her young son's accomplishments. When he told her that he had won an honorable prize for his first philosophical thesis, "Note on the Fourfold Root of Sufficient Reason," his mother's answer was "I did not know that you were interested in botany." After this experience, it is not surprising that young Schopenhauer developed an intense hatred for women and a distrust of them.

In keeping with his cynical and haughty general personality development, Schopenhauer was opposed to the popular revolutionary movements of his time. Yet what did this lonely hater of people in general, of women, and of the suppressed classes in particular teach in his writings?

In his *Notes on the Basic Principles of Ethics*, he teaches that "all human beings are alike and identical in a metaphysical sense," that "all virtues and ethical values arise from the intuitive knowledge of human equality," and that "sympathy and compassion" are the "basis of justice and of all ethical concepts."

If one reads Schopenhauer's *World as Will and Idea* under the viewpoint of reflections of the author's unresolved difficulties in living and of his unfulfilled longings, one will find many data to corroborate my thesis that this schizoid, paranoid philosopher succeeded in converting his unfulfilled longing for the unattainable into the eternal spiritual monument which is his philosophical writings.[8]

Talking about Schopenhauer takes the investigation of the assets of people with mental difficulties out of the realm of my personal experience into the realm of world-famous examples to which every reader could add any number from his own knowledge. Let me recall the great mentally disturbed poets Hoelderlin, Lenau, and Oscar Wilde; the writers Edgar Allan Poe and Charlotte Brontë; and the composers Schumann and Tchaikovski. Think also of the mental difficulties of the great painter Van Gogh, torn throughout his life between art and religion and driven from the gray monotony of his Dutch homeland by an irresistible long-

8. For a short orientation on Schopenhauer's life and work see Irwin Edman, *The Philosophy of Schopenhauer* ("Modern Library" ed.) His collected papers have been translated into English by Haldane, Saunders, Bullock, and Thompson.

ing for the sun, "not its rays, but the sun itself!" As a result of this compulsive longing, he went south—southern France—in search of the sun. Under the influence of his religious longing and his striving for the sun, he built the sunflower-covered, bright-yellow "House of Friendship," where artists were supposed to live and work together in the spirit of original Christian communism. His vision did not materialize, but his unfulfilled and eternally unreconciled longings for life and love, sun, religion, and art were converted into the creativeness as a result of which he gave the world, within two years, the incredible collection of colorful paintings which are so widely known.

When, at last, the artist Gauguin came to visit and live with Van Gogh in the "House of Friendship," the visit was a complete and very painful failure. This was taken by Van Gogh as a definite proof that his dreams of unifying art and friendship, love, sun, and religion could not be fulfilled. He broke down and was hospitalized voluntarily. Several paintings of the mental hospitals where he lived, the portrait of one of his attendants, and one later of his psychiatrist friend, Dr. Gachet, are creative monuments of the time of his illness. Only his very last paintings show clear marks of mental disorder in the great artist, who was to end his life a prey of his difficulties in living. The lonely, disillusioned, mentally disordered artist shot himself while leaning against the lonely tree which we all know from several of his paintings.[9]

I have mentioned the composer Robert Schumann as another example of a person who converted the liabilities of a serious mental disorder into assets of eternal creative value. This schizophrenic artist was so withdrawn, seclusive, and disinclined to talk that, instead of talking, he started very early to depict his emotional experiences in musical compositions. This statement is not my interpretation of his works but comes from the composer's statements. It holds, for instance, for his lovely piano compositions "Scenes from Childhood," or even more so for "The Davidities' March," in which he musically depicted the various aspects of his own personality as he experienced them: he is Florestan, the passionate fighter, on the one hand; Eusebius, the melancholy dreamer, on the other; and Master Raro, the umpire who observes his split in personality.

9. From the vast literature on Van Gogh, the classical biographical study by Julius Meier-Graefe should be mentioned, translated into English by John Holroyd Reece (2 vols.), published in 1922 and 1926 by the Medici Society, London and Boston; in 1928 by Payson and Clarke, New York; in 1933 by Harcourt, Brace, New York; and in 1936 by Michael Joseph, London. An excellent short biography and evaluation of Van Gogh's work, with first-rate reproductions of his paintings in color and in black and white is Wilhelm Uhde's *The Life and Work of Vincent Van Gogh* (Vienna and New York: Phaidon Press). There is a novel based on the life of Vincent Van Gogh by Irving Stone, *Lust for Life* ("Modern Library" ed.). Pathographical studies have been done by Jaspers, "Strindberg and Van Gogh," *Research in Applied Psychiatry* (1922), p. 5; and by Walther Riese, "Vincent Van Gogh in der Krankheit," *Grenzfragen des Nerven und Seelenlebens,* Vol. CXXV (Munich: J. F. Bergmann, 1926).

Another outcome of Schumann's schizoid verbal inarticulateness was his use of the great poetry of some of his contemporaries in courting his wife and expressing his love to her. This is, according to the statements in some of his letters to his mother, how he came to use the famous poetry of others as texts for the composition of many of his famous songs, "Frauenliebe und Leben," and so on.[10]

Schumann's dislike for speaking may also be held responsible for his being the only composer of his time, except Richard Wagner, to write an opera without recitatives. This opera, *Genoveva*, is not one of Schumann's great compositions. Schizophrenic artist that he was, he was too little interested in dramatics, in contrast to lyrics and epics, to write good opera. Nothing but the overture to *Genoveva* is performed today. However, the composition of operas without recitatives has been of real importance in the further development of this style of composition.

In reflecting on Schumann's life and art in relationship to his mental disturbance, I would consider that his career as composer was, comparatively speaking, a happy outcome of his illness. After having tried his wings as writer and as lawyer, he decided to become a pianist. In order to do away with one of the technical problems of every pianist—how to accomplish independence in action of the fourth and fifth finger—he built a queer little device, such as only a schizoid person would evolve, and practiced on it with fanatical determination until he had ruined the function of his forth and fifth fingers, thus bringing to an end any possible career as a pianist. From what is known of Schumann's history and of the few recitals he gave, it could be assumed that he would not have become too successful a concert pianist anyhow because of his schizoid lack of contact with and interest in his audience. Certainly, Schumann's mental difficulties were responsible for the fact that the world is the richer for one more great composer, whatever the expense to his contemporaries in the loss of a pianist.[11]

To add a few more examples of those people greatly handicapped in mind, but with equally great assets, the development of which is due to their handicaps, let us take first the inarticulate, at times practically mute, schizophrenic dancer Nijinsky. He used bodily movement instead of spoken words, which failed him, as a means of self-expression in the highest style of the art. Most readers, at least those who are interested in the art of dancing, may remember some of the delightful performances by this schizophrenic artist which carried him to world-wide fame—"Le Spectre de la Rose," "Afternoon of a Faun," "Les Sylphides," and so on.

10. Those readers who are musically interested may have learned to appreciate these songs in recent years while hearing them sung by Marian Anderson.

11. For biographical data about Robert Schumann see Wasiliewsky, Fuller Maitland, or Patterson. For his letters see *The Life of Robert Schumann Told in His Letters*, trans. May Herbert (1902), and *Letters of Robert Schumann*, trans. Hannah Bryant (1907).

The nature of his mental illness may be considered as one of the very sources of the impressive specificity of his art.[12]

Psychiatric experience teaches that there is, in general, a connection between schizophrenia and the choice of dancing as an artistic expression. For example, several of the most talented students of Mary Wigman's School of Dance, Dresden, had, as I know from personal experience, difficulties in living of the schizophrenic type. One of them, a resident of one of the war-torn southern European countries, had a mental breakdown when war conditions deprived her of the possibility of expressing herself to people by dancing, and recovered when she was able to resume her work and her art after the end of the war. Many institutions for the mentally disordered use artistic dancing successfully in the treatment of schizophrenics. I hope some artistic and psychological expert will find it worth his while, in the near future, to undertake further research on the problem of the fascinating relationship between schizophrenia and the dance.

To conclude the consideration of famous people whose assets were in causal connection with their mental difficulties, let me discuss a few people whose accomplishments were not in the field of arts.

Clifford Beers emerged from the serious experience of many years of mental illness and hospitalization with the writing of his autobiography, *A Mind That Found Itself*, a classic among the biographies of the mentally disturbed. Sensitized by his own experience to the needs of the mentally ill and to the necessity for preventive measures in this field, he became the founder, first, of the mental hygiene society in his home state, Connecticut, and, subsequently, the founder of the American and later of the international mental hygiene movements. He also interested Henry Phipps in donating the funds for the first psychiatric hospital connected with a medical school in this country. Thus he became, in spirit, one of the cofounders of the Henry Phipps Psychiatric Clinic, Johns Hopkins Medical School in Baltimore.[13]

Anton T. Boisen, formerly a research associate at the Chicago Theological Seminary and chaplain at Elgin Hospital, recovered from several severe schizophrenic episodes, which he masterfully describes in his most worthwhile theological and philosophical study, *The Exploration of the Inner World*. His experience as a psychiatric patient and as a theologian led him to promote clinical psychiatric training of theological students, he himself being the first one to get such training. He felt that psychiatric training was desirable for students of theology, because, with

12. Romola Nijinsky, *Nijinsky* (New York: Simon & Schuster, 1934); Arnold Haskell and Walter Nouvel, *Diaghileff: His Artistic and Private Life* (New York: Simon & Schuster).

13. Clifford Beers, *A Mind That Found Itself* (New York: Longmans, Green & Co.; rev. ed., New York: Doubleday, 1948).

such training, future ministers would be better equipped to help their parishioners if they got into emotional difficulties and, even more so, because he knew that a person who is trained in the right approach to the emotional problems of the mentally sick will automatically be better equipped to understand the emotional vicissitudes in the lives of the mentally healthy. In other words, Anton Boisen operated on the thesis that the difference between the mentally healthy and the mentally disturbed is one of degree only.

In addition, Boisen has published a number of most interesting contributions to the psychopathology of the mental disturbance which he himself had to undergo, and to the correlation between psychiatric and religious experience which was the background of his own creative development.[14]

One more little-known but great personality should be mentioned among those who recovered from severe mental disturbance and succeeded in making an asset of their experience: the anonymous "Late Inmate of the Glasgow Royal Asylum for Lunatics at Gartnavel," to whom I owe, by the way, the title of this paper. In his booklet, *The Philosophy of Insanity*, he expresses as early as 1860, when prejudice against mental illness was still overwhelmingly greater than it is now, his conviction that the difference between the mentally healthy and the mentally disturbed is one of quantity only. His own experience as an inmate of a mental hospital helped him, for instance, to come to as wise and modern a conclusion as the following: "What constitutes insanity?" he asks. "This is a question not easily answered, for the line which separates sanity from insanity is invisible, and there are as many kinds and degrees of the disease as there are sufferers."

"I am, and have been for years," he says in another place, "intimately acquainted with men, indeed I number some of them among my particular friends, whose advice on many subjects I would ask and take, and yet they are subject to delusions which totally unfit them, and, to all appearance, will ever unfit them, from residing outside the walls of a lunatic asylum." And at another place: "Of all men we [that is, those who have been mentally disturbed] should be the first to put, wherever it can bear it, a charitable construction upon the motives and actions of others —the last to judge, the last to condemn. The very brute extracts wisdom from suffering—why should not we? The dog burns his foot, and ever after looks askance at the fire."

In the spirit of such insight, the great anonym writes down what he remembers from the time of his own mental illness and of his hospital-

14. Anton T. Boisen, *The Exploration of the Inner World* (Chicago: Willet, Clark, 1936) ; "Types of Dementia Praecox—a Study in Psychiatric Classification," *Psychiatry*, I (1938), 233–36; "Economic Distress and Religious Experience—a Study of the Holy Rollers," *ibid.*, II (1939), 185–94; "The Form and Content of Schizophrenic Thinking," *ibid.*, V (1942), 209–18. These are only some of the great number of Boisen's contributions.

ization, fully aware of a definite purpose: "I purpose to note down," he says, "a few of my recollections concerning my thoughts and actions while under the influence of the disease, in the hope that they may be useful to those whose business it is to watch over the insane, and a warning to those who, through ignorance or recklessness, abuse their minds, till the tortured spirit, like a fire-begirt scorpion, turns upon itself and stings." At another place: "This subject is to me decidedly painful, but I do hope that my treatment of it may be a means of encouraging friends to persevere in their attention to relatives who are thus afflicted, and in this hope I have told my plain truthful story, and who knows but that it may tend to soften the prejudices which almost everyone entertains against such as I; and I may add, for the consolation of the afflicted and their friends, that a fit of insanity does not necessarily permanently injure either the feelings, or the intelligence of the person, after the fit has passed."[15]

I have said that I borrow the title for my paper from the above-quoted author. Yet he called his booklet *The Philosophy of Insanity*, and I call my paper "Remarks on the Philosophy of Mental Disorder." This difference in wording is not only a formal one but also one of content. When psychiatrists talk about insanity, it has more or less the connotation of incurability; the expression "mental disorder" is therefore preferable, for even serious mental disturbances can potentially be treated successfully with intensive psychotherapy, it is now believed.

This leads me to discuss the first of the four statements on which I planned to elaborate in this paper—that severely mentally disturbed people can be approached with the methods of modern intensive psychotherapy.

Until about twenty years ago, it was the conviction among psychiatrists and psychoanalysts, guided by such classical teachers as Kraepelin and Bleuler and psychoanalysts like Fenichel and Schilder, that psychotherapy with seriously disturbed—psychotic—persons could not be done.[16] Freud predicted in 1904 that it might be possible to treat the severely mentally disordered with intensive psychotherapy if, despite

15. I have quoted verbatim from this precious little book because it was out of print at the time this paper was being written; it is now being reprinted by Greenberg, New York: *The Philosophy of Insanity—by a Late Inmate of the Royal Asylum for Lunatics at Gartnavel* (Edinburgh: Maclachlan & Stewart; London: Houlston & Wright; 40 St. Enoch Square, Glasgow: William Love, 1860). It contains so much of the wisdom which modern psychiatrists have still to learn and to teach today, eighty-six years after the anonymous former inmate of a mental hospital learned it from his own experience and felt called upon to teach it.

16. Emil Kraepelin, *Clinical Psychiatry* (New York: William Wood Co., 1904), pp. 21–29; Eugen Bleuler, *Dementia Praecox* (Leipzig and Vienna: Franz Deuticke, 1911); Otto Fenichel, *Outline of Clinical Psychoanalysis* (New York: W. W. Norton & Co., 1934), pp. 313–62; Paul Schilder, *Introduction to a Psychoanalytic Psychiatry* (New York: Nervous and Mental Disease Pub. Co., 1928).

basic difficulties as he saw and outlined them in 1914, psychoanalytic technique could be successfully adapted to their specific needs.[17]

Since then the attitude of many psychotherapists has changed. Under the leadership of Adolf Meyer, William Alanson White, and, above all, Harry Stack Sullivan in this country, a number of American psychoanalysts and psychotherapists with psychoanalytic orientation have done intensive psychotherapy with psychotics, especially in the psychoanalytical hospitals—Chestnut Lodge (D. M. Bullard), Forest Sanitarium (J. Steinfeld), Menninger Clinic, The Haven (L. Bartemeier), and others.[18]

By "intensive"—psychoanalytically oriented—psychotherapy, I mean communication between two people through spoken words, gesture, and attitude, the psychiatrist and the psychiatric patient, with the goal that both may learn to understand the troublesome aspects of the patient's life and bring them and their hidden causes to the patient's awareness, so that his living may be facilitated and his difficulties in living may be alleviated, if not eliminated. In order to accomplish this goal, the patient must verbalize his problems to and investigate them with another trained and experienced person, the psychiatrist. As he does so, he may be freed from his difficulties in living to the extent to which he will be able to become aware of, and therefore capable of handling, his interpersonal relationships.[19] The psychiatric predecessors thought that it was not possible to realize such a procedure with seriously mentally disordered people, because they felt, first, that no workable doctor-patient relationship—"transference"—could be established with the psychotic; second, that most of his communications were not understandable to the psychiatrist; and, third, that the psychotic's tendency toward health and his wish for change were not sufficient to work with.

17. Sigmund Freud, *On Psychotherapy*, in *Collected Papers* (London: Hogarth Press, 1924), Vol. I, and *On Narcissism—an Introduction*, in *Collected Papers* (London: Hogarth Press, 1925), Vol. IV.

18. Adolf Meyer, *The Nature and Conception of Dementia Praecox* ("Dementia Praecox Monographs" [Boston: Gorham Press, 1911]) ; William Alanson White, *Medical Psychology—the Mental Factor in Disease* (New York: Nervous and Mental Disease Pub. Co., 1931) ; *Outlines of Psychiatry* (New York: Nervous and Mental Disease Pub. Co., 1935) ; Sullivan, *op. cit.*, see "Therapeutic Conceptions," pp. 87–117; "Modified Psychoanalytic Treatment of Schizophrenia," *Am. J. Psychiat.*, XI (1931), 519–40.

In European countries, Federn of Vienna, Fairbairn of Edinburgh, Ernst of London, Hollos of Budapest, and Boss of Zurich were among those who tried modified psychoanalytic psychotherapy with hospitalized psychotics: Paul Federn, "The Analysis of Psychotics, *Internat. J. Psychoanal.*, XV (1934), 209–14; W. R. D. Fairbairn, "A Revised Psychopathology of the Psychoses and Psychoneuroses," *Internat. J. Psychoanal.*, XXII (1941), 250–79; and "Endopsychic Structure Considered in Terms of Object-Relationships," *ibid.*, XXV (1944), 70–93; E. Boss, personal communication from Dr. Ruth Charlotte Cohn, New York (Swiss literature not yet available) ; Kurt R. Eissler, "Limitations to the Psychotherapy of Schizophrenia," *Psychiatry*, VI (1943), 381–91; M. G. Ernst, "A Psychotherapeutic Approach in Schizophrenia," *J. Ment. Sc.* (1940), pp. 668–74; F. Fromm-Reichmann, "Transference Problems in Schizophrenics," *Psychoanalyt. Quart.*, VIII (1939), 412–26; "Recent Advances in Psychoanalytic Therapy," *Psychiatry*, IV (1941), 161–64.

19. Sullivan, *op. cit.*

As I have shown in the introductory fragment of psychotherapeutic contact with the catatonic woman-poet, the assumption that such rapport cannot be established is untenable. The error in judgment of the classical psychiatrists seems to have been due to the withdrawn, detached, and sometimes aggressively hostile attitude which many mentally disturbed people show. This attitude was considered to be the result of a primary impenetrable grandiose self-engulfment—"narcissism." Modern psychiatric research shows that the seclusive, haughty, seemingly unapproachable attitude of these people is a secondary result of very early serious warping of their relationships with the people significant in their environment in infancy and childhood, with more or less consistent subsequent thwarting pressure in the same direction until they eventually break down. It is in order to forego the repetition of further painful interpersonal experiences that these people withdraw into the detachment and regress to the infantile, self-sufficient attitude which prevented the older psychiatrists from trying to reach them.

In addition, these psychiatrists were hesitant to cope with the sometimes active assaultiveness of the inarticulate psychotic, which seemed unpredictable and not understandable to them. Since modern psychotherapists have learned to understand the background of the psychotic's seclusive attitude from his early history and have learned that his communications can be understood in principle, they are able to establish a workable doctor-patient relationship with him.[20]

Let me illustrate by telling how the initial rapport with the catatonic woman-poet was established. We had our first interview while the young woman was still greatly disturbed, suicidal and actively assaultive, hallucinated and delusional. She opened the conversation by saying, "Dr. Bullard [the superintendent of the hospital] says I should talk with you; maybe the two of us could hit it off all right; and my brother [a psychiatrist] says that you have written something about people like myself, so that he thinks you will be able to understand me. By the way, could I read it? And my parents brought me all the way north from Argentina because they want me to be treated in this hospital." Realizing that this was the girl's way of testing out whether or not I intended to deal with my superintendent's patient, or with the sister of a colleague of mine, or with the daughter of her parents, who would pay the bills, or with herself in her own right, I responded that neither Dr. Bullard nor the patient's brother or parents would decide whether or not she and I could get along with each other, that we had to try to find out in our own right whether each of us felt that she could talk to the other and understand each other's language,[21] and whether she would feel that I could be

20. Fromm-Reichmann, "Transference Problems in Schizophrenics," and "Preliminary Note on the Emotional Significance of Stereotypes in Schizophrenics"; J. Hollos, *Hinter der gelben Mauer* (Bern: Huber); G. Schwing, *Ein Weg zur Seele des Geisteskranken* (Bern: Huber); Sullivan, "Affective Experience in Early Schizophrenia," *Am. J. Psychiat.*, VI (1927), 468–83; "Research in Schizophrenia," *ibid.*, IX (1929), 553–67.

21. The patient was in full command of the English and Spanish languages.

of use to her in understanding and alleviating her difficulties. The girl's question as to whether she should read my publications was answered in the negative, for it did not necessarily follow that I would understand her difficulties because I had understood those of others.

This elimination of the interference of any third person, with the establishment of our professional relationship and the definition of the goal of such a relationship, made it possible for the patient to talk to me immediately about her complaints. This she indicated by then asking whether I could explain to her why it was that she felt "so hazy and dizzy" all the time and whether I could tell her what to do about it. Thus a workable relationship was established with a seriously disturbed, catatonic person.

The same can be done with even very hostile and inarticulate people.

Several years ago, a very disturbed, inarticulate young male patient was on the disturbed ward of this hospital. He had been seen for regular psychotherapeutic interviews over a long period of time by one of our male physicians. During this time I had seen him only casually, passing the time of day with him when I came to visit other patients on the ward. As the progress of this young man was not deemed satisfactory, change to a female psychotherapist was decided upon. When first I invited myself to a psychotherapeutic interview with the young man, he became violently assaultive and refused to see me. All I could do to protect myself was to retire quickly. Was this a not-understandable or an unpredictable response on the part of the patient? I did not think so. For a year or longer, I had paid no special attention to him. All of a sudden, I got good and ready to speak to him without being given the opportunity by him to explain the reasons. Why should he be ready to have us talk to each other just because I was? Realizing that his reluctance was justified and that, being the inarticulate patient he was, he could not express it other than in assaultive action, I subsequently went to see him daily for 3 months, telling him outside the door of his room that I came on the ward to see him, and only him, and that I was waiting for him to become ready to give us a chance to try useful therapeutic interchange. After 3 months, he invited me in, confirmed my interpretation of his previous reluctance, and a workable relationship was established.

The second reason which prevented classical psychiatrists from believing that intensive psychotherapy with psychotics could be done successfully—namely, that the communications of the mentally disturbed were not understandable and perhaps meaningless—has been refuted by implication in what has been said thus far. If the concept is correct, that the psychotic's mental experiences and modes of expressing them are different only in degree and not in kind, his communications must, in principle, be as meaningful and potentially understandable as are those of the "healthy." The previously discussed parallels between dreams and psychotic productions and the preceding examples of establishing contact between two psychotics and myself bear witness to this.

Hence the psychiatrist has to listen to the communications of the mentally disturbed and try to understand them, irrespective of whether or not he can always grasp their meaning. If he cannot understand them, he still owes the respect to the mentally disordered person to know that his communications are practically always self-meaningful. The psychiatrist as the participant observer in the psychotherapeutic interchange with the psychotic must have a well-developed self-respect. If he has, he can afford acceptance of the fact that the mental patients can convey ideas to him which make no sense to the psychiatrist, who is supposed to be "in his right mind"—ideas which are evidently meaningful to the patient, who is allegedly "out of his mind." This is where classical psychiatrists and psychoanalysts failed their psychotic patients. If the modern psychotherapist is able to accept this experience without any lowering of his security, psychotherapeutic collaboration between him and his patient will be possible. It is not necessary for the psychiatrist to understand the meaning of everything that the mentally disordered patient tries to convey to him. In his dealings with neurotics, he does not grasp the meaning of every dream which the neurotic may report; nor do "healthy" people "understand" all that is said to one another. However, in either situation, the psychiatrist is required to realize that the productions are potentially meaningful. The following are a few examples, illustrating the difference between the ways of communication of the mentally disturbed and the mentally healthy.

One of the central pathogenic problems of the catatonic woman-poet was an unrecognized jealousy of her baby sister, which was greatly justified by the preference given to this newcomer by her environment, but of which the patient was totally unaware. Various therapeutic efforts to make her see it had not been acceptable to her. One day Margherita discovered that I had just gotten a new history of art. I asked her whether she wished to look up something in it, and she answered by showing me some reproductions of the work of the painter Cézanne. Being sure that her choice was not accidental but quite meaningful, yet not knowing what the meaning might be, I asked her whether she had ever seen any of Cézanne's original paintings, upon which she told me the following story: When she was seventeen or somewhat younger, her parents had taken her, the younger sister, and one brother to Madrid, where the family had seen some of Cézanne's originals. When they arrived at the Spanish border two days before reaching Madrid, her brother, who had to attend to their *triptyques,* left the car in which they were traveling on what appeared to be an abandoned railroad track. Suddenly a train approached on this track. Instantly, Margherita moved to the driver's seat, turned on the ignition, and moved the car off the track just in time. The first thing that came to her attention afterward was that her parents had grabbed the younger sister and were bestowing affection upon her as a sign of their great relief. Hearing this story, I was supposed to guess by implication that Margherita's parents, in their happiness at seeing the younger sister safe, had forgotten to thank Margherita, whose presence of mind had saved the lives of the whole family. This was the patient's way of admitting to the psychiatrist that she had at last become aware of her jealousy of the younger sister—an awareness which henceforth could be used for therapeutic purposes.

Another example of the psychotic's particular means of communication:

One day, toward the end of the treatment, Margherita and I read and discussed some of her favorite poetry as a means of finding out about some emotional experiences of hers which were expressed in the poetry. At one point, I failed to hear her convey signs of her apprehension in terms of one of the poems. I only realized it afterward, when I noticed an expression of utter sadness and disappointment upon her face. I apologized for my lack of alertness, stating that I realized such failures in alertness to be inevitable at times in our psychotherapeutic dealings and encouraging her to make me aware of them, if she could, whenever they occurred. The next day, Margherita brought me a little gift, stating that this was to express her appreciation for our discussion of the poetry. Realizing that a schizophrenic, as a rule, will not bother to account for the plausibility of his actions, I knew that this was not the real reason for Margherita's having brought the gift. I was supposed to guess that what she really was grateful for was my frank admission of my failure in alertness.

So much for the means of expression of the mentally disturbed and the psychiatrist's potential ability to understand.

As to the lack of a tendency toward health which made classical psychiatrists despair of trying to do verbalized psychotherapy with the mentally disordered, it was shown that there is a tendency toward health in every human being, as discussed in the section on the two-sided motivation of mental symptoms. I maintain with Sullivan that there is as much of a tendency toward health in the mentally or physically ill as there is a tendency toward intake of food and liquids in the hungry and thirsty.[22] In some mental patients, a spontaneous wish for change and recovery is found. In others, such a wish can be aroused on the basis of their tendency toward health, unless life has so little in store for them that they cannot be expected to become interested in being able to cope with its vicissitudes.

There is, however, one imperative presupposition to be entertained by any psychotherapist who wants to be useful to the mentally disordered in their rehabilitation. He must have sufficient insight into and respect for the special needs of the specific personalities of these people to realize that he is not called upon to guide them toward adjustment conforming with the conventionalities of the culture. To a mentally disturbed person, recovery means being sufficiently aware of his previous difficulties in interpersonal relationships that he may become able to

22. Sullivan, *op. cit.*

reach out for that which means security and satisfaction to him, be it ever so different from the conventional patterns of interpersonal relationships in his culture.

Most justifiably, there has been much discussion about the as yet deplorably small number of recoveries of the mentally disordered under intensive psychotherapy. This has been attributed chiefly to lack of psychiatric skill and knowledge. It is my conviction and the conviction of my psychiatric friends that the greater responsibility must be referred to the sad fact that most psychiatrists have more respect for the society which pays them for their services than for the patients who need their help and guidance. These psychiatrists work, advertently or inadvertently, toward the recovery of a mental patient in terms of a conventional adjustment to society rather than in terms of his individual needs.

The schizophrenic woman-poet, for example, from whose treatment history many examples in this paper are taken, was not treated with the goal of having her make an adjustment to the social standards and requirements of her family group, much less to living with her parents, whose main interest was playing a role in "society" in the capital city of their country. Nor was the appraisal of her state of mental health made dependent upon the question of whether or not this schizoid personality, with her great legitimate need for privacy and at times aloneness, would make a successful marital adjustment. Treatment came to an end when she knew enough about her early and present interpersonal relationships to be able to get along with people when she met them as a social human being, instead of evading them because she dreaded them, as she had done previously. She has been able to form some relationships of durable intimacy, and she has found security in these relationships, in her creative work, and in some worthwhile pastimes.

Now to come to the discussion of my fourth and last point: the influence of one's dealings with the mentally disturbed on one's contacts with the emotionally healthy. When one realizes how many mentally sick or mentally handicapped persons are able to convert their previous liabilities into really worthwhile assets, once they have succeeded in turning the destructive aspects of their difficulties in living into constructive aspects of life, the attempt at trying to help these people to attain such goals appears most gratifying, even though, at present, psychiatrists are not at all successful in their therapeutic efforts with all of them.

There are other reasons which make the dealings of the so-called healthy with the mentally disordered most worthwhile. If psychiatrists could learn to apply the sensitive and cautious, yet spontaneous, respectful, and alert, considerateness which is required in their dealings with the schizophrenic to their relationships with their fellow men in general, it would constitute a most rewarding improvement of human relationships in this culture.

If society could learn something from the schizophrenic's lack of any need or wish for plausibility or magic use of apologetic rationalization, it would make for much greater directness and frankness in human interrelationships.

Mentally disturbed persons who have withdrawn from their environment are refreshingly intolerant of all kinds of cultural compromises; hence they inevitably hold the mirror of the hypocritical aspects of the culture in front of society.

For all these reasons, it can be exceedingly valuable to deal with psychotic people for all those psychiatrists who are willing to learn from their psychotic fellow men. Considering relationships with mental patients from this viewpoint, it is no overstatement to say that the mentally sick, who allegedly have lost their minds in their interpersonal struggles, *may* be useful to the mentally healthy in really finding *their* minds, which are all too frequently lost, as it were, in the distortions, the dissociations, the hypocritical adaptations, and all the painful hide-and-seeks which modern culture forces upon the mind of man.

However, this may become possible *only* if "mentally disturbed" and "mentally stable" people are no longer considered different in kind but only in degree and if no moral disqualification is attached to mental disorder. Then and only then will so-called healthy, but too well-adjusted, people become capable of hearing with respect and with a consequent gain in growth, maturation, and inner independence the message which comes to them from some of the culturally uncompromising and mentally disordered persons—a message none the less valuable because at times the price of their nonconformity is painful episodes of mental disturbance.

(2)

NOTES ON THE HISTORY AND PHILOSOPHY
OF PSYCHOTHERAPY

Psychotherapy is as old as recorded medical history. In the course of the centuries, psychotherapeutic methods changed back and forth. Sometimes there were changes from persuasive to supportive and suggestive techniques, at other times to witch-hunting, incantations and prayers, and other expulsory methods. All these methods were designed to free the diseased person from the mental disease which was then conceived of as an isolated entity, poured into or imposed on the mentally sick individual. "The figures, through whom mental healing evolved, ran the gamut of monks and medicine men, saints and sinners, kings and quacks, physicians and specialists" (7).

At the time of the German Renaissance and under Paracelsus' influence this concept changed (70, 103). Mentally disturbed people were given the status of sick individuals. "The sacred art of medicine must be practised on men and for men," as Johan Weyer put it in the sixteenth century. "This holds," he said, "regardless of whether they suffer from physical or from mental disease." No longer should physicians attribute disease to strange and extraneous spiritual forces or gods. "Something must have happened within the individual if his fantasies are abnormal" (Weyer, in 103).

Only after this change of concept regarding mental illness and regarding the mentally ill had been accomplished, i.e., after "psychotherapy like other arts and sciences had passed through two of its stages of evolution, the mystical and the taxonomic" (57), could the first roots of rational psychotherapy be planted.

Incidentally, it should be noted that the shifts in status given to the mentally disturbed run parallel to general political developments in various countries:[1] In progressive and liberal periods the philosophy governing people's attitudes toward the mentally disturbed was one of looking at them as sick fellow men who were in need of care and treatment and whose care and treatment were a public responsibility.

Reprinted from *Progress in Psychotherapy* (New York: Grune & Stratton, Inc., 1956).

1. Erich Fromm, lecture presented at the 1949 scientific memorial gathering for H. S. Sullivan, held by the William Alanson White Institute of Psychiatry, Psychology and Psychoanalysis in New York (unpublished).

This observation remains correct, irrespective of the fact of which we all are painfully aware, that there has been and still is a far cry from the insight into the need of our mentally disturbed fellow men for care and treatment to its adequate realization.

In reactionary periods and countries, the mentally sick were considered useless parasites. The Nazis, e.g., committed indiscriminately first compulsory sterilization and later mass murder on the inmates of their mental hospitals, without investigating the question of curability.

Modern intensive psychotherapy and modified psychoanalytic treatment for the application to the psychotic inmates of mental hospitals was, of course, not acceptable in a country like Nazi Germany, which had banned the teachings of Freud, of his precursors and his successors, from the scientific and the therapeutic scene. A systematic development of the treatment of psychotics with modified psychoanalytic psychotherapy was formulated by Moreno and other students of psychodrama (60). It was then promoted by Schilder (82), Kempf (51a), Federn (21–23), Sullivan (87–92), Whitehorn (99–101), Bychowski (9), Eissler (14–17), Hill (47), Katan (50–51), J. N. Rosen (76), Wexler (97–98), Arieti (3), and this writer (33–36, 38), to mention only some of the principal protagonists.

Before this modern development of the dynamic psychotherapy of psychotic patients could be inaugurated, two older erroneous psychiatric concepts had to be disproved. One was the error in Kraepelin's teachings about the therapeutic inaccessibility of schizophrenic people (patients suffering from dementia praecox in his terminology), because their communications were unintelligible; the other was the error inherent in Freud's assumption that the schizophrenic's narcissism prevents him from establishing a therapeutically valid patient-doctor relationship. Once this was done, intensive psychotherapy with psychotics could be started. To have done so is one of the contributions of American psychiatry to recent developments in psychotherapy.

In progressive democratic countries, the following basic philosophy of psychotherapy as a procedure "based on common sense and intuitive understanding of human nature"[2] (3) has been accepted since Paracelsus: that man in distress can get help by various types of curative contacts with other trained and allegedly healthy men. This concept prevails in the first refined modern description of planned psychotherapy, Pinel's *Traitement moral,* which was published at the end of the eighteenth century. In this book Pinel laid down the first foundation of a systematic psychological therapy of mental disorders (70).

The next important development in psychotherapy was medical hypnotherapy. It was promoted at the beginning of the nineteenth century by

2. Franz Alexander, *Progress in Psychotherapy,* p. 82.

Mesmer (104) and given a scientific orientation by Braid and Liébault (70, 103).

The use of hypnosis for treatment and research introduced a new principle into medicine: *l'action de la morale sur le physique* ("the influence of the mind on the body"). In fact, one could say that the research of the mind-body aspects of those days is the cradle of modern psychosomatic psychotherapy.[3]

Before medical hypnotherapy entered the picture, the whole orientation of medicine throughout its history was based on the assumption of somatic supremacy. In addition to the above-mentioned authors, Tuke, Charcot, and Forel "brought about a new scientific and clear understanding of the mental processes underlying hypnosis and suggestibility"; they also introduced the principle that the neuroses were treatable emotional disturbances (Charcot), and they used their experiences with the treatment of psychoneurosis as a steppingstone in their attempt to gain a general understanding of human behavior and its motivations in the mentally healthy as well as the mentally sick (Bernhein, Tuke). Incidentally, this constitutes the first (known) endeavor in the history of psychiatry to understand the behavior and motivation of the mentally healthy on the basis of psychopathological knowledge and experience, an approach with which some decades later Freud was to be so successful.

In the second part of the nineteenth century, Janet increased the knowledge of hypnosis and wrote a fine description of a psychotherapy of hysterical and neurotic disturbances. He was the first psychiatrist to discover and describe unconscious psychodynamic mechanisms. He failed, however, to accept the consequences of his insight, and in the end held on to the doctrine that hysteria was the result of a constitutional weakness of the mind and nervous system. Thus he bore out Zilboorg's statement (103) that "it is difficult to rise above the age to which one has pledged one's loyalty."

Before Charcot and Janet, people's principal psychotherapeutic interest was focused on the treatment of psychotics and of hysterics with a dramatic symptomatology. Their successors in the psychotherapeutic field—Freud, Adler, Jung, and their disciples—were, in the initial stages of their work, concerned mainly with the treatment of neurotics.

As we see it now, both neurotic and psychotic patients can be treated with psychotherapy. In my personal opinion, the basic principles underlying intensive psychotherapy apply to all types of mental illness, regardless of the differences in technique required in the psychotherapeutic approach to various types and various degrees of mental disturbance and emotional distress.

The older concepts of planned rational psychotherapy which I have

3. It was inaugurated by Georg Groddeck (42) and followed up in more recent years by Dunbar, the Chicago Psychoanalytic Institute, Weiss and English and others.

quoted so far were, above all, different from modern psychotherapy in their conception of the roles attributed to the two participants in the psychotherapeutic process—the patient and the helper. They were concerned with the mentally sick person only as an object of the therapeutic efforts of the doctor. The doctor's functions were viewed only in terms of the adequate application of his psychotherapeutic skills and powers to his patient. Psychotherapy was not conceived of in terms of any active participation of the patient, much less in terms of any mutual interpersonal interaction between doctor and patient.

Recent developments in psychotherapy, however, have been increasingly marked by the insight that the therapeutic contact between man and man, patient and trained expert, should be a mutual and collaborative one. Observation and investigation of the personality of the doctor as well as of the patient have become significant parts of psychotherapy, and the scrutiny of the modes of interaction between patient and doctor are now considered to be an integral part of the psychotherapeutic process.[4] Freud's concept of the therapeutic process in terms of "transference" (the real and the irrational aspects of the patient's relationship to the therapist), "resistance" (the dynamic repetition of the patient's reluctance to recover anxiety-evoking experiences), and "countertransference"[5] (the real and the irrational aspects of the doctor's relationship to the patient) is the most clearly formulated expression of this development (25–28). Moreno's conduct of the therapeutic interview between patient and helper in psychodrama is another outcome of this point of view (61). Muncie's description of the attitude of the psychobiologic school, and of its founder, Adolf Meyer, also illustrates well this general change in the psychotherapeutic position.[6] Sullivan's definition of the psychiatrist's role in the psychotherapeutic procedure as "participant-observer" is another expression of this development (87, 88). Wolberg demonstrates how much can be learned in hypnotherapy about transference phenomena.[7] Among other modern authors, Whitehorn should be quoted here with his statement: "Radical psychotherapy is essentially a cooperative task, in which success depends ultimately upon the patient, the psychotherapist serving primarily as an expert assistant" (99).

Does it appear redundant to note at this point that transference and countertransference have, of course, played a great role at all times and in all types of psychotherapy, even though not recognized or consciously utilized for psychotherapeutic purposes? In recent years Masserman and other students of animal behavior could demonstrate the significance of

4. Louis Cholden, *Progress in Psychotherapy*, p. 239.

5. Don Jackson elaborates on the less well-known modern conceptions of countertransference in his contribution, *ibid.*, p. 234.

6. Wendell Muncie, *ibid.*, p. 119.

7. Lewis R. Wolberg, *ibid.*, p. 217; see also Harold Rosen (75).

transference and countertransference even in their work with animals (57).

At the present period of psychotherapeutic development, it can be stated that, inaugurated by Freud, all schools of psychotherapy and of dynamic psychiatry pay great attention to the therapeutic use of the patient-doctor relationship.[8] If I speak of dynamic psychiatry I am referring to a type of psychiatry whose "most elementary implication is," to put it in Whitehorn's words, that "psychological experience does make a difference in the subsequent behavior of the human being" (99). I may follow the 1952 Conference on the Psychiatrists' Training and Development with a more explicit definition: "Psychodynamic psychiatry accepts the functional significance of emotion. A fundamental postulate of psychodynamics, which is a predictable science, is that most of the significant activities of human beings are motivated and goal-directed in persisting long-term patterns and that the immediate meaning of an action requires for its adequate understanding the context discernible in the over-all meaning of the biography of the organism." The other basic postulate of psychodynamics is that an appreciable part of human motivations "remains implicit or perhaps quite unconscious, and unconscious motivation may be in direct and severe conflict with conscious motivation. The systematic investigation of unconscious processes is one of the most important procedures in psychodynamic study" and psychodynamically oriented psychotherapy (65).

In quoting this statement I do not overlook the difference between human psychodynamics and the physical sciences, which Whitehorn emphasizes: "Human experience," he says, "is not the science of merely passive endurance of the present, desire or dread of the future, it is also active striving toward some goal. This active striving distinguishes psychodynamics from the physical sciences, such as hydrodynamics" (100).

Irrespective of their differences in other aspects of psychotherapeutic technique and methodology, most, if not all, schools of psychodynamic psychotherapy agree about the fact that the investigation of the interaction between patient and doctor should take precedence over the evaluation of all other aspects of the patient's communications. To follow this rule does not mean, however, to reintroduce old psychiatric ideas of a special type of psychotherapy, "relationship therapy," as Levine suggests in his otherwise excellent, informative survey of the various psychotherapeutic methods (54). We would rather say that "relationship therapy" is inherent in all types of modern psychodynamic psychotherapy.

Stressing the particular significance of the patient-doctor interaction implies recognition of the important role which should be attributed to

8. Alexander, Cholden, Jackson, Kubie, Lidz, *Progress in Psychotherapy*, pp. 111, 82, 239, 234, 87, 102.

communication in general by dynamic psychiatrists and psychotherapists. This refers to the interpersonal as well as to the sociologic implications of communication theory. Ruesch and Bateson (77) offer the outstanding expression of this trend in psychotherapy in their book.[9]

One of the causes for the delay of psychoanalytic writers and practitioners in becoming aware of and paying attention to the doctor's and the patient's collaborative relationship and communication was the older conception of psychotherapy as the treatment of mental symptoms and not of mentally sick people. The ancient Chinese wisdom had been forgotten, according to which "disease is rarely localized, but generally affects the entire human being . . . disease is often associated with behavior" (95). For many centuries the concept of the totality of disease was destroyed, and disease meant "no longer what happened to the whole man, but what happened to his organs" (99), until Paracelsus, Weyer, Vives, and More promoted the changes in conception which we have described before (103). The modern position of the philosophy of dynamic psychotherapy is well characterized by Whitehorn's statement, "one treats persons, not schizophrenia, or depression" (99). Before Whitehorn, Adolf Meyer "abandoned the concept of individual diseases which dominated the Kalbaum-Hecker-Kraepelin tradition," and began to speak of "reaction types" and "the total personality reaction in all its aspects." Such concepts were, according to Meyer, "the only basis for a proper understanding of the patient."[10] Leon Saul (79) adheres to the same concept when he describes neuroses and psychoses "not as entities but as ways of reacting."[11] Walter Riese has published a fascinating and thoughtful historical and philosophic review of these developments (71) and will continue with his publications on the subject (70, 72) in his forthcoming *History of Psychiatry*.

The rediscovery of mental disease as a reaction of the total personality and the discovery that the treatment of mental disease is carried on by the interchange between two persons, the doctor and the patient, was intensified as psychiatrists began, under Freud's influence, to investigate and understand emotional illness and mental symptoms genetically and causally, in terms of their partially unknown psychological roots. In the course of this research, psychiatrists learned about two psychopathologically and therapeutically important sets of facts in people's interpersonal development. First, they came to know about the great role which the significant people in a person's past history, especially infancy and childhood, play in the genesis of mental illness. Second, they learned to realize that the patient repeats consciously and/or unconsciously with

9. Jurgen Ruesch, *ibid.*, p. 180.

10. See Muncie's paper, *ibid.*, p. 119.

11. Martin has elaborated on this topic in his discussion of Karen Horney's "holistic" approach (*ibid.*, p. 170).

the therapist the vicissitudes of his early relationships and that he endows the doctor with the personality trends and other characteristics which he first encountered in the significant people of his past life.

Following Freud's teachings, the clarification of these transferred interpersonal experiences of the mental patient with the therapist became a focal point of psychotherapeutic endeavor, thus reinforcing the position that the patient-doctor relationship is the backbone of the psychotherapeutic procedure. At the same time, the therapists themselves learned to strive for awareness of their own conscious and unconscious emotional counterreactions to their patients, lest these interfere with an unbiased approach to the patient's therapeutic needs.

This therapeutic philosophy should produce an attitude of respect and a sense of equality between doctor and patient. The doctor should learn to accept with humility the knowledge that the difference between the emotional problems of the mentally healthy and the emotional difficulties in living of neurotics and psychotics is much more one of degree than one in kind. As Henry Brosin puts it, "the observations that every man during some period of his early development has the potentialities for behaving, thinking and acting in patterns much like those utilized by a schizophrenic, manic, obsessive, or phobic patient alter considerably the attitude of the investigator toward the phenomena of bizarre behavior" (8). This elevation of the mental patient from the ranks of an object of therapy to a partner of the therapist is also one of the central doctrines of existentialist analytic psychotherapy.[12]

The same position is emphasized by Zilboorg's statement, "mental disease . . . is . . . a function of everything that is in us—our remotest past, our life-experience, our loves, our hatred" (103), which paraphrases H. S. Sullivan's memo to psychiatrists and psychotherapists that "we are all more simply human than otherwise" (87). Moreno's discovery and development of psychodrama as a valid and powerful psychotherapeutic method is a significant outcome of the same philosophy.[13] All these statements impress me as being like an application to psychology of Claude Bernard's biologic principle that there is no essential difference between health and disease. Incidentally, he developed this doctrine more than a century ago. Four centuries before Claude Bernard and five centuries before Freud, Sullivan, and Zilboorg, Vives and More were sufficiently unafraid of being "unscientific" to state: "Man should be treated with the same tolerance and respect accorded to any other natural phenomenon. Such tolerance is fundamentally a form of love, a mode of identifying oneself with others" (103). Much to the detriment of the growth and development of the science and art of psychotherapy, too many of Vives' and More's successors in psychotherapy have refrained

12. Binswanger, *ibid.*, p. 144.
13. See Moreno's own description, *ibid.*, p. 37, and his previous publications (60–62).

from such insight and formulation, for fear of their unscientific, emotional connotations.

The conception of human behavior and motivation as the outcome of environmental influences and the concept of the therapeutic value of environmental modifications lead to another modern development in the history and philosophy of psychotherapy. Environmental influences come from a person's parents, family, teachers, playmates, classmates, etc., as well as from his general social and cultural environment, be it directly or through the medium of the significant people of his immediate milieu. Two trends in psychotherapy have developed as a result of this insight.

First, psychiatrists have learned to include patients' relatives in their treatment program (86), either in joint patient-relative group-therapy (1)[14] or by giving or asking colleagues or social workers to give information and therapeutic advice about the patients' condition to their relatives. This is a must in the case of more seriously disturbed persons. Their relatives need advice about how to approach the patient best, for their own sake and for the benefit of the patient.

Second, most modern psychiatrists feel that these influences must be studied and understood in the frame of reference of societies and cultures other than those to whose specific influence the person in question has been exposed. It is therefore felt that, to be fully effective, the principles of psychiatry and psychotherapy must be studied in the framework of the social sciences, cultural anthropology, and other behavioral sciences (29–31, 49, 52, 63, 83–85).

In spite of some of its inherent interpersonal difficulties, which Redlich and Brody have recently outlined (68), we shall have to "turn to history, sociology, and anthropology and combine them with the medicine we have learned," as Zilboorg puts it (103). Thus interdisciplinary research has become an increasingly significant part of research in psychotherapy. Mabel Cohen has elaborated on the subject in *Psychiatry*, the journal founded by H. S. Sullivan which concerns itself more than other psychiatric periodicals with the connection between psychotherapy and other behavioral sciences (11). Sullivan worked as a staunch promoter of interdisciplinary research in psychiatry, but at the same time, he cautioned about the dangers (87, 93).[15] Moreno's *Sociometry* is another psychiatric journal which pays great attention to the interdisciplinary ramifications of psychiatry.

The reader will find reflections of this modern trend of psychotherapy in a number of papers. Another outcome of the increasing insight into the necessity of paying attention to the psychology of mental patients as members of social units is the growing use of group therapy and

14. See also Moreno, *Progress in Psychotherapy*.

15. This topic was also discussed in his seminars with psychiatrists and in his contribution to the discussions of UNESCO, Paris, 1949.

psychodrama, practiced as such and jointly with other psychotherapeutic methods. They are presented by Ziferstein and Grotjahn, Shugart and Loomis, Moreno, Yablonsky and Enneis, in Friedemann's review of psychotherapy in Switzerland, in Kelnar and Sutherland's review of the British situation, and in Schindler's report about psychotherapy in Austria.[16]

The increase in attention which has been given to the importance of the social setting in which treatment takes place is another practical outcome of the recognition given by modern psychotherapists to the significance of patients' environments. The book by Stanton and Schwartz (85), the work of our British colleagues, Jones and Reese, on which Kelnar and Sutherland comment, Sivadon's and Tosquelles's work, to which Favez-Boutonnier refers in her review of psychotherapy in France,[17] and the most interesting work of Querido in Amsterdam (67) are outstanding examples of this trend in modern psychotherapy. To summarize: the modern psychotherapeutic position may be well defined with the statement that mental patients have to be understood and treated in their dual quality of being unique and at the same time essentially alike (54, 78, 87).[18]

Unfortunately, some psychiatric authors who have clearly seen these social issues and have utilized them in psychotherapeutic research and practice have called themselves and have been labeled by their colleagues as "culturalists." By this label they have been implicitly put in contrast to the "biologists," i.e., those psychotherapists who stress the biologic aspects of the human organism and personality. I consider this conceptual dichotomy an unfortunate one. Actually, "modern dynamic psychiatry . . . has demonstrated systematically . . . that man lives his life as a biological unit" and that "environmental processes which interfere with people's mental well-being may include such things as inadequate food, water, oxygen, as well as inadequate love, disruption of an interpersonal relation, or the restrictions of a society" (19). As a matter of fact, "since human experience is always bound up with the processes occurring in a living organism, even the relations between fundamental biological problems and the general problems of philosophy must be regarded as very intimate" (55).

To repeat, then, I believe that all human beings, hence all mental patients, should be conceived of as psychobiologic units. There is sufficient experimental support for the validity of this concept. To mention only a few examples, I would like to bring the interesting experiments of Hebb and Lilly to the reader's attention (46, 56). These authors were able to produce experimentally psychobiologic experiences of loneliness.

16. *Progress in Psychotherapy*, pp. 248, 256, 265, 24 and 324, 149, 318, 277, 267.
17. Juliette Favez-Boutonnier, *ibid.*, p. 284.
18. See also Jules H. Masserman, *ibid.*, p. 188.

Also, schizophrenic-like reactions are produced in apparently mentally healthy persons by the administration of drugs, such as mescaline and, more recently, lysurgic acid (80). The well-known somatic concomitants of many emotional experiences and the findings of psychosomatic medicine point in the same direction.

Only if we realize the interlinkage between the biologic and the cultural approach, can we begin to hope that it will sooner or later be possible to establish a "valid frame of reference for comparison" of the various psychotherapeutic schools, such as narcoanalysis, narcosynthesis, hypnoanalysis, etc. As a matter of fact, I feel the time has come for serious attempts along those lines. As Whitehorn puts it, "Fortunately there are, at the present time, many evidences of the desire among psychotherapists of divergent traditions to seek a common basis for the validation of results and to aim at the formulation of principles held in common."[19] David McK. Rioch has set an interesting example for this type of approach in his article "Theories of Psychotherapy" (74). This research should not be done in the spirit of peacemaking in the sense of hiding the legitimate differences among various psychotherapeutic methods and techniques. The scientific issues and merits of the different schools should be compared with two purposes in mind: first, such procedure would further progress in developing the scientific aspects of psychotherapy; second, it should do away with the self-imposed isolation of many psychotherapists. For lack of communication with their colleagues, these people indulge in self-imposed reverie to the effect that theirs is *the* one method of treatment for all patients. I agree with Knight, when he states that psychiatrists who operate on that assumption "are practising poor psychotherapy" (53).

That brings us to the discussion of our next topic, the validity of psychotherapy as a science. We said that the essence of all modern psychotherapeutic endeavor is the interpersonal exchange between two people, patient and psychiatrist. That means that the medium in which the psychotherapist operates has a complex pattern which includes all the variables and intangibles inherent in each of the two persons and in their interactions. Hence he operates by the strength of data which are comparable only within the limits of these variables. Transference and countertransference and the "unscientific" experiences of identification, empathy, and intuition with their various experiential components constitute specific elements in the doctor-patient relationship which defy, at least partly, scientific description and evaluation (2). Yet I agree with Zilboorg that "our aim is to replace intuition with understanding," and to convert the intuitive truths with which all psychotherapy works by necessity into scientific truths, so that they may become "public

19. Diethelm (13) and Hinsie (48) have also made significant contributions in this direction.

property . . . ready to be used, tested, questioned, probed and experimented with by anyone else who is interested in science" (103).

I am working on a research project on intuitive processes in the psychotherapist who works with schizophrenics (in collaboration with Marvin Adland, Don Burnham, Harold Searles of Chestnut Lodge, and Alberta Szalita of New York) which aims precisely at this goal (36). There is much justification in Zilboorg's warning to the effect that "when we talk about psychotherapy we must be clear whether we talk about an art, a series of theoretical propositions, or a scientific system" (103).

As far as the awareness and the conscious understanding of transference and countertransference are concerned, the whole psychoanalytic literature is full of papers which treat this subject. Alexander, Cholden, Ziferstein and Grotjahn, Kubie, Lidz, Rogers, and Zilboorg pay special attention to it. Balint has most aptly emphasized the problem when he says that the doctor must learn, as best he can, to know "the pharmacology of his most important drug—himself."

Another hurdle which psychotherapy has to overcome on its road to becoming more scientific is set up by the very genesis of modern psychodynamic psychotherapy. Once Breuer and Freud discovered the psychogenic nature of the paralysis of their first patient by encouraging the cathartic abreaction of the patient's emotional problems, "this meant that for the first time in the history of psychology . . . a therapeutic agent . . . led to the discovery of the cause of the illness (103). The psychogenic nature of many somatic manifestations of mental disorder must be explored by new methods, in addition to the empiric fact that these symptoms can be favorably influenced or resolved by psychotherapy (as in the case of the paralysis of Freud and Breuer's patient).

In spite of all the data about the present limitations of psychotherapy as a scientific discipline, there is no reason for feeling discouraged about the outcome of our efforts in this direction. "While there is now a widespread recognition that more and better research in psychiatry is badly needed," as David Hamburg states in a recent publication (43), there also are many tools available by means of which psychiatrists can try to do this research. Hoch has suggested some methods in his paper in *Progress in Psychotherapy* (p. 72). Rioch says, in a paper which concerns itself with psychiatry as a biologic science: "No science is better than its art, and a science of human behavior is dependent for its growth on the artists who develop new operations" (73).

Let us take a look, then, at the attempts that psychotherapists have made so far toward improving the status of their art as a science. During the last years, sound recording has been used by an ever increasing number of psychotherapists. Moreno mentions its early use in his psychotherapeutic work (62). Rogers describes its utilization for many years by the members of his group in his paper in *Progress in Psychotherapy*

(p. 199).[20] These recordings serve the double purpose of offering material for study and reconsideration to the psychotherapist himself and, by making the recordings available to others, of breaking through the dangerous privacy which is inherent in individual psychotherapy by its very nature. Discussions of psychotherapeutic interviews at hospital staff meetings and in seminars and personal supervision aim at the same purpose. Yet anybody who has followed Donald Bloch's suggestion to jot down what he remembers of a recorded interview and to compare his notes with his recording knows about the inevitable limitations of these discussions.[21] Psychotherapists are subject to the universal human phenomenon which Nietzsche described: "This is what I did, says my memory, I cannot possibly have done this, says my conscience. And the memory yields." Incidentally, Freud used this quotation in his elaboration on the dynamics of repression (25).

Motion pictures have been used in recent years mainly for educational purposes (64), one-way screens for training purposes. The utilization of motion pictures for the investigation of the wide area of non-verbal communication between patient and doctor constitutes a research project dear to the hearts of many dynamic psychotherapists. Birdwhistell's recent publications on the analysis of body motion and gesture should prove most helpful in any investigation of non-verbal communication (5). Linquistic investigation and interpretation of psychotherapeutic interviews have been recently planned by various groups of psychotherapists.[22]

There has been much concern about the danger that recordings may make the psychiatrist and the patient self-conscious and that they may cramp the psychiatrist's psychotherapeutic style, if not actually interfere with his therapeutic effectiveness. In our experience with a staff of twenty psychiatrists at Chestnut Lodge the initial period of self-consciousness was overcome after the first few recordings were done. Subsequently the machine was forgotten. To facilitate the process of forgetting that it is operating (and/or to protect it from violation by disturbed psychotics), one may put a secretary in charge of operating it

20. Among other publications of and on recorded psychotherapeutic interviews, I should like to mention the following ones as characteristic examples: Gill, Newman, and Redlich, "The Initial Interview in Psychiatric Practice" (39) ; "Coordinated Research in Psychotherapy" done by seven members of Rogers' group of non-directive psychotherapists (69) ; Will and Cohen's report of "A Recorded Interview in the Course of Psychotherapy" (102) ; Cohen *et al.*, "A Personality Study of Successful Naval Officers" (12) ; Eldred *et al.*, "A Procedure for the Systematic Analysis of Psychotherapeutic Interviews"(18).

21. Personal communication.

22. At the Center for Advanced Study in the Behavioral Sciences, Stanford, California, Norman McQuown recently linguistically interpreted the recording of Otto A. Will's psychotherapeutic interview with a patient which was published in *Psychiatry* (102). McQuown's study will be published shortly.

outside the wired consultation room. Patients' permission should be secured.

Another significant contribution to the scientific understanding of psychiatry and psychotherapy comes from experiments with animals, if they are done by people who are mindful of the danger of arriving at wrong conclusions by anthropomorphizing the reactions of their subjects.[23]

The introduction of psychological testing as an important diagnostic and prognostic adjunct should also gradually help to make psychotherapy a more scientific discipline.

To repeat, this comparison of the methods used by the various schools should not be undertaken in the spirit of making peace among the various psychotherapeutic schools. There are valid reasons for most variations and differences, whether they stem from contrasting theoretic viewpoints or practical convictions or from differences in the personalities of the psychotherapists. Muncie quotes Adolf Meyer's attitude toward the problem: "The doctor's view can probably never be wholly separated from his own personality structure despite the widespread belief that he acts as a mirror to the patient's philosophy."[24] What should, however, be accomplished is a continuous and thorough job of comparing the data on the strength of which the various schools operate in theory and therapy. "Political" issues should be entirely eliminated from the scientific scene. They have beclouded the scientific horizons all too frequently in the past, when discussions among representatives of various psychotherapeutic schools were inaugurated. Set up in the right scientific spirit, such discussions should greatly contribute to progress in the scientific and practical aspects of psychotherapy.

The proponents of the various psychotherapeutic schools will speak for themselves and their respective schools in their contributions to this book, *Progress in Psychotherapy*.* Therefore, I will only add a word about the general differences and similarities in definition and goals of psychotherapy.

Modifying Freud's original recommendations along the lines of his interpersonal conception of psychiatry, Sullivan suggests the use of the following instrumentalities: the scrutiny of the patient's and the psychiatrist's personalities and the patient's symptomatology in terms of investigating all phases of the interpersonal reactions between doctor and patient in their own right and in their genetic and historical significance, with repeated discussion and rediscussion of the pathogenic topics ("working through" in Freud's terminology). Special attention should

23. See the work of Masserman, Gantt, Liddell, and others; for reference see Masserman (57).

24. Muncie, *Progress in Psychotherapy*, p. 119.

* [See p. 25 for source of this paper.—ED.]

be paid to patients' defenses both against accepting insight into the results of these discussions and against the doctor who is instrumental in their discovery (Freud's "resistance"). By all these means the patient is expected to gain conscious knowledge of, and curative insight into, the history and the dynamics of his symptomatology and into the dynamics of his operations with the psychiatrist. By virtue of this insight, he learns eventually to understand his interpersonal operations. If and when this task is accomplished, a patient should have gained a sufficient degree of lasting insight into his interpersonal operations and their dynamics to enable him, in principle, to handle them adequately without professional help. Another criterion for a patient's recovery from mental illness and emotional trouble is, according to Sullivan, the patient's ability to experience himself as the same person whom other people see in him. If we apply this experience to the relationship of the recovered patient with the doctor, it means that patient and doctor should, in essence, agree in their evaluation of the former patient's personality, his assets and his liabilities (87, 88).

This presupposes, of course, that the patient's transference, the doctor's countertransference experiences, and the patient's "parataxic distortions" (Sullivan) regarding people and interpersonal situations have been successfully dissolved. Whitehorn, who defines psychotherapy as "the art of combating disease and promoting health by mental influences," follows Freud and Sullivan in essence, when he says: "In the more successful cases, it appears that psychotherapy achieves its success through modifying a patient's basic interpersonal attitudes, in a direction and to a degree which enables a patient to conduct his life more effectively, with satisfaction and without serious neurotic or psychotic symptoms." Whitehorn calls psychotherapy which aims at this goal, "radical psychotherapy" (101).

I have not offered any specific classical psychoanalytic formulations of psychotherapeutic goals, first, because they are implied in the formulations of other psychodynamic schools which were originally inaugurated by classical psychoanalysis, and, second, because I assume that readers of this book are familiar with classical psychoanalytic conceptions.[25] Incidentally, as a result of the recent elaborations on the theoretic conceptions of ego psychology (20, 44, 45) and of its practical applications to therapy by classical psychoanalysis, the difference between the psychotherapeutic technique which classical psychoanalysts use and the technique employed by other psychoanalytic and psychodynamic schools has become much lessened in scope and significance.

To mention a few more suggestions which seem significant to me for the accomplishment of favorable psychotherapeutic results: Wheelwright

25. The symposium on the goals of psychoanalytic therapy (*Internat. J. Psychoanal.*) gives an adequate picture of this subject (94).

recommends, with Jung, as an important ingredient of all psychotherapeutic endeavor, the encouragement of the healthy aspects of personality by concentrating on the constructive side of their neurotic manifestations.[26] As a result of this philosophy, he warns against making "adaptation" in its own right a psychotherapeutic goal—adaptation and adjustment being the false gods of the frightened citizens of our disturbed world. Whitaker has something similar in mind when he advocates encouragement of patients' tendency toward growth, growth having been experienced by every patient in his premorbid life.[27]

As most psychiatrists realize, and as the reader can learn by going through this book, there are, of course, many psychotherapeutic methods which set themselves the more limited goal of curing patients' symptoms and of promoting their social adjustment. Some of them aim for a limited focal amount of insight for their patients, but they do not operate in the framework of Whitehorn's radical psychotherapy. These methods (e.g., brief psychotherapy, suggestive and supportive psychotherapy,[28] hypno- and narcoanalysis) and the acceptance of their limited goals are no doubt indicated and justified in certain types of patients. However, these patients have to be carefully selected as to diagnosis and personality. Therapists who do so should avoid the danger that their choice of therapeutic method and their selection of patient may be determined by a personal pessimistic attitude toward all aspects of living, of which they may be unaware, or, more specifically, by the dim outlook which they harbor with regard to the prognoses and general potentialities of the mentally sick.

The aims of the collaborative endeavor in which a psychotherapist engages with his patient if he works with intensive dynamic psychotherapy should be the following, regardless of the "school" to which the therapist belongs: The patient is expected to become free from mental symptoms, especially from excess anxiety, and free to utilize his innate tendencies toward personal growth and maturation, unhampered by greed, envy, and jealousy. He should also be free for a creative expansion of his personality and for striving for self-realization. He should be able to give and accept love and tenderness and to form durable relationships of emotional and physical intimacy (33).

All this cannot be accomplished once and for all, even by a fully successful course of psychotherapy. Growth and maturation, striving for freedom from anxiety and for freedom to accept oneself and to love others, are the outgrowth of a continuous experience in living (28a). Nobody will be spared the vicissitudes in living which will time and

26. Joseph Wheelwright, *Progress in Psychotherapy*, p. 127.

27. Carl Whitaker, *ibid.*, p. 210.

28. I am referring here to "supportive" therapies as an independent method, not to the supportive element which is, as Levine (*ibid.*) points out, inherent in all psychotherapy.

again tax his equanimity and, in the case of a former mental patient, his capacity to weather such vicissitudes without relapsing. Treatment, if it is successful, should enable the recovered patient to enjoy the good aspects of his life and to endure the bad ones, without resurgence of neurotic or psychotic symptomatology and without giving rise to unbearable anxiety.

There may be some readers who have gained the impression that a fulfilment of the enumerated goals of psychotherapy may contribute too much to the development of egocentric personalities. I would like to remind those readers of Fromm's paper on "Selfishness and Self-Love" (32) and of Whitehorn's statement that "mankind is provided with a sound biological foundation for altruistic interpersonal attitudes, which is of the highest importance for individual human satisfaction and for human society" (101). It is precisely for this reason that psychotherapy need not concern itself with helping patients to get "adapted or prepared for the occupational and family group" (40). Human beings are basically social animals. Patients who have attained the above-mentioned results from psychotherapy will therefore automatically reach out for the fulfilment of the requirements of group adjustment—not as goals per se, but as parts of a successful and happy way of living with their social group.

All psychotherapeutic methods have in common the necessity to understand and fight the excess anxieties of mental patients. I say "excess anxieties," because mild degrees of anxiety in our culture are "the common fate of all," whether we are mentally healthy or disturbed. These mild degrees of anxiety are not necessarily detrimental; they are danger signals, and frequently constructive (26, 37, 41).

In this atomic age the struggle with our anxieties has grown quite severe, especially since the first bombs were dropped on Hiroshima and Nagasaki. This event made the destructive "gains" from nuclear physics so painfully real that, since then, great fear reigns in the minds of our contemporaries. This fear is too tremendous to be faced by healthy as well as by mentally disturbed people. Both try to keep this anguish and apprehension of terrific outer danger in repression and/or to convert it into anxiety, the fear of inner danger. No matter how painful the experience of severe anxiety is, it is less threatening than the fear of becoming a victim of atomic warfare.[29] It seems to me that this may well be the reason for the marked increase in scientific interest and in scientific and non-scientific publications on the subject of anxiety during the last decade (4, 37).[30]

29. Frieda Fromm-Reichmann, discussion of fear and anxiety in the atomic age, in Franz Alexander's multidisciplinary seminar on "Changes in Personality during the Last Fifty Years," at the Center for Advanced Study in the Behavioral Sciences, Stanford, California, October–December, 1955, unpublished.

30. For further publications see bibliographies of Fromm-Reichmann (37).

An increasing number of people have responded to this constellation by turning for help to religion. Clergymen and psychiatrists all over the country have shown an ever growing interest in exchanging their scientific and practical experiences and philosophies (66, 96). But only a limited number of people receive satisfactory answers to and solutions of their fears and anxieties from religion. For this reason, psychotherapists are called upon to realize and act upon the statement with which I would like to conclude these notes on the history and philosophy of psychotherapy: If there was ever a time when people were in need of psychotherapy and of psychotherapists who are themselves well aware of and able to cope with their own fears and anxieties, the atomic age represents this period in the history of our culture.

References

1. ABRAHAM, JOSEPH, and VARON, EDITH. *Maternal Dependency and Schizophrenia: Mothers and Daughters in a Therapeutic Group.* New York: International Universities Press, 1953.

2. ALEXANDER, FRANZ. "The Therapeutic Application of Psychoanalysis." In: *Mid-Century Psychiatry.* Edited by ROY R. GRINKER. Springfield, Ill.: Charles C Thomas, 1953.

3. ARIETI, SILVANO. *Interpretation of Schizophrenia.* New York: Robert Brunner, 1955.

4. AUDEN, W. H. *The Age of Anxiety.* New York: Random House, 1946.

5. BIRDWHISTELL, RAY L. *Introduction to Kinesis (An Annotation System for Analysis of Body Motion and Gesture).* Louisville, Ky.: University of Louisville Press, 1954.

6. BREUER, JOSEPH, and FREUD, SIGMUND. "The Psychic Mechanism of Hysterical Phenomena." In *Studies in Hysteria.* New York and Washington: Nervous and Mental Disease Pub. Co., 1936.

7. BROMBERG, WALTER. *Man above Humanity.* Philadelphia: J. B. Lippincott Co., 1955.

8. BROSIN, HENRY. "Contributions of Psychoanalysis to the Study of Psychoses." In *Dynamic Psychiatry.* Edited by FRANZ ALEXANDER and HELEN ROSS. Chicago: University of Chicago Press, 1952.

9. BYCHOWSKI, GUSTAV. *Psychotherapy of Psychosis.* New York: Grune & Stratton, 1952.

10. COBB, STANLEY. *Emotions and Clinical Medicine.* New York: W. W. Norton & Co., 1950.

11. COHEN, MABEL B. "Research in Psychiatry," *Psychiatry,* XVII (1954), 297–98.

12. COHEN, R. A. (with COHEN, M. B., HALPERIN, A., OHANESON, E. M., and WILL, O. A.). *A Personality Study of Successful Naval Officers.* Washington: Office of Naval Research, 1951.

13. DIETHELM, OSKAR. *Treatment in Psychiatry.* New York: Macmillan Co., 1936.

14. EISSLER, KURT R. "Notes upon the Emotionality of a Schizophrenic Patient and Its Relation to Problems of Technique," *The Psychoanalytic Study of the Child*, VIII (1954), 199–251.
15. ———. Remarks on the Psychoanalysis of Schizophrenia, *Internat. J. Psychoanal.*, XXXII, 139–56. Reprinted in BRODY, EUGENE B., and REDLICH, FREDERICK C., *Psychotherapy with Schizophrenics*, pp. 130–67. New York: International Universities Press, 1952.
16. ———. "Limitations to the Psychotherapy of Schizophrenia," *Psychiatry*, VI (1943), 381–91.
17. ———. "Notes upon Defects of Ego Structure in Schizophrenia," *Internat. J. Psychoanal.*, XXXV (1954), 141–46.
18. ELDRED, S. H., *et al.* "A Procedure for the Systematic Analysis of Psychotherapeutic Interviews," *Psychiatry*, XVII (1954), 337–45.
19. ENGEL, GEORGE L. "Homeostasis, Behavioral Adjustment and the Concept of Health and Disease." In *Mid-Century Psychiatry*. Edited by ROY R. GRINKER. Chicago: University of Chicago Press, 1953.
20. ERIKSON, ERIK H. "Ego Development and Historical Change," *The Psychoanalytic Study of the Child*, II (1946), 359–96.
21. FEDERN, PAUL. *Ego Psychology and the Psychoses*. New York: Basic Books.
22. ———. "Psychoanalysis of Psychoses," *Psychiat. Quart.*, XVII (1941), 246–57, 480–87.
23. ———. "Principles of Psychotherapy in Latent Schizophrenia," *Am. J. Psychotherapy*, I (1947), 129–44.
24. FREUD, ANNA. *The Ego and the Mechanisms of Defense*. New York: International Universities Press, 1946.
25. FREUD, SIGMUND. *A General Introduction to Psychoanalysis*. New York: Liveright, 1935.
26. ———. *The Problem of Anxiety*. New York: W. W. Norton & Co., 1936.
27. ———. *Further Recommendations in the Technique of Psychoanalysis: Observations on Transference-Love*. In *Collected Papers*, II, 377–91. London: Hogarth Press, 1946.
28. ———. *The Dynamics of the Transference*. In *Collected Papers*, II, 312–22. London: Hogarth Press, 1946.
28a. ———. "Analysis Terminable or Interminable," *Internat. J. Psychoanal.*, XVII (1937), 373–405.
29. FROMM, ERICH. *Escape from Freedom*. New York and Toronto: Rinehart & Co., 1941.
30. ———. *Man for Himself*. New York and Toronto: Rinehart & Co., 1947.
31. ———. *The Sane Society*. New York and Toronto: Rinehart & Co., 1955.
32. ———. "Selfishness and Self-Love," *Psychiatry*, II (1953), 507–23.
33. FROMM-REICHMANN, FRIEDA. *Principles of Intensive Psychotherapy*. Chicago: University of Chicago Press, 1950.
34. ———. "Psychoanalytic Psychotherapy with Psychotics," *Psychiatry*, VI (1943), 277–79.

35. ———— (with COHEN, M. B., BAKER, G., COHEN, R. A., and WEIGERT, E.). "An Intensive Study of Twelve Cases of Manic-depressive Psychosis," *Psychiatry*, XVII (1954), 103–37.

36. ———— (with ADLAND, M., BURNHAM, D., SEARLES, H., and SZALITA, A.). "Clinical Significance of Intuitive Processes of the Psychoanalyst," *J. Am. Psychoanal. A.*, I (1955), 5–88.

37. ————. "Psychiatric Aspects of Anxiety." In *An Outline of Psychoanalysis*. New York: Random House, 1955.

38. ————. "Psychotherapy of Schizophrenia: Academic Lecture," *Am. J. Psychiat.*, III (1955), 1, and her other papers on the psychotherapy of schizophrenics.

39. GILL, MERTON, NEWMAN, RICHARD, and REDLICH, FREDRICK C. *The Initial Interiew in Psychiatric Practice*. New York: International Universities Press, 1954 (published with phonograph records).

40. GOLDSTEIN, KURT. "The Idea of Disease and Therapy," *Rev. Religion*, XIII (1947), 229–40.

41. ————. *Human Nature in the Light of Psychopathology*. Cambridge: Cambridge University Press, 1940.

42. GRODDECK, GEORG. *The Book of the It*. New York: Funk & Wagnalls, 1950.

43. HAMBURG, DAVID. "Review of the Recent Publications on Psychosomatic Medicine," *Psychiatry*, XVIII (1955), 391–98.

44. HARTMANN, HEINZ. "Comments on the Psychoanalytic Theory of the Ego," *The Psychoanalytic Study of the Child*, V (1950), 74–96.

45. HARTMANN, HEINZ, KRIS, E., and LOWENSTEIN, R. "Comments on the Formation of Psychic Structure." In *The Psychoanalytic Study of the Child*. Edited by GREENACRE, PHYLLIS, *et al.* New York: International Universities Press, 1946.

46. HEBB, D. O. "The Problem of Consciousness and Introspection." In *Brain Mechanisms and Consciousness: A Symposium*. Springfield, Ill.: Charles C Thomas, 1955.

47. HILL, LEWIS B. *Psychotherapeutic Intervention in Schizophrenia*. Chicago: University of Chicago Press, 1955.

48. HINSIE, LELAND E. *Concepts and Problems of Psychotherapy*. New York: Columbia University Press, 1937.

49. KARDINER, A. *The Psychological Frontiers of Society*. New York: Columbia University Press, 1945. And his previous publications quoted there.

50. KATAN, MAURITZ. "Structural Aspects of a Case of Schizophrenia," *The Psychoanalytic Study of the Child*, V (1950), 175–211.

51. ————. "The Importance of the Non-psychotic Part of the Personality in Schizophrenia," *Internat. J. Psychoanal.*, XXV (1954), 119–23.

51a. KEMPF, E. I. *Psychopathology*. St. Louis: C. V. Mosby Co., 1920.

52. KLUCKHOHN, CLYDE, MURRAY, H. A., and SCHNEIDER, D. M. (eds.). *Personality in Nature, Society, and Culture*. New York: Alfred A. Knopf, 1953.

53. KNIGHT, ROBERT P. "A Critique of the Present Status of Psychotherapies," *Bull. New York Acad. Med.*, XXV (1945), 100–114. Reprinted in

Psychoanalytic Psychiatry and Psychology. New York: International Universities Press, 1950.

54. LEVINE, MAURICE. "Principles of Psychiatric Treatment." In *Dynamic Psychiatry.* Edited by FRANZ ALEXANDER and HELEN ROSS. Chicago: University of Chicago Press, 1952.

55. LILLY, RALPH. *General Biology and Philosophy of the Organism.* Chicago: University of Chicago Press, 1945.

56. ———. "Effects of Physical Restraint and of Reduction of Ordinary Levels of Physical Stimuli on Intact, Healthy Persons." Presented at Group for Advancement of Psychiatry, 1955. To be published in GAP Reports.

57. MASSERMAN, JULES H. *Principles of Dynamic Psychiatry.* Philadelphia: W. B. Saunders Co., 1946.

58. ———. "Principles of Psychiatric Treatment." In *Dynamic Psychiatry.* Edited by FRANZ ALEXANDER and HELEN ROSS. Chicago: University of Chicago Press, 1952.

59. ———. *The Practice of Dynamic Psychiatry.* Philadelphia and London: W. B. Saunders Co., 1953.

60. MORENO, JACOB L. *Who Shall Survive? Foundations of Sociometry, Group Psychotherapy, and Sociodrama.* New York: Beacon House, 1934 (1953), and his other publications mentioned there and in his papers in this book.

61. ———. *Psychodramatic Treatment of Psychoses.* ("Psychodrama Monographs," No. 15.) Beacon, N.Y.: Beacon House, 1945.

62. ———. "A Frame of Reference for Testing the Social Investigator," *Sociometry,* Vol. III (1950).

63. PARSONS, T., and BALES, R. F. *Family, Socialization, and Interaction Process.* Glencoe, Ill.: Free Press, 1953.

64. POWDERMAKER, FLORENCE. *Guide to Utilization of Films on Psychotherapeutic Interviewing.* Washington: Veterans Administration Department of Medicine and Surgery.

65. SPECIAL COMMISSION ON PSYCHODYNAMIC PRINCIPLES. *The Psychiatrist, His Training and Development.* 1952 Conference American Psychiatric Association. Washington, 1953.

66. GOLDSTON, JAGO (ed.). *Ministry and Medicine in Human Relations.* New York: International Universities Press.

67. QUERIDO, ARNE. "Organization and Function of a Mental Hygiene Department, *Internat. Health Bull., Geneva,* II (1950), 13–18.

68. REDLICH, FREDERICK C., and BRODY, EUGENE B. "Emotional Problems of Interdisciplinary Research in Psychiatry," *Psychiatry,* XVIII (1955), 233–39.

69. ROGERS, C. R., RASKIN, N. J., SEEMAN, J., SHEERER, E. T., STOCK, D., HAIGH, G., HOFFMAN, A. E., CARR, A. C. "A Coordinated Research in Psychotherapy," *J. Consult. Psychol.,* XIII, 3.

70. RIESE, WALTHER. "An Outline of History of Ideas in Psychotherapy," *Bull. Hist. Med.,* XXV (1951), 5.

71. ———. *Conception of Disease: Its History, Its Versions, and Its Nature.* New York: Philosophical Library, 1955.

72. ———. "History and Principles of Classification of Nervous Disease," *Bull. Hist. Med.*, XVIII (1945), 465–512.
73. RIOCH, DAVID McK. "Psychiatry as a Biological Science," *Psychiatry*, XVIII (1955), 313–21.
74. ———. "Theories of Psychotherapy." In *Current Trends in Psychological Theory*. Pittsburgh: University of Pittsburgh Press, 1951.
75. ROSEN, HAROLD. *Hypnotherapy in Clinical Psychiatry*. New York: Julian Press, 1953.
76. ROSEN, JOHN N. *Direct Analysis*. New York: Grune & Stratton, 1953.
77. RUESCH, JURGEN, and BATESON, GREGORY. *Communication: The Social Matrix of Psychiatry*. New York: W. W. Norton & Co., 1951; *see also* Ruesch's papers in *Psychiatry*, XVI, 215–43; XVIII, 1–18, 323–30.
78. SAUL, LEON. "The Nature of Neurotic Reaction," *J. Am. Psychol.*, CVI (1950), 547–48.
79. ———. *Bases of Human Behavior*. Philadelphia: J. B. Lippincott Co., 1951.
80. SAVAGE, CHARLES. "Lysurgic Acid and Diethylamide (LSD-25): A Clinical Psychological Study," *Am. J. Psychiat.*, CVIII (1952), 896–900, and the other papers published by him and his group which are quoted there.
81. SCHAFER, ROY. "Psychological Test Evaluations of Personality Change in Intensive Psychotherapy," *Psychiatry*, XVIII (1955), ¹75–92. (This is one of the most recent publications in the field. For older publications see its bibliography.)
82. SCHILDER, PAUL. *Introduction to Psychoanalytic Psychiatry*. New York: International Universities Press, 1951.
83. SCHWARTZ, MORRIS S., and SCHWARTZ, C. G. "Problems in Participant Observation," *Am. J. Sociol.*, LX (1955), 343–53, and M. S. Schwartz's other papers quoted there.
84. STANTON, ALFRED H., and SCHWARTZ, MORRIS. "Medical Opinion and the Social Context in the Mental Hospital," *Psychiatry*, XII (1949), 243–49.
85. ———. *The Mental Hospital*. New York: Basic Books, 1954.
86. STERN, EDITH A. (with the collaboration of SAMUEL W. HAMILTON). *Mental Illness: A Guide for the Family*. New York: Commonwealth Fund, 1942.
87. SULLIVAN, H. S. *Conceptions of Modern Psychiatry*. New York and Toronto: W. W. Norton & Co., 1954.
88. ———. *The Interpersonal Theory of Psychiatry*. New York: W. W. Norton & Co., 1953.
89. ———. "Affective Experience in Early Schizophrenia," *Am. J. Psychiat.*, VI (1927), 468–83.
90. ———. "Research in Schizophrenia," *ibid.*, IX (1929), 553.
91. ———. "The Relation of Onset to Outcome in Schizophrenia." In *Schizophrenia (Dementia Praecox)*, pp. 10–111. Baltimore: Williams & Wilkins, 1930.
92. ———. "The Modified Psychoanalytic Treatment of Schizophrenia," *Am. J. Psychiat.*, XI (1931), 519.

93. SULLIVAN, H. S. "Notes on Investigation, Therapy, and Education in Psychiatry and Their Relations to Schizophrenia," *ibid.*, XXVII (1947), 271–80.

94. GLOVER, FENICHEL, STRACHEY, BERGLER, NUNBERG, BIBRING. "Symposium on the Theory of the Therapeutic Results of Psychoanalysis," *Internat. J. Psychoanal.*, XVIII, Parts 2 and 3 (1937).

95. VEITH, ILZA, and WITZLEBEN, HENRY VON. "Psychiatric Thought in Chinese Medicine," *J. Hist. Med. Allied Sc.*, X (1955), 261–68.

96. WEIGERT, EDITH. "Love and Fear: A Psychiatric Interpretation," *J. Pastoral Care*, Vol. II (Summer, 1951).

97. WEXLER, MILTON. "The Structural Problems of Schizophrenia: Therapeutic Implications," *Internat. J. Psychoanal.*, XXXII (1951), 157–66.

98. ———. "The Structural Problems of Schizophrenia: The Role of the Internal Object," *Bull. Menninger Clin.*, XV (1951), 221–34. Reprinted in BRODY, EUGENE B., and REDLICH, FREDERICK C., *Psychotherapy with Schizophrenics*. New York: International Universities Press, 1952.

99. WHITEHORN, JOHN C. "Psychodynamic Considerations in the Treatment of Psychotic Patients," *University of West Ontario M. J.*, XX (1951), 27–41.

100. ———. "Psychodynamic Approach to the Psychoses." In *Dynamic Psychiatry*. Edited by FRANZ ALEXANDER and HELEN ROSS. Chicago: University of Chicago Press, 1952.

101. ———. *Psychotherapy: Modern Trends in Psychological Medicine.* New York: Paul C. Hoeber, 1956.

102. WILL, OTTO A., and COHEN, ROBERT A. "A Report of a Recorded Interview in the Course of Psychotherapy," *Psychiatry*, XVI (1953), 263–82.

103. ZILBOORG, GREGORY. *A History of Medical Psychology.* New York: W. W. Norton & Co., 1941.

104. ZWEIG, STEFAN. *Mental Healers.* London: Cassell & Co.

II

On Psychoanalysis and Psychotherapy

(3)

RECENT ADVANCES IN PSYCHOANALYTIC
THERAPY

In order to discuss recent advances in psychoanalytic therapy, I wish to review briefly certain basic psychoanalytic concepts which have been accepted by all psychoanalysts. The working-of-the-mind is understood to be a result of dynamic interaction between the unconscious and the conscious parts of the mind, whereby _conscious_ and _unconscious_ express not only a degree of consciousness but also a difference in the quality and means of expression. Mental health is established by harmonious interaction between the conscious and unconscious mental processes and by generous adaptation of conscious and unconscious drives and desires to the standards of conscience, on the one hand, and to the requirements of the outer world and the relationships with fellow men, on the other.

Traumatic interference with harmonious interrelations of the mental systems comes from drives and desires which are incompatible with the personal or environmental standards, either as such or because they are linked with frustrated infantile desires and drives whose memories are retained throughout life in the unconscious. Thus a person develops defenses against those drives and desires which threaten his peace, in order to avoid such interference. Because the drives are so powerful, these defenses are never quite successful, and the resulting emotional and mental illnesses are compromises between rejected drives and rejecting mental forces.

The aim of psychoanalytic therapy is to bring these rejected drives and wishes, together with the patient's individual and environmental moral standards, which are the instruments for his rejections, into consciousness and in this way place them at his free disposal. In doing this the conscious self becomes strengthened, since it is no longer involved in the continuous job of repressing mental content from awareness. The patient can then decide independently which desires he wants to accept and which he wishes to reject, his personality no longer being warped or dominated by uncontrollable drives and moral standards. This process permits growth and maturation.

Presented at a symposium on Recent Advances in Therapy in Neurology and Psychiatry before the March, 1941, meeting of the Maryland Psychiatric Society, Baltimore.

Reprinted from _Psychiatry: Journal of the Biology and Pathology of Interpersonal Relations,_ Vol. IV, No. 2 (May, 1941). Copyright by The William Alanson White Psychiatric Foundation, Inc.

The methodology of psychoanalytic therapy lies in the patient's learning to understand his problems intellectually and emotionally while re-experiencing them and working through the dynamics of his conflicts, as they are activated in the interrelationship with the analyst. This relationship itself becomes an object of investigation and interpretation for therapeutic purposes.

Recent advances in psychoanalytic therapy are due first to changing conceptions of the nature of drives elaborated by various modern psychoanalysts. These newer conceptions have not been accepted by a large group who still believe in all the classical concepts originated by Freud.

Freud thought at first that, except for hunger, all drives were of a sexual nature, and later that there were two types of drives, the erotic and the destructive, whereby he used the term *sex* in his own broad sense.

Freud's concepts were seemingly influenced by the culture of the times in which they were conceived: during the instinctivistic and materialistic trends in natural science and medicine and the sexual prudishness of the Victorian age.

Modern psychoanalysts do not, of course, deny that sexual and destructive drives are many times among those which lead up to neurotic and psychotic developments. We believe, however, with Horney, Hill, Sullivan,[1] and others that there are also other powerful drives and desires at the foundation of neurotic and psychotic conflicts. These other powerful drives and desires are used by persons, individually, as a defense, in their efforts to adjust to a competitive world and to gain self-assertion among their fellow men; examples are the need for love and dependence —frequently used as a means of domination—the quest for power, the need for prestige and perfection, and reactive hostility and resentment against those who frustrate the realization of these and other drives.[2]

These drives and desires may or may not have sexual implications— their investigation and interpretation along sex lines is frequently of no therapeutic value to the patient. His need is to see their defensive character, and these and similar drives are frequently just as incompatible with the official standards of our present culture and its repercussions in the individual conscience and, therefore, just as much subject to rejection as were the forbidden sexual drives at the time of Freud's discoveries.

1. Karen Horney, *The Neurotic Personality of Our Time* (New York: W. W. Norton & Co., 1937), and *New Ways in Psychoanalysis* (New York: W. W. Norton & Co., 1939) ; Lewis B. Hill, "The Use of Hostility as Defense," *Psychoanalyt. Quart.*, VII (1938), 254–64; Harry Stack Sullivan, "Socio-psychiatric Research: Its Implications for the Schizophrenia Problem and for Mental Hygiene," *Am. J. Psychiat.*, X (o.s. 87) (1931), 977–91, and "Conceptions of Modern Psychiatry," *Psychiatry*, III (1940), 1–117.

2. The latter is in contradistinction to Freud's concept of the primary existence of destructive drives, the so-called *death instinct*. There are some of us who definitely do not agree with the concept of the death instinct.

This leads to the discussion of another advance in psychoanalysis due to the clarification of Freud's concept of *reality*.

Freud speaks of an objective "reality" of the outside world in contradistinction to the private and frequently unreal inner world of the neurotic. While he clearly points out how greatly the person's immediate surroundings are determined by changing environmental influences, he neglects to see that the same holds true for the world at large, which is dependent on the changes of culture and is lacking in any universal and eternal psychological character.

The "reality" to which, for instance, a Vienna girl of the upper middle classes had to adjust in the period before the first World War is a long way from the "reality" to which an American salesgirl has to adapt herself in this year of 1941.

To give another example: such Freudian concepts as the girl's envy of the boy's genitalia or the boy's competitive hatred for his father and his sexual attraction to his mother hold true and are valuable in therapy with many patients of our particular Western patriarchal culture. Yet they are not found in matriarchal cultures, and we know that they are social concepts and have no universal and biological significance.

Another result of modern sociologic thinking in analysis is shown in Sullivan's concept of a person's adjustment to reality in terms of adaptation to interpersonal relationships.[3] Such a concept was unacceptable in the early days of psychoanalysis because at that time all human relationships were studied only from their sexual aspect.

Our better understanding of the role of human relationships in general goes with more realistic concepts of the special relationship between patient and psychoanalyst.

Freud taught that, ideally, the analyst, as nearly as it is possible, must be a blank to the patient. This is to help the patient express himself more freely about the therapist as his catalytic agent and to transfer to him and work through with him all the unresolved emotional reactions which he has previously felt toward other people. It also makes it at times possible for the patient to use the psychoanalyst as his new conscience while revising his own moral standards which have interfered.[4]

In many ways this concept of the relationship between patient and analyst has proved to be of great value to the patient, and even more so to the analyst. He has learned to understand how many of the patient's emotional reactions are determined by the therapeutic situation rather than by the person of the therapist. This insight enables him to accept

3. The research work done by the Chicago Psychoanalytic Institute on gastrointestinal syndromes as an expression of the patient's give-and-take relationship to his surroundings should be mentioned in this connection.

4. Although it is accepted by many psychoanalysts, Freud's doctrine that this conscience with its conscious and unconscious traits is an independent part of the mind seems to some of us more interesting as hypothesis than as proved fact.

the patient's hatred without counterhostility, his love and appreciation without personal response or conceit; thus it protects both patient and therapist from inappropriate reactions on the part of the analyst.

To this extent the analyst's reaction would be all right. But, if he went further, his aloofness would also become a means of protection against his patient's legitimate reactions to him as a person, whether resentment if he blundered or appreciation when he struck the right chord.

As Ferenczi[5] and his disciples have pointed out at various times, we know now that, being unreal, it is a dangerous pretense to think that one of two partners—the analyst—can remain a shapeless nonentity to the other—the patient—in the course of a therapeutic procedure whose very essence is an intimately interpersonal experience and whose aim is the patient's re-establishment of real contacts in a real world.[6]

Hence our attitude now is to help our patients, in neutrality, to re-experience and re-evaluate emotional reactions. However, we do not spend all our time in an atmosphere of unreal self-protective irresponsibility.

That, of course, does not mean that the analyst will talk about his personal life, personal viewpoints, or emotions to the patient. He will avoid unreasonable emotional counterreactions, and he will not use the patient to serve his own needs instead of the patient's.

Sexual feelings toward the analyst may come up. The analyst who has gone through analysis himself will meet these feelings as he does the patient's other emotional reactions. According to our recent insight, their frequency has been overrated, as have the sexual drives as a traumatic factor in general, and their significance is frequently misinterpreted.

Sex feelings, or expression of such feelings, come up many times as a defense, on the one hand, or, on the other, as an expression of insecurity in patients who do not know how to express attachment or how to ask for reassurance other than in terms of sex.

In principle, all these interpersonal reactions come up in the course of every psychotherapeutic procedure, if not between all patients and physicians. The difference between the psychoanalytic and other psychotherapeutic methods is that analysis asks that the patient and the therapist be aware of and make use of them for the purposes of treatment. Other methods may neglect to see them or may deny their existence.

Another change in psychoanalytic therapy is due to our changed attitude toward interpretations. When analysis was first used, we believed in interpreting every expression of repressed unconscious memories or experience as soon as we could get hold of it in terms of Freud's instinctiv-

5. Sándor Ferenczi, *Further Contributions to the Theory and Technique of Psycho-analysis* (London: Hogarth Press, 1926), pp. 177–238.

6. Helen McLean offered suggestions along this line in a paper on "The Art of Psychoanalysis" presented at the meeting of the Washington-Baltimore Psychoanalytic Society, February 8, 1941.

istic content and vocabulary. We expected these interpretations to be followed immediately by the neurotic patient's relinquishing the symptoms connected with the material pointed out. We have since learned that these expectations were ill founded. A wide variety of suggestions and warnings as to timing and content of interpretations have been offered; for example, that interpretations are to be made only if the patient's present relationship with the analyst is positive enough to grant their acceptance or only if the material is connected with the patient's relationship to the analyst, preferably in its negative phases.

At present many analysts feel an increasing inclination to become more thrifty with interpretations from fear of unduly intellectualizing the patient's experience in analysis. Left alone, the patient will discover the unconscious meaning of many of his experiences without interpretation. Freud warned us to bear in mind that analysis is a procedure designed to cure the patient, not to show him how clever his analyst's interpretations are. It is to be noted that the content of interpretations has altered in accordance with the changing concepts. The avoidance of scientific terms is recommended.

The most important progress has come from learning to deal not only with the rejected, unconscious material and the unconscious rejecting forces but also from exposing defenses in the patient's conscious personality. The previously mentioned defensive drives provide an example. Thus we approach the patient and his problems on a more realistic level and stress the dynamics of his actual relationships and reactions toward his environment. This, of course, does not mean that we neglect to search for and to study his unconscious background.

All modern analysts accept the classical belief in the paramount importance of confronting the patient with the *non*-conscious sources of his mental life, and of rediscovering and working through unconscious material, most of them in the great therapeutic significance of rediscovering forgotten childhood memories. Others, like Horney, wonder about the need and wisdom of stressing the childhood memories.

In short, our notions of the therapeutic value, timing, and contents of interpretations are fluctuating, analysis is moving, and final decisions are to be derived from further experience.

Another advance in analysis comes from a change in the choice of patients. During the last fifteen years attempts have been made to adjust the analytic method to the needs of psychotic patients. Results are still far from satisfactory, but the research under way, while not yet as helpful as we wish, is at least increasing our understanding of psychotic and neurotic processes.

As Freud predicted, the classical conversion hysteria has practically disappeared. Now we understand and treat psychosomatic conditions on a deeper level than previously.

The ever increasing number of neurotic characters has created a new group of patients. Their analyses are long and difficult. A lack of markedly severe symptoms makes it difficult for them to accept treatment. Moreover, the concealed disintegrative forces and their fondness for themselves concentrate resistance to changes in their personality.

Yet successful character analyses are most encouraging; and, since there is no other psychotherapeutic method which enables real changes in character, this seems to be the field reserved for psychoanalytic therapy for a long time to come.

Many other persons, especially those who do not ask for more than a cure of isolated symptoms, should be submitted to shorter psychotherapeutic methods which are simpler and less expensive than the psychoanalytic procedure in its present state of development.

Recent advances in psychoanalytic treatment come from reviewing the instinctivistic concepts of human drives and desires; from giving more consideration to the cultural and realistic aspects of the patient's outer world, his personal relationships in general and with the analyst; from putting more stress than previously on the exposure of conscious defenses of the self; and from including psychoses, psychosomatic syndromes, and neurotic characters in the list of those who may receive psychoanalytic treatment.

(4)

INSIGHT INTO PSYCHOTIC MECHANISMS
AND EMERGENCY PSYCHOTHERAPY

War psychotherapy is of rather recent origin. Its use as we know it to-day was first initiated during the Russian-Japanese War and expanded during World War I. In order not to pack this paper with a large burden of literature, I may mention at this point a review of the literature on war psychiatry until 1940 done by Meyer Maskin under the auspices of the William Alanson White Foundation (1).

The additional experience which had unfortunately to come with the Spanish Civil War and the present world war was the need for emergency psychiatry of the civilian victims of modern total warfare. In dealing with this new art and science we are faced with two problems of equally great significance: (a) What can we learn from our experience in peacetime psychiatry that may improve the speed and efficiency of emergency psychotherapy? and (b) What contributions from our experience in emergency psychotherapy can be made to general psychiatry as a healing art and as a science of human relationships?

In view of the cultural values for which this country and her allies wish to fight, it may be an encouraging sign on a bleak horizon and may help to raise the morale of physicians and patients if we look at our emergency duties from both aspects, as highly practical and as scientific and cultural. Let me therefore offer some suggestions from both angles which have come to me in regard to the mutual influence of insight into psychotic mechanisms and emergency psychotherapy.

Among the papers which have been published so far, I was especially impressed by one written by the British psychiatrist, Dr. Felix Brown of Oxford, "Civilian Psychiatric Air Raid Casualties" (2). Like Gillespie (3), whom most of you heard recently during his stay in this country, Brown mentions two surprising facts which were observed during the air raids on the British Isles: (a) the small number of psychiatric casualties, which in fact were so infrequent that many hospitals which had been prepared for psychiatric air-raid casualties were soon converted to gen-

Read before the Section on Neurology and Psychiatry of the Maryland Psychiatric Society, February 5, 1942.

Reprinted from *Medical Annals of the District of Columbia*, Vol. XII, No. 3 (March, 1943)

eral hospital use, and (b) the immediate cure of acute emotional disturbances such as shock, indicated by tremor, dilated pupils, severe tachycardia, fear and anxiety states, and transient hysterical reactions, such as limp, semistuporous states, conditions of acute fright, and conversion symptoms.

If patients suffering from these reactions could be seen by the psychiatrist immediately after the trauma, be it at the place where the accident occurred, the air-raid shelter, or the casualty station, and if they were encouraged to give immediately the whole history of the trauma and their emotional reactions to it, complete cure of their acute emotional reactions could be accomplished. Also endurance of later air raids was improved.

They were, of course, approached tactfully, reassuringly, and cautiously but were pressed to fill every possible gap in the history of their accident and their emotional reactions to it, no matter how distressing it seemed to recall it. Only if the patients were too dazed to speak, was history-taking delayed.

Once the psychiatrist had succeeded in making the air-raid victim talk about everything pertaining to the accident, the patient was put to sleep. The choice and the amount of sedatives were determined by the severity of the victim's experience and the seriousness of his emotional reactions. Milder cases were put to sleep at the casualty station for something like 3 hours by small doses of chloralhydrate or potassium bromide and then sent home. More serious cases stayed for 1 day and night, others for something like a week at the hospital, with sleep of 13 hours during the night and 2 or 3 hours twice a day by means of 6 grains of nembutal, $7\frac{1}{2}$ grains of sodium amytal, or evipan narcosis. Additionally, morphine and hyoscine were given in very disturbed cases.

All acute psychiatric casualties which were treated in this way recovered immediately and completely, no matter how severe the actual accident had been. Psychoneuroses with more permanent symptoms developed only if and when it was impossible for the victims to be seen by the psychiatrist immediately after the accident, so that there was time to force the memory of the traumatic experience out of their awareness. It is this act of making the air-raid victims talk in detail and explicitly about the accident and its emotional repercussions immediately after it has happened that Brown considers the crucial point of treatment. He fully recognizes that the victim cannot overcome the pathogenic influence of the traumatic experience without being given the benefit of complete relaxation and extensive sleep after the discussion; but he is anxious to have the victims talk before he puts them to sleep, because he wants to hinder "repression" and to encourage immediate integration of the traumatic experience.

To repeat, in all psychiatric air-raid casualties in which the method of immediate thorough discussion of the accident and the victim's emotional reactions to it, with subsequent sedation, could be accomplished, complete cure was obtained. Chronic psychoneuroses were observed only when immediate history-taking was impossible. Psychoses were observed only in predisposed personalities.

In military psychotherapy similar experience has been gathered. Some military psychiatrists recommend immediate history-taking from the air-raided soldier as Brown does from the civilian air-raid victims. Others suggest psychocatharsis with or without hypnosis. Still others recommend sodium amytal ($7\frac{1}{2}$ grains) to be given very slowly intravenously in doses which help the patient to relax sufficiently to express himself without putting him to sleep. All these treatment suggestions have the common basic idea of getting the traumatic experience into the open as quickly as possible after it has taken place, thus hindering the patient from forcing it out of awareness and turning it into a repressed, and hence pathogenic, emotional experience.

I said that we were surprised when we heard Brown's and Gillespie's reports. And yet those of us who are trained in modern genetic and dynamic psychiatry should not have been surprised at all. We should have expected the gratifying results of a method of treatment which is altogether based on our modern knowledge of the genesis of peacetime neuroses and psychoses. Modern psychiatry teaches, as you know, that there are traumatic emotional experiences at the basis of every psychoneurosis or psychosis. There are, above all, frustrating childhood experiences which are too hard for the child to face, much less to integrate, either because of the actual severity of the experience or because of its significance in fantasy or because of the child's unfavorable environmental or constitutional background, which has made him hypersensitive toward the vicissitudes of life. Therefore, the infantile mind tries to make these experiences ineffective by forcing them out of awarness (by "repressing" them). However, that does not mean that they really disappear. No emotional experience which we undergo at any time of our life can actually vanish. Yet, if we do not dare, or are unable, to face it and to integrate it and it is, instead, pushed out of awareness, it remains, as it were, like an emotional foreign body at the bottom of our mental organism. So do the repressed unhappy childhood experiences. The result is that the child's reactions to these early thwarting experiences do not integrate with the maturing process of the rest of the self, so that the person, as he grows up, will not be able to take further thwarting experiences and frustrations as they come to him in later life on the same level of maturity that he has otherwise attained at the time. Instead, he will face them with the immature emotional equipment he possessed at the time he was first repressing early emotional injuries. Furthermore, he will add the pain and hurt experienced in the early times to the hardship of every later painful experience, because there was no opportunity to assimilate and digest the first thwarting experiences because of their early repression. Hence any further disappointment or frustrating experience in later life is standing not only for itself but also for the first early emotional traumata, and for all subsequent frustrations with which they are tied up by the mutual bond of the initial traumata. Consequently, the endurance of warp and frustration is considerably diminished for such a person. Sooner or later, one of the disappointments he may have to undergo will represent the last link in a chain of unintegrated injuries which will at last lead up to emotional sickness.

What are psychiatrists doing to treat these conditions? We try to help the patient to revive the initial repressed traumatic experiences, to relive them with the psychiatrist, to discuss and rediscuss them with him; and we expect that it will contribute to the patient's final cure if he succeeds at last in facing the initial "repressed" traumatic experiences, in getting emotional and intellectual insight into their working, and eventually in integrating them, so that they are no longer interfering with his ability to meet the vicissitudes of later life.

If it is true that the repression of early traumatic experiences is paramount among the causes for neurotic and psychotic developments in peacetime, then we understand that keeping an air-raid victim from repressing his traumatic experience when it arises safeguards him against the development of a later emotional disturbance. And if it is true that repression of previous traumatic experiences is responsible for a person's lessened tolerance for similar ones which he may have to undergo subsequently, we understand that safeguarding against repression and helping in the conscious integration of one traumatic air-raid experience will make for increased endurance of later ones.

Now as to the other "surprising" observation of our British colleagues —the comparatively small number of psychiatric air-raid casualties—let us see whether our experience in peacetime psychiatry offers ways of understanding and explaining this observation also.

The theory of the genesis of mental disturbances we have given so far holds true for both neuroses and psychoses. In the genesis of various types of psychoses, we find an additional important fact which may throw some light on the experience of the British psychiatrists in emergency psychiatry. It seems that they do not fall sick simply because of the unbearable repetition of very early infantile warping experience but also because of the tremendous amount of resentment, rage, anger, and hostility they develop in response to these and the subsequent thwarting experiences that life has inflicted on them. This hostility calls in turn for a tremendous insecurity, in part for fear of hostility from the surroundings. Hence fear of their own hostility and fear of hostility from other people play a great role in the etiology of these psychoses. Proof of this hypothesis came to us while observing patients whose recovery was largely encouraged if they were given the opportunity to get rid of their excess hostility by expressing it fully to the psychotherapist and to be freed from their fear of hostility in other people by the experience of never meeting any of it in their contacts with their psychotherapist.

What bearing has this experience on our understanding of the unexpectedly small number of psychiatric air-raid casualties? To feel hostility which has to be repressed and to be afraid of hostility in other people make for serious mental disturbances in peacetime. The air-raid victim has not only no reason to keep his hostility from his awareness, but hostility against a foe who inflicts the air-raid accidents on him is expected and required. Also, since there cannot be any repressed fear of outside hostility, because the victim's hostility is the overt response to the hostile act inflicted on him by the enemy, two important reasons for the rise of mental disturbances in peacetime—fear of the patient's own repressed hostility and of hostility in his fellow men—are out of the question in psychiatric air-raid casualties.

In addition, there is one other factor: peacetime neuroses or psychoses arise from personal emotional traumata experienced by the individual patient, and his emotional response to it is a highly personalized one. Most peacetime neurotics and psychotics feel distinctly that nobody else will feel and react the way they do, and they are very reluctant to compare notes with their neighbor, as it were. The contrary holds true for air-raid victims: the air raid itself, as well as the common reaction of hostility and resentment against the enemy which it arouses, is a group experience which one victim shares with the next. This fact constitutes another safeguard against serious mental disturbances after air raids.

This insight has been used by the British psychiatrists in their therapeutic efforts with their psychiatric air-raid casualties. As soon as the victims were cured from the acute traumatic shock, they were encouraged to join their fellow victims in the emergency group work necessary during or after an air raid.

This leads to one further explanation of the small number of psychiatric casualties as offered by the Canadian psychiatrist Scott in his paper, "The Soldier's Defense and the Public Attitude" (4). Scott states that the number of psychiatric casualties among the armed forces has also been smaller than expected. He thinks that it is partly due to the forced inactivity of the trench warfare during World War I; i.e., he considers the increased military activity to be a safeguard against psychiatric casualties among soldiers, just as the psychiatrists for civilian air-raid victims believe also when they use group activity for therapeutic and prophylactic purposes.

Scott mentions one more reason for the decrease in the number of psychiatric casualties among soldiers which we also consider valid for civilians, namely, the change in the cultural attitude toward fear and anxiety now as compared with twenty-five or thirty years ago. Formerly a soldier who felt fear and anxiety had to do all he could to hide it from his fellow soldiers, if not from himself. Otherwise, he would be stigmatized as a coward in his own mind and in the evaluation of his comrades and superiors. Nowadays any soldier is supposed to know, and is allowed to admit to himself and to others, that he is frightened when his life and health are threatened. This does not make him a coward in his own eyes or in those of his comrades or superiors. In this war the soldier is supposed to fight, not because he does not know any fear, but in spite of his fear.

The same holds true for the civilian air-raid victim. He too may be frightened, yet, because of our present cultural attitude, fear and anxiety need not be suppressed. Therefore, they do not work as pathogenic agents. Many times the contrary may be true. Fear and anxiety are something which the individual air-raid victim has in common with the rest of the air-raided community. As a frankly admitted emotional group experience, fear and anxiety may safeguard against mental sickness, as does the open expression of group hostility.

So far we have discussed the contribution of psychiatric disturbances in peacetime to the understanding of emergency psychotherapy. Now to our second question: What contributions to peacetime psychiatry are to be gained by Brown's and Gillespie's experience with psychiatric air-raid casualties?

The favorable psychotherapeutic results which the authors obtained by safeguarding their patients against repression encourage further emphasis on those modern pedagogic and medical teachings which advocate frank unrepressed emotional expression in healthy children as a safeguard against the rise of neuroses and psychoses in later life.

Sleep treatment as used by Brown and Gillespie with psychiatric air-raid victims has been given in peacetime psychotherapy to psychoses only. The good results with emergency cases lead to the question whether sleep treatment of peacetime neuroses may be indicated after an actual severe traumatic emotional experience, as well as in cases of seriously upsetting revival and reliving of highly traumatic material from the past in the course of psychotherapy. Further investigation of this question as a possible means of shortening peacetime psychotherapy of neuroses appears promising.

One very important factor in the psychiatric treatment of air-raid casualties has not been sufficiently stressed in the British literature. That is the question of the therapeutic significance of the personal relationship between the psychiatrist and the air-raid victim.

It has been said that the results in civilian emergency psychotherapy are, by and large, better than in military psychotherapy. The fact that the soldier, unlike the civilian, has no immediate gain from his recovery has been made responsible for this difference. We believe that there is another more important reason. As mentioned before, the crucial part of modern peacetime psychotherapy is the discussion of, and the patient's insight into, his interpersonal relationship with the psychotherapist with all its ramifications. This relationship is built up on the background of our knowledge that the mentally sick are different from so-called healthy people (including the psychiatrist) only by degree and not in kind. On the background of this attitude, a natural, spontaneous, and matter-of-fact relationship between patient and doctor should be developed which makes it possible for the patient to overcome his reluctance and inhibitions toward entering into a therapeutic discussion of his problems and conflicts and toward using the psychiatrist as a catalytic agent for his previous traumatic interpersonal experiences.

While the doctor's attitude should be completely free from sentimentality or overfriendliness, it is self-evident that the condition sine qua non of any such psychotherapeutic procedure is that the doctor meet the patient on an equal level and not in the spirit of any pre-established authority other than that of his medical and psychiatric training and experience. The military psychiatrist will have a hard time making his patients trust his intention to meet them as equals. Being a commissioned officer, he is in danger of remaining a superior in the soldier's mind, much as he may consciously try to ignore the military situation while in psychotherapeutic contact with his patient. That is what Colonel Porter seems to have in mind when he mentions in his paper "The Military Psychiatrist at Work": "he must possess tact to a superlative degree" (5). At the present time the Navy tries to dispose of these difficulties somewhat better than the Army by having the physicians wear doctor's uniforms while working, by encouraging the sailors to address the physicians as "doctor" instead of using their military title, and by having the physicians address each other as "doctor" rather than according to their military rank. See also Gillespie's "Psychological Effects of War on Citizen and Soldier" (3).

I had the opportunity to follow up the work of a young psychotherapist, a medical officer in the Army, who tried to do consistent psychotherapy with a private before his dismissal. Even though the soldier knew he would be dismissed from the army, treatment was not successful because the patient was not able to take any therapeutic suggestions in their own right. No matter how the psychiatrist put his suggestions, the soldier took them as orders given to him by his superior; beneficial or not, he had to follow them. Any reasonably free discussion of the patient's relationship with his doctor and superior seemed impossible.

On the other hand, a report came to me from a psychiatrist who worked at one of the large recruiting centers of the country and who succeeded in convincing the recruits that he actually wanted to meet them on an equal level. Realizing that the future soldier, being examined by the psychiatrist, would be as suspicious and sensitive as any psychiatric patient under treatment, the doctor tried to convey to his recruits the idea of a wholesome mutual interpersonal relationship on the basis of equality, by certain intangibles in attitude and gestures rather than by spoken words. He knew from his psychiatric experience with the mentally sick how frequently people feel that words are used not only to convey the real meaning of things but also to cover it up. The soldiers believed him, and he was said to have seen and evaluated two and a half times as many recruits in a given time as his less experienced and less gifted colleagues. What is true for the approach to recruits in psychiatric examinations will be just as true and perhaps more so for the therapeutic approach to the soldier. This means that successful psychotherapy can be done only on the basis of a successful patient-physician interrelationship. The military situation between medical officer and non-commissioned soldier-patient is an obstacle to its establishment. This interference does not exist for the psychiatrist who treats civilian air-raid victims. I believe this to be the main reason for the better results in their treatment versus those in military psychiatry.

Brown and Gillespie do not explicitly elaborate on the question of their personal interrelationship with their successfully treated air-raid victims. Nonetheless, one gains the firm conviction from the atmosphere of Brown's paper that their skill in establishing the right kind of human attitude toward and the right kind of interrelationship with their patients has been one of the decisive reasons for their success.

In addition to its therapeutic value, there is another reason why non-authoritarian psychiatric guidance on the basis of a valid doctor-patient relationship is of paramount significance in our days. To some patients the individual experience of that type of relationship may serve as illustration and symbol of the general idea for which combatant and non-combatant victims are supposed and are willing to suffer and to fight, real human interrelationships in the spirit of freedom and democracy versus totalitarian submission and versus authoritarian leadership.

References

1. MASKIN, M. "Psychodynamic Aspects of War Neuroses," *Psychiatry*, IV (1941), 97.
2. BROWN, F. "Civilian Psychiatric Air-Raid Casualties," paper read by Dr. Frank Luton at the 1940 meeting of the Southern Psychiatric Association, Nashville, Tennessee.
3. GILLESPIE, R. D. *Psychological Effects of War on Citizen and Soldier.* (Salmon Lectures.) New York: W. W. Norton & Co., 1942.
4. SCOTT, W. C. M. "Soldier's Defence and Public's Attitude," *Lancet*, II (1941), 271.
5. PORTER, W. C. "Military Psychiatrist at Work," *Am. J. Psychiat.*, XCVIII (1941), 317.

(5)

NOTES ON PERSONAL AND PROFESSIONAL
REQUIREMENTS OF A PSYCHOTHERAPIST

The average psychiatrist who has acquired some knowledge of the principles of intensive psychotherapy has studied mainly the psychotherapeutic process and the problems concerning the patient's personality. Unless he has undergone psychoanalytic training, not much attention has been given to the investigation of his personality. Unless the psychotherapist is widely aware of his own interpersonal processes, so that he can handle them for the benefit of the patient in their interpersonal therapeutic dealings with each other, no successful psychotherapy can eventuate.

It is to the immortal credit of Sigmund Freud that he was the first to understand and describe the psychotherapeutic process in terms of an interpersonal experience between the patient and the psychiatrist and that he was the first to call attention to and study the personality of the psychotherapist as well as the patient's and their mutual interpersonal relationship. Only those psychotherapists who have done psychotherapy both before and after being acquainted with Freud's concepts will be able to realize the full extent of the significance of his discovery of the laws governing the interpersonal exchange between psychotherapist and patient. I personally remember only too well the time when I dealt psychotherapeutically with mental patients before I was acquainted with Freud's teachings. I realized, with distress, that something went on in the patients' relations with me, and in my relations with them, which interfered with the psychotherapeutic process. Yet I could not put my finger on it, define it, or investigate it. What a relief it was to become acquainted with the tools furnished by Freud for investigation into the awareness of the doctor-patient relationship. Prior to these discoveries, psychiatrists had been in the dark, both to the detriment of their patients and to the disadvantage of their professional self-respect.[1]

Reprinted from *Psychiatry: Journal of the Biology and Pathology of Interpersonal Relations*, Vol. XII, No. 4 (November, 1949). Copyright by The William Alanson White Psychiatric Foundation, Inc.

1. Sigmund Freud, *A General Introduction to Psychoanalysis* (New York: Liveright Pub. Corp., 1935), chap. xxvii on "Transference," and chap. xxviii on "The Analytic Therapy." See also Freud, "On Psychotherapy" (1904), *Collected Papers*, I, 249-63; "The Dynamics of the Transference" (1912), *ibid.*, II, 312–22; "Further Recommendations in the Technique

The debt of gratitude to Freud for his discovery of the need to study the doctor-patient relationship, in regard to the patient's as well as the doctor's part in it, still holds true, regardless of the fact that Freud and his disciples subsequently nullified part of its far-reaching implications. As we know, Freud taught that all our relationships with other people, including the relationship of the mental patient with his doctor, are patterned by our early relationships with the significant people of our environment in infancy and childhood. Our later interpersonal difficulties have to be understood in terms of these early interpersonal tie-ups. The vicissitudes of the patient's experiences with the doctor in particular have to be investigated and understood for psychotherapeutic purposes. Since they are transferred from unresolved difficulties in interpersonal relationships with the significant people of the patient's early life, they are "transference" experiences.

Countertransference experiences, in their turn, as they may come up and interfere with the psychotherapeutic process, must be investigated, understood, and, if possible, eliminated in terms of their being transferred from the early interpersonal experiences of the doctor with the significant people of *his* infancy and childhood.

It is true that the patterns of our later interpersonal relationships are built up in our early lives, are repeated in our later lives, and can be understood through the medium of their repetition with people in general and through the medium of the mutual aspects of the doctor-patient relationship in particular. There is, however, danger of carrying this insight too far. At the present developmental phase of dynamic psychoanalytic psychiatry, we still believe that it is not only helpful but indispensable for psychotherapeutic success to study the patient's and the psychiatrist's mutual relationships in terms of their repetitional characteristics. But we keenly feel that this should not be done to the point of neglecting to scrutinize the reality of the actual experience between therapist and patient in its own right. This viewpoint is also inherent in Freud's original teachings. But his transference doctrine gave an opening to explain away the facts of actual experiences between the therapist and the patient here and now. In practice, this has at times carried with it the danger of inducing therapists to neglect the significance of the vicissitudes of the actual doctor-patient relationship versus its transference aspects.

There is another point of departure from Freud's original "transference" conceptions in the concepts of psychoanalytic psychotherapy as they are outlined here. This non-agreement stems from the fact that our thinking does not coincide with Freud's doctrine of the ubiquity of

of Psychoanalysis: Observations of Transference-Love" (1915), *ibid.*, II, 377–429; and *New Introductory Lectures on Psychoanalysis* (1915) (New York: W. W. Norton & Co., 1933), chap. vi on "Explanations, Applications, and Orientations."

the Oedipus complex, the positive (sexual) attachment to the parent of the opposite sex, with concomitant rivalrous hatred for the parent of the same sex. Consequently, we do not try to understand, as a foregone conclusion, therapists' difficulties in their relationships with patients and vice versa as repetitions of their unresolved Oedipus constellations.[2]

Harry Stack Sullivan has introduced the term "parataxis" instead of "transference" and "countertransference." Parataxic interpersonal experiences are distortions in people's present interpersonal relationships. They are conditioned by carry-overs of a person's previous interpersonal experiences, prevalent from infancy and childhood but not always or necessarily from entanglements with his parents.

So much for the discussion of the concepts of transference and countertransference and parataxis in their relevance for the understanding of the interpersonal processes of the psychotherapist. From this explanation it follows that the interpersonal processes of the psychotherapist, as a private and as a professional person, must be investigated and recognized both in regard to the possibility of their being distorted as "countertransference," as "parataxic" experiences, and in regard to the present interpersonal situation. This is one reason for requiring a personal psychoanalysis as part of the training for doing intensive psychotherapy.

What, then, are the basic requirements as to the personality and the professional abilities of a psychotherapist? If I were asked to answer this question in one sentence, I would reply: "The psychotherapist must be able to listen." This does not appear to be a startling statement, but it is intended to be just that. To be able to listen to and to gather information from another person, in this other person's own right, without reacting along the lines of one's own problems or experiences, of which one may be reminded perhaps in a disturbing way, is an art of interpersonal exchange which few people are able to practice without special training. To be in command of this art is by no means tantamount to actually being a good psychotherapist, but it is the prerequisite for all intensive psychotherapy.

If it is true that the therapist has to avoid reacting to the patient's data in terms of his own life, this means that he must have enough sources of satisfaction and security in his non-professional life to forego the temptation of using his patients for the pursuit of his personal satisfaction or security. If he has not succeeded in getting the personal fulfilments in life which he wanted and needed, he should realize this. His attitude toward the sources of dissatisfaction and unhappiness in his life must then be clarified and integrated to the extent that they do not interfere with his emotional stability and with his ability to concentrate upon listening to the patient. This is a second reason for making a per-

2. Patrick Mullahy, *Oedipus Myth and Complex* (New York: Hermitage Press, 1948); see "The Family Complex," pp. 26–27.

sonal psychoanalysis a training requirement for a psychotherapist. Additional reasons will be discussed later.

The statement that the patient should not be a source of satisfaction and security to the psychotherapist is, of course, not in reference to their actual, overt dealings with each other, since it is common knowledge that the professional relationship between psychiatrists and patients precludes any sort of non-professional mutual intimacy. What I am referring to is the danger that the discontented psychotherapist may use in fantasy the data collected from the patient as a substitutive source of satisfaction.

For example, a patient may tell a therapist who has just experienced an unhappy love relationship about problems of a similar nature. The psychiatrist should be sufficiently detached from his own problems that he does not relate himself to the patient's experience and indulge in an orgy of self-referral.

Or: A woman-psychoanalyst, who has passed the menopause and who regrets having had only one child, hears about the third or fourth pregnancy of one of her patients. There should be no preoccupation with the denial of her own wishes intruding into her concentration upon the patient's report of her pregnancy.

Again: A patient relates to the psychiatrist his progress in a happy courtship. The psychiatrist, having in mind the lack of glamour in his own life, may use the patient's account as one might use fiction or screen romance, as a starting point for fantasies of his own, projecting himself into the role of the patient or of the patient's partner instead of concentrating exclusively upon listening to the patient in his own right.

The same sort of experience may take place as a patient relates success or failure in prestige in any field. Whenever wishes or ambitions, fulfilments or failures, similar to those in the psychiatrist's career are touched upon, he has to counteract the danger of using the patient's narrative as a starting point for dream satisfactions of his own instead of using its narration as a source for collecting further helpful data about the patient. Although this ultimate goal has already been stated in the Hippocratic oath, the psychotherapist will only rarely be able, of course, to fulfil this ideal. Should he be unable to do so, he is expected to be aware of it, so that he can safeguard against the possibility of undesirable therapeutic consequences. This holds true for fantasies in the realm of both satisfaction and security.

In speaking about "satisfaction" and "security" as the two goals of fulfilment that man pursues, I follow Sullivan's definition.[3] "Satisfaction," he says, is the result of fulfilments in the realm of that which

3. Harry Stack Sullivan, *Conceptions of Modern Psychiatry* (Washington, D.C.: The William Alanson White Psychiatric Foundation, 1947).

has to do with the bodily organization, the glandular processes, such as satisfaction of hunger, sexual gratification, need for sleep, and avoidance of physical loneliness. "Security" refers to the fulfilment of that which has to do with the cultural equipment of a person, the word "cultural" referring to everything that is man-made. Security, then, means fulfilment of a person's wishes for prestige and his being able to use his powers, skills, and abilities successfully for interpersonal goals within the range of his interests.

How, then, does the psychotherapist's need for satisfaction and security bear upon his ability to listen, in addition to the previously discussed danger of allowing the material received from the patient to arouse his own fantasy?

Satisfaction of hunger has been mentioned as the first necessary fulfilment; that, in our culture, means to have or to earn the money with which to buy food. The psychotherapist earns this money by means of his professional dealings with his patients. In that sense, practicing his profession is a legitimate source of satisfaction for him. What he has to safeguard against, however, is making psychotherapy with one patient the sole source of his satisfaction. In order to avoid having this happen, it is recommended that, in starting private practice, the young psychiatrist begin psychotherapy with two patients or combine intensive psychotherapy with one patient with additional psychiatric activities of another type, such as part-time institutional work, teaching, consultations, and so on. However unimportant this may seem to the inexperienced, psychotherapy with only one patient as the single source of income may be easily doomed to failure.

Sexual gratification has been quoted as the second goal of satisfaction in man's life. The psychotherapist has to safeguard strictly against using the patient, actually or in fantasy, for the pursuit of lust, so that sexual fantasies with regard to the patient or the partners the patient mentions or identification with the patient or his partners in their sexual experiences does not interfere with the psychotherapist's ability to listen.

Needless to say, man's third goal of satisfaction—his need for sleep—should not be sought by the psychotherapist while attending to his professional obligations. But, unfortunately, I am giving away no secret when I state that there are therapists who fall asleep while they are supposed to be listening to their patients, especially if the psychiatrist sits behind the patient and they do not see each other. There are even rationalizations in the psychiatric dictionary for such unforgivable errors in procedure—such as "I fall asleep only if the patient produces irrelevant material and wake up as soon as the patient's productions become relevant." In marked contrast to such flimsy rationalization, I wish to emphasize strongly my viewpoint that the answer of the therapist to the patient's producing irrelevancies is not to take a nap but to listen sufficiently alertly that he can interrupt and direct the patient toward the production of more relevant material. This statement implies a change of attitude with regard to the technique of "free associations" as used in classical psychoanalysis. I will elaborate on this topic later. If the psychiatrist indulges in napping during the psychotherapeutic interview, it interferes with his ability to listen and to conduct the interview adequately. It also has the implication of lowering the patient's self-respect as the doctor evidences how little interested he is in the patient and his communications. This may turn out to be quite disastrous to the psychotherapeutic process, because the self-esteem of a psychiatric patient is very low to begin with. His lack of self-respect, his insecurity, is, as a rule, wittingly or unwittingly, one of the reasons for his needing psychotherapy.

One of the important principles of intensive psychotherapy is that the psychiatrist endeavor not to hurt the patient's self-respect unnecessarily. The classical psychoanalytic setup of the doctor sitting behind the patient, who is lying on the couch, may imply the danger of encouraging any inclination on the part of the psychiatrist to drowse. At the time when the technique and methods of classical psychoanalytic therapy were developed, this position was considered desirable, to facilitate a state of complete relaxation in the patient, which would make it possible for him to associate freely and to eliminate embarrassment while relating delicate and painful material. Moreover, the founder of classical psychoanalysis, Sigmund Freud, felt that he personally was not up to having patients look at him eight hours daily, and he assumed that many of his colleagues might have the same difficulty.[4]

Since then, psychoanalytic insight and technique have undergone a great development. To many psychoanalytic psychiatrists it now appears that the psychiatric knowledge of the dynamics of mental processes has grown to the point where it is not necessary, as a rule, to gain an initial acquaintance with the patient's psychopathology by listening to his free associations over a period of time before any active psychotherapeutic intervention may be administered.[5] In addition, many topics, the communication of which was formerly fraught with extreme hesitancy and shyness, have gradually lost the connotation of embarrassment for most people in this culture during the last fifty years. Indeed, it is because of Freud's teachings that there is today a more normal attitude toward the discussion of formerly prohibited sexual subject matter. Suggestions on technique, which he originally made to conform with the sensitivities of his contemporaries, are therefore now outdated by the very results of his teachings.

4. Freud, *A General Introduction to Psychoanalysis.*
5. F. Alexander, T. French, *et al., Psychoanalytic Therapy: Principles and Application* (New York: Ronald Press Co., 1946).

As to the hardship for the psychotherapist in being gazed at daily for eight hours, I believe that there were two reasons, both of which can be discounted today. One was that the therapist was liable to share the embarrassment of his patient while listening to difficult communications. The second was the original psychoanalytic concept, according to which the psychotherapist was supposed to show no signs whatsoever of reacting to, or participating in, the patient's communications. The more colorless and the more inanimate the countenance of the psychotherapist appeared, the more nearly he approached the idea of serving the patient as a recording machine on which he could record whatever was on his mind. This inanimate attitude also served as a safeguard against the psychoanalyst's becoming personally involved with his patients and with the emotional experiences which they were reciting. The consistent control of facial expression, posture, and gestures which the psychoanalyst had to exert under these conditions made it very hard indeed for him to be exposed to his patients' visual scrutiny all day long.[6]

Nowadays many psychoanalysts no longer think of the psychotherapist as being unresponsive to and only a mirror of the patient's utterances. We consider him a participant-observer in the psychotherapeutic process. Also, we do not believe that it is necessary or desirable for the psychiatrist to bar responsive reactions of spontaneity from the psychotherapeutic scene, as long as his responses cannot be used by patients as a means of orientation inadvertently guiding their productions and behavior. Also they must, of course, be genuine responses to the patient's communications and not colored by his private collateral experiences.

With these two concepts in mind, I consider it, by and large, much more desirable to have an arrangement which makes it possible for both the patient and the therapist to look at each other or not, as the occasion may warrant. Prohibiting the use of visual contact as an aid in the therapeutic process is an unnecessary deterrent and makes for an unreal situation. This holds true especially for psychotic patients, whose lack of orientation in the outer world has to be counteracted by the visible and audible reality of another person.[7]

As to the fourth goal of human satisfaction—the avoidance of physical loneliness—it goes without saying that the patient should not be used for its achievement. This does not mean advocating that the psychiatrist be an obsessional denizen of our culture, wherein touching another person or being touched by him is considered taboo unless there is an intimate relationship. The contrary is true. At times it may be wise and indicated to shake hands with a patient or, in the case of a very dis-

6. Frieda Fromm-Reichmann, "Recent Advances in Psychoanalytic Therapy," *Psychiatry*, IV (1941), 161–64.

7. Frieda Fromm-Reichmann, "Psychoanalytic Psychotherapy with Psychotics," *ibid.*, VI (1943), 277–79.

turbed person, to touch him reassuringly or not to refuse his gesture of seeking affection and closeness. However, it is always recommended that one be thrifty with the expression of any physical closeness in one's psychotherapeutic contacts.

Stating that occasional gestures of physical closeness are a part of directed psychotherapeutic endeavor does not, however, mean that physical intimacy is ever recommended where it is not carried out for the well-defined needs of the patient, that is, for strictly psychotherapeutic reasons. A psychotherapist who is lonely must watch that his own need for physical closeness does not interfere with his coming to the right conclusions about the patient's needs. He must safeguard against a lack of alertness in listening due to this interference of his own unresolved needs.

Security operations should interfere with the psychiatrist's ability to listen just as little as do his personal needs for satisfaction. The psychiatrist who needs the individual patient to build up his prestige and to prove to himself that he is able to use his powers and his skills successfully will be in danger of trying to impress his patient instead of being impressed by the patient's needs and trouble. This could hold true especially for the young psychiatrist, who must try to counteract his own insecurity in two ways which will interfere with his ability to listen. First, he may feel called upon to hide his insecurity by displaying professional pompousness. Such an endeavor is highly undesirable; in fact, it may doom the psychotherapeutic procedure to failure. As stated before, every mental patient suffers from an impairment in self-assurance; that is, he is insecure and anxious. This being so, he will be most sensitive to the attempts of other persons at hiding their insecurity. If this other person is the psychotherapist, the therapist's own ill-disguised insecurity will add to the patient's anxiety. The patient will not feel free to confide in the psychiatrist and to believe in his ability to listen. Psychotherapeutic collaboration will be defeated.[8]

The young psychiatrist who may feel called upon to try to impress his patients might keep in mind, furthermore, how unnecessary this is because the patients who come to see him want help. They expect him to be competent to offer this help because of his training or because he has been recommended by a successfully treated patient or by an older psychiatrist. Patients tend toward health, and they are lonely. Their wish for help, their tendency toward health, and their loneliness are much more important to them than the chronological or professional age of the person to whom they turn for this aid.

The second way in which the psychiatrist may try to bolster his inse-

8. Incidentally, psychiatrists who got their training in central Europe and who are doing psychotherapy in this country now should keep in mind that their Anglo-Saxon patients will resent any display of pompousness even more than their European patients did.

curity, namely, by cultivating his patients' dependence and admiration, is therefore equally unnecessary. This may interfere with the psychiatrist's ability to listen even more than the direct display of pompousness. The cultivation of such attitudes pushes his patients into a state of dependence instead of working toward their growth, independence, and an ability to use their own judgment. To put it differently, the psychiatrist duplicates the demands for unqualified love and acceptance of authority which the parents or other significant adults of the patient's childhood may have imposed on him, to his detriment. In Freud's terminology, he artificially cultivates the patient's positive transference. As he does so, he can be reasonably certain that contrary results will be obtained in the long run. The patients will resent the psychiatrist's interference with their tendency toward and wish for growth and independence which are among the reasons for which they came to see the doctor, and they will hate their would-be helper for failing them. In other words, the psychiatrist's attempts at artificially cultivating his patient's positive transference will necessarily breed a negative attitude in the patient toward the psychiatrist.

Some unfortunate results of the need of the insecure psychiatrist to use the patient as a test tube for his skills and powers should be mentioned at this point. Such a psychiatrist may be so preoccupied with the idea that his patients have to get well for the sake of his reputation that he will listen to them and conduct treatment in such a way that he deafens himself against and disregards the patient's real needs and striving for improvement. Or the insecure psychiatrist may feel that the patient must understand whatever the doctor feels called upon to point out, disregarding the question of whether or not the patient is ready to follow at the time. In the same vein, he may answer the patient's failure to understand with an intensified irritation, which, in turn, will certainly becloud the legitimate issues of the psychotherapeutic process.

Moreover, the patient is liable to feel that he is being used as a means of strengthening the psychiatrist's reputation rather than as an object of treatment in his own right; this attitude could well be conducive to the failure of treatment.

In this connection, I recall the unhappy neurotic son of a powerful and influential father, whose life was dedicated solely to the increase of his father's prestige and reputation. He expected everyone with whom he came in contact to function only in order to impress his influential father or to be seeking prestige as his father did. Of course, the patient expected his physician to behave accordingly. "If I get well," he volunteered in his first interview, "it will be quite a feather in your cap." The psychiatrist was fortunately not preoccupied with his reputation, so that he heard the patient and the implications of his sarcastically polite remark. Much to the patient's surprise, he replied with serious simplicity that his reputation was established to his own satisfaction, independent of failure or success with one or another single patient. He added, as soon as the patient gave him an opening, that he was not interested in impressing the patient's father but solely in an attempt to be of use to the patient in his own right, if and when he cared for psychotherapeutic collaboration. Many years later, when the patient at last reached the goal of recovery, he dated the beginning of successful psychotherapy to this conversation.

Other insecure psychiatrists may insist on their patients' doing and accomplishing things before they are ready. The patients may try to do so in an attempt to please and encourage their doctors, while they themselves become discouraged by the failure of their premature efforts. Most assuredly, the patient should *not* be put into the position of having to reassure the doctor. Fortunately, there are patients who are able to see and verbalize this danger. The psychiatrist who is not too preoccupied in his quest for gaining security at the expense of his patients may be able to hear their warning.

This admonition against the doctor's pushing a patient in a certain direction for the doctor's benefit should not be mistaken for a general cautioning against the therapeutic validity of any pushing of patients, sometimes against their own wish and conviction. In some types of patients, whose cases cannot be discussed here, such active procedure is indicated and useful.

The preoccupation of the insecure psychiatrist with the need to assert himself at the expense of his patient has another unfortunate outcome: namely, the fantasy that the patient may be "clay in the hand of the builder" and that he can mold him according to his own image. Such wishes may lead the doctor into fantasies about non-existing similarities between him and his patients. These fantasies will make him resistant to obtaining a real picture of these patients' personalities and of their specific difficulties in living. The patients will be expected to accept or work out the same solutions for their personal problems as those which the therapist has decided upon for his life. They will not get the help they need in searching for their own answers.

In other cases the patients are expected to accept the psychiatrist's set of personal values instead of being encouraged, with therapeutic validity, to find their own sets of values and to learn to follow them independently.

From all this it follows that the psychiatrist must have a reasonably stable self-esteem to avoid psychotherapeutic blundering. This offers another reason for the necessity of the psychiatrist's undergoing a personal psychoanalytic inventory before he undertakes intensive psychotherapy with others.

There is one more reason why the psychiatrist's self-respect is of paramount significance for the therapeutic procedure. If it is true that one's ability to respect others is dependent upon the development of one's self-respect, then it follows that only a self-respecting psychotherapist is capable of respecting his patients and of meeting them on the basis of mutual human equality. The self-respecting psychiatrist will keep in mind that he is superior to his patients only by his special training and experience, and not necessarily in any other way. His patients may or may not have greater personal assets than he has. The fact that a person needs psychiatric help in handling his difficulties in living by no means constitutes any basic inferiority. Only the psychiatrist who realizes this is able to listen to his patients in such a way that there may be a psychotherapeutic success.

The psychiatrist's respect for his patients will also help to safeguard against the previously mentioned mistake of assuming an attitude of personal "irrational authority" instead of listening and conducting therapy in the spirit of collaborative guidance. This irrational authoritarian behavior will be harmful not only because it interferes per se with the patient's tendency toward growth and maturation but also, and more important, because it constitutes a traumatic repetition of the authoritarian aspects of the cultural pattern of behavior in general, and of the parental pattern in particular, to which most mental patients have been harmfully subjected in their past.[9]

This is not intended to rule out the therapist's taking a firm and definite stand as an expert who establishes his "rational authority" in his psychotherapeutic suggestions. But it does rule out the therapist's taking advantage of the unhappy, intimidated, and overdependent patient's inclination to put him, as a person, on an authoritarian pedestal. For many psychiatrists the temptation to do so may be present as a means of getting even with annoying authoritarian domination to which they themselves have been subjected by their parents, teachers, or superiors and anonymously by society at large.

If the psychiatrist is self-respecting and has respect for his patients, his ability to listen will also not be impaired by fantasies of omniscience or perfectionism. He will realize that he is not called upon to be a magician who is expected to perform psychotherapeutic miracles; he will be able to admit mistakes, limitations, and shortcomings as they occur.

Insecure and self-righteous psychiatrists cannot endure their failure to understand one or another of their patient's communications, without developing feelings of anxiety or resentment. These psychotherapists cannot understand that the mental patient, who is supposed to be out of his mind, may say meaningful things which the psychiatrist, who is supposedly in his right mind, cannot understand.

9. Erich Fromm, *Escape from Freedom* (New York and Toronto: Farrar & Rinehart, 1941) ; *Autorität und Familie* (New York: Institute of Social Research; Paris: Alcan, 1937), German with English and French abstracts of each contribution.

This statement may seem redundant to those psychoanalysts who work with ambulatory neurotics only. The psychiatrist who works with disturbed psychotics, however, will be faced time and again with his inability to follow the contents of the communications of his patients. This holds true despite the fact that psychiatrists learned from Freud to revise the teachings of classical psychiatry, which stated that most psychotic utterances made sense neither to the patient nor to the psychiatrist. It is not necessary, however, to understand all a patient's utterances. The disturbed patient, as a rule, does not mind if the psychotherapist fails to understand the contents of his communications as long as the doctor is frank about it and does not make false pretenses. The therapist has to approach all of them, including the non-intelligible psychotic productions, the way he approaches the dreams of the healthy and of the neurotic. He expects to understand some of them and to be at a loss as to the meanings of others; yet he realizes that most of them are meaningful for the dreamer.

There was a time when we psychoanalysts became overenthusiastic about the discovery of the potentially meaningful communications of our patients. This drove psychoanalytic psychotherapy in the false direction of concentrating on the contents of patients' communications and of overrating the psychotherapeutic usefulness of understanding them. This held true for the inadvertent communications of the neurotic, his slips and other phenomena, which Freud has described so masterfully under the heading of the "Psychopathology of Everyday Life," as well as for the productions of the psychotics.[10] That time has passed, and we are now more interested in the origin, the timing, and the dynamics of neurotic and psychotic productions as a psychotherapeutic signpost, without eliminating, of course, our interest in the actual contents and our attempts at understanding.

To illustrate: A hospitalized paranoid schizophrenic in her middle thirties, who had been overtly disturbed for thirteen years, started tending toward recovery after many months of intensive psychotherapy. One of her main symptoms until then had been the delusion of the appearance of "The Line." As yet the patient had not told the psychotherapist what "The Line" was; it may have been that she did not even know herself. However, she succeeded, upon the inquiry of the therapist, in telling him, each time, what event preceded the appearance of "The Line," until they finally discovered what type of events in the patient's life created the appearance of "The Line." "The Line" disappeared, and its elimination seemed to have contributed greatly to the general improvement in the patient's condition.[11]

This example should remind the psychiatrist of two important facts: first, his interest in research should be secondary to his eagerness in dis-

10. Freud, *A General Introduction to Psychoanalysis.*

11. For an extensive discussion of this case see Herbert Staveren's "Suggested Specificity of Certain Dynamisms in a Case of Schizophrenia," *Psychiatry,* X (1947), 127-35.

covering data strictly pertinent to his psychotherapeutic obligations; second, he should not be pertinacious in searching for and in conveying understanding to the patient at the expense of observing what is going on in the patient. There is frequently no therapeutic advantage in doing so. As Freud said, "The psychoanalyst's job is to help the patient, not to demonstrate how clever the doctor is."

The warning against fantasies of omniscience and perfectionism, as they interfere with the psychiatrist's ability to listen freely to the patient and to admit mistakes, does not necessarily mean in all cases that the psychotherapist should feel obliged to admit his mistakes to his patients. The patient carries enough of his own worries without the therapist's increasing them, much less using his patient as father-confessor and burdening him further by an ill-advised concept of sincerity, prompted by the doctor's worry regarding his mistakes. What really matters is that he be able to admit his mistakes frankly to himself, so that he can operate with his insight.

On the other hand, there are many times and situations when it is wise and therapeutically useful to comment on his errors to the patient in a matter-of-fact and non-masochistic manner.

Sometimes it may be wise for the psychiatrist, should he anticipate difficulties which could arise from specific contrasts between his and the patient's personality makeup, to formulate this possibility to the patient, pointing out the danger of their interference with psychotherapeutic progress. The following experience exemplifies this:

A very brilliant, clever, and shrewd psychopath, all of whose interpersonal relationships were in terms of power manipulations only, was told after the first two interviews that the psychiatrist considered himself to be reasonably intelligent but much less clever and shrewd than the patient. The psychiatrist explained that it would be easy enough for the patient to put something over on him, should he choose to use his superior shrewdness and cleverness for that purpose. It was then suggested to him that he make his choice between using the psychiatrist for what help he had to offer or as a target for his shrewd manipulations. In spite of this warning which the psychiatrist had offered for both the patient's and his own benefit, the patient succeeded more than once in deluding the psychiatrist during the course of the treatment. Since this was foreseen, it was easy to fall back on the initial statement whenever it became necessary to disentangle any of the patient's shrewd, though unconstructive, power manipulations.

The psychiatrist's sense of security undergoes the greatest test of endurance when he is subjected to the mental patient's display of hostility. I am not in agreement with the teachings of classical analysis, according to which people are born to be hostile and aggressive—that is, with Freud's teachings on the death instinct.[12] In this hostile world of ours,

12. Freud, *Beyond the Pleasure Principle* (London: International Psycho-analytical Press, 1922).

however, every person, and certainly every mental patient, has sufficient reason for learning to develop reactions of hostility. Mental patients react with hostility to the hostile behavior and the shortcomings of the significant adults in their environment, including the failures of the therapist, and they transfer onto him their anger and their resentment engendered by previous experiences. Furthermore, they interpret the therapist's behavior and communications along the lines of their unfavorable past experience with other people. Hence it follows that every mental patient will have to express a marked degree of hostility in the course of his interpersonal dealings with the therapist. This being so, psychotherapy can be successful only if the psychiatrist is secure enough himself that he will be able to deal adequately with the hostile reactions of his patients.

There is another inevitable source of patients' hostile reactions against the psychotherapist. This stems from the bipolarity in the dynamics of mental disorder. Mental symptoms are an expression of a patient's anxiety. At the same time, they constitute a defense against anxiety, an attempt at warding it off.[13] A patient's attitude toward the psychotherapist is inevitably a reflection of this twofold meaning of the symptoms. The doctor who fights a patient's symptomatology is the object of his patient's friendly feelings, inasmuch as the patient's attitudes are motivated by his inherent tendency toward regaining health. At the same time, a mental patient will cling to his symptomatology because of its defensive quality. Therefore, the psychiatrist is also the target of the patient's hostility because his therapeutic endeavors are aimed at depriving him of these defenses. Insights into the dynamic bipolarity of the symptomatology of mental patients should help the psychiatrist to endure these hostile outbursts, which are determined by the function and not by the personality of the therapist.

Some psychiatrists seem to believe that they can exhibit their unadulterated willingness to listen constructively to the patient's outbursts of hostility by inviting him, in so many words, to "express his hostility." This does not work, of course. First, one is not likely to follow any suggestion of a person toward whom one feels angry or resentful, let alone the invitation to express one's resentment. Second, it is not likely to be followed because no one actually feels or thinks about his anger in terms of "hostility." The very use of this abstract term is apt to make the patient feel that his anger, his rage, his fury, his resentment, and so on are minimized or not taken seriously when referred to as "hostility." Therefore, the psychiatrist who invites his patient to express hostility protects himself, wittingly or unwittingly, from becoming the actual target of this hostility.

13. Frieda Fromm-Reichmann, "Remarks on the Philosophy of Mental Disorder," *Psychiatry*, IX (1946), 293–308.

Other therapists may have learned to brace themselves in order to endure a patient's openly hostile onslaught in a psychotherapeutically valid, that is, personally detached, way. These same physicians may, however, not be able to live up to the professional standards in listening to their angry patients if this anger is expressed in the mitigated form of criticism of the doctor's personal or professional performances. Psychiatrists who do therapy with hospital or clinic patients may be tempted to argue away hostile invectives against their institutions. The need to be on the defensive and to be loyal regarding the places with which they are connected may blind these psychiatrists to the fact that more often than not the patient may only seemingly criticize or resent the hospital or the clinic while actually using the institutions as targets for the expression of negative feelings which are directed against the therapist as a part of this institution.

Another common way of being misled about a patient's hostility or critical judgment stems from complaints about other doctors who have treated him. The temptation to feel flattered at being considered better than the colleagues mentioned may induce the therapist's inattention to the fact that his colleagues are used by the patient merely as a screen to express negative feelings or judgment about others while he is actually talking about his present psychotherapist.

The therapist may feel his security all the more threatened by his patient's direct or veiled criticism if and when he feels that it is objectively justified. It is most desirable for a therapist to feel sufficiently secure both as a person and in his work that he may be able to listen and to discriminate correctly between justified and unjustified criticism. If he recognizes it as correct, he should be able to take it at its face value and to learn from it. If he considers it unjustified, he should be able to listen, with his attention and his subsequent inquiries focused on the emotional reasons for the patient's need to criticize.

Hypersensitivity to justified or unjustified appreciation or deprecation of his abilities, due to lack of self-respect, will particularly interfere with a therapist's constructive contacts with some groups of psychotics. Because of their marked anxiety, these people have developed a consistent watchfulness of their environment and great alertness regarding interpersonal experiences. Therefore, they are frequently capable of emotional eavesdropping, as it were, on other persons, including their psychotherapist. From the gestures, attitudes, inadvertent words and actions of the physician, the psychotic may, at times, gain an empathic awareness of certain personality aspects of which the therapist himself may not be aware. Well-developed security is necessary for the therapist to be able to listen without resentment to his patients' comments on these, more often than not, undesirable personality trends of which he may have been previously unaware.

Where there is lack of security, there is anxiety; where there is anxiety, there is fear of anxieties in others. The insecure psychiatrist is therefore liable to be afraid of his patients' anxiety. Hence he may not want to hear about their anxiety and their anxiety-provoking experiences. He may thwart the patient's tendency to submit these experiences to psychotherapeutic investigation by feeling called upon to give premature reassurance to the patient because he needs reassurance himself. In doing so, he is liable to obstruct his patients' verbalizations and the investigation of important emotional material. Moreover, to the patient the doctor's anxiety represents a measuring rod for his own anxiety-provoking qualities. If the doctor is very anxious, the patient may take that as a confirmation of his own fear of being threatening, that is, "bad." In other words, the doctor's anxiety decreases the patient's self-esteem.

The statement that the psychiatrist should be able to endure a patient's hostile outbursts in word and action is by no means identical with the suggestion that he ought to grant every patient the freedom to express his hostile impulses at random. Many neurotics, especially hysterics, indulge in verbalized and play-acted hostile dramatizations, be it in overobedience to misinterpreted psychoanalytic writings or with the idea of testing the psychiatrist's endurance or of delaying constructive psychotherapeutic collaboration. In such cases the psychiatrist should interfere with the patient's display of hostility. Note, however, that he does so for the benefit of the patient and the psychotherapeutic process and not because of his own anxiety.

On the other hand, it is true that even psychiatrists with a reasonably well-developed sense of security may at times run into patients who evoke fear or anxiety in them. This may happen in connection with verbal reports about anxiety-producing material as well as in connection with actual acts of violence. The psychiatrist is liable to treat these patients along the line of his own anxieties, instead of facing the anxiety of the patient in a therapeutically valid manner.

In the case of threatening or real violence in action, the psychiatrist is justified and required to express firmly his unwillingness to be its target. He should also see to it that adequate precautionary measures are taken. This attitude is advocated not only for the sake of the doctor's own protection but just as much for the sake of the protection of the patient against actions, the later recall of which leads to self-derogation and self-depreciation.

When the doctor's anxiety is due to verbal productions or where there is failure to produce relief for himself by precautionary measures, the anxious psychiatrist should suggest to the patient that he change psychotherapists and help him to do so, unless the doctor is able to discover unconscious reasons for his anxiety, which he is able to resolve psychoanalytically.

If the psychiatrist has the good luck not to be afraid of assaultive patients and to be able to listen to their hostile outbursts without impairment of his sense of security, this will have two beneficial consequences. First, the very fact that the doctor does not become frightened will mitigate the patient's fear of his own aggression and, therefore, modulate his actual assaultiveness, which has been, in part, fear-born to begin with; second, the psychiatrist's fearless reception of the patient's outbursts may lead to subsequent valid therapeutic developments, as in the following case of a very disturbed, assaultive, catatonic woman-patient:

She had been under intensive psychotherapy for one and one-half years without ever showing active assaultiveness toward the therapist. One day she came into the office and remained standing by the desk, instead of taking a seat as was her usual habit. Asked about the reason for this, she answered with considerable feeling, "You will admit that I have never done anything to you or to your things during all the time that I have come to see you here, no matter how upset I might have been. Today, I will knock all of your things off the desk and then I will knock you down. You had better call your maid to protect you." Fortunately, the psychiatrist was not afraid, so that she was able to say, firmly and calmly, that she would not call anyone in for her protection. Had she asked for help against a patient who threatened assaultiveness but showed no real evidence of action, instead of concentrating on the case of the patient's threatened assaultiveness, she might easily have jeopardized the chances of further treatment. So the doctor decided to cope with the situation as follows: She realized, she said, that the patient could easily knock her down, should she choose to do so, since she was younger, stronger, taller, and more agile than the doctor. She hoped, however, that the patient would prefer to tell her about the reasons for her hostile mood. To this suggestion the patient replied, with great emphasis, that this was not the time for her, an American-born woman, to discuss things with a (recently naturalized) German doctor. "Don't you know that there is a war on?" she continued. "The Americans and the Germans at the front do not talk things over, they fight." There followed another invitation to ask the maid in for the doctor's protection, then a suggestion on the doctor's part to the effect that the former difference in the patient's and the doctor's nationality could not be the reason for the patient's fighting mood. The doctor reminded the patient of the fact that, in their previous contacts, she had never found the patient to be prejudiced in favor of Americans who had immigrated many generations ago rather than recently. She also mentioned that the patient had always known of the doctor's German origin and that previously this fact had not interfered with their psychotherapeutic intercourse. The patient maintained her threatening attitude and posture for about three-quarters of an hour before giving in to the doctor's repeated, insistent requests to discuss the real reasons for her being upset. Then, at last, the patient said with considerable feeling that one of the attendants on the ward had called her a "filthy, dirty homosexual." The psychiatrist immediately expressed her genuine concern and her intention to investigate and remedy the situation. The patient was now completely calm. She sat down, lighted a cigarette, and said, "It is no longer necessary to investigate the incident." She then looked at her watch, regretted the amount of time she had spent on her outburst of hostility, and suggested that at least the last few minutes of the interview should be used for serious psychotherapeutic work.

The basic cause for the patient's disturbance had not been the fact of the attendant's calling her a homosexual, per se, but that, from the implication of such abuse, the hospital and its staff considered homosexuality to be "filthy and dirty." To her, this attitude was in direct contradiction to the therapist's initial statement during their first interview, that homosexuality was nothing of which to be ashamed or any reason for hospitalization, provided that it did not impair the patient's security of living among the average prejudiced inhabitants of this culture. Hence the attendant's abuse carried with it the connotation that the psychiatrist had been insincere when stating her own and the hospital's unprejudiced attitude regarding homosexuality. Therefore, the patient's emotional investment in the incident was immediately withdrawn as the psychiatrist divorced herself from any identification with the offender. The whole incident was subsequently utilized for a psychotherapeutically important investigation of the doctor-patient relationship, with its implications regarding the patient's relationship with other people.

There is another therapeutically undesirable consequence of a psychiatrist's insecurity which can come from a handicap that plays a great role in the personality development and interpersonal attitude of many people—I mean the fear of being ridiculed. The fear of ridicule is so universally characteristic of human kind because of the social interrelatedness of its members that it is not infrequently used as a pedagogical deterrent by parents and teachers. As a matter of fact, there are some Indian tribes who use it as the only means of acculturating their children and of raising them to respect and accept the mores of the tribe.[14]

The psychotherapist may be afraid of appearing ridiculous in the eyes of his colleagues or of the secretaries of his clinic. A patient may walk out on him or be markedly late for his interviews. The doctor may fear the ridicule of other patients or of the nurses on the ward, as a disturbed hospital patient soils his suit by throwing food at him, by spitting at him, by smearing feces on him, or if a patient tries to lock the doctor into the room, and so on. It would, of course, be greatly desirable for the doctor to be able to overcome his fear of ridicule. As a matter of fact, if he could, he would automatically take the wind out of the sails of those in whose eyes he fears to appear ridiculous. But it cannot be expected that he will always be able to conquer this fear. The quest for prestige in our culture is so great that it will interfere with some doctors' efforts to become desensitized to it. What can be expected, however, is that the

14. Fromm, *Autorität und Familie.*

trained psychotherapist be aware of his fear and try to work through it or, if unsuccessful, that he create a treatment setup which enables him to evade situations which threaten him with the ridicule of his associates.

The need of an insecure psychiatrist to draw security from a virtuous adjustment to the conventionalities of his time and from a quest for approval from "the good and the great" may turn out to be another agent interfering with his ability to listen in a therapeutically valid fashion.[15] This type of dependence gives rise to the danger that the psychiatrist consider the changeable man-made standards of the society in which he lives to be eternal values to which he and his patients must conform. Therefore, his ability to listen and to help will be limited as his patients try to discover to what extent and in what way each of them needs to adjust to the cultural requirements of his time. He will be desensitized to the patient's personal needs because of preoccupation with his own dependency on the society and culture of his era and its transitory values. As I have pointed out elsewhere, this may render him practically incapable of guiding certain types of patients:

The recovery of many schizophrenics and schizoid personalities, for example, depends upon the psychotherapist's freedom from convention and prejudice. These patients cannot and should not be asked to accept guidance toward a conventional adjustment to the customary requirements of our culture, much less to what the individual psychotherapist personally considers these requirements to be. The psychotherapist should feel that his goal in treating schizoid personalities is reached if these people, without hurting their neighbors, are able to find for themselves the sources of satisfaction and security in which they are interested. This presupposes, of course, that these patients have acquired, through inner freedom and independence from public opinion, under the guidance of their psychotherapist, the ability to live their own lives irrespective of the approval of their neighbors.[16]

On the other hand, there are, of course, many other types of patients —neurotics, for example—whose personalities are potentially in accord with the requirements and values of this culture; their lack of adjustment is part of the symptomatology and should be subject to change through treatment. Many of them are eternal adolescents who refuse to grow up and who, therefore, try to maintain the defiant attitude of teen-agers toward that which represents to them the demands of the adults, against whom they rebel. These patients make it equally necessary for the therapist to be reasonably independent of social conventionality and evaluations in his own right, just as does the first group. Unless he is, there is danger of his becoming irritated by and defensive against the juvenile or adolescent rebellion of his adult neurotic patients, instead of recog-

15. Fromm, *Escape from Freedom.*

16. Frieda Fromm-Reichmann, "Notes on the Development of Treatment of Schizophrenics by Psychoanalytic Psychotherapy," *Psychiatry,* XI (1948), 263–73.

nizing it for what it is and treating it without undue emotional expenditure.

To summarize: Security and inner independence from the authoritarian values attributed to the conventional requirements of our culture are indispensable for the therapist who wants to guide his patients successfully toward finding out about the degree of cultural adjustment that is adequate for their personal needs.

In early psychoanalytic literature some authors claimed that the psychoanalyst should be free from any evaluational goals while dealing with his patients. To my mind, this holds true only for the psychiatrist's own personal evaluational systems pertaining to religion, philosophy, political viewpoints, and other questions of "Weltanschauung" which he would not expect to be, or to become, the evaluational goals of his patients. It is not correct to say, however, that there is no immanent set of values connected with the goals of psychotherapy.[17] Treatment, of course, is aimed at the solution of the patient's difficulties in living and of the symptomatology for the cure of which he seeks the help of the psychiatrist. Ideally, these goals will be accomplished by aiming psychotherapeutically at the development of growth, maturation, and inner independence of the patient; at his potential freedom from fear, anxiety, and the entanglements of greed, envy, and jealousy in his interpersonal relationships; and at his capacity for self-realization and for forming durable relationships of intimacy with others and of giving and accepting mature love. I define "mature love," with Fromm and Sullivan, as the state of interpersonal relatedness in which one is as concerned with the growth, maturation, welfare, and happiness of the beloved person as one is with one's own.[18] This capacity for mature love presupposes the development of a healthy and stable self-respect.

By "self-realization" I mean a person's ability to use his talents, skills, and powers to his satisfaction within the realm of his own freely established realistic set of values. Furthermore, I mean the patient's ability to reach out for and to find fulfilment of his needs for satisfaction and security, as far as they can be attained without interfering with the needs of his fellow men. K. Goldstein's concept of "self-actualization" and Fromm's concept of the "productive character" covers what I have tried to establish here as the ideal goal of psychotherapy.[19]

In the classical psychoanalytic literature, insufficient attention has been given, so far, to the concept of self-realization as a great source, if not the greatest source, of human fulfilment. Freud has referred to it in

17. Fromm-Reichmann, in Fromm, *Autorität und Familie*; also Erich Fromm, *Man for Himself* (New York and Toronto: Rinehart & Co., 1947).

18. Sullivan, *op. cit.*, Fromm, "Selfishness and Self-Love," *Psychiatry*, II (1939), 507–23.

19. K. Goldstein, *Human Nature in the Light of Psychopathology* (Cambridge: Harvard University Press, 1937); Fromm-Reichmann, "Notes on the Development of Treatment of Schizophrenics by Psychoanalytic Psychotherapy."

his teachings on secondary narcissism and ego ideal formations, but he has dealt more with the investigation of the origin than with the elaboration of the psychological significance of the phenomenon.[20] I will refrain from going into theory at this point and restrict myself to emphasizing "self-realization" or "self-actualization" as a practical psychotherapeutic goal of paramount importance. Last but not least, the combined personality study and treatment which constitute psychotherapy should furnish the patient with the tools for the maintenance of his stability during periods of uncertainty, frustration, and unhappiness as they are bound to occur in everyone's life. The psychotherapist should not be afraid of being aware or of admitting that these are the basic standards which guide him in his therapeutic dealings with his patients, no matter how eager he may be to establish his personal evaluational neutrality.[21]

Some psychoanalysts set up the genital maturity of the patient as a criterion for his recovery, meaning his ability to be orgastically potent in heterosexual intercourse. They believe that the signs of recovery, herein outlined, will accompany or result from genital maturity.[22] I believe it to be the other way around. That is to say, a person who is reasonably free from anxiety, greed, envy, and jealousy and who is able to experience interpersonal intimacy will be capable of expressing this in terms of satisfactory sexual activities.

The suggestion that the psychotherapist be guided by these ethical goals of treatment is not intended to supersede my initial suggestion that otherwise he must safeguard against any interference with his professional attitude by his personal sets of ethical values in terms of matters of "Weltanschauung." It is self-evident that this does not mean that he should not verbalize evaluations to the patient. It should be emphasized, however, that ideally the psychiatrist keeps these types of personal evaluations sufficiently apart from his professional life to avoid their inadvertent emanation. The danger of the influence of such ever present evaluational attitudes on the patient's development is increased by the specific state of emotional dependence which characterizes the relationship of the mental patient with his psychotherapist while he is under treatment. This state of dependence per se makes the patient most sensitive to all his physician's verbalized and non-verbalized communications. The dependence and alert sensitivity are increased by the laws governing the patient's relationship with the psychiatrist. They bring about the patient's tendency to transfer onto the psychiatrist the previous attitudes of dependence which he has felt toward those in authority

20. Freud, *The Ego and the Id* (London: Hogarth Press, 1935), and "On Narcissism: An Introduction" (1914), *Collected Papers*, IV, 30–59.

21. Sullivan, *op. cit.*; and Fromm, *Escape from Freedom* and *Autorität und Familie*.

22. O. Fenichel, *Problems of Psychoanalytic Technique* (Albany, N.Y.: Psychoanalytic Quart., Inc., 1939); W. Reich, *The Function of the Orgasm* (New York: Orgone Institute Press, 1942).

in his past, and, last but not least, they account for his tendency to interpret the doctor's actual utterances along the lines of past life-experiences with significant people. Rightly or wrongly, the patient will, as it were, read between the lines of what the psychotherapist actually wishes to convey. The therapist must be prudent so as not to misuse the great sphere of influence granted him by his patients, much tempted though he may feel at times to use dependent attitudes of patients as a means of imbuing them with his own personal set of values. It would be quite easy to feel flattered by the patients' trust and dependence rather than to remain alert to the fact that their insecurity, hence overdependence, is part of the disturbance for which they seek treatment.

The emanation of the psychiatrist's general system of ethical values is not the only example of the possibility of inadvertent communication of his viewpoints and its influence on the course of treatment. The emanation of the doctor's evaluation of and judgment about the symptomatology of his patients may turn out to be of equally great importance. I could illustrate this in terms of the history of stool-smearing in classical psychiatry, on the one hand, and in terms of Menninger's, Simmel's, and my own published psychoanalytical observations, on the other.[23]

This inadvertent empathic conveyance to the patient of the psychiatrist's standards plays an important role in many more areas of the treatment situation. Many rules and regulations regarding the psychoanalytic setup, which cannot be discussed in detail at this point, have been established to facilitate the patient's and the psychiatrist's successful collaboration in intensive psychotherapy. It has been recommended that one should, by all means, avoid interruptions of psychotherapeutic interviews by actual interference or by accidental distractions, such as environmental noises. It has also been recommended that one make it a rule not to see one's patients outside the scheduled interviews, professionally or otherwise. These and other regulations are very helpful indeed in maintaining a therapeutically constructive doctor-patient relationship. The degree of good or evil consequences which results from violating these rules depends, however, mainly, if not solely, upon the degree of disturbance which such refraction creates in the minds of patient and therapist.[24]

This becomes significantly understandable if one remembers how the same principle holds true in all our interpersonal relationships, beginning with the initial relationship between mother and infant. Much has

23. K. Menninger, "Psychoanalytic Psychiatry: Theory and Practice," *Bull. Menninger Clin.*, IV (1940), 105–23; Ernst Simmel, "Die psychoanalytische Beandlung in der Klinik." *Internat. Ztscher. Psychoanal.*, XIV (1928), 352–70 (translation in *Internat. J. Psychoanal.*, X [1929], 70–89) ; Fromm, *Autorität und Familie*.

24. Alexander *et al.*, *op. cit.*; Fromm-Reichmann, "Recent Advances in Psychoanalytic Therapy," and "Problems of Therapeutic Management in a Psychoanalytic Hospital," *Psychoanalyt. Quart.*, XVI (1948), 325–56.

been said, for example, about the time element in bowel training for children. We now know that it is not the time element but the attitude of the mother who does the bowel training that is of paramount importance for the personality development of the child. By the same token, it is primarily the attitude of the psychiatrist who handles the rules and regulations governing the therapeutic interviews and only secondarily the maintenance or infraction of these regulations that makes for the difference between psychotherapeutic success and failure.

There is one more interpersonal problem of the psychiatrist which is pertinent to this discussion before I conclude the investigation of the psychotherapist's personal and professional requirements for correct handling of the doctor-patient relationship and the psychotherapeutic process: that is, the question of the psychiatrist's like or dislike for a patient. Of course, it is his privilege to refuse acceptance of a patient for treatment if and when he feels that he dislikes him as a person. Once he does accept the patient, however, these categories are void of meaning in his professional dealings with patients. If a person comes to see the psychiatrist, this implies a need for changes in his personality, and if the psychiatrist accepts a person for treatment, this means that he recognizes that person's need for change and that he hopes to be instrumental in the patient's ultimately accomplishing these necessary changes. This being so, the question of whether or not the patient, in his present mental condition and with his present personality trends, is to the psychiatrist's liking is beside the point.

The great significance which dynamic psychiatry attributes to the environmental factors and to the interpersonal traumata which help shape people's personalities is another factor, which should happily forestall the rise of the problem of like or dislike for his patients in the mind of the psychiatrist. As he learns about the historical data which are responsible for the characterological development and for the psychopathology of the patient, the temptation to make a moral evaluation with the implication of acceptance or non-acceptance will be replaced by genetic understanding and therapeutic curiosity.

If a therapist feels that he likes or dislikes a patient who is under treatment, the reasons, as a rule, are not due to the patient's type of personality per se. The psychiatrist may like a patient who is making satisfactory progress in treatment, thereby augmenting his self-appreciation and his prestige; he may dislike a patient whose treatment has become stagnant, because that may express doubts of his skill on the part of the patient and, even worse, within the doctor's own mind.

These statements are not identical with the suggestion that every therapist should expect to be capable of treating persons suffering from any type of personality disorder. The contrary is true. In the course of his psychiatric career and with the aid of his supervised psychotherapeutic work, the psychotherapist should learn what types of patients respond best to his personality as it colors his type of therapeutic approach.

Of course, there are no rules of unfailing psychiatric validity to guide therapists in the difficult selection of suitable patients.

Here are a few examples, taken from a host of similar ones, merely offered as signposts for a general orientation. A markedly schizoid psychotherapist may have a difficult and unsuccessful time with patients suffering from marked manic and depressive mood-swings and vice versa. A very maternal psychotherapist may needlessly get under the skin of an aloof patient, who struggles for independence from a mother's domineering overprotection. Psychotherapists who like to reap the harvest of their collaborative therapeutic endeavor with patients in a not too distant future will do better work with neurotics than with psychotics, where psychiatric attention is more focused on timeless therapeutic curiosity and research interest. Anxious or forbidding personalities may not be helpful to patients suffering from anxiety states. Psychiatrists with markedly ingratiating or propitiating needs had best refrain from working with the suspicious paranoid patients.

In concluding, I wish to summarize my suggestions as follows:

It has been stated that the psychotherapist is expected to be stable and secure enough to be consistently aware of and in control of that which he conveys to his patients in words and mindful of that which he may convey by empathy; that his need for operations aimed at his own security and satisfaction should not interfere with his ability to listen consistently to patients, with full alertness to their communications per se and, if possible, to the unworded implications of their verbalized communications; that he should never feel called upon to be anything more or less than the participant-observer of the emotional experiences which are conveyed to him by his patients.

On the surface, these rules seem obvious and easy to follow; yet they are not. As a matter of fact, they are offered to show the ideal goals for which the psychotherapist should strive. In actuality, none of us will be consistently able to live up to all of them. We have to bear in mind that no amount of inner security and self-respect protects the psychiatrist from being as much a subject of and vulnerable to the inevitable vicissitudes of life as is everyone else. This being the case, it is equally obvious that it may be difficult at times for each psychotherapist to maintain the unadulterated role of the detached and alert participant-observer of his patients. Indeed, it requires special personal training to be able to do so. The personal psychoanalysis which, for training purposes, has been repeatedly recommended in these pages as a requirement for the person who wishes to do intensive psychotherapy must also be recommended for reasons of the psychiatrist's personal development. It will help him to become sufficiently aware of his own problems and enable him to handle his interpersonal relationships, at large, and therefore his professional relationships with his patients in particular, so that the first will not interfere with the latter. His personal analysis will serve as a valid means of acquainting him with the dynamic significance of his own early developmental history and his early patterns in interpersonal relationships as integrating factors of his personality structure. This will improve his ability to keep the vicissitudes of his personal life apart from his professional life. It will also increase his skill in helping patients to discover dissociated and repressed elements of their history and to recognize transference and parataxic factors in their present interpersonal experiences with the therapist and others. And so it is, because of the interrelatedness between the psychiatrist's and the patient's interpersonal processes and because of the interpersonal character of the psychotherapeutic process itself, that any attempt at intensive psychotherapy is fraught with danger, hence unacceptable, when not preceded by the future psychotherapist's personal analysis.

(6)

RECENT ADVANCES IN PSYCHOANALYSIS

Before any discussion of recent advances in psychoanalysis is attempted, a brief review should be given of some basic concepts of classical psychoanalysis versus its modifications in recent modern dynamic psychoanalytic conceptual thinking, so that a useful frame of reference may be established.

Advances achieved in psychoanalysis in recent years are in relation to these conceptions, to the method and technique of therapy, and to the types of patients who can be treated by psychoanalytic psychotherapy (1).

BASIC PSYCHOANALYTIC CONCEPTS

Psychoanalysis understands the functioning of the human mind as the result of the dynamic interaction between mental operations on various levels and with different qualities of awareness (Freud: conscious, preconscious, unconscious). Thoughts and feelings which are incompatible with the standards of a person himself or with those of significant people in his environment or of his culture at large may be barred from awareness and recall ("repressed," "dissociated") because of the effect of anxiety they would produce, were they to remain in awareness. Unknown to the person, these repressed experiences remain alive in his mind and influence his thoughts, feelings, and actions. At times, this is the reason for people's expressing things which are seemingly not meaningful. As psychoanalysts have learned to realize that the origin of these expressions is on other levels of awareness, hence qualitatively different from those in which the person communicates, they have learned to understand that all mental and emotional manifestations are meaningful and, at least potentially, understandable.

This dynamic conception of the operation of the human mind is in contrast to the preanalytic, descriptive, psychiatric approach to an understanding of the working of the mind as a static entity. Poets and philosophers, of course, have known for centuries about the functional dichotomy of the human mind. It is the scientific discovery of its application to psychiatry and to psychology and, more specifically in the context of this paper, of its medical application to psychiatry, to psy-

Reprinted from *Journal of the American Medical Women's Association*, IV, No. 8 (August, 1949), 320–26.

chotherapy, and to medicine at large (psychosomatic medicine) that I am discussing here.

To gain an understanding of human personality as characterized by psychoanalytic dynamic psychiatry, the functioning of the personality must be explored and understood genetically, that is, from its total history. The early developmental history of infancy and childhood plays a predominant role in the formation of character and personality and especially in the formation of patterns of human interrelationships. This early history is understood in terms of three elements complementing one another. They are the constitution, or that which a person brings with him; the influences of external circumstances at large; and, most of all, the specific important interpersonal experiences of the infant and young child with the significant people of his early environment. The latter play a portentous role, because of the duration and extent of the biological and psychological dependence of the human.

Unknown to the person, this pattern formation and its reappearance hold true also for the early traumatic interpersonal experiences which have been subjected to the process of dissociation or repression. Because they have been dissociated, there can be no participation of such experiences in the growth and maturation of the rest of the personality. Their reflection in the interpersonal experiences of later life is the salient feature of many distorted evaluations plus the mental patient's unwitting, compulsive search for their repetition. Whether the connection of these early, unclarified interpersonal experiences is with love, hatred, pain, anxiety, or other feelings and emotions, their transference to the people of one's later life plays a very important role in all relationships.

So much, in brief, about the generally accepted basic psychoanalytic concepts of the functioning of the human mind and personality. I shall endeavor now to outline briefly a few highlights of the various psychoanalytic conceptions of human developmental history because they form the frame of reference for all genetically oriented psychoanalytic psychotherapy.

Developmental History

The early developmental history as conceived by Freud is psychosexual in nature (2–5). He understands the various phases of a person's development to be the outcome of a response to the lust obtainable and the interpersonal expression available by means of the bodily zones of food intake and elimination. Consequently, Freud speaks of an oral, anal, and phallic state of one's pregenital psychosexual development, all of which precede the ability of a person to feel genital lust. The sexual energy manifesting itself in these psychosexual pregenital and genital interests and activities, Freud calls "libido." He conceives the course of character development and personality in its ultimate mentally healthy outcome to be the result of this libidinal energy having run a complete and uninterrupted course, from the early oral state to the time at which the human gains the ability to feel primarily genital lust in relation to another person of the opposite sex.

According to Freud, a person matures as he learns to take care of the desexualization of his pregenital libido by means of sublimation, reaction formation, overcompensation, etc. Subsequently, he develops the capacity for orgastic genital experiences with a mature person of the opposite sex.

Oedipus Complex

Maturing begins with the Oedipus complex, the situation in which the genitalization of libido is felt in connection with a tender and sexual affection for the parent of the opposite sex and concomitant feelings of rivalry and hatred for the parent of the same sex. The Oedipus constellation in the mentally healthy is resolved by the child's tendency to use the parent of the same sex as a model for its own further developmental patterns and ideal formations and the parent of the opposite sex as a person through whom it learns to develop friendly interpersonal relationships.

The ability to amalgamate feelings of emotional tenderness and of sexual attraction toward one and the same person is considered another evidence of matureness. Freud views love as an outcome and a concomitant feeling of sexual attraction to another person.

In the course of neurotic character development, according to Freud's concepts, the progress of libidinal energy from oral to genital primacy is interrupted and incomplete. The libidinal charge is fixated emotionally at one of the pregenital levels of the psychosexual development. Also, the neurotic person has not succeeded in overcoming the early conflicts of the original Oedipus constellation. According to Freud, these early conflicts constitute one universally valid reason for the later development of neurotic disorders.

The doctrine of the ubiquitousness and the sexual nature of the Oedipus complex has been revised by many psychoanalytic authors and cultural anthropologists, e.g., by Boehn (6), Fromm (7), Malinowski (8), and Mullahy (9). They would demonstrate, first, that in matriarchal societies it may not be the father but an uncle who is the target for the little boy's hatred; second, that the boy's hatred against the father, where encountered, is much more frequently based upon his resentment of the authoritative prerogatives of the father figure and/or his envy of the interpersonal intimacy between the father and mother than upon a sexual origin.

Sullivan viewed the various phases of the developmental history in terms of the interpersonal experiences characteristic of each of these phases of development (10). He referred to the period of infancy, the childhood period, the juvenile era, preadolescence, and, as a last developmental phase, adolescence.

The period of infancy he considers to be the time during which the human is in contact with the mothering one by empathic linkage, the state of non-verbal contact through non-sensory channels that is characteristic of the early mother-infant relationship. In varying degrees, empathy may operate in people throughout their lives. It is the quality by means of which non-verbalized, meaningful communication is frequently successful and its operation becomes therapeutically important in the psychiatrist's dealings with his mental patients, especially with mute or inarticulate ones.

Sullivan characterizes the childhood period by the development of mutual, verbalized communication, contentment in a communal life with authoritarian adults, and more or less personalized pets, toys, and other objects.

The juvenile era is characterized by maturation of the need for compeers and of one's talents for such interpersonal phenomena as co-operation, competition, and compromise.

Preadolescence is a time during which the need for a chum to love is a predominant interpersonal factor. Love, as defined by Sullivan and by Fromm (11), is the state of relatedness in which a person is as interested in the loved one's well-being, satisfaction, and security, growth, and maturation as he is in his own.

Adolescence is the period that is characterized by the process of puberty, gradually producing a maturing sense of self-realization. This is the time when there is a need to break away from the authoritative people of childhood in a rather dramatic way, via the detour of exchanging them for dependence upon and admiration for one's heroes and heroines. In this way the ability to form independent evaluational judgments is finally gained, and ultimately the capacity is developed for establishing durable relationships of intimacy.

PSYCHIATRY—THE SCIENCE OF INTERPERSONAL RELATIONSHIPS

This interpersonal concept of the developmental history is an illustrative part of Sullivan's total doctrine of psychiatry as being the art and science of interpersonal relationships, which means that human personality functions and can be understood only in terms of a person's actual or fantasy relationships and through the medium of a person's contacts and exchange with others.

The emotional importance of the bodily zones of intake and elimination and of their functions during early life is not denied, of course, by any of the modern psychoanalytic psychiatrists (12, 13). However, many of them do not believe that character and personality trends can be understood as the outcome of various forms of desexualization, as has been described in the review of the basic classical psychoanalytic concepts. Fromm, for instance, sees the fundamental basis of character formation in the specific kind of relatedness of a person to the world as it is molded in childhood by the family, the psychic agent of society. His concept of a receptive, exploitative, hoarding, and marketing character versus a productive character who is able "to use his powers and to realize the potentialities inherent in him," in a positive, life-furthering sense is illustrative of his approach.

We see from these concepts, then, that modern developmental psychoanalytic theory is characterized by the maintenance of the paramount significance of the total developmental history and by the negation of its classical psychosexual interpretation.

Freud's conception of the emotional significance of immediate environmental influences for the understanding of human personality and for the treatment of human psychopathology has been broadened in the direction of the inclusion of cultural influences on a general scale versus his otherwise predominantly biological approach to human psychopathology. The concepts of Fromm (12, 14), Horney (13, 15), Kardiner (16), Sullivan (10, 17), and others on the Oedipus constellation may serve as an example for this development.

PSYCHOANALYTIC CONCEPTS OF ANXIETY

Another expression of the changes and advances in psychoanalytic thinking and therapy is with regard to some mental symptoms, among them the most outstanding one—anxiety. The study of the concepts of anxiety as developed in the various schools of psychoanalytic thinking is of the greatest importance for any student and practitioner in the field, since the understanding and adequate handling of the patient's anxiety plays a crucial role in all psychopathology and hence in all psychoanalytic psychotherapy.

Freud has defined anxiety in his early writings as the correlate of repressed libidinal strivings. Later he saw it as a person's fear at the realization of culturally unacceptable inner strivings (18). This definition is similar to the one Sullivan gives in his interpersonal frame of reference (10, 19). In Sullivan's definition, anxiety is the discomfort which the child learns to feel at the disapproval of the significant adult who first uses the arousal of this discomfort as a tool while training the child to abide by the basic requirements of acculturation. With great variations as to the threshold of endurance, anxiety remains effective throughout people's lives in response to disapproval from important people which interferes with the individual's security and prestige. Sullivan has taught the understanding of all mental disorders as an expression of and an attempt at warding off anxiety. Horney speaks of four principal modes of defense against anxiety: affection, submissiveness, power, withdrawal. She teaches that the craving for affection, for power, and for control plays a paramount role in the development of neuroses and neurotic personalities.

Where there is anxiety, there is insecurity; where there is insecurity, there is lack of self-respect; where there is lack of self-respect, there is lack of respect for others. Anxiety causes impairment of relatedness to others, fear of friendliness in giving and taking, loneliness, and hostility —all well-known symptoms in mental patients.

This brief outline of psychoanalytic concepts may suffice as a background for the following discussion of the recent advances in the method and technique of psychoanalytic psychotherapy and the types of patients who may be treated by modern, dynamic psychoanalytic psychotherapy.

ETIOLOGY OF MENTAL DISORDER

In the light of the dynamic and genetic conceptions of the working of the mind, human psychopathology is understood by all dynamic psychiatrists as the outcome of early warp, thwarting experiences, and severe frustrations in relation to a significant person in the infant's or child's environment. In the upbringing of our present day, circumscribed as it is by family life, as a rule it is a parent who is responsible for warping experiences the threat of which is too great to be offset by other benign influences. The type of emotional disturbance which a person develops will depend upon the timing of the first decisive blow of a set of such traumatic experiences and upon the presence or absence of other benign or malignant interpersonal influences. Many emotional experiences of his later life will be undergone, actually or by his interpretation, as if they were really repetitions of the original traumata in the childhood setting.

In other words, whenever a person who has undergone too severe or too frequent early traumatic experiences is exposed to later life-experiences engendering pain, hostility, anxiety, etc., he has to cope not only with the actual experience as such but, in addition, with its repetitional validity. This repetitional aspect stems from his early dissociated—therefore, never satisfactorily integrated—traumatic experiences, with all their immature misevaluation and their concomitant anxiety.

In order to avoid misunderstanding, I wish to state at this point that, in discussing the psychopathological effects of keeping emotional experiences from awareness, I do not mean to say that all dissociative or repressed processes are psychopathological in nature. The contrary is true. Man depends upon successful dissociations and processes of selective inattention for the mastery of his psychobiological existence.

It is the surplus of painful and anxiety-arousing emotional experience whose barring from awareness creates psychopathological problems. If a patient's original traumatic material is brought to awareness in psychotherapy, it can be submitted to revaluation on the present level of the patient's matureness, anxiety can be relieved, and recent traumatic experience can be freed from the additional weight of non-integrated previous experience. Hence the bringing to awareness and the subsequent evaluation of repressed material must be an integral part of the psychotherapeutic process, just as will the investigation of those feelings the reflection of which will be transferred to the people of one's later life.

PSYCHOANALYTIC PSYCHOTHERAPY

In the situation of psychoanalytic psychotherapy these feelings, unknown to the patient himself, will be transferred to the psychotherapist, and so they can be studied *in statu nascendi* by psychiatrist and patient. Otherwise, treatment must be directed toward resolving psychopathological repression and dissociation and understanding the patient's difficulties in terms of his developmental history. This aim is attained by using the following psychotherapeutic tools: collecting data from the patient regarding biographical and historical facts which the patient is able to offer; his presenting problems, previous problems, and crisis situations; biographical data, especially regarding his developmental history; his private mental experiences, such as dreams and daydreams, hallucinatory and delusional experiences.

The means for collecting the data are listening intelligently, as a participant-observer, to all that the patient has to say; asking simple, meaningful, and pertinent questions; encouraging associative thinking; and picking up marginal thoughts and physical sensations, where direct information is failing. Further therapeutically valid material presents itself in the repetition and reactivation, during treatment, of the powers which originally motivated the patient's dissociative procedures. As mentioned before, this also takes place and is of the essence for therapeutic use in the vicissitudes of the doctor-patient relationship, in its real and in its distorted, "parataxic," aspects—in classical terminology, in the patient's "transference" experiences. Once the pertinent data are carefully collected, interpretive collaboration between the patient and the psychotherapist follows, with regard to the understanding of the hidden meaning of the previously dissociated material, as to its genetics, dynamics, and content.

Interpretation

Interpretation means translating into the language of awareness, and thereby bringing into the open, what the patient communicates, without being conscious of its contents, its dynamics, its revealing connections with other experiences, or the various implications pertaining to its factual or emotional background.

At the present state of development in psychoanalytic psychotherapy, special interpretive attention is given to the clarification of the dynamic significance of the defense mechanisms, the security operations which the anxious mental patient uses, wittingly or unwittingly, in his dealings with his fellow men, including the psychotherapist. These security operations are directed against real or alleged anxiety-producing threats to the patient's safety and prestige. This makes it advisable for great attention to be paid to the actual interpersonal experiences of the patient in his everyday life, both prior to and during the treatment situation. Special attention should be paid to the crises which precipitated his entering treatment and which may recur while he is undergoing psychotherapy (15, 10, 29).

Part of the previously hidden meaning of the patient's material reveals itself, and some of his dissociations resolve themselves by the mere process of relating the data to the doctor, that is, by bringing his hitherto private covert experiences into contact with outward reality. Another part gets clarified in the course of the interpretive investigation of the patient's security operations. Only what remains unclarified by these two devices should be uncovered and revalued by direct interpretation of content. By and large, content interpretation, per se, is not considered so important today as it was in the early years of psychoanalysis, and it is used with ever increasing thriftiness, caution, and discrimination.

No cure is accomplished, according to present classical and modified psychoanalytic knowledge, by any single, one-time understanding of any single symptom or any single previously dissociated experience. All emotional experiences which are made accessible to the patient's awareness and mature emotional judgment have to be recognized and accepted ("worked through") repeatedly in various contexts. In doing so, psychiatrist and patient should be guided by what gradually emerges as the patient's central problem. Working through should be continued until the time is reached when the intellectual understanding of this problem, of its previously dissociated causes, and of its various interlocking mental and emotional ramifications is gradually transformed into real creative emotional insight.

Free Associations

The encouragement of the patient's "free associations" is considered to be the backbone of classical psychoanalytic therapy. It is designed to eliminate the patient's conscious control over his mental productions, thus bringing out previously repressed and dissociated material.

Since the psychoanalytic doctrine and method were first conceived, an impressive body of knowledge and experience has been collected concerning the modes of operation and expression used in interpersonal processes outside awareness. Therefore, many modern dynamic psychotherapists do not feel the indiscriminate use of the so-called method of "free association" to be a basic requirement in psychoanalytic therapy. This marks another change in psychoanalytic therapy.

Many psychoanalysts feel that a sufficient amount of recognizable dissociated material comes to the surface and may rise into awareness in more directed psychotherapeutic interchange and directed, focused associative thinking.

Dream Interpretation

Scientific dream interpretation continues to be considered an important means of understanding many thoughts and feelings that the patient cannot express while awake, because of the fact that, during sleep, control and censorship of his mental processes are eliminated or at least greatly reduced. The extent to which dream interpretation may be used in any single psychotherapeutic process depends upon the therapeutic usefulness of both the nature of a patient's dreams and the understanding and interpretive skill of the psychotherapist.

Didactic Psychoanalysis

Emphasis may be placed upon the fact that the extent and nuances of the use of the various psychotherapeutic tools in each course of treatment will, of necessity, be codetermined by the assets and liabilities of both persons concerned, the patient and the doctor as participant-observer. This being so, a personal psychoanalysis is among the training requirements for any psychiatrist who wishes to do psychoanalytic psychotherapy.

Setup in Psychoanalytic Psychotherapy

The tendency to give more therapeutic attention to actual realities in the patient's life is responsible for several practical changes in the treatment situation. Among recent changes is the relinquishment, by many psychoanalysts, of the binding rule that the patient must lie on the couch, the doctor seated invisibly behind him. As now understood by many psychoanalytic psychotherapists, this arrangement interfered, for quite a number of patients, with an experience of reality and with the spontaneity of the exchange between patient and doctor. This feeling of reality and the spontaneous interchange should be encouraged, notwithstanding the maintenance of the strictly professional character of the doctor-patient relationship. Many psychoanalysts allow patients to sit or to lie down, whichever way seems to work best with each patient. With some patients this may be decided upon at once for the entire course of treatment; with others, changes of position once or repeatedly may be advisable during the course of the treatment.

BRIEF PSYCHOTHERAPY—GROUP PSYCHOTHERAPY

Other recent changes in psychoanalytic psychotherapy stem from research and practical endeavor directed toward shortening the psychoanalytic process with a carefully selected group of patients. Important work in that direction is under way at one of the leading psychoanalytic training centers in this country, the Chicago Psychoanalytic Institute (20, 21). The successful introduction of psychoanalytic concepts into group psychotherapy as it has been developed in many psychotherapy centers during and after the last war should also be mentioned in this connection (22, 23, 24).

PSYCHOSOMATIC MEDICINE

The technique of psychoanalytic psychotherapy was originally created for special application to psychoneuroses. Treatment of physical symptoms was in terms of an interpretive approach to the "conversion symptoms" of the hysteric (2–5). Modern developments in psychosomatic medicine are due mainly to psychoanalytic research (25–27). Two sets of results, which have become of great significance for practically all branches of modern medicine, stem from this advance in psychoanalytic development. One is the psychotherapeutic approach to the emotional roots of the etiologic factors of somatic symptomatology, where symptoms and syndromes were previously approached in terms of their clinical appearance. The other is the finding of certain laws governing the correlation between certain types of psychoneurotic personalities and their choice of bodily disturbances. The psychosomatic significance of high blood pressure, gastric ulcers, and the various types of colitis, asthma, and hay fever is by now known to every physician as representative of these findings.

PSYCHOSIS

There is one more important progressive step in psychoanalytic psychotherapy, which is signified by a modification in the technique of psychoanalysis for the application to the psychoses (28–34). An early attempt at doing classical psychoanalysis with a manic-depressive was made by Abraham (35). Recently, research and therapeutic endeavor focused around the manic-depressive group have been carried out in England (36). In this country, severely disturbed schizophrenics have been approached with modified psychoanalytic techniques. This became possible because of the previously described recent changes in psychoanalytic technique and as a result of the two afore-mentioned great discoveries of psychoanalytic psychiatry: that all mental manifestations, including those of the mentally disordered, are potentially meaningful and that there is interpersonal interaction between any two people who meet, including the mentally disturbed patient and the psychotherapist.

Out of this grew the psychopathologically significant insight that the difference between healthy, neurotic, and psychotic people is much more one of degree than one of kind; that the mentally handicapped may have assets which may not be found in the healthy and that the healthy may have liabilities not duplicated in the mentally disturbed (36). In brief, that we are all "much more simply human than otherwise" (10).

Some psychoanalytic psychiatrists hope that it is not too optimistic to harbor the dream that this psychiatric insight may in time develop into a small contribution toward improving the mutual understanding between the people of the disturbed world of today.

References

1. FROMM-REICHMANN, FRIEDA. "Recent Advances in Psychoanalytic Psychotherapy," *Psychiatry*, IV (May, 1941), 161–64.
2. FREUD, SIGMUND. *A General Introduction to Psychoanalysis*. New York: Boni & Liveright, 1920.
3. BRILL, A. A. *The Basic Writings of Sigmund Freud*. New York: Modern Library, 1938.
4. HENDRICKS, IVES. *Facts and Theories of Psychoanalysis*. New York: Alfred Knopf, 1939.
5. FENICHEL, OTTO. *Outline of Clinical Psychoanalysis*. New York: W. W. Norton & Co., 1934.
6. BOEHN, FELIX. *Internat. Ztschr. Psychoanal.*, XII (1926), 66–79. (Not translated.)
7. FROMM, ERICH. In ANSHEN, RUTH NANDA (ed.), *The Family, Its Function and Destiny: A Synthesis*, chaps. xvii, xix. New York: Harper & Bros., 1949.
8. MALINOWSKI, B. *Sex and Repression in Savage Society*. New York: Harcourt, Brace & Co.; London: Kegan Paul, Trench, Trubner & Co., 1927.
9. MULLAHY, PATRICK. *Oedipus Myth and Complex*. New York: Hermitage Press, Inc., 1948. Offers orientation on the attitude of all psychoanalytic schools to the problem.
10. SULLIVAN, H. S. "Conceptions of Modern Psychiatry: William Alanson White Memorial Lectures," *Psychiatry*, III (February, 1940), 1–117. Reprinted as monograph by the William Alanson White Psychiatric Foundation, Washington, D.C., 1947.
11. FROMM, ERICH. "Selfishness and Self-Love," *Psychiatry*, II (November, 1939), 507–23.
12. ———. *Escape from Freedom*. New York and Toronto: Farrar & Rinehart, Inc., 1941.
13. HORNEY, KAREN. *The Neurotic Personality of Our Time*. New York: W. W. Norton & Co., 1937.
14. FROMM, ERICH. *Man for Himself: An Inquiry into the Psychology of Ethics*. New York: Rinehart & Co., 1947.

15. HORNEY, KAREN. *New Ways in Psychoanalysis*. New York: W. W. Norton & Co., 1939.
16. KARDINER, ABRAM. *The Individual and His Society*. New York: Columbia University Press, 1939.
17. SULLIVAN, H. S. "A Note on the Implications of Psychiatry, the Study of Interpersonal Relations, for Investigations in the Social Sciences," *Am. J. Sociol.*, XLIII (1937), 848–61.
18. FREUD, SIGMUND. *The Problem of Anxiety*. New York: W. W. Norton & Co., 1936.
19. SULLIVAN, H. S. "The Meaning of Anxiety in Psychiatry and in Life," *Psychiatry*, I (1948), 1–13.
20. ALEXANDER, FRANZ, FRENCH, THOMAS M., *et al. Psychoanalytic Therapy*. New York: Ronald Press Co., 1946.
21. *Proceedings of the Psychotherapy Council*. Chicago: Psychoanalytic Institute, 1946.
22. ABRAHAM, JOSEPH. "Group Psychotherapy: Remarks on Its Basis and Application," *M. Ann. District of Columbia*, XVI (1947), 612–16.
23. ACKERMAN, N. W. "Dynamic Patterns in Group Psychotherapy," *Psychiatry*, VII (1944), 341–48.
24. SLAVSON, S. R. *An Introduction to Group Therapy*. London and Oxford: Commonwealth Fund, 1943.
25. *Journal of Psychosomatic Medicine*. Baltimore, Md.: Williams & Wilkins Co.
26. DUNBAR, H. F. *Emotions and Bodily Changes*. New York: Columbia University Press, 1938.
27. WEISS, E., and ENGLISH, O. S. *Psychosomatic Medicine*. Philadelphia and London: W. B. Saunders Co., 1943.
28. SULLIVAN, H. S. "Environmental Factors in Etiology and Course under Treatment of Schizophrenia," *M. J. & Rec.*, CXXXIII (1931), 19–22.
29. ———. "Therapeutic Investigations in Schizophrenia," *Psychiatry*, X (1947), 121–25.
30. FEDERN, P. "Psychoanalysis of Psychoses," *Psychiat. Quart.*, XVII (1943), 3–19.
31. ———. "Principles of Psychotherapy in Latent Schizophrenia," *Am. J. Psychotherapy*, I (1947), 129–44.
32. FROMM-REICHMANN, FRIEDA. "Transference Problems in Schizophrenics," *Psychoanalyt. Quart.*, VIII (1939), 412–26. Reprinted in *Contemporary Psychopathology*, ed. S. S. TOMKINS. Cambridge, Mass.: Harvard University Press, 1943.
33. ———. "Psychoanalytic Psychotherapy with Psychotics," *Psychiatry*, VI (1943), 277–79.
34. ———. "Notes on the Development of Treatment of Schizophrenics by Psychoanalytic Psychotherapy," *ibid.*, XI (1948), 263–73.
35. ABRAHAM, K. *Selected Papers*, pp. 473 ff. ("International Psychoanalytical Library," No. 13.) London: Hogarth Press, 1948.
36. KLEIN, MELANIE. "A Contribution to the Psychogenesis of Manic-depressive States," *Internat. J. Psycho-analysis*, XVI (1935), 145–74.
37. FROMM-REICHMANN, FRIEDA. "Remarks on the Philosophy of Mental Disorder," *Psychiatry*, IX (1946), 293–308.

(7)

PERSONALITY OF THE PSYCHOTHERAPIST AND
THE DOCTOR-PATIENT RELATIONSHIP

There is agreement about some basic requirements which a psychiatrist must fulfil in order to build a valid therapeutic relationship with his patients, with the goal of contributing constructively to the solution of the patient's difficulties in living. First, the psychiatrist should have his own problems in living reasonably well solved, or he should at least be sufficiently aware of them that they do not interfere with his ability to listen constructively to patients. If that is accomplished, the previous or present problems of the psychiatrist may serve as a useful adjuvant in an experiential personal frame of reference in his work with the patients —so long as he guards against using them for wayward overidentification.

Second, the psychiatrist should be able to handle impacts upon his own narcissism and on his personal and professional vanity without uncalled-for, unconstructive counterreactions. This includes his ability to handle frustrations in the therapeutic process, patients' hostile outbursts against him, and the eavesdropping of sensitive patients upon expressions of the hidden peculiarities of his personality.

Let me illustrate by a consultation which I had with several younger colleagues. One spoke of a psychotic patient who had done remarkably well in treatment for several months, to her own and her doctor's satisfaction, and who felt threatened by an oncoming relapse. "You have not understood anything I have ever said to you, doctor," the patient said, angrily and in despair. The doctor, accepting the patient's remark verbatim, was very disappointed but responded, so he thought, with patience and understanding. "Then we must go over these things again," he said. Whereupon he received a resounding and painful smack in the face from the patient. The mark it left still showed. Feeling that the patient deserved to be "punished" for such an uncalled-for act of hostility, the doctor gave her shock treatment.

What had happened to the doctor was that the relapse of a patient who had done well up to a point brought about a sense of severe frustration in him. Her statement that his lack of understanding was the cause of this relapse hit his professional pride and self-appreciation. Under the twofold impact of a frustrating experience and a blow to his nar-

These papers were delivered at a round-table discussion at the annual meeting of the American Psychiatric Association in Atlantic City, N.J., on May 15, 1952.

Reprinted from *American Journal of Psychoanalysis*, Vol. XIII, No. 1 (1953).

cissism, the doctor misinterpreted the patient's statement that she felt misunderstood as meaning that he had failed to understand the single issues under discussion. He therefore implied that things could be improved by rediscussion of these single items. The patient, becoming desperate by such miscarriage of her complaint, distrusted her ability to verbalize her meaning, and regressed to the language of gestures. The doctor retaliated by punishing the patient.

My disagreement with the doctor's reaction to the patient's assault does not imply the suggestion that he should take the patient's hostile outburst without restricting her. It is certainly to be recommended that assaultiveness be prevented for the sake of the doctor's self-protection and even more so for the sake of the patient's self-respect. However, the psychiatrist's attitude toward the patient should not be dictated by his feelings of frustration and/or hostility which patients' communications may elicit in him.

Such an attitude presupposes a great amount of emotional security on the part of the psychiatrist. This sense of security is often mentioned, therefore, as a prerequisite for all constructive psychotherapeutic intervention. What has *not* been mentioned sufficiently, however, is that no one is, can be, or should be completely secure emotionally; so, of course, there should be no quest for complete security on the part of the psychiatrist.

Life ends with death, the timing and causes of which are unpredictable. This fact is, actually and symbolically, the last expression of the fact that there are unknown forces which govern our lives. A psychotherapist who does not know and integrate this fact and who dreams about complete emotional security, an unreal attainment in life, cannot guide his mental patients to wholesome, constructive testing and evaluation of reality or to a constructive adjustment to it. In other words, acceptance of emotional insecurity, which is the acceptance of a certain amount of anxiety in the lives of the psychiatrist and his patients, is one of the constructive forces in the psychotherapeutic process. When the psychiatrist refers to a mental patient's anxiety as the central object of treatment, he should think only of the excess anxiety suffered by mental patients, not of the milder degree of anxiety which we all have to accept and to integrate. As a matter of fact, anxiety as a signal of forthcoming danger is not detrimental but helpful and constructive in coping with the vicissitudes of life.

In the special case of anxiety which may be aroused in the psychotherapist by a patient, this may constitute a most crucial constructive adjuvant in spotting and in coping with the patient's problems that brought about the anxiety. The prerequisite for this constructive use of both the doctor's and the patient's anxieties for therapeutic purposes is that the doctor be secure enough emotionally to create and further the psychotherapeutic process in the spirit of a "we experience," as one patient recently called it.

For a while, this patient happened to be the only hospital patient I treated. She repeatedly reported speculations among her fellow patients as to the reason for her having been selected for treatment by me as the senior staff member and about the envy that ensued from this choice. When I teasingly asked her when and how she would have to prove to me, and to her envious fellow patients, that her senior psychiatrist was no "hot shot," the patient's response was to the effect that I had successfully counteracted her impulses in that direction by establishing our therapeutic relationship as a "we" experience. "I simply say to the patients who ask me how you do it, that you don't do it by magic but that the two of us work at it very hard together."

What has been said about the psychotherapist's ability to see the constructive aspects of a certain degree of anxiety in himself and in his patients holds equally true for his attitude toward other symptoms of the mental patient. Symptoms must be understood and therapeutically approached, not only as an expression of a mental illness, but also as an attempt of the patient to fight the illness. For instance, consider regression. This symptom constitutes not only a withdrawal to an earlier developmental level but also an attempt to cope on this level with tasks which are congruent with the sick person's reduced ability to attack the task more maturely.

Again, let us look at hallucinations and delusions. They constitute not only failures or distortions of sensory perceptions but also attempts to externalize inner problems and to solve them by a confrontation with outward reality.

It has been recommended and accepted by the various psychoanalytic schools that the psychotherapist should be analyzed, so that he can learn to know from his own experience the conscious and unconscious dynamics of his psychological functioning, his narcissism, anxieties, hostilities, etc. I believe that there is a potent additional reason for the desirability of the psychiatrist's analysis: he should learn from his own experience to believe in the possibility of psychological change in himself and in others.

This belief in change goes together with, and is inherent in, the psychiatrist's knowledge of, and belief in, potential human competence and man's tendency toward health. It is this competence and motivation toward health that constitute one of the most constructive aspects in psychotherapy, if the psychiatrist knows how to use it. Most patients know or expect that they can recover from their mental disorder. The despair which mental patients express at times in this connection does not, as a rule, refer to their fear of not being able to get well but rather to their fear of not finding the right doctor to help them. The psychiatrist who misinterprets the patient's despair may do so because of his own lack of belief in their potentiality for change. He then makes the same mistake as parents do who are blind and do not live up to the expectations of their children, who undergo growth and change.

The inner knowledge that emotional changes are possible, which is alive in most mental patients, is frequently accompanied by their fear of and defenses against this change. Every psychiatrist is well acquainted with the defenses that obsessional patients, for instance, develop against imminent changes from within and without. Change is a threat to the routine of living to which they are accustomed.

One of my previously psychotic patients who was living independently outside the hospital but was still under psychotherapy became suddenly panicky one day when she heard me use the word "change." Intensive investigation of this unexpected reaction on the part of a patient, who was aware of and enjoyed the great changes she had already undergone, disclosed the following reason for her panic. The degree of difference between her past and present life was brought sharply into focus by the psychiatrist's use of the word "change." She was momentarily filled with the fear of losing the continuity between her two worlds, between her previous and her present self.

In summary, the belief in and knowledge of the potentiality for change in mental patients, the knowledge of their fear of it, and the skill in the psychiatrist's ability to handle defenses against it constitute a central constructive part of all valid psychotherapy.

The question of the psychiatrist's belief in potential human competence leads up to the discussion of my next point: the problem and the constructive aspects of values in psychotherapy. In the past we were taught that there should not be any values inherent in psychotherapy. At the present time psychiatrists realize and accept the fact that the goals of psychotherapy constitute the values inherent in psychotherapeutic philosophy. These goals are the patient's growth and maturation: a reasonable security and freedom from anxiety; self-realization; the ability to give and receive love, to share values, and to engage in intimate interpersonal relationship, including sexual ones, with sufficient security to eliminate greed, envy, and jealousy (Alexander, Fromm-Reichmann, Horney, Kubie, Sullivan, Whitehorn). In the judgment of this writer, there is no constructive psychotherapy unless the psychiatrist's operations are guided by this set of values. However, it should never be confounded with the personal set of values accepted by, and governing the life of, any individual psychiatrist. From the above-mentioned concept of human competence, it follows that, in the course of a constructive therapeutic process, mental patients must learn to discover and to establish their own sets of values. That means that, in the course of their treatment, patients must find out for themselves which ways and contents serve them best for their self-realization; in what direction their growth and maturation should go; to what type of person they should relate or with whom they should share values.

The psychotherapist will be a valuable aid to patients in their efforts to build up a constructive life if he keeps this in mind and does not interfere with patients' growth and ultimate independence by giving himself the narcissistic gratification of playing father or God to them. His task is not to play up to his own needs for self-aggrandizement but to help patients to become mentally healthy, self-respecting persons.

The last point I wish to take up is the role of conventionality in the doctor-patient relationship and in the psychotherapeutic process. Conventions are man-made rules to facilitate the smooth running of relationships between people who are not close enough to one another, or independent enough of one another, to set up their own patterns of interpersonal dealings. In other words, conventionalities were originated for convenience and were intended to be so accepted for use by people in their everyday living with one another. The psychotherapist should keep in mind that conventions have been made for the convenience of people, not people for the observance of conventions. And so he should be able to recognize the relative—as it were, purely teleological—value of conventionalities. He must know that adherence to conventionalities should never be used as a measuring rod for mental health.

To illustrate, among the factors upon which the recovery of manic-depressive patients depends is their learning to relinquish the overevaluation of conventionalities which they have learned from their upbringing and to exchange them for a personal set of values developed on their own initiative.

Schizophrenics, however, must learn not to use anticonventionality as a weapon. But their psychotherapists must learn that schizophrenic patients can get well without adherence to the accepted mores of our culture and society. A former schizophrenic, for example, may choose to live in a certain degree of withdrawal, perhaps remain unmarried, or select other unconventional ways of living. All this is all right as long as his mode of living enables him to function adequately and without detriment to the people around him.

Constructive psychotherapeutic help is given by a psychiatrist who accepts emotional insecurity in himself and in his patients as a legitimate part of life itself and who is able to use his own anxieties as they may arise during the psychotherapeutic process as a means of spotting the patient's anxieties which elicited his own; who knows about and believes in the inherent competence and tendency toward health of mental patients, the constructive aspects of their symptomatology, and their potentialities for emotional change; who accepts guiding evaluational principles inherent in the philosophy of psychotherapy but who is free from the need to introduce his personal set of values in the psychotherapeutic work with patients; and who is able to recognize the relative value of conventionalities and to refrain from using patients' adherence to them as a measuring rod for their state of mental health.

(8)

PSYCHOANALYTIC AND GENERAL DYNAMIC
CONCEPTIONS OF THEORY AND OF
THERAPY: DIFFERENCES AND
SIMILARITIES

A psychoanalyst who might be asked to give very briefly the essential principles of psychoanalysis could say that the recognition of the significance of childhood history for personality development, the teachings of transference and resistance, and, above all, the establishment of the unconscious as an integral part of the human mind constitute the essence of psychoanalysis.

Freud (11) says in the *History of the Psychoanalytic Movement* that every psychiatrist who accepts the validity of these three doctrines may consider himself a psychoanalyst. At the present developmental state of psychoanalysis, the acceptance of the paramount significance of anxiety for the dynamic understanding of human personality should be added as the fourth requisite of an analyst.

In the spring of 1952 a Conference on Psychiatric Education took place at Cornell University, under the auspices of the American Psychiatric Association, the American Association of Medical Colleges, and the United States Public Health Service, Division of Mental Health (2). For the first time in the history of modern psychiatry an extensive statement on "Principles of Dynamic Psychiatry" was prepared for this conference by a joint commission of psychoanalysts and other dynamic psychiatrists. The three conceptions mentioned above have been recognized in this statement as forming an integral part of the operating principles in dynamic psychiatry.

While classical analysts as well as dynamically oriented psychiatrists accept these principles as to their dynamics, the various schools of thought differ in regard to the interpretation of their meaning. Freud (10, 12) saw childhood development as a psychosexual one. Freud and Abraham (1) speak about the two oral, the two anal, the urethral, and the phallic phases of childhood development. Dynamic psychiatrists conceive of childhood development in terms of the developmental phases of

Reprinted from the *Journal of the American Psychoanalytic Association*, Vol. II, No. 4 (October, 1954).

the child's interpersonal relationships. They speak about infancy as the period when the child cannot yet use language as a means of communication; they consider childhood as the period when life centers around the relationship to and the verbalized communication with the parents and siblings; and they speak about the juvenile era as the period when competition, co-operation, and compromise with one's compeers are established. These developmental phases are followed, for example, in Sullivan's interpersonal conception (40, 41) by preadolescence as the time during which the need for a beloved chum is a predominant factor and adolescence as the period characterized by the onset of puberty, by a gradually maturing sense of self-realization, by the need to replace previous authorities by new heroes, and subsequently by the capacity for independence and for the establishment of durable relationships of intimacy.

The afore-mentioned Commission on Psychodynamic Principles (2) differentiated these periods as infancy up to twelve or fifteen months; early childhood, from two to four years, as the phase of elementary domestic socialization; middle childhood, the latency period of classical analysis, as the phase of communal socialization. Puberty and adolescence are characterized in the report of the commission by the onset of biological, reproductive, and social maturation, reconsideration of values, and social learning, which develop in the adolescent the ability to foresee and meet the problems of adulthood.

In spite of these differences between the psychosexual and the interpersonal theories of childhood development, there are two points in the concepts of both groups where there is a meeting of minds. One: although proponents of general psychodynamics do not share with classical analysts the concept of the sexual interpretation of the developmental phases connected with the zones of intake and elimination, both groups do share the conception that the processes of intake and elimination (food, urine, bowel movements) are used by infants and children for the purpose of non-verbal interpersonal communication. For this reason Sullivan (40, 41) encompasses the zones of intake and elimination in his general conception of "zones of interaction" (he also speaks of auditory and visual zones of interaction). Classical analysts, however, refer to the zones of intake and elimination as "erotogenic zones" (10, 12). Fairbairn's (5–7) psychoanalytic research should be mentioned in this connection, since it contains important elements similiar to Sullivan's approach.

The second point in question is the following: the differentiation between the sexual conceptions of childhood development by classical analysts and the interpersonal theory of dynamic psychiatrists is, in part, one of definition rather than one of actual conceptualization. Freud (10, 12) decided to call "sexual" all those partial, pregenital, emotional, and physical manifestations in infants and children which are later unified in a person's genital sexuality, and he made the point that this was a matter of definition stemming from his genetic approach to all human manifestations, including sexual ones. [Should we recall at this point that in the *New Introductory Lectures* Freud (14) refers to the instinct theory as "our mythology"?] Non-analytic dynamic psychiatrists use the concept "sexual" only in connection with actual or fantasied erotic experiences with other people.

So much about the important points of partial agreement about dynamic developmental conceptions. There remain the basic differences between the classical analytic concept of personality development as the outcome of the vicissitudes of psychosexual energies and the dynamic psychiatrist's conception of personality development as the outcome of the vicissitudes of early interpersonal relationships in general.

The consideration of the second essential concept, originally mentioned, which general dynamic psychiatry and classical psychoanalysis have in common now brings us to a discussion of the similarities and differences between both schools of thought in the concepts of transference and resistance. The dynamics of transference as the revival and repetition with contemporaries, and especially with the psychotherapist, of all the characteristics of one's early modes of relating to the significant people of one's earlier life are equally accepted by both groups. Their inclusion as an integral part of dynamic principles met with the nearly unanimous approval of the eighty-six psychiatrists (including twenty-four psychoanalysts) who participated in the Conference on Psychiatric Education (2).

The difference lies in the conceptions of the content matter of the transferred material. The psychoanalytic doctrine of the universality of the Oedipus complex in its sexual interpretation is, as we know, not accepted by other dynamic psychiatrists. There is no psychiatrist who doubts the predominant importance of the interpersonal patterns developed in the relationship of infant and child with his parents as the most significant people of his early life. However, most dynamic psychiatrists conceive of the love and attachment to the one parent as not being necessarily a sexual one, and of the hatred or resentment against the other parent as not necessarily stemming from sexual rivalry. Jealousy of the closeness of the parents and envious resentment of the authority attributed to one of the parents are among the non-sexual interpretations which the Oedipus constellation has found in general dynamic psychiatry. Needless to say, these differences between the conceptions of both groups regarding the content material of transference make for a difference between the content meaning and the interpretation of transference phenomena in the general dynamic frame of reference and their meaning and interpretation in the framework of classical analysis. In psychoanalytic philosophy it always entails the transfer of the sexual entanglements of the Oedipus constellation onto people in general, and especially onto the psychoanalyst. Recent publications by Gitelson and by Lampl-de Groot in the symposium on "The Re-evaluation of the Oedipus Complex" (18) should be studied in this connection.[1]

We continue with a discussion of the similarities and differences in conceptualization and therapeutic utilization of a third essential concept accepted by both groups. All dynamic psychiatrists share with classical analysts the concept of conscious and unconscious motivations and drives and the understanding of the operations of the human mind as a product of their interaction. This statement includes, of course, the agreement of various psychodynamic schools as to the great theoretical and therapeutic significance of the interpretation of dreams and as to the technical usefulness of free associations in psychotherapy with psychoneurotics. The utilization of dreams and free associations in the treatment of psychotics, however, is not an unqualified one. I have elaborated on this point in previous publications (16, 17). The content meaning of both phenomena—dreams and free associations—is, of course, interpreted differently by each school in accordance with its difference in the general conceptualization of the unconscious.

To follow up this difference: many dynamic psychiatrists do not accept Freud's concept of the existence of a primary innate unconscious to which mental experiences are added, which become secondarily unconscious by repression; nor have many dynamic psychiatrists included Freud's concept of the preconscious. Rather than wish for material which has actually become unconscious by repression, these psychiatrists think in terms of mental content which is temporarily or permanently barred from awareness, that is, which has been dissociated, but all-of which can be recalled under adequate emotional circumstances. This process of dissociating material which is easily available to recall can be observed especially in psychotherapy with schizophrenics.

In the early development of classical analysis, this conceptual difference used to find its reflection in marked differences in handling the resistance of patients in the therapeutic process. For reasons which we shall presently discuss, it has become much less so in the period of recent developments of ego psychology and of the psychoanalysis of the functions of the ego.

In Freud's conception (12), resistance is the patients' objection to the recall of previously repressed material; as such, it is also directed against the psychiatrist who is instrumental in promoting the recall. This used to be considered the curative center of the therapeutic endeavors of the classical psychoanalyst. At present, however, both groups put therapeutic emphasis primarily on the investigation of the anxiety aroused by un-

1. Special differences in the therapeutic technique of handling transference phenomena, which various psychoanalysts have developed, cannot be discussed in the framework of this paper. Franz Alexander as one of its main proponents discusses them in his own contribution, "Psychoanalysis and Psychotherapy," *J. Psychoanalyt. A.*, II, No. 4 (1954), 722–33.

earthing repressed material and the anxiety operating in the relationship with the therapist who helps patients to resolve repressive processes. Psychotherapeutic interest is focused only secondarily on the content of what has been repressed. In other words, both groups have shifted the center of their therapeutic interest from the investigation of the content of the operations of the id to the investigation of the dynamics of the operations of the ego. The panel on "Technical Implications of Ego-Psychology and Character Analysis" under Bibring's chairmanship at the 1948 midwinter meetings of the American Psychoanalytic Association (3); the work of Hartmann, Kris, and Loewenstein; and Erikson's papers on this subject at the 1950 annual meetings in Detroit (4, 22, 23, 27–30) are especially representative of the development of ego psychology in classical psychoanalytic therapy. Incidentally, Wilhelm Reich (33) suggested and anticipated this development in his early contributions.

Among the reasons for this shift in therapeutic emphasis among analysts, the historical fact should be mentioned that Freud's original concepts of analytic therapy and theory were gained from his experience with the psychoneuroses, mainly hysteria, whereas the majority of the patients with whom we work now are character disorders and obsessionals, as well as many borderline cases and outright psychotics. The repressed and dissociated material of these patients is somewhat more easily available to consciousness than that of the hysteric. Their anxieties are greater than those of the hysteric and in the borderline cases and the psychotics not infrequently nearer to the surface. These facts, I believe, explain in part the psychoanalytic shift in therapeutic emphasis from unearthing repressed material and investigating its meaning, to the investigation of its dynamics. This includes, above all, therapeutic concern with the manifestations of the anxiety aroused by the resolution of repressed material and the patients' operations with the therapist. At this point, then, the theoretical and therapeutic conceptions of classical psychoanalysts and other dynamic psychiatrists run in close dynamic confluence.

Inasmuch as the analytic shift of emphasis is codetermined by the change in the type of patients from whom psychoanalytic experiences have been derived, this development, I believe, represents one part of the change which Freud anticipated when he expressed the hope that the technique of psychoanalytic therapy would eventually be modified to become applicable to the narcissistic neuroses, to the psychoses (9).

This remarkable capacity of Freud to promote and anticipate modifications and changes in psychoanalytic conceptualization and technique seems to me to be something which we all should take to mind and emulate. Psychoanalysts should not put Freud unfairly on the pedestal of indiscriminate acceptance and adoration on which another great teacher of the nineteenth century, Karl Marx, was put by his disciples. Marx countered these attempts with his famous statement: "Moi, je ne suis pas marxiste" ("I am not a Marxist"). Let us remember that Freud also said in spirit, time and again, "I am a Freudian, but not a Freudist." He shows this in his constant work on changes and improvements in his psychological concepts.

Freud's changing viewpoints about the dynamics of anxiety—the fourth and last concept which we wish to discuss in our context—is especially representative of his courage and freedom to change, even to reverse himself. In *The Problem of Anxiety*, Freud (13) repudiates his original libidinal concept of anxiety as a correlate of repressed sexual desires. There he redefines anxiety as the discomfort felt by a person who, in response to the inner realization of formerly repressed, unacceptable drives and wishes, is afraid of punishment, of castration. With this definition, the psychoanalytic conception of anxiety has been brought nearer to the concepts of other dynamic psychiatrists. Sullivan (38–41), to mention this dynamic psychiatrist first, shares with Freud the concept of the anxiety-arousing power of unacceptable thoughts, feelings, wishes, and drives. But, in the framework of his interpersonal conception, he sees the expected punishment for these forbidden inner experiences as entailed in the anticipated disapproval of the significant people of an anxious person's early life and of their emotional successors in his present life. This viewpoint is also offered by Whitehorn, in his remarks as chairman of the Commission on Psychodynamic Principles (2). "Expectations of social disapproval or social sanctions," he says, "are extremely important determinants of anxiety in human beings and domesticated animals." However, Whitehorn calls these expectations only *determinants* of anxiety and does not offer them as a full explanation of the dynamics of anxiety. In his contribution to the same report, Theodore Lidz has stigmatized *total* definitions of anxiety as the result of fear of anticipated disapproval as oversimplifications. I agree with this viewpoint.

I have asked myself, therefore, time and again for an additional, or a more satisfactory, explanation of the most significant emotional content of people's anxieties which causes the self-disapproval and the fear of punishment and disapproval by others and which may be held responsible for the importance of anxiety in the current analytic and dynamic concepts. In going over the literature on anxiety in children and adults, from M. Klein (26), Sharpe (35), and Spitz (37) to Ferenczi and Rank (8), Freud (13), Rado (32), Sullivan (38–41), Fromm (15), Horney (24, 25), and Silverberg (36), it seems that the feeling of powerlessness, of helplessness in the presence of inner dangers which the individual cannot control constitutes in the last analysis the common background of all further elaborations on the theory of anxiety. Briefly outlined, this led me to develop the following hypothesis which might be acceptable to both psychoanalysts and other dynamic psychiatrists.

The most universal source of inner helplessness in adults, I believe, stems from their unresolved fixations to the emotional entanglements with significant persons of their early lives—in our culture, of course, mainly with parents during childhood. The result of these fixations is that people compulsively appraise other people in terms of their ancient childhood patterns of living, judgments, and expectations. They act upon and respond to people in line with these misconceptions. Many times people are half-aware of their erroneous judgments, expectations, and behavior, yet are helpless in their attempt to change. This is due to their lack of awareness of the unconscious roots of their compulsive need to repeat old patterns of relatedness and of living, i.e., of the unresolved fixations to their early ways of living with the significant people of their childhood. This helplessness in the face of the need for change of anachronistically distorted patterns meets with discontent and disapproval by oneself and others and also frequently with hatred against anonymous and indefinable forces or, personified, against the people of the past who seem responsible for one's being held back against one's will. This powerlessness in the face of repetition compulsion versus change and in the presence of its concomitant uncontrollable hatred produces deep emotional insecurity in people. That is, it is the cause and the expression of anxiety.

Could it be that this helplessness in the presence of the task of utilizing normal learning processes in the service of psychological change and growth is one and the same as the anxiety which Kurt Goldstein (19, 20) has described in his brain-injured soldiers? Faced with a task which they recognize as requiring something of them but which they cannot accomplish for reasons unknown to them, namely, their neurological brain injury, they too become the prey of an abject feeling of helplessness, of nothingness, of a "catastrophic reaction," as Goldstein has called their anxiety. A similar definition of anxiety has recently been offered by Juergen Ruesch (34), who derives it from his experiences with people under stress.

It is my conviction that any further development of psychoanalytic and psychodynamic conceptions and therapeutic techniques will have to come from a further development of the understanding and the therapeutic utilization of the problem of anxiety. At present, Grinker (21) and Rado (32) and their groups are searching for further answers to this problem. The proceedings of the thirty-ninth annual meeting of the American Psychopathological Association, edited by Zubin and Hoch (42), and Rollo May's (31) monograph on anxiety, give an adequate picture of the present state of our knowledge of anxiety. Freud has given us a signpost for a fruitful direction of further investigations on the subject by teaching us to understand dynamically all mental symptomatology in its polar significance as an expression of and as a defense against anxiety.[2]

2. A more extensive elaboration on this topic was offered in a monograph, "Notes on the History and Philosophy of Psychotherapy," in *Progress in Psychotherapy* (New York: Grune & Stratton, 1956).

To conclude and summarize: Four basic analytic and dynamic principles—the significance of childhood development, the concepts of the unconscious and of transference and resistance, and the problems of anxiety—have been briefly outlined from the viewpoint of their conceptual and therapeutic similarities and differences in the framework of classical analysis and of dynamic psychiatry, to help our orientation in this much discussed field.

References

1. ABRAHAM, K. "A Short Study of the Development of the Libido Theory" (1911). *Selected Papers on Psycho-analysis.* London: Hogarth Press, 1927.
2. AMERICAN PSYCHIATRIC ASSOCIATION. *Psychiatry and Medical Education.* Washington, D.C.: A.P.A., 1952.
3. BIBRING, E., *et al.* "Technical Implications of Ego-Psychology and Character Analysis," *Bull. Am. Psychoanal. A.,* Vol. V (1949).
4. ERIKSON, E. *Childhood and Society.* New York: W. W. Norton & Co., 1950.
5. FAIRBAIRN, W. R. D. "Endopsychic Structure Considered in Terms of Object Relationships," *Internat. J. Psychoanal.,* XXV (1944), 70–93.
6. ———. "Object Relationships and Dynamic Structure," *ibid.,* XXVII (1946), 30–37.
7. ———. *Psychoanalytic Studies of the Personality.* London: Tavistock Pub., Ltd., 1952.
8. FERENCZI, S., and RANK, O. *The Trauma of Birth.* New York: Robert Brunner, 1953.
9. FREUD, S. (1904). *On Psychotherapy.* In *Collected Papers,* I, 249–63. London: Hogarth Press, 1924.
10. ———. (1905). "Three Contributions to the Theory of Sex." In *The Basic Writings of Sigmund Freud.* New York: Modern Library, 1938.
11. ———. (1914). "On the History of the Psycho-analytic Movement," *Collected Papers,* I, 287–359. London: Hogarth Press, 1946.
12. ———. (1917). *A General Introduction to Psychoanalysis.* New York: Liveright, 1935.
13. ———. (1926). *The Problem of Anxiety.* New York: W. W. Norton & Co., 1936.
14. ———. (1932). *New Introductory Lectures on Psychoanalysis.* New York: W. W. Norton & Co., 1933.
15. FROMM, E. *Escape from Freedom.* New York: Rinehart & Co., 1941.
16. FROMM-REICHMANN, F. *Principles of Intensive Psychotherapy.* Chicago: University of Chicago Press, 1950.
17. ———. "Notes on the Development of Treatment of Schizophrenics by Psychoanalytic Psychotherapy." In *Specialized Techniques in Psychotherapy.* Edited by G. BYCHOWSKI and J. L. DESPERT. New York: Basic Books, 1952.
18. GITELSON, M., LAMPL-DE GROOT, J. Symposium: "The Re-evaluation of the Oedipus Complex," *Internat. J. Psychoanal.,* XXXIII (1952), 4.
19. GOLDSTEIN, K. *The Organism.* New York: American Book Co., 1939.

20. ———. *Human Nature in the Light of Psychopathology*. Cambridge, Mass.: Harvard University Press, 1940.
21. GRINKER, R. R. *Psychosomatic Research.* New York: W. W. Norton & Co., 1953.
22. HARTMANN, H. "Psychoanalysis and Developmental Psychology," *The Psychoanalytic Study of the Child*, V, 7–17. New York: International Universities Press, 1950.
23. ———. "Technical Implications of Ego Psychology," *Psychoanalyt. Quart.*, XX (1951), 15–30.
24. HORNEY, K. *The Neurotic Personality of Our Time*. New York: W. W. Norton & Co., 1937.
25. ———. *New Ways in Psychoanalysis*. New York: W. W. Norton & Co., 1939.
26. KLEIN, M. *Developments in Psycho-analysis: Contributions to Psychoanalysis, 1921–45*. London: Hogarth Press, 1948.
27. KRIS, E. "Notes on the Development and on Some Current Problems of Psychoanalytic Child Psychology," *The Psychoanalytic Study of the Child*, V, 24–44. New York: International Universities Press, 1950.
28. ———. "Ego Psychology and Interpretation in Psychoanalytic Therapy," *Psychoanalyt. Quart.*, XX (1951), 15–30.
29. LOEWENSTEIN, R. M. "Conflict and Autonomous Ego Development during the Phallic Phase," *The Psychoanalytic Study of the Child*, V, 47–52. New York: International Universities Press, 1950.
30. ———. "Ego Development and Psychoanalytic Technique," *Am. J. Psychiat.*, CVII (1951), 617–21.
31. MAY, R. *The Meaning of Anxiety*. New York: Ronald Press Co., 1951.
32. RADO, S. "On the Psychoanalytic Exploration of Fear and Other Emotions," *Tr. New York Acad. Sc.*, XI (1952), 7.
33. REICH, W. *Character Analysis*. New York: Nevill, 1947.
34. RUESCH, J. "The Interpersonal Communication of Anxiety," *Symposium on Stress*, pp. 154–64. Washington, D.C.: Walter Reed Army Medical Center, 1953.
35. SHARPE, E. *Collected Papers on Psychoanalysis*. New York: Harcourt, Brace & Co., 1929.
36. SILVERBERG, W. *Childhood Experience and Personal Destiny: A Psychoanalytic Theory of Neurosis*. New York: Springer Pub. Co., 1952.
37. SPITZ, R. A. "Anaclitic Depression," *The Psychoanalytic Study of the Child*, II, 313–42. New York: International Universities Press, 1946. (See also Spitz's other articles in this annual series of books.)
38. SULLIVAN, H. S. "The Meaning of Anxiety in Psychiatry and in Life," *Psychiatry*, XI (1948), 1–13.
39. ———. "The Theory of Anxiety and the Nature of Psychotherapy," *ibid.*, XII (1949), 3–12.
40. ———. *Conceptions of Modern Psychiatry*. 2d ed. New York: W. W. Norton & Co., 1954.
41. ———. *The Interpersonal Theory of Psychiatry*. New York: W. W. Norton & Co., 1953.
42. ZUBIN, J., and HOCH, P. *Anxiety*. New York: Grune & Stratton, 1950.

III

On Schizophrenia

(9)

TRANSFERENCE PROBLEMS IN

SCHIZOPHRENICS

Most psychoanalytic authors maintain that schizophrenic patients cannot be treated psychoanalytically because they are too narcissistic to develop with the psychotherapist an interpersonal relationship that is sufficiently reliable and consistent for psychoanalytic work (1, 12, 13). Freud, Fenichel, and other authors have recognized that a new technique of approaching patients psychoanalytically must be found if analysts are to work with psychotics (2, 6, 8, 16, 19, 31–36). Among those who have worked successfully in recent years with schizophrenics, Sullivan, Hill, and Karl Menninger and his staff have made various modifications of their analytic approach (14, 17, 21–25, 28, 29).

In our work at the Chestnut Lodge Sanitarium we have found similar changes valuable. The technique we use with psychotics is different from our approach to psychoneurotics (3, 4, 32, 33). This is not a result of the schizophrenic's inability to build up a consistent personal relationship with the therapist but is due to his extremely intense and sensitive transference reactions.

Let us see, first, what the essence of the schizophrenic's transference reactions is and, second, how we try to meet these reactions.

In order to understand them, we must state those parts of our hypothesis about the genesis of these illnesses that are significant for the development of the patient's personal relationships and thus for our therapeutic approach.

We think of a schizophrenic as a person who has had serious traumatic experiences in early infancy at a time when his ego and its ability to examine reality were not yet developed. These early traumatic experiences seem to furnish the psychological basis for the pathogenic influence of the frustrations of later years. At this early time the infant lives grandiosely in a narcissistic world of his own. His needs and desires seem to be taken care of by something vague and indefinite which he does not yet differentiate. As Ferenczi (7) noted, they are expressed by gestures and movements, since speech is not yet developed. Frequently, the child's desires

Read before the forty-first annual meeting of the American Psychoanalytic Association, Chicago, May, 1939.

Reprinted from the *Psychoanalytic Quarterly*, Vol. VIII, No. 4 (October, 1939).

are fulfilled without any expression of them, a result that seems to him a product of his magical thinking.

Traumatic experiences in this early period of life will damage a personality more seriously than those occurring in later childhood, such as are found in the history of psychoneurotics. The infant's mind is more vulnerable, the younger and less used it has been; further, the trauma is a blow to the infant's egocentricity. In addition, early traumatic experience shortens the only period in life in which an individual ordinarily enjoys complete security, thus endangering the ability to store up, as it were, a reasonable supply of assurance and self-reliance for the individual's later struggle through life. Thus such a child is sensitized considerably more toward the frustrations of later life than by later traumatic experience. Hence many experiences in later life which would mean little to a "healthy" person and not much to a psychoneurotic mean a great deal of pain and suffering to the schizophrenic. His resistance against frustration is easily exhausted.

Once he reaches his limit of endurance, he escapes the unbearable reality of his present life by attempting to re-establish the autistic, delusional world of the infant; but this is impossible because the content of his delusions and hallucinations is naturally colored by the experiences of his whole lifetime (9–12, 21–25).

How do these developments influence the patient's attitude toward the analyst and the analyst's approach to him?

Because of the very early damage and the succeeding chain of frustrations which the schizophrenic undergoes before finally giving in to illness, he feels extremely suspicious and distrustful of everyone, particularly of the psychotherapist, who approaches him with the intention of intruding into his isolated world and personal life. To him the physician's approach means the threat of being compelled to return to the frustrations of real life and to reveal his inadequacy to meet them or—still worse—a repetition of the aggressive interference with his initial symptoms and peculiarities which he has encountered in his previous environment.

In spite of his narcissistic retreat, every schizophrenic has some dim notion of the unreality and loneliness of his substitute delusionary world. He longs for human contact and understanding, yet is afraid to admit it to himself or to his therapist for fear of further frustration. That is why the patient may take weeks and months to test the therapist before being willing to accept him.[1]

However, once he has accepted him, his dependence on the therapist is greater, and he is more sensitive about it than is the psychoneurotic because of the schizophrenic's deeply rooted insecurity; the narcissistic, seemingly self-righteous attitude is but a defense.

Whenever the analyst fails the patient from reasons to be discussed

1. Years in the case reported by Clara Thompson (27).

later—one cannot at times avoid failing one's schizophrenic patients—it will be a severe disappointment and a repetition of the chain of frustrations that the schizophrenic has previously endured.

To the primitive part of the schizophrenic's mind that does not discriminate between himself and the environment, it may mean the withdrawal of the impersonal supporting forces of his infancy. Severe anxiety will follow this vital deprivation.

In the light of his personal relationship with the analyst it means that the therapist seduced the patient by giving him a bridge over which he might possibly be led from the utter loneliness of his own world to reality and human warmth, only to have him discover that this bridge is not reliable. If so, he will respond helplessly with an outburst of hostility or with renewed withdrawal, as may be seen most impressively in catatonic stupor.

One patient responded twice with a catatonic stupor when I had to change the hour of my appointment with her; both times it was immediately dispelled when I went to see her and explained the reasons for the change. This withdrawal during treatment is a way the schizophrenic has of showing resistance and is dynamically comparable to the various devices which the psychoneurotic utilizes to show resistance.[2]

The schizophrenic responds to alternations in the analyst's defections and understanding by corresponding stormy and dramatic changes from love to hatred, from willingness to leave his delusional world to resistance and renewed withdrawal.

As understandable as these changes are, they nevertheless may come as quite a surprise to the analyst, who frequently has not observed their source. This is in great contrast to his experience with psychoneurotics, whose emotional reactions during an interview he can usually predict. These unpredictable changes seem to be the reason for the conception of the unreliability of the schizophrenic's transference reactions; yet they follow the same dynamic rules as the psychoneurotics' oscillations between positive and negative transference and resistance. *If the schizophrenic's reactions are more stormy and seemingly more unpredictable than those of the psychoneurotic, I believe it to be due to the inevitable errors in the analyst's approach to the schizophrenic, of which he himself may be unaware, rather than to the unreliability of the patient's emotional response.*

Why is it inevitable that the psychoanalyst disappoint his schizophrenic patients time and again?

The schizophrenic withdraws from painful reality and retires to what resembles the early speechless phase of development in which consciousness is not yet crystallized. As the expression of his feelings is not hin-

2. Edith Weigert-Vowinckel (30) observed somewhat similar dynamics in what she calls the "automatic attitudes" of schizoid neurotics.

dered by the conventions he has eliminated, so his thinking, feeling, behavior, and speech—when present—obey the working rules of the archaic unconscious (26). His thinking is magical and does not follow logical rules. It does not admit a *no*, and likewise no *yes;* there is no recognition of space and time. I, you, and they are interchangeable. Expression is by symbols; often by movements and gestures rather than by words.

As the schizophrenic is suspicious, he will distrust the words of his analyst. He will interpret them and the analyst's incidental gestures and attitudes according to his own delusional experience. The analyst may not even be aware of these involuntary manifestations of his attitudes; yet they mean much to the hypersensitive schizophrenic, who uses them as a means of orienting himself to the therapist's personality and intentions toward him.

In other words, the schizophrenic patient and the therapist are people living in different worlds and on different levels of personal development with different means of expressing and of orienting themselves. We know little about the language of the unconscious of the schizophrenic, and our access to it is blocked by the very process of our own adjustment to a world that the schizophrenic has relinquished. So we should not be surprised that errors and misunderstandings occur when we undertake to communicate and strive for rapport with him.

Another source of the schizophrenic's disappointment arises from the following: since the analyst accepts and does not interfere with the behavior of the schizophrenic, his attitude may lead the patient to expect that the analyst will assist in carrying out all the patient's wishes, even though they may not seem to be to his interest or to the analyst's and the hospital's in their relationship to society. This attitude of acceptance, so different from the patient's previous experiences, readily fosters the anticipation that the analyst will try to carry out the patient's suggestions and take his part, even against conventional society, should occasion arise. Frequently, it will be wise for the analyst to agree with the patient's wish to remain unbathed and untidy until he is ready to talk about the reasons for his behavior or to change spontaneously. At other times he will, unfortunately, be unable to take the patient's part, without being able to make the patient understand and accept the reasons for the analyst's position.

For example, one day I took a catatonic patient who asked for a change of scene to a country inn for lunch, another time to a concert, and a third time to an art gallery. After that he asked me to permit him with a nurse to visit his parents in another city. I told him I would have to talk this over with the superintendent and, in addition, suggested notifying his people. Immediately he became furious and combative because this meant that I was betraying him by consulting with others about what he regarded as a purely personal matter. From his own detached and childlike viewpoint he was right. He had given up his isolation in exchange for my personal interest in him, but he was not yet ready to have other persons admitted to this intimate relationship.

If the analyst is not able to accept the possibility of misunderstanding the reactions of his schizophrenic patient and, in turn, of being misunderstood by him, it may shake his security with his patient.

The schizophrenic, once he accepts the analyst and wants to rely upon him, will sense the analyst's insecurity. Being helpless and insecure himself—in spite of his pretended grandiose isolation—he will feel utterly defeated by the insecurity of his would-be helper. Such disappointment may furnish reasons for outbursts of hatred and rage that are comparable to the negative transference reactions of psychoneurotics, yet more intense than these because they are not limited by the restrictions of the actual world.

These outbursts are accompanied by anxiety, feelings of guilt, and fear of retaliation, which, in turn, lead to increased hostility. Thus is established a vicious circle: we disappoint the patient; he hates us, is afraid we hate him for his hatred, and therefore continues to hate us. If, in addition, he senses that the analyst is afraid of his aggressiveness, it confirms his fear that he is actually considered to be dangerous and unacceptable, and this augments his hatred.

This establishes that *the schizophrenic is capable of developing strong relationships of love and hatred toward his analyst.*

"After all, one could not be so hostile if it were not for the background of a very close relationship," said one catatonic patient after emerging from an acutely disturbed and combative episode.

In addition, I believe that *the schizophrenic develops transference reactions in the narrower sense,* which he can differentiate from the actual interpersonal relationship.

A catatonic artist stated the difference between the two kinds of relations while he was still delusional and confused when he said pointing to himself, "There is the artist, the designer and the drawer," then, looking around my office at the desk and finally at me, "the scientist, the research worker, the psychiatrist. . . . As to these two my fears of changes between treatment and injury do not hold true. Yet there is also something else between us—and there is fear of injury and treatment—treatment and injury." Then he implored me: "Understand! Try to be psychic—that will constitute real communism between us" (here using a political symbol to indicate a personal bond).

Another instructive example was given by an unwanted and neglected middle child of a frigid mother. He fought all his life for the recognition denied him by his family. Ambitious, he had a successful career as a researcher. During the war he was called to a prominent research center some distance from his home. Ten years later, after several frustrating repetitions of his childhood conflicts, he became sick.

The first eighteen months of his analysis were spent in a continuous barrage of hatred and resentment. He would shout: "You dirty little stinking bitch" or "You damned German Jew; go back to your Kaiser!" or "I wish you had crashed in that plane you took!" He threatened to throw all manner of things at me. These stormy outbursts could be heard all over the hospital.

After a year and a half he became less disturbed and began to be on friendly terms with me, accepting willingly some interpretations and suggestions. Asked about his hatred of me, he said, "Oh, I think I did not actually hate you; underneath I always liked you. But when I had that call to the Institute—do you remember?—I saw what the Germans had done to our men, and I hated you as a German for that. Besides, mother, far from being proud of me as you would have expected, hated me for going instead of staying home and supporting her pet, my younger brother. You were mother, and I hated you for that. My sister, although living near the Institute, did not even once come to see me, although she had promised to. So you became sister, and I hated you for that. Can you blame me?"

From these examples can one doubt that the schizophrenic demonstrates workable transference reactions?

As the usual psychoanalytic approach is effective only with psychoneurotics, what modifications are necessary in our current technique in order to meet the particular needs of schizophrenics?

Contact with the schizophrenic must begin with a long preparatory period of daily interviews (as in psychoanalysis with children), during which the patient is given the opportunity of becoming acquainted with the analyst, of finding out whether the analyst can be of value to him, and of overcoming his suspicion and his anxiety about the friendship and consideration offered to him by the analyst. After that the patient may gain confidence in his physician and at last accept him.

One patient shouted at me every morning for six weeks, "I am not sick; I don't need any doctor; it's none of your damned business." At the beginning of the seventh week the patient offered me a dirty, crumpled cigarette. I took it and smoked it. The next day he had prepared a seat for me by covering a bench in the yard, where I met him, with a clean sheet of paper. "I don't want you to soil your dress," he commented. This marked the beginning of his acceptance of me as a friend and therapist.

Another very suspicious patient, after two days of fear and confusion ushering in a real panic, became stuporous for a month—mute, resistive to food, and retaining excretions. In spite of this rather unpromising picture, I sat with him for an hour every day. The only sign of contact he gave to me or anyone was to indicate by gestures that he wanted me to stay; all that he said on two different days during this period was: "Don't leave!"

One morning after this I found him sitting naked and masturbating on the floor of his room, which was spotted with urine and sputum, talking for the first time, yet so softly that I could not understand him. I stepped closer to him but still could not hear him, so I sat down on the floor close to him, upon which he turned to me with genuine concern: "You can't do that for me, you too will get involved." After that he pulled a blanket around himself saying, "Even though I have sunk as low as an animal, I still know how to behave in the presence of a lady." Then he talked for several hours about his history and his problems.

Finally I offered him a glass of milk. He accepted the offer, and I went to get it. When I came back after a few moments his friendliness had changed to hostility, and he threw the milk on me. Immediately he became distressed: "How could I do that to you?" he asked in despair. It seemed as though the few minutes I was out of the room were sufficient time for him to feel that I had abandoned him.

His confidence was regained by my showing that I did not mind the incident. And for eight months of daily interviews he continued to talk. Unfortunately, he was then removed from the sanitarium by his relatives.

This also serves to illustrate the difference between the schizophrenic's attitude toward time and ours. One patient, after I told him I had to leave for a week, expressed it thus: "Do you know what you are telling me? It may mean a minute and it may mean a month. It may mean nothing; but it may also mean eternity to me."

Such statements reveal that there is no way to estimate what time means to the patient; hence the inadvisability of trying to judge progress by our standards. These patients simply cannot be hurried, and it is worse than futile to try. This holds true in all stages of treatment (15).

This was brought home to me by a catatonic patient who said at the end of five months of what seemed to me an extremely slow movement in the direction of health: "I ought to tell you that things are going better now; but [with anxiety in his voice] everything is moving too rapidly. That ought to make us somewhat skeptical."

As the treatment continues, the patient is asked neither to lie down nor to give free associations; both requests make no sense to him. He should feel free to sit, lie on the floor, walk around, use any available chair, lie or sit on the couch. Nothing matters except that the analyst permit the patient to feel comfortable and secure enough to give up his defensive narcissistic isolation and to use the physician for resuming contact with the world.

If the patient feels that an hour of mutual friendly silence serves his purpose, he is welcome to remain silent: "The happiness to dare to breathe and vegetate and just to be, in the presence of another person who does not interfere," as one of them described it.

The only danger of these friendly silent hours is that the patient may develop more tension in his relationship with the analyst than the patient can stand, thereby arousing great anxiety. It belongs among the analyst's "artistic" functions, as Hill has called them (14), to sense the time when he should break his patient's friendly silence.

What are the analyst's further functions in therapeutic interviews with the schizophrenic? As Sullivan (24) has stated, he should observe and evaluate all the patient's words, gestures, changes of attitudes and countenance, as he does the associations of psychoneurotics. Every single production—whether understood by the analyst or not—is important and makes sense to the patient. Hence the analyst should try to understand and let the patient feel that he tries.[3] He should, as a rule, not attempt to prove his understanding by giving interpretations because the schizophrenic himself understands the unconscious meaning of his productions better than anyone else.[4] Nor should the analyst ask questions when he does not understand, for he cannot know what trend of thought, far-off dream, or hallucination he may be interrupting. He gives evidence of understanding, *whenever he does*, by responding cautiously with gestures or actions appropriate to the patient's communication; for example, by lighting his cigarette from the patient's cigarette instead of using a match when the patient seems to indicate a wish for closeness and friendship.

"Sometimes little things like a small black ring can do the job," a young catatonic commented after I had substituted a black onyx ring for a silver bracelet I had been wearing. The latter had represented to him part of a dangerous armor of which he was afraid.

What has been said against intruding into the schizophrenic's inner world with superfluous interpretations also holds true for untimely suggestions. Most of them do not mean the same thing to the schizophrenic that they do to the analyst. The schizophrenic who feels comfortable with his analyst will ask for suggestions when he is ready to receive them. So long as he does not, the analyst does better to listen. The following incident will serve as an illustration:

A catatonic patient refused to see me. I had disappointed him by responding to his request that someone should spend the whole day with him by promising to make arrangements for a nurse to do so instead of understanding that it was I whom he wanted. For the following three months he threatened me with physical attack when I came to see him daily, and I could talk with him only through the closed door of his room.

Finally he reaccepted me and at the end of a two-and-a-half-hour interview stated very seriously: "If only you can handle this quite casually and be friendly and leave the young people [the nurses] out of it, I may be able to work things out with you." The next day in the middle of another hour of confused hallucinatory talking, he went on: "This is a great surprise to us. There were lots of errors and misunderstandings between us, and we both learned quite a bit. If you could arrange for me to see my friends and to spend more time on an open ward, and if you remain casual, we might be

3. Diethelm also stresses this viewpoint (5).

4. LaForgue (18) attributes the cure of a case of schizophrenia to his interpretive work with the patient. According to my experience, I believe it was due to his sensitive emotional approach and not the result of his interpretations.

able to co-operate." It is scarcely necessary to say that we acted in accordance with his suggestions.

In contrast to fortunate experiences like these, there will remain long stretches on every schizophrenic's lonely road over which the analyst cannot accompany him. Let me repeat that this alone is no reason for being discouraged. *It is certainly not an intellectual comprehension of the schizophrenic but the sympathetic understanding and skilful handling of the patient's and physician's mutual relationship that are the decisive therapeutic factors.*

The schizophrenic's emotional reactions toward the analyst have to be met with extreme care and caution. The love which the sensitive schizophrenic feels as he first emerges and his cautious acceptance of the analyst's warmth of interest are really most delicate and tender things. If the analyst deals unadroitly with the transference reactions of a psychoneurotic, it is bad enough, though as a rule not irreparable; but if he fails with a schizophrenic in meeting positive feeling by pointing it out, for instance, before the patient indicates that he is ready to discuss it, he may easily freeze to death what has just begun to grow and so destroy any further possibility of therapy.

Here one has to steer between Scylla and Charybdis. If the analyst allows the patient's feelings to grow too strong without providing the relief of talking about them, the patient may become frightened at this new experience and then dangerously hostile toward the analyst.

The patient's hostility should ideally be met without fear and without counterhostility. The form it sometimes takes may make this difficult to do. Let it be remembered, however, that the less fear patients sense in the therapist, the less dangerous they are.

One patient explained this to me during the interviews we had in her postpsychotic stage of recovery. "You remember," she said, "when you once came to see me and I was in a wet pack and asked you to take me out? You went for a nurse and I felt very resentful because that meant to me that you were afraid to do it yourself and that you actually believed that I was a dangerous person. Somehow you felt that, came back, and did it yourself. That did away with my resentment and hostility toward you at once, and from then on I felt I could get well with you because if you were not afraid of me, that meant that I was not too dangerous and bad to come back into the real world you represented."

Sometimes the therapist's frank statement that he wants to be the patient's friend but that he is going to protect himself, should he be assaulted, may help in coping with the patient's combativeness and relieve the patient's fear of his own aggression.

Some analysts may feel that the atmosphere of complete acceptance and of strict avoidance of any arbitrary denials which we recommend as

FRIEDA FROMM-REICHMANN

a basic rule for the treatment of schizophrenics may not accord with our wish to guide them toward reacceptance of reality. We do not believe that is so.

Certain groups of psychoneurotics have to learn by the immediate experience of analytic treatment how to accept the denials that life has in store for each of us. *The schizophrenic has, above all, to be cured of the wounds and frustrations of his life before we can expect him to recover.*

Other analysts may feel that treatment as we have outlined it is not psychoanalysis. The patient is not instructed to lie on a couch, he is not asked to give free associations (although frequently he does), and his productions are seldom interpreted other than by understanding acceptance.

Freud says that every science and therapy that accepts his teachings about the unconscious, about transference and resistance, and about infantile sexuality may be called psychoanalysis. According to this definition, we believe that we are practicing psychoanalysis with our schizophrenic patients.

Whether we call it analysis or not, it is clear that successful treatment does not depend on technical rules of any special psychiatric school but rather on the basic attitude of the individual therapist toward psychotic persons. If he meets them as strange creatures of another world whose productions are not understandable to "normal" beings, he cannot treat them. If he realizes, however, that the difference between himself and the psychotic is only one of degree and not of kind, he will know better how to meet him. He will be able to identify himself sufficiently with the patient to understand and accept his emotional reactions without becoming involved in them.

To summarize: *Schizophrenics are capable of developing workable relationships and transference reactions, but successful psychotherapy with schizophrenics depends upon whether the analyst understands the significance of these transference phenomena and meets them appropriately.*

References

1. ABRAHAM, KARL. "The Psychosexual Difference between Hysteria and Dementia Praecox." In *Selected Papers*. London: Hogarth Press, 1927.
2. BRILL, A. A. "Schizophrenia and Psychotherapy," *Am. J. Psychiat.*, Vol. IX, No. 3 (1929).
3. BULLARD, D. M. "Organization of Psychoanalytic Procedure in the Hospital" (to be published in *J. Nerv. & Ment. Dis.*).
4. ———. "The Application of Psychoanalytic Psychiatry to the Psychoses" (to be published in *Psychoanalyt. Rev.*).
5. DIETHELM, OSKAR. *Treatment in Psychiatry*. New York: Macmillan Co., 1936.
6. FENICHEL, OTTO. *Outline of Clinical Psychoanalysis*. New York: W. W. Norton & Co., 1934.

7. FERENCZI, SANDOR. "Stages in the Development of the Sense of Reality." In *Contributions to Psychoanalysis.* Boston: Richard G. Badger, 1916.
8. FREUD, SIGMUND. *On Psychotherapy.* In *Collected Papers,* Vol. I.
9. ———. *The Loss of Reality in Neurosis and Psychosis.* In *Collected Papers,* Vol. II.
10. *Neurosis and Psychosis.* In *Collected Papers,* Vol. II.
11. ———. *Psycho-analytic Notes upon an Autobiographical Account of a Case of Paranoia (Dementia Paranoides).* In *Collected Papers,* Vol. III.
12. ———. *On Narcissism: An Introduction.* In *Collected Papers,* Vol. IV. 4th ed. London: Hogarth Press, 1946.
13. ———. *A General Introduction to Psychoanalysis,* Lecture XVI. New York: Liveright Pub. Co., 1935.
14. HILL, LEWIS B. "Treatment of the Psychotic Ego." Read before the annual meeting of the American Psychiatric Association, St. Louis, May, 1936.
15. HINSIE, LELAND E. *Treatment of Schizophrenia.* Baltimore: Williams & Wilkins Co.
16. JELLIFFE, SMITH ELY. "Predementia Praecox," *Am. J. M. Sc.,* 1907, p. 157.
17. KAMM, BERNHARD. "A Technical Problem in the Psychoanalysis of a Schizoid Character," *Bull. Menninger Clin.,* Vol. I, No. 8 (1937).
18. LAFORGUE, RENÉ. "A Contribution to the Study of Schizophrenia," *Internat. J. Psychoanal.,* Vol. XVIII, Part 2 (1936).
19. MULLER, MAX. *Über Heilungsmechanismen in der Schizophrenie.* Berlin: S. Karger.
20. SCHILDER, PAUL. *Entwurf zu einer Psychiatrie auf psychoanalytischer Grundlage.* ("Internationale Psychoanalytische Bibliothek," No. XVII.) Vienna: Internationaler Psychoanalitische Verlag.
21. SULLIVAN, HARRY STACK. "The Oral Complex," *Psychoanalyt. Rev.,* Vol. XII, No. 1 (1925).
22. ———. "Affective Experience in Early Schizophrenia," *Am. J. Psychiat.,* Vol. VI, No. 3 (1927).
23. ———. "Research in Schizophrenia," *ibid.,* Vol. IX, No. 3 (1929).
24. ———. "The Modified Psychoanalytic Treatment of Schizophrenia," *ibid.,* Vol. XI, No. 3 (1931).
25. ———. "Sociopsychiatric Research: Its Implications for the Schizophrenia Problem and for Mental Hygiene," *ibid.,* Vol. X, No. 6 (1931).
26. STORCH, ALFRED. *The Primitive Archaic Forms of Inner Experiences and Thought in Schizophrenia.* ("Nervous and Mental Disease Monograph Series," No. 36.) New York: Nervous and Mental Disease Pub. Co.
27. THOMPSON, CLARA. "Development and Awareness of Transference in a Markedly Detached Personality," *Internat. J. Psychoanal.,* Vol. XIX, Part 3 (1938).
28. TIDD, CHARLES W. "Increasing Reality Acceptance by a Schizoid Personality during Analysis," *Bull. Menninger Clin.,* Vol. I, No. 5 (1937).
29. ———. "A Note on the Treatment of Schizophrenia," *ibid.,* Vol. II, No. 3 (1938).

ANN

30. WEIGERT-VOWINCKEL, EDITH. "A Contribution to the Study of Schizophrenia," *Internat. J. Psychoanal.*, Vol. XIX, Part 3 (1938).
31. WAELDER, ROBERT. "Schizophrenic and Creative Thinking," *Internat. J. Psychoanal.*, Vol. VII (1926).
32. WEININGER, B. "Psychotherapy during Convalescence from Psychosis," *Psychiatry*, Vol. I, No. 2 (1938).
33. ———. "The Importance of Re-educational Therapy in Recovered Psychotic Patients" (to be published).
34. WHITE, WILLIAM A. "Study on the Diagnosis and Treatment of Dementia Praecox," *Psychoanalyt. Rev.*, Vol. VIII (1917).
35. WHITE, WILLIAM A., and JELLIFFE, SMITH ELY. *The Modern Treatment of Nervous and Mental Diseases*. Philadelphia: Lea & Febiger.
36. WHITE, WILLIAM A. *Outlines of Psychiatry*. Washington: Nervous and Mental Disease Pub. Co., 1935.
37. LEWIS, NOLAN D. C. *Research in Dementia Praecox*. Scottish Rite of Freemasonary for the Northern Masonic Jurisdiction of the United States of America, 1936.

(10)

A PRELIMINARY NOTE ON THE EMOTIONAL
SIGNIFICANCE OF STEREOTYPIES
IN SCHIZOPHRENICS

Modern psychiatrists have departed from the teaching of classical psychiatry that the schizophrenic was one with whom interpersonal contact could not be established and whose means of expression, whether in speech or in action, had no meaning for himself and could not be understood by others. We are no longer satisfied with the conscious and intellectual approach to the intriguing question of schizophrenic communication, since it offers no help in our efforts to establish therapeutic contact. We learned from Freud to look for the unconscious and the emotional meaning rather than the conscious and the intellectual significance of speech and action, and from Sullivan to approach every psychiatric problem in terms of the patient's interpersonal relationships. Hence we now view all that the schizophrenic says or does as a distorted expression of some kind of positive or negative relationship to his surroundings and his therapist. We know that each of his communications is significant, no matter how unreasonable it may appear from the conscious and intellectual aspect, and we use this knowledge in modern psychotherapy with schizophrenics.

While there have been some publications on the emotional meaning of the schizophrenic language, from psychiatrists and from former schizophrenic patients, there is one form of schizophrenic expression whose emotional significance has been little discussed: the stereotypies. It is hoped that the following observations of schizophrenic patients in prolonged interviews may contribute to their understanding.

A catatonic patient who was lying in bed during our interviews would at various times gently stroke his blanket while a tender expression would light his otherwise rather rigid face. When he felt that I had noticed it, these gentle, purposeful strokes would change into compulsive and mechanical movements, endlessly repeated. The tender facial expression would simultaneously become withdrawn, if not actually hostile.

After spending several hours with him on various days, I discovered that

Reprinted from the *Bulletin of The Forest Sanitarium* (now The Forest Hospital, Des Plaines, Ill.), Vol. I, No. 1 (April, 1942).

the tender blanket stroking was brought forth each time by a reaction from me, which indicated and conveyed to him my understanding something of his cryptic schizophrenic speech or gesture.

Another patient would shyly smile, and for a split second his rigid catatonic facial expression would turn into a warm and grateful one, when he felt that I understood the hidden meaning of what he wanted to convey. As soon as he felt observed, his smile turned into an endless barrage of compulsive laughter. After accepting this without comment for more than a year of daily interviews, I finally asked the patient whether his loud, compulsive laughter was due to a wish to hide the friendly smile and joy at being understood. He nodded "Yes" quite seriously and indicated by his whole behavior that he understood.

After this, he changed once more from a friendly smile to detached compulsive laughter, but suddenly stopped in the middle of it. When I commented on my not wanting to deprive him of this means of expression as long as it met his needs, he seriously shook his head. Since then the compulsive laughter has disappeared, although other catatonic behavior has continued. (I am still working with the patient. The incident related happened two years ago.)

Another patient, who had a highly prized statuette of Nephrotete in her room, hid it at one of our interviews while she became verbally hostile, saying that I was not to have the privilege of looking at it. After becoming reconciled to me, she put the statue back in place, and, with a warm and tender expression, she repeatedly caressed it gently as long as she felt unobserved. The moment she noticed that I looked at her, the face assumed an expression of colorless indifference. She rubbed the statue with rigid stereotyped movements and said in a matter-of-fact tone "I put some oil on it to preserve the finish."

After this I gently stroked the statue myself, venturing to comment: "It feels nice and soft like an understanding friend whom one may like to touch." The patient's face lighted up. The compulsive rubbing changed into gentle purposeful stroking. Then she turned the face of the statue toward me, next moved the whole statue over to me and finally said: "I am glad you like her."

She, too, expressed friendliness and warmth toward me as long as she felt unobserved, hid her feelings behind a screen of indifference when observed, and eventually admitted her friendliness via the medium of her statue, only after being safely reassured as to my understanding and acceptance.

It would seem to me that the stereotypic blanket stroking of the first patient, the catatonic laughter of the second, and the compulsive rubbing of the statue by the third follow the same pattern. The first patient strokes the blanket, the third, the statue, _instead of being tender toward the person whose understanding they enjoy. They feel the need to hide this disguised evidence of their tenderness until they are sure of being understood._ The second patient hides his friendly smile behind a screen of catatonic laughter, as soon as he feels that his friendliness is noticed.

These experiences, which could easily be multiplied, indicate that the seemingly meaningless and inappropriate stereotyped actions of schizophrenics are meaningful, as are the rest of their communications. They serve to screen the appropriate emotional reactions which are at their bottom. Unless we are with the patient over sufficiently long periods of time, we may have the opportunity to see only the manneristic screening without discovering what it hides.

Why does the schizophrenic feel this compulsive need to hide his feelings? A catatonic patient once formulated the answer to this question perfectly for me. I was silently wandering around the grounds of our sanitarium with the patient, who was at that time on very good terms with me. Suddenly he became frightened and tried to get away from me. The reasons were unknown to me. The next day I asked him about it. "We run away from fear of another rebuff," was his immediate reply. "This is the clue to each and every one of our reactions."

Every psychiatrist knows how true that is. One of the causes of the schizophrenic's illness seems to be due to a real or imagined traumatic rebuff in very early infancy, followed by a chain of similar traumata which the patient experiences either actually or in fantasy. He is conditioned and sensitized by the first traumatic infantile rebuff to the point that many later experiences are a traumatic repetition of his first rebuff to him. While ill, he meets this danger by defensive speech, attitude, and action. One of them is the stereotypies.

According to this hypothesis, the three patients were afraid to let me see their friendly feelings. Showing them meant running the risk of not getting an understanding acceptance or response to their friendly reactions, the mere possibility of which represented another rebuff.

If this explanation is valid, we should be able to confirm it by finding it applicable to schizophrenic means of expression other than the stereotyped actions; and indeed we do.

The schizophrenic's indirect or distorted use of verbal expression may be understood similarly. To illustrate: a schizophrenic who previously had used my foreign accent as a rationalization for his antagonism during several hostile episodes, acknowledged one day an interpretation that pleased him, by asking "Are you from Cambridge?" I did not immediately understand what he wanted to tell me, and simply denied. Whereupon the patient who actually knew from where I came, insisted on my being from Cambridge, and finally added: "I knew a girl who came from Cambridge; maybe I was not sufficiently introduced to her."

What he wanted to express was that he liked me and my comments that day and that he no longer resented me as he had when he complained about my accent. Hence he claimed I was a girl with the famous faultless Harvard accent. When I denied this, he said he was not sufficiently introduced to me, i.e., I did not know him or understand sufficiently what he wanted to convey to me.

His defense against the risk of a rebuff is to give evidence of friendly feelings toward me by making a statement he knows to be wrong. If I do understand his roundabout way of expressing his friendly appreciation, fine. If I do not, he need not take it as evidence of non-acceptance and rebuff, for he has carefully worded his own acceptance of me in such a manner that he can refer my lack of response to his own cryptic ways of expression.

Another example: A catatonic patient had tried at various times to set paper on fire in his room when given matches to light a cigarette. Since then matches had been denied to him.

One day, when he seemed quite relaxed, I handed him matches while staying with him. I wanted to increase his self-reliance by giving evidence of trusting him. He played around with them, stroked them, then put the red package of matches close to the red trimming of his pajamas and said, "Look, how it matches; don't you like that?" After a pause of ten minutes he continued: "I feel these days quite a bit like setting something on fire. That has nothing to do with *them* [meaning evidently him and me], but *they* [pointing to the door and meaning other people on the ward] don't understand what it means."

He does not dare to express plainly his pleasure at being trusted. Nor does he venture to say in so many words that he will show his appreciation of my attitude by controlling his compulsion to set things afire while I am with him. Hence he displaces the expression of his pleasure, leaving it up to me to understand or misunderstand his grateful delight, and protects himself from feeling rebuked, should I misinterpret. In addition, he talks of him and myself as "they," instead of "we," which leaves an opening for me to understand that he means *us* and an opening for him not to be hurt if I don't.

These examples may suffice to support the hypothesis that the reason for stereotyped actions as for indirect or distorted verbalizations in schizophrenics is due to their wish to remain cryptic and ambiguous for defensive reasons. The danger of being misunderstood against which they protect themselves is identical to them with the risk of "another" painful rebuke.

While distortion and indirectness in verbal communications are used for the screening of both friendliness and hostility, I have seen no cases thus far in which stereotyped actions were used to cover up resentment or hostility.

Further investigations must show whether—and, if so, why—it is actually only the danger of expressing friendliness or also the fear of expressing hostility which furnishes the incentive to the schizophrenic to screen his feelings by stereotyped actions.

To summarize: schizophrenic stereotypies serve frequently to cover up friendly feelings which call for a favorable response. They are a means of defense against non-acceptance and rebuff.

(11)

PSYCHOANALYTIC PSYCHOTHERAPY WITH PSYCHOTICS: THE INFLUENCE OF MODIFICATIONS IN TECHNIQUE ON PRESENT TRENDS IN PSYCHOANALYSIS

Changes in seven technical requirements of classical psychoanalysis have been made in psychoanalytic psychotherapy with psychotic patients. I shall describe these modifications of classical procedure as they have developed in practice, and I shall discuss their possible implications for a modified analytical approach to the non-psychotic patient.

The Couch

The couch regulation is neither understood nor followed by the psychotic patient. Sitting behind the patient in the beginning of treatment is contraindicated; it is too unreal, for the psychoanalyst is the bridge to external reality. Indeed, it may be necessary for the psychoanalyst to sit on the floor with the psychotic patient in order to hear what he has to say, or it may be appropriate for the physician to sit on a desk—where the patient has settled in a threatening posture—to show that he is unafraid.

It is beneficial and relaxing for *some* neurotic patients to lie on the couch in the classical manner; it may be quite the contrary—and artificial—for *others*, depending on their habits and life-histories. Accordingly, that position is recommended which allows the patient and analyst to look at each other whenever the patient desires.

Seated behind the patient, the psychoanalyst may, or may not, listen; the patient's thoughts may, or may not, "wander away" from the interpersonal relation with the invisible, silent physician.

Freud remarked that *he* could not endure to have patients gazing at him for eight hours. This suggests a change in the eight-hour system rather than the maintenance of invisibility for those who share Freud's

A contribution to a symposium on "Present Trends in Psychoanalytic Theory and Practice" presented at the forty-fifth meeting of the American Psychoanalytic Association, May 11, 1943, Detroit, Michigan.

Reprinted from *Psychiatry: Journal of the Biology and Pathology of Interpersonal Relations*, Vol. VI, No. 3 (1943). Copyright by the William Alanson White Psychiatric Foundation, Inc.

feeling. Personally, I have found a ten- or fifteen-minute interval between interviews most helpful.

"Victrola-Record" Attitude

The classical "Victrola-record" attitude does not meet the therapeutic needs of the psychotic patient. His attitudes of "What is the use?" and "I don't care" toward the outer world—be it from despair, defiance, or indifference—require the attention of a psychiatrist who is careful to show that he is genuinely concerned with the patient's welfare and that he is methodically trying to re-establish the lost spontaneity of the patient in active interaction, strictly within the reference frame of doctor-patient relations. This can scarcely be accomplished without the alertness and spontaneity of the doctor.

Lack of spontaneity also appears with the non-psychotic. It should never be countered by a corresponding attitude in the analyst. Indeed, as a therapeutic indication, this "Victrola-record" attitude may but mask the analyst's personal timidity.

Free Association

It is quite unnecessary to encourage free association with psychotic persons. They spontaneously exhibit the attitudes and the ability for free expression which the psychoanalyst seeks to establish in neurotic patients by means of free association.

Classically, the technique of free association was the most helpful psychoanalytic device by means of which the non-psychotic patients' conventional selection of material was interdicted and the unconscious roots of his personality problems were exposed.

With increased experience, insight, and skill in the practical utilization of psychoanalysis, it is frequently possible to proceed quickly toward the same goal by an utterly unconventional, direct, and precise questioning.

Interpretation

Psychotic productions confirm the psychoanalytically acquired knowledge of—and are in principle like—the means of expression that people use when awareness is greatly reduced, as in the crepuscular states of utter fatigue; before falling asleep; the language of the dream during sleep; the language of myths, fairy tales, and legends.

Generally, many psychotic patients understand their productions far more clearly than does the psychoanalyst; it may therefore be crudely redundant for the psychoanalyst to explain what he believes he has understood. Rather, the psychoanalyst should indicate by a relevant response or an appropriate reaction when he understands, without compulsion to be omniscient. It is in no sense beneficial for the patient to feel that the doctor resents his lack of clarity. Many single communications require no explanations, while it is always necessary to interpret the dynamic processes in the etiology of the psychotic illness.

The need for interpretive activity in the work with non-psychotic patients has also diminished. Many psychoanalytic insights—previously accessible only to psychoanalysts—have become generally known to the well-educated layman. In this connection, Freud's prophecy concerning the decrease—if not the disappearance—of classical hysteria due to the spread of insight about many conversion symptoms may be recalled.

Today the interpretation of content has been in large measure abandoned; interpretations regarding transference, resistances, and defenses have been reduced. The modern patient requires less interpretive help than did his predecessor. Moreover, there is danger of producing antitherapeutic self-consciousness by excessive or untimely interpretations—a fact which has been insufficiently emphasized in the literature. Certainly, it may be said that recent experience in the treatment of psychotic patients validates the modern trend toward caution and thriftiness in the use of interpretation.

Repressed Content

The pathogenic problems and the contents of repression are neither all sexual in nature nor all due to hostility, as advocated for a while by some psychoanalysts. All the emotion, feelings, thoughts, impulses, and fantasies which the psychotic person has experienced regarding significant people during his past and present life, or which persist in their ideal formations, may become pathogenic problems and contents of repression if they are incompatible with his private standards—the social standards of significant persons in his past or present environment. It is not the biological aspects of sexuality but the pathological features of their interpersonal relations which more frequently create sexual problems.

From his experience with the psychotic person the psychoanalyst has also been compelled to discover the non-sexual causes and contents of repression in the neurotic patient; but it is to be remembered that Freud's teachings, which had removed the ban against sexual material, made this discovery possible.

Parenthetically, emphasis should be placed on the fact that, while the interpretation of psychological data from the patient's current life-situation, in terms of the biological experiences of his infancy, may increase their palatability, it may, and it often does, decrease their therapeutic efficacy.

"Acting Out"

"Acting out" is often a necessary preliminary in the psychotic person's initial interviews with the psychotherapist. If the physician attempts to force verbal expression, he may destroy the beginning rapport with inarticulate patients and defeat any possibility of further treatment. If "acting out" is what one has during the interview, it should be utilized for therapy.

The experience thus gained requires careful consideration of the question as to whether psychoanalysts in all cases attempt to suppress "acting out" by neurotic patients during interviews for the sake of established therapeutic aims or whether the prohibition is often exercised in fear of what the patients will do if the acting is permitted.

The Psychoanalyst's Values

Psychoanalysts pretend in vain that their values are irrelevant in therapy or influentially non-existent in the psychotherapist. There are legitimate values for every psychoanalyst. Unless he is clear on the importance and relevance of unconventional standards, he is not likely to be alert to how his own values compare with conventional evaluations which are promoted by the society that pays him for his services.

The psychoanalyst's legitimate set of values should be the patient's growth and maturation of personality and helping the patient to gain the freedom and the courage to fulfil his needs and wishes as long as it can be done without hurting his neighbor. These ideals are held consciously by some therapists, more unwittingly by others.

Psychotic or neurotic, the patient has been conditioned by a pathogenic life-history to distrust the sincere interest of others in his freedom, growth, and maturation—an experience which constitutes another confirmation of the paramount importance of the history of the patient's infantile and childhood development. Success or failure in treatment may therefore depend on the psychoanalyst's ability to convey convincingly, yet with little verbalization, his interest in his patient's growth.

The psychoanalyst's insight regarding his own evaluations of conventions—that are still being suffered by the patient—may be the only key to successful analysis with the psychotic or largely facilitate the outcome with the neurotic patient.

(12)

PROBLEMS OF THERAPEUTIC MANAGEMENT
IN A PSYCHOANALYTIC HOSPITAL

Psychoanalytic therapy has been used in the treatment of hospitalized psychotics for about twenty years. During this time there has been much thought and discussion about how to change and adapt conventional state-hospital management to the requirements of a psychoanalytic hospital.

We are still far from having all the answers; hence I feel that the best I can do is to outline some of the questions, with the tentative answers which have emerged so far from discussions among our staff members, from the exchange of opinion among psychoanalytic hospitals, and from the literature which has been published on the subject. This may contribute to further clarification of administrative psychotherapy and may provoke further constructive discussion.

The psychoanalyst who works with psychotics in a psychoanalytic hospital realizes more than do his colleagues in other mental hospitals that undue curtailment of the patients' freedom—i.e., misuse of authority by previous authoritative figures, especially by the parents in the patients' childhood and by their later representatives in society—is most frequent among the reasons for the rise of mental disturbance. Therefore, he is inclined to give the patients as much freedom and as many privileges as possible, and he will try to force on them the least number of regulations and restrictions. However, the hospitalized psychotic's conception of and need and desire for freedom are not identical with those of the healthy person. How, then, can the hospital reduce a freedom which the psychotic is incapable of utilizing judiciously, without repeating the old traumatic authoritarianism? In other words, how does the psychiatrist succeed in granting to the psychotic the right amount of privileges for the time of his hospitalization?

The psychotic patient who needs hospitalization has not been capable of living without guidance and help; thus, admission to an institution is frequently a great relief from the unbearable burden of managing independently and of making decisions.

The psychoanalyst is aware that, in our culture, all his patients have

Reprinted from the *Psychoanalytic Quarterly*, Vol. XVI, No. 3 (July, 1947).

had imposed overauthoritative restrictions of their freedom by at least one parent, if not both, or other important adults in their childhood. Many patients have subsequently been forced to submit to similar authoritative pressure from later parental surrogates in school, college, or work or by society at large. The latter may be the interpretation which those who have been severely thwarted in their early lives cannot help giving to their later interpersonal experiences. The therapist may therefore be inclined to counteract such traumatic influences by giving them the gift of more freedom than the psychotic patient can handle. While it is most undesirable for the psychiatrist to create additional frustrations in a thwarted psychotic's life, he cannot undo the evil consequences of the past merely by safeguarding against their repetition. The evil influences of the past have to be counteracted by recollection, "working through," re-evaluation, and integration of what happened in early life in terms of the present. The psychotherapist's attitude alone will not accomplish this.

The psychotherapist's conception of "freedom and independence," which he may cherish for himself, may not seem at all desirable to his psychotic patient, who may sense that the psychoanalyst or other staff members expect him to be desirous of the type of freedom that they want for themselves. If the psychotic is protected from developing wishes for freedom which are of the psychiatrist's making, he will ask less frequently for privileges which he cannot handle and be spared the frustration of being granted privileges and having them withdrawn; also, the psychiatrist will make fewer errors in handling the patient's privileges.

The psychiatrist should, of course, not be overconcerned with the conveniences of hospital routine or with his own prestige when conducting a patient's therapeutic management. He should not lack the courage to give the psychotic a chance when he believes that the patient is ready to derive therapeutic benefit from it, even if a repeal of these privileges may become necessary later on. This may or may not reflect unfavorably on the therapist's judgment in the eyes of the patients or of the staff which is inconvenienced by it.

I remember two patients who were temporarily more upset after they were taken for a shopping trip and to the movies than they had been during a long period of hospitalization without privileges. The administrative psychotherapists and the other staff members thought that a great mistake had been made. In the course of the further treatment of both patients, however, it became apparent that these trips, disturbing as they had been at the time, had, in the long run, meant a great, legitimate encouragement to the patients. This subsequently facilitated and speeded their collaboration in psychoanalytic therapy. I also remember the three or four patients who misused their privileges, ran away, and discontinued treatment. The psychoanalytic hospital has such patients, as does any hospital.

The newcomer on the staff of a psychoanalytic hospital will find himself easily misled in the evaluation of a patient's ability to handle town privileges, for the reason that even a very disturbed, delusional, or hallucinated paranoid or disoriented patient may, on the surface, appear ✓ rather well composed and rational as compared with an equally disturbed patient in another type of mental hospital. This is due to the consistent interpersonal exchange and rational, verbalized contacts which are offered to the patients by all the staff members of the psychoanalytic hospital and particularly by the psychoanalytic therapist.

The attitude of the psychotic toward his own difficulties and toward many problems in therapeutic management is determined to a large extent by the attitude of the members of the hospital staff, particularly of the psychiatrists. How can staff members in a psychoanalytic hospital use this influence for the benefit of the psychotic, and how can they prevent its working hardship on the patient? This is the problem of the general significance of attitudes and evaluations which the psychiatrist communicates directly or inadvertently in his contacts with psychotic patients.

Be we healthy, neurotic, or psychotic, we are all bound by the acknowledged or tacit code of values of our fellow men, especially those to whom we are tied by any kind of dependent relationship. The psychoanalyst knows how this cultural pattern is re-experienced and magnified under the special conditions of the transference. The former psychoanalytic opinion that there is no workable transference with psychotics has been reversed (17). We know now that the contrary is true. The psychotic's relationship with the psychoanalyst and his empathic sensitivity to his environment and to the psychoanalyst's personality are often much more intense than the transference reactions of average neurotics. By the same token, he is more sensitive to and dependent upon the psychiatrist's and the hospital's attitudes and judgments than is the average healthy or neurotic person in our culture toward the attitudes of his fellow men.

It frequently happens that physicians, nurses, and other institutional personnel are justifiably afraid of a psychotic patient because of threatening or assaultive behavior. Some psychotics are skilled in playing upon the vulnerabilities and sensitivities of some staff members or sometimes sense unfriendly feelings of staff members for which they expect retribution. In the first case, the patients have to be managed, of course, by physically capable, skilful personnel, able to control them with a minimum of force. Psychotherapy by psychiatrists or nurses can be instituted only when the patient's assaultive tendencies are under adequate control.

Sometimes outbursts of physical violence are a negativistic response to orders given by the personnel or by the physicians and can at times be stopped by rescinding the orders that aroused them. An attempt at doing so is therefore recommended whenever the safety of the patient, of other patients on the ward, or of the personnel is not endangered. Hostile words or threatening attitudes sometimes evoke fear or anxiety in the psychotherapist. The patient senses the doctor's or the nurse's discomfort, no matter how skilfully dissimulated, and will derive a feeling of unworthiness, if not despair, from the realization that he evokes fear and anxiety in people on whom he relies for change and recovery.

A patient who, while in a pack, had been given psychotherapeutic interviews throughout a period of agitation and assaultiveness was one day removed by me from the pack in compliance with her insistent request. When asked, after her recovery, whether she recalled any experience that she believed responsible for regaining her mental health, the patient's prompt response was that her recovery started the day I took her out of the pack, which meant to her that she was not too dangerously terrifying, after all (17).

Excepting active violence requiring physical control, it is best for psychotherapists and psychiatric nurses to stay away from patients of whom they are afraid; they are liable to manage the patient according to their fears and anxieties instead of being guided by the needs of the patient (21, 22). I do not mean that psychiatric personnel should or could avoid being fearful of certain psychotic patients; however, since psychoanalytic therapy is an experience between two people, it will depend upon the personality and the emotional problems of both the psychotic patient and the psychotherapist and on the interplay between them (transference and countertransference) as to whether or not fear and anxiety will interfere. It is wise to replace the nurse or psychiatrist who becomes frightened of a patient with another who does not, without, of course, implication of reproach. If, however, the member of the staff recognizes that there are unconscious reasons for his anxiety and he is able to overcome it by uncovering these reasons, then it will not be necessary to replace him. If the psychiatrist or the nurse wants to continue work with a patient despite fear, he should speak about it with the patient. Once the therapist is aware and not ashamed of his fear and is free to make it a topic of discussion with the patient, it does not necessarily interfere with his usefulness.[1]

For example, a patient hit me and asked me the next day whether or not I resented his having done so (17, 18). My answer was that I did not mind his hitting me as such because I realized that he was too inarticulate to express, other than by action, the well-founded resentment he felt against me at the time. "However," I went on, "I do resent being hurt, as everyone does; more-

1. Great demands are made upon the training, skill, and endurance of the psychiatric nurses, who—unlike the psychotherapist—spend not one but eight hours daily with psychotic patients. These special problems which arise for nurses who work in psychoanalytic hospitals have been discussed by various authors (10–12, 23, 24, 27, 28, 34–36).

over, if I must watch lest I get hurt, my attention will be distracted from following with alertness the content of your communications." The patient responded by promising spontaneously not to hit me again, and he kept his promise despite several severely hostile phases through which he was still to progress.

Another problem in the hospital management of patients which is greatly influenced by the attitude of the staff is the question of how long to keep a patient on, or when to transfer him to, a closed ward. Every mental hospital should strive to develop a sound policy with regard to the therapeutic functions of its closed wards for disturbed patients. If it is the sincere conviction of the members of the staff that the function of the disturbed ward is only therapeutic and by no means punitive and if transfers to closed wards are administered exclusively for therapeutic reasons, hospital patients will have no feeling of humiliation, frustration, or resentment and will have no sense of discrimination or ostracism on the part of the staff and open-ward patients. Our patients will, at times, ask voluntarily to be transferred temporarily to the disturbed ward, as they feel the need for protection from acting out uncontrollable destructive impulses against themselves or their fellow patients.

One of the most impressive examples illustrating the great influence that the psychotherapist's inner attitude toward psychiatric symptomatology has on the therapeutic prospect of the hospital patient is the history of the psychiatric evaluation of the symptom of smearing feces. Formerly this was considered a symptom of grave prognostic significance in any psychotic patient. Since psychoanalysts have learned to approach this symptom in the same spirit of investigating its psychopathology and its dynamics as they approach any other symptom, it has lost its threatening aspects.

A schizophrenic young woman was given to compulsive anal masturbation, followed by touching herself and her therapist with her hands, which were soiled with fecal matter. The psychoanalyst could not help resenting having her arms and her dresses soiled by the patient. She dreaded therapeutic interviews with the girl until she decided to wear worn-out, long-sleeved washable dresses while seeing this patient. There followed a marked feeling of relaxation on the part of the psychoanalyst, to which the schizophrenic girl responded immediately by ceasing to smear feces. Soon she was able to participate in therapeutic discussions of the dynamics of her compulsory anal masturbation and to discontinue it. She has since recovered from her severe mental disorder.

Every psychoanalyst knows about parallel, though less dramatic, experiences with neurotic patients. The patients reacted to any interruption of interviews as a major disaster as long as the psychoanalyst conveyed by his own attitude that it was; likewise, they objected to emergency telephone calls or noises outside as serious interferences with the therapeutic procedure. When the psychoanalysts learned to be relaxed and matter-of-fact about the inevitable interferences, the neurotic patients no longer minded occasional interruptions.

It used to be considered most important that patients in analysis have not even an accidental meeting with the analyst outside his office; consequently, the patients reacted to any such accidental meeting with intensive emotional reactions. This does not mean the advocacy of relinquishing the principle of a strictly professional relationship between doctor and patient or a denial of the wisdom of avoiding extra-professional meetings with certain patients who are, at times, so overwhelmed by their current problems that they should be protected from any possibility of additional emotional complexities. The quality and number of these difficulties are largely dependent upon whether the psychoanalyst expects them to occur and whether he creates the expectation of their occurrence in the patient. The psychoanalyst is justified in safeguarding his private life and his leisure against professional interference, provided—if the issue arises—that he gives the patient no false rationalizations as reasons. However, the psychoanalyst who feels so keenly about his personal needs that he cannot endure making occasional exceptions is not suited for psychotherapy with hospitalized psychotics. There is no place in psychoanalysis—be it in ambulatory or hospital practice—for a state of splendid isolation to maintain the patient's transference-glorification of his therapist to bolster the latter's security. If the therapist permits this to happen either deliberately or unwittingly, the patient will suffer. As the psychoanalyst makes rounds, he will meet his psychotic psychoanalytic patients on the wards. Quite often, if the psychoanalyst feels securely comfortable about it, it will prove beneficial to the psychotic to meet the psychiatrist in a social atmosphere which is less conventional and nearer to the requirements of reality than psychoanalytic interviews.

Psychotic patients whose condition warrants hospitalization may have to be seen more frequently than their scheduled psychoanalytic interviews, when emergencies, such as panic, arise. Whenever this happens while the psychoanalyst is busy with another patient, he may interrupt the interview without disturbance if he has no conflict about it himself. If he gives his patient frankly and matter-of-factly the reason for the interruption, the patient, as a rule, not only will not mind but will often react with an increased sense of security from the seriousness and sense of responsibility with which his psychoanalyst meets the emotional needs of his patients when an emergency arises. Psychotics seldom either take advantage of such considerateness or try unnecessarily to force the psychiatrist to interrupt work with other patients for their benefit. Unlike the neurotic, particularly the hysteric, these patients are too sick and suffer too much to play tricks on, or inconvenience, the psychiatrist whose help they need.

The psychoanalytic hospital should be a therapeutic community. "Social adjustment" to this community should not be forced prematurely upon the psychotic patient. For schizoid personalities, it should not even be made a goal. The staff (physicians, psychologists, nurses, occupational therapists, social workers) should be trained to help with a successful solution of this problem under the special guidance of an administrative and a psychoanalytic therapist assigned to every patient.[2] How can that be accomplished?

Enthusiasm in applying a new type of psychoanalytic therapy to a new type of patient originally led to overemphasis on psychoanalytic treatment above all other aspects of hospital treatment. The psychoanalysts on the staff treated "their patients," knew other patients, if at all, from staff presentations, and left therapeutic administration to the younger psychiatrists, who, in turn, were not doing any psychoanalytic therapy. This hierarchy was damaging to the self-esteem of the administrative psychiatrist and detrimental to his prestige among patients and personnel. The psychoanalysts did not make rounds or participate in social activities, partly because their time was filled with analytic hours, partly because they did not want to meet *their* patients outside their scheduled interviews.

Incidentally, staff members of a psychoanalytic hospital should not refer to "Dr. X's patients" but to "Mr. A on Ward B." All patients are in need of the help of the hospital's therapeutic facilities, including the help offered by the psychoanalysts of the hospital. Psychoanalysts are familiar with the magic power of words. Moreover, some psychoanalysts will be better liked, others less well liked, by the members of the hospital staff, especially by the nurses. Dr. X's patient may more easily suffer the positive and the negative reflections of the degree of appreciation which the nurses feel for the doctor if he is referred to as the patient of Dr. X than if he is just a resident of a ward.

In the present state of our limited skill and experience, the number of favorable results with modified psychoanalytic therapy of psychotics remains small. William Alanson White's suggestion that the causes for "spontaneous recoveries" be investigated has not been widely followed. The psychoanalyst should join the administrative therapist as part of the therapeutic hospital community, which is a factor in these "spontaneous recoveries," even at the expense of his time with individual

2. The terms "psychoanalysis" and "psychoanalytic therapy" and "intensive psychotherapy" are used alternately and synonymously to indicate that the psychoanalytic approach to the psychotic is different from the psychoanalytic therapy of the neuroses, yet constitutes a modification and amplification of techniques in psychoanalytic therapy whose development Freud predicted in 1904 (13).

patients (46).[3] He should make rounds on the wards, visit the shops, and participate in some of the social activities in the hospital, and he should do a little more than just pass the time of day with responsive patients whom he happens to meet on the grounds, thus contributing to the "spontaneous" recovery of one or another patient who is not under personal analysis.

The staff members of all psychoanalytic hospitals agree that it is desirable to have a psychoanalytic therapist and an administrative therapist for every patient. The psychoanalyst analyzes the patient, the administrator assuming responsibility for privileges, visitors, participation in recreational and occupational therapy, diet, medical care, medication. Originally, this division in responsibilities was an attempt to apply in a hospital the conventions of the psychoanalytic treatment of ambulatory neurotics. Experience proved it to be right for other reasons as well.

A schizophrenic woman patient who suffered from delusions of food poisoning used some factual information about the handling of the cows or the milk on the hospital farm—which did not conform to the standards of her farm relatives—to corroborate her fears. The patient tried repeatedly to get the psychoanalyst involved in a discussion of the merits of her data which she held responsible for her fear of drinking hospital milk. This she used unwittingly to evade investigation of the mechanism of her delusions. The psychoanalyst recommended that she discuss her complaints with the administrative therapist, whom he informed about the problem. With this help the patient's delusion was relieved without discouraging her therapeutic need to test reality.

A schizophrenic, who had attempted suicide by swallowing lye previous to her admission to the hospital, required dilatation of an esophageal stenosis at regular intervals. She made an issue about the physician by whom, and the place where, the dilatation should be done. In having this problem managed by the administrative psychiatrist, the psychoanalyst was free to investigate and bring to consciousness problems of personality and irrational implications. Action and decision by the administrative therapist, who arranged the necessary practical details, could not, of course, be delayed until the patient could analyze the related problems.

Some hospitals have designated the responsibility for the administrative therapy of all patients to one psychiatrist on the staff; others had all their psychoanalytically trained psychiatrists do psychoanalysis with some patients and administrative psychotherapy with others, giving each patient a psychoanalyst and an administrative therapist. We felt, after

3. I want to state my agreement with those psychiatrists who feel as William Alanson White did, that few, if any, among the recoveries of hospitalized mental patients which are accomplished without psychotherapy are actually spontaneous. The attitude of the personnel, the atmosphere of the hospital, and the interchanges among fellow patients are contributing factors in these recoveries. It was the thorough investigation of these factors which White wanted to encourage.

some years of experimentation, that this led to the encouragement of an unrealistic, overindividualized, and, at times, too demanding attitude in some types of patients, like alcoholics and psychopaths; therefore, we have recently assigned the patients of each ward to one administrative therapist.

Experiments with administrative group therapy are being made, with the participation of the nurse in charge of the ward, in which all patients of the ward who can are encouraged to join. This seems to counteract successfully the danger of overindividualization and reduces, at least to a certain extent, the rivalry between competitive patients for the time of the administrative therapist. One hardship for some patients is the change in administrative psychiatrist each time they are transferred from one ward to another; however, the degree of this hardship is, by and large, proportional to the attitude of the staff toward it, in keeping with our observation that the patient's reactions depend much on the attitudes of the staff. The time that the administrative therapist spends with each patient is determined by the patient's state or by the nature of a practical problem for which a solution may have to be found. To develop sufficient insight, skill, and psychiatric wisdom to sense when a patient actually needs the time for which he is asking and to know when it is prudent to reduce the time spent with a patient who wishes the doctor's attention without being able to use it constructively are among the difficulties of administrative psychiatry.

Administrative group therapy on wards affords the opportunity of learning something about the environment in which the hospitalized patient lives. Insight into the dynamics of personal relationships on the ward are therefore as important for the psychoanalytic investigation of the patient's difficulties as is the home environment for the understanding of the psychology of ambulatory patients.

The psychotic patient is most sensitive to the violation of the personal confidences he may intrust to his psychoanalyst. Once a relationship between him and the psychoanalyst is established, he wants, as a rule, to think of it as a strictly private experience. Generally speaking, it seems that most psychotics take it for granted, at least as long as they are seriously disturbed (hallucinated, delusional), that everybody in their environment knows about their experiences. How can the hospital staff resolve this contradiction? How can the psychotic's problems be discussed among the members of the medical staff, the nursing staff, the social workers, and the occupational therapists without violating the patient's quest for privacy?

Psychoanalytic interviews are scheduled for set periods, regardless of the nature of the therapeutic problem. Both successful psychoanalytic therapy and successful administrative therapy are dependent upon constructive exchanges of opinion between the patient's two therapists and on intelligent information about the patient imparted to the nursing staff.

It has been said that such exchange of opinion is unfair because the psychoanalyst betrays the patient's confidence. I am of the opinion that— if he is sufficiently in contact with reality to give any thought to the problem—a patient whose condition is serious enough to warrant hospitalization expects the joint therapeutic endeavors of the staff of the hospital. He soon comes to know that there are conferences of the medical and nursing staffs to discuss patients' problems. The therapeutic value of discussing a patient's problems and needs among members of the staff is far greater than an indiscriminate allegiance to a non-therapeutic concept of confidence, the sanctity of which is overestimated in our culture. This information should be used only to help in the understanding of the patient's needs and problems and thus to facilitate nursing care and administrative decisions.

Nurses have greater tolerance and less fear of difficult patients if they are kept abreast of the dynamics of the patient's psychopathology in terms of progress or retardation, as the case may be. The psychoanalyst finds it useful at times to introduce information he obtains from other staff members into interviews with his patient, especially if it deals with emotionally important material which the patient omits to report.

In our hospital, for example, there is a weekly staff meeting for the discussion of new admissions and current administrative problems. In addition, there are two weekly conferences, with participation of the whole medical staff and one or two charge nurses, for a clinical presentation, discussion of the psychological mechanisms of progress or failure in psychoanalytic and administrative therapy, and discussion of the present status of the patient and of further psychoanalytic technique, therapeutic management, and nursing care. When there are disagreements between the administrative and the psychoanalytic therapists about managing a patient, the decision lies with the staff. Weekly, one of the physicians confers about a patient with the nurses and the recreational and occupational therapy workers. Every month there is a meeting of the entire therapeutic hospital staff at which the occupational therapy department presents a patient for general discussion. All the supervising nurses, some of the practical nurses, and the recreational and occupational therapists have been or are being psychoanalyzed.

New patients are visited by the superintendent and the director of psychotherapy prior to their first clinical presentation to the staff. The admission conference comes to a tentative conclusion about the choice of a psychoanalyst for the new patient. Psychoanalysts who have hours available have interviews with the new patient. Final decision is made by the staff, and, if possible, consideration is given to the patient's preference.

No patient is subjected to the ordeal of appearing at any of the staff conferences. Patients do not convey, as a rule, a true picture of the nature of their difficulties when "performing" before a group. If a patient expresses the desire to be presented to the staff, it usually proves the patient's lack of serious intent regarding treatment, change, and recovery. If he seriously wants to give vent to and to get help regarding doubts, grievances, or complaints about treatment, management, personnel, or physicians, he is encouraged to ask for an interview with the superintendent or the director of psychotherapy. Such interviews are always granted and arranged for with the patient's therapists.

It is important that the psychoanalytic work with every psychotic patient be supervised, to avert complications of transference and countertransference. These may occur more easily among psychotics than they do in psychoanalysis of neurotics because modified psychoanalytic therapy of psychotics is still in a state of experimentation. The long duration of the treatment, the special intensity of the analyst's work, and the heavy emotional display in word and action on the part of some of the patients are additional items which invite transference and countertransference difficulties of a specific quality and complexity.

Despite the many local, national, and international meetings at which this subject has been discussed ever since it was introduced as a requirement in psychoanalytic training, the criteria for establishing what constitutes good analytic supervision remain highly controversial. At one of our staff conferences we listened to the recording of a psychotherapeutic interview with a psychotic.[4] When the staff members were asked for suggestions, none approached the interpersonal problems involved in the same way.

A woman patient succeeded in making me afraid of her. She threatened repeatedly to hit me, throw stones at me, or to get me jammed in the door as I entered or left the room; however, nothing much actually happened except for a few slaps in my face. Having worked with potentially more dangerously aggressive male and female patients without being afraid, I knew that there were unconscious reasons for my fear of this patient. Following a discussion of this negative countertransference of mine, I became conscious of the reasons, upon which it subsided.

After the discussion, I met the patient on the grounds of the hospital, and she greeted me as usual, shouting, "God-damn your soul to hell." I replied, "For three months you have successfully tried to frighten me, yet neither you nor I have gotten anything out of it, so why not stop it?" "All right," she said, "God-damn your soul to—heaven!" "That would not help you either, because if I should die, I could not try to be of use to you." By then she had become aware that my fear, which had been an offense to her, was gone; she bent to the ground, picked a flower, and handed it ceremoniously to me, say-

4. Both the recording and the discussion were, of course, not done without asking explicitly for the patient's permission.

ing, "OK, let us go to your place and let's do our work there," which we did. Constructive psychotherapeutic collaboration between the patient and me was resumed.

After conferring with the administrative therapist, each patient's participation in hospital activities is invited, but not pressed, by nurses and occupational and recreational therapists. Most patients will volunteer participation when they are emotionally ready for it. The atmosphere calls for it, as a matter of fact. Precaution against pushing participation in group activities is especially indicated in the case of catatonic schizophrenics. It takes a good deal of psychiatric experience and empathy to know how much the reluctance of these people to take part in group activities is the outcome of a psychotic dread of and a defensive withdrawal from others and how much it is due to the need for partial aloneness.

Similar caution should be taken against forcing the psychotic to be "co-operative." The idea has to be brought home, by word and action, to those patients who can listen that they are members of the human community which the hospital represents, with privileges and obligations. Co-operation makes for smoothly running wards, but it is not infrequently the sign of a patient's hopeless submission. Co-operative behavior may be deterioration (44). What appears to be co-operation is frequently the psychotic's defense, designed to lead personnel into leaving him alone. To many psychotics, suggestions from members of the staff are identical with the arbitrary aggression to which they were subjected in their childhood. If they come at a time when the patient is not ready to verbalize and work through his resentment of them in psychoanalytic interviews, negative therapeutic results are the inevitable consequence. The administrative therapist should keep in mind that advice and suggestions, though at times useful and needed, are always liable to increase the patient's state of dependence upon him and the institution and his resentment and hatred of this dependency.

For these reasons, it is wise, in principle, to be rather thrifty with advice to psychotics, as all psychoanalysts are trained to be in their therapy with neurotics. Discussion should be useful to any patient with whom communication is possible, as long as it remains an exchange of opinion. If a patient continues to be defiant, the therapist has to seek the reasons for such behavior: Is it something in his personal attitude? Is the patient's defiance directed against the hospital or against the psychoanalyst, from whom he displaces it, to the administrative therapist? Is the patient's defiance a defense against a positive attachment to the therapist or to the hospital? The therapist or nurse will not pose these questions to the patient but will use them as a means of orientation for his technique in handling the patient's defiance.

There are only three types of behavior which make administrative

[148]

interference with psychotics imperative: first, suicidal and homicidal acts; second, running away (psychotics); third, sexual relationships between patients.

From suicide, every psychiatrist knows, there is no absolute protection. Suicidal patients are placed on closed wards, where special nurses and the removal of all dangerous implements serve at least to safeguard the patient as best one can and to remind him of the psychiatrist's and the whole staff's serious intention to do so. It may also facilitate keeping alive what is left of the suicidal person's own tendencies toward life and health. We have found it helpful in some cases to admit frankly to a patient our inability fully to protect him from his suicidal impulses unless there is some tendency toward life left which we can try to reinforce by our protective measures.

A patient who refuses to eat should not be tube-fed unless there is actual danger of starvation. It has always the implication of temporarily desocializing the patient. It is a seriously traumatic experience, and the psychiatrist should wait before forcing it on a psychotic until it becomes inevitable for physical reasons. The patient should be encouraged by making his tray especially attractive; his food should be left with him over a long period of time, even though this may inconvenience the nurses on duty. The regular meal may be replaced by a sandwich which may be left in the patient's room indefinitely. Some patients who refuse food from fear of being poisoned may be induced to eat if the nurse or the psychiatrist invite themselves to share a meal.

The limitation of psychoanalytic interviews to one-hour periods does not make sense to the psychotic, who has no sense of time. The same holds true for the psychoanalyst's passive acceptance of a psychotic's failure to keep his appointment. There may be hours when the psychotic cannot communicate anything; at other times he may be so productive that it works great hardship to interrupt him, as in the not infrequent event of his becoming communicative at the end of an interview. But the psychoanalysts' need to keep their time schedule makes such limitations inevitable. What is the attitude of the psychoanalyst toward the hospitalized psychotic who refuses to keep his psychoanalytic appointment?

When a psychotic refuses to come for his interview, it is, as a rule, wise to go to see him on the ward and, if necessary, stay with him for the scheduled duration of the interview, even if he remains uncommunicative the entire time. This is recommended because the psychoanalyst has no way of knowing initially why a psychotic refuses to keep his appointment, whether the psychotic's "resistance" can be analyzed, or whether his refusal calls for immediate action. Suspicious schizophrenics may want to test whether the psychoanalyst will come to see

FRIEDA FROMM-REICHMANN

them, despite their refusal to go to see him. One patient was reluctant to come to see the analyst because she did not want to leave her special nurse, to whom she was jealously attached, so that the nurse would not take care of other patients. Acknowledging this, she asked for the psychoanalyst's help in resolving this possessive attachment. Another patient, a traveling salesman, sent the message, "Tell her I won't see her today. I'll see her tomorrow." His reason was not that he did not want to see me that day but that he wanted to get even with me for saying each time at the end of the interview, "I'll see you tomorrow." This was the formula customers used who wanted to get rid of him. A stuporous catatonic with whom I sat through many mute hours would break through his muteness to say, "Stay," each time I changed my position.

Sometimes it happens that an otherwise communicative psychotic refuses to come to his interview because he feels he needs time to digest the material discussed in previous hours before he is ready to continue. If, on investigation, this appears to be so, it may be wise to follow the patient's suggestion. Either the psychotic has different ways of expressing reluctance and resentment, or he needs more of the psychiatrist's help to give them expression, than does the neurotic. If the psychoanalyst is successful in getting the psychotic to state his reluctance and the reasons for it, this may counteract outbursts of violence.

The traditional one-hour interviews do not, as a rule, meet the needs of the psychotic. As was pointed out above, the psychotic has no conventional sense of time and cannot help defying the psychotherapist's attempt at making their communicative efforts time-bound. The psychotherapist must try, as a rule, to keep his interviews with each patient on a set schedule because of his scheduled obligations to the others. The rule or rationalization that the psychotherapist must keep rigidly to schedule with his patients to emphasize the professional character of the doctor-patient relationship does not work with psychotics. The decision as to when to terminate a psychotherapeutic interview should be determined by the patient's clinical needs in the judgment of the psychiatrist and not by a compulsive attitude about time.

Some psychotherapists are experimenting with working three times weekly with hospitalized psychotics only, seeing them for longer or shorter periods as the need may be, the remainder of their working week being spent with ambulatory patients. The experiences derived from these experiments are still of too short duration to draw conclusions.

The great benefits experienced by some psychotic patients from having their doctors give them psychotherapeutic interviews of several hours' duration have been most rewarding (20, 39, 40). A thwarted, schizoid personality had gone for twenty years through several schizophrenic episodes. Once we talked without interruption for three hours. The patient was deeply moved, and was temporarily less rigid. "I wish somebody had talked to me that way

[150]

twenty years ago; then I would not have turned out to be the person I am now," this rather inarticulate patient commented.

Another example is furnished by an equally uncommunicative catatonic girl. One day, after sitting mutely through the greater part of her scheduled psychotherapeutic interview, appearing quite grieved and depressed, she succeeded, toward the end of the hour, in starting to talk about what she considered the causes of her sadness. I allowed her to continue. When she had finished, she said warmly, quite in contrast to her usual rigid manner and look: "I realize that you kept me overtime. I needed it today. I am very grateful, and I can accept it from you. Maybe that is progress." In subsequent interviews the girl discussed freely the reasons for her unhappiness, referring repeatedly to the prolonged interview and its beneficial influence on her relationship with the psychoanalyst and on her improved ability to collaborate in our mutual psychotherapeutic endeavor.

An objection to prolonged, special interviews is that psychotics who have suffered in part the consequences of thwarting and warping experiences of a lifetime, are exceedingly sensitive to disappointment, and one interview lasting several hours may pave the way for painful disappointment, unless the psychoanalyst takes every possible precaution to make it clear to the patient that this cannot be the regular pattern for their therapeutic relationship.

Some years ago, I saw a young catatonic, at his urgent request, for prolonged evening interviews during a recess in my teaching activities. When the classes reconvened, I had to change the appointments with the catatonic to shorter daytime interviews. Unfortunately, I had not succeeded in impressing the temporary character of our evening appointments sufficiently on the young man; hence he added this disappointment to some previous minor grievances, complained eventually about all of them, and discontinued psychotherapeutic collaboration. There is enough evidence in the patient's treatment history to believe that this unfortunate incident was paramount among the causes for my ultimate therapeutic failure.

To remain alert, spontaneous, and yet cautious continuously for many hours with a rigid and poorly communicative person is an extremely fatiguing experience. The psychiatrist should not avoid fatigue in the pursuit of his professional duties, but he must be able to keep free from resentment toward the patient and must learn to avoid undue expectations or demands as to its therapeutic results. He should have an unmasochistic awareness of the limits of his endurance, and he should not overstep the margin; otherwise, what seems to be an unusually devoted therapeutic effort will work nothing but hardship on the patient and the therapist.

The timing of psychotherapy with hospitalized psychotics is a controversial question. Some psychoanalysts advocate not seeing psychotics for psychoanalytic interviews while they are acutely upset. I do not agree with this viewpoint. While the patient is acutely distressed he needs evidence of the psychiatrist's willingness to be therapeutically useful just as much as, if not more than, at other times; moreover, appointments during these episodes do not constitute a waste of time and effort, even if little is said and nothing is worked through. The fact that the psychoanalyst has observed the patient's disturbed episodes and that he has not shown any sign of disapproval or rejection greatly facilitates referring to them and making psychoanalytic use of them in the interviews which follow (46).

If a patient is so actively assaultive that the psychoanalyst feels threatened, and his attention is distracted by considerations of self-protection, the patient should be seen in a pack. One can explain to most patients the reason for seeing them while they are in packs. This is preferable to seeing such patients with an attendant present because of its inevitable interference with psychoanalytic therapy, which is, in essence, an experience between two people.

Every psychotic patient suffers from a serious loss of self-respect, no matter how disguised; his low self-esteem is hidden behind a mask of narcissistic self-sufficiency, haughtiness, seclusiveness, or megalomania; therefore, he needs reassurance and acceptance. Indiscriminate reassurance, however, will be met with suspicion or taken as a sign of lack of understanding. Indiscriminate acceptance and warmth will clash with many psychotics' distrust and fear of intimacy. What, then, is the desirable way for the psychoanalyst and the other members of the hospital staff to approach the hospitalized psychotic?

The psychotic's low self-esteem and his self-recriminations, as well as his apprehension that his words and actions are liable to produce fear and anxiety in those around him, may call forth quick reassurance from the therapist or the nurses. Frequently, however, these may feel the need for reassurance in their own behalf. This problem is familiar to every psychoanalyst who treats ambulatory patients; however, the reactions of hospitalized psychotics are frequently more conducive to indiscriminate reassurance because they are more frightening to the patient and to the psychiatrist. No matter what the motivation may be, such direct reassurance is more ill advised with the psychotic than it is with neurotics.

A seclusive and withdrawn catatonic became suddenly overtly anxious and upset after the nurse had told him that she could not see why such a well-meaning, friendly, and good-hearted fellow as he had to remain in seclusive isolation. He offered in explanation: "They say I am a menace and I frighten them." The patient, it proved, had sensed the nurse's anxious discomfort about his asociability and his inaccessibility. He therefore understood that her invocation of all his allegedly good social qualities was her need to reassure *herself* as well as him about the frightening potentialities of his culturally unacceptable aloneness.

Patting a psychotic on the back shakes the belief of a suspicious psychotic in the sincerity of the psychiatrist, and, even if the patient is reassured, nothing much is accomplished psychotherapeutically. This too ready reassurance may mean that the psychiatrist does not understand the seriousness of the patient's predicament and may prevent subsequent psychoanalytic investigation and resolution.

A psychotic may, for example, be able to put into words his murderous impulses. If the psychoanalyst or the psychiatric aids are too hasty in drawing the patient's attention to the great difference between thought and action, etc., the psychoanalyst may never again hear about the patient's very real fear of homicide. If, however, someone says, in effect, "I wish you could let me know sometime what hardships you endured from other people to arouse murderous impulses in you," then, with good luck, the patient may submit the related events to psychoanalytic therapy.

Knowing that the damaged self-esteem of psychotics is often associated with a developmental history of being unloved and unwanted, the psychotherapist may want to be helpful by showing great appreciation, friendship, or even love, only to discover that too much friendliness clashes with the psychotic's marked fear of closeness. If a psychotic is able to respond to friendliness, it may come to mean so much to him that he becomes reluctant to reveal his difficulties for fear of losing the friendship of the psychiatrist or nurse. Too much appreciation by the psychiatric helper may be interpreted as an acknowledgment of the patient's compliance rather than as an acceptance of his personality in its own right. Too much gentleness may be conceived as flattery, as a lack of respect, or, even worse, as an expression of condescension. When the psychiatric staff is warned against displaying too much friendliness and warmth, they should also be warned against the opposite extreme. If too little acceptance is shown to the previously thwarted psychotic, it will be a repetitive traumatic "other rebuke," as one patient put it (18). Sometimes it may be wise and desirable to give reassurance to the patient by showing one's respect for him and his developmental possibilities or by showing dissatisfaction with his failures, implying one's expectation that he can do better.

A young woman with a right-sided hemiplegia, mental retardation, and traumatic epilepsy from birth came to the hospital at the age of seventeen. She had learned to do all types of needlework with her left hand with considerable skill, and she was evidently accustomed to be commended for it by everybody who saw it. The first time I saw her doing some elaborate embroidery, I turned it to the reverse side, which did not look at all tidy. I commented that one who had her obvious skill could certainly improve the appearance of the reverse side. Many years later, after she had succeeded in making great progress in improving her life and her personal relationships under modified psychoanalytic therapy, she volunteered the information that her success was due to my initial remark about her embroidery. This had convinced her that she was not just being patted on the back and made her believe that I had confidence in her potentialities for growth and maturity.

Psychiatric personnel should keep in mind to what degree many psychotics are sensitive that the appreciation of their accomplishments is made at the expense of their personality per se.

A sculptor, whose work I wanted to evaluate for its psychological and artistic aspects, seemed very pleased when I first told him that I had traveled to his home town to see his sculpture. He answered some questions about his work, although he was as a rule quite uncommunicative. At the next interview, this catatonic was more disturbed than he had been for some time. Eventually he said with great emphasis, "I warned you yesterday not to go on with this; but it seems you didn't hear me." We never found out whether he had warned me without my hearing or whether it was only a fantasy. What we did learn was that my psychoanalytic discussion of his art meant to him that I was now interested only in his work and not in him.

An inexperienced psychotherapist suggested to a schizophrenic patient that he and the patient were friends. "Oh, no," the patient replied emphatically, "we are not; we hardly know each other and, besides, you want me to change; so how can you say that you are a friend of the person I am *now*." The hospitalized psychotic should be given respect and friendliness based on the knowledge that the difference between the psychotic, the neurotic, and the "healthy" psychotherapist is only one of degree and not of kind. This should extend to seemingly unimportant details, such as calling the patients by their last names with appropriate prefixes, unless they specifically ask to be called by their first names, or until the duration of the mutual acquaintance with psychiatrists and nurses brings this about in the natural course of events.

What is the attitude of a psychoanalytic hospital toward the administration of chemical sedation? Psychoanalytic therapy aims at bringing into awareness the unconscious roots of the problems of the mentally disturbed. Pharmacological sedation beclouds alert awareness of what happens during disturbed episodes and reduces the psychotic's ability to work through and understand it, either at the time or later. While it furnishes relief from states of acute tension, it may delay permanent relief through recovery by psychoanalytic insight. Hospitalization should provide for psychotics the opportunity of going through their disturbed episodes with as little restrictive interference as possible; hence it follows that a minimum of chemical sedation is desirable. There are, however, psychotic states of such severity or states of grave disturbance of such prolonged duration or prolonged states of such degree of anxiety that it would constitute an error in medical judgment to ask of the patient to endure them without any pharmacological help. The same holds true for prolonged states of sleeplessness, not only because of the increase in anxiety which may result from a succession of sleepless nights but also because of the resulting state of fatigue (44). The physical condition of a patient who suffers from prolonged agitation may be endangered by overexertion unless he is temporarily sedated, and a patient may become so noisy that he must be quieted for the sake of the other patients. If and when possible, continuous baths and packs deserve preference over chemical sedation except with patients whose anxiety increases under restrictive measures; otherwise, hydrotherapy proves quite helpful if administered strictly as a therapeutic and not as a punitive measure. Some patients experience a great relief from tension if they are given something to eat, be it before retiring or as they feel threatened by sleeplessness in the course of the night.[5]

There should never be a standing order for daily or nightly sedation. Every patient's need for sedation should be reviewed and reconsidered daily according to the nurses' day and night reports and consultations with the administrative therapists, sometimes in conjunction with the psychoanalytic therapists. On the basis of these consultations, those psychotics who suffer from the above-mentioned conditions are given sedatives at night or, in grave cases, during the day. All attempts aimed at quieting disturbed psychotics routinely should be barred from the therapeutic management of the psychoanalytic hospital.

Some nurses and administrative therapists favor giving sedatives to newly admitted patients to offset states of anxiety which may arise in the first night after their admission. I believe these states can and should be counteracted by general psychotherapy. All staff members who have initial contacts with a patient on the first day should make a point of indoctrinating him about the philosophy and the goals of the hospital; the responsibility of the nurses, attendants, and physicians; and the functions of the admitting physician, the administrative therapist, and the psychoanalytic therapist. As a rule, the patient comes to the hospital for intensive psychotherapy. He should be told, therefore, that some initial examinations must be completed and that the medical staff and the patient must become acquainted with one another before the choice and appointment of his psychotherapist can be accomplished.

To patients who are seemingly not in contact upon their admission, part of such information may be conveyed through attitude and gestures, if not in speech. If this indoctrination is adequately done by the organized joint efforts of the staff members, the patient's adjustment to his stay in the hospital may be greatly facilitated and the rise of initial states of anxiety successfully counteracted.

5. Research should be done regarding the question of how much the sedative effect of food intake is due to its infantile pattern of procuring material protection and security, how much oral intake per se conveys a sense of security, and how much physiological reasons are responsible.

The relatives of a psychotic are, as a rule, among those responsible for
—though frequently not guilty of—the beginning of the mental disturbance; hence many psychiatrists are inclined to cut down as much as possible on the patient's and the physician's contacts with the relatives, although the hospitalized patient needs the visits of his relatives for the
sake of his prestige and self-respect. The psychiatrist needs their help in
securing collateral information, and he should try to teach them how best
to get along with the sick member of the family.

In working with psychotics, psychoanalysts learn that they need the
collaboration of relatives. It should be kept in mind that a relative, unlike a patient, has no opportunity to develop a workable transference relationship with the psychiatrist; therefore, it is much harder for him to
follow any of the psychiatrist's suggestions than it is for the patient;
moreover, relatives may have good reasons to dislike the psychiatrist or
to fear him, as they realize that the patient has told the psychiatrist about
the hardships occasioned him by the family. While the relative may feel
badly about this, the psychiatrist, in his turn, should keep in mind that
the relative's being instrumental in the rise of unhappy developments in
the patient's life does not necessarily imply his being responsible for, or
guilty of, having brought about these unfavorable developments; they
may have come into being because of actions or attitudes which the relative assumed because he actually did not know better.

The psychiatrist should be alert to a tendency to see relatives not objectively but through glasses dimmed by his countertransference to his
patient. It is therapeutically beneficial to side with the patient, at least at
the beginning of the treatment. Especially with a psychotic, it must be
made clear that he is being treated because he wants treatment and not
because his relatives want him to have it. Nevertheless, it will neither be
for the patient's benefit nor help the psychiatrist in getting along with
the patient's relatives, if he sides with the patient at the expense of correct and unbiased evaluation of the data that the patient offers regarding
his relatives and his relationships with them. In addition, the psychiatrist ought to remember that he may have to make allowances for the
relatives' possible resentment of a mentally ill family member and for
ambivalences about the patient's treatment and recovery.

With all these considerations in mind, it will work a minimum of hardship on the psychiatrist to establish a constructive relationship with the
relatives, by which the patient may be greatly benefited. The psychiatrist
should, as a rule, be able to secure reliable collateral information from
the relatives of the psychotic and to get them interested in accepting suggestions regarding their approach to and attitude toward the psychotic
member of the family. Recently we have succeeded in influencing the
course of the treatment of some psychotic patients most favorably by
teaching the mothers, through personal interviews and letters, how to
alter their behavior toward the patients.

As to the visits of relatives and friends with hospitalized psychotics, institutional psychotherapists have been inclined, by and large, to eliminate or curtail them if they seemed to make the patients more disturbed. This practice seems undesirable to me because it encourages prejudice and makes for weird fantasies regarding mental hospitals. Of more importance than this is the repeated experience which every hospital psychotherapist has with the majority of the patients: the visit of their relatives may disturb and upset them temporarily. While discussing an impending visit, they may seriously consider declining to see their relatives. Yet, as the visitor actually arrives, it becomes evident that a great number of patients have wanted the visit after all. The sense of belonging, the heightening of their self-respect, and the increased prestige in the eyes of other patients caused by visits from relatives and friends mean so much to the hospitalized psychotic that he should not be deprived of them, although the patients, at times, have to pay with a seeming temporary setback in their progress. Autobiographical accounts of previously hospitalized people who have recovered point in the same direction (2, 6, 7).

In the small number of cases in which visits are inadvisable, whether because of a relative's inability to approach the patient adequately or because of the reluctance of the patient to see him, the staff of this hospital will encourage the relatives to visit the hospital. We encourage them to see the superintendent, the administrative and the psychoanalytic therapists, and sometimes the head nurse and the ward nurse. That way, we hope to counteract prejudice and ill feeling and to obtain and give valuable information for the patient's benefit.

The role of the relative is, of course, less important in the lives of ambulatory psychoanalytic patients, who try to free themselves from their infantile ties with the significant relatives of their childhood, than it is in the lives of psychotic people whose difficulties in living are so great that they need hospitalization. They must, of necessity, remain dependent upon other people, at least for the duration of their hospitalization.

References

1. ANDERSON, CARL. "Project Work: An Individualized Group Therapy," *Occupational Therapy*, XV (1936), 265.
2. ANONYMOUS LATE INMATE OF THE GLASGOW ROYAL ASYLUM FOR LUNATICS AT GARTNAVEL. *Philosophy of Insanity*. Glasgow, 1860. Reprinted: New York: Greenberg Publisher, 1947.
3. BULLARD, DEXTER M. "The Application of Psychoanalytic Psychiatry to the Psychoses," *Psychoanalyt. Rev.*, XXVI (1939), 526–34.
4. ———. "Experiences in the Psychoanalytic Treatment of Psychotics," *Psychoanalyt. Quart.*, IX (1940), 493–504.
5. ———. "The Organization of Psychoanalytic Procedure in the Hospital," *J. Nerv. & Ment. Dis.*, XCI (1940), 697–703.

6. BEERS, CLIFFORD. *A Mind That Found Itself.* New York: Longmans, Green & Co., 1917.

7. BOISEN, ANTON. *The Exploration of the Inner World.* Chicago and New York: Willett, Clark & Co., 1936.

8. CHAPMAN, ROSS. "Psychoanalysis in a Psychiatric Hospital," *Am. J. Psychiat.*, XCI (1935), 1093–1101.

9. EISSLER, KURT R. "Limitations to the Psychotherapy of Schizophrenia," *Psychiatry*, VI (1943), 381–91.

10. ERICKSON, ISABEL. "The Nursing Problems in the Psychiatric Hospital," *Hospitals*, XI (1937), 58–62.

11. ———. "The Psychiatric Nurse," *Am. J. Nursing*, XXXV (1935), 351–52.

12. ———. "The Psychiatric Nursing Care of Manic Depressive and Schizophrenic Psychoses," *Trained Nurse and Hosp. Rev.*, XCVIII (1937), 587–92.

13. FREUD, SIGMUND. *On Psychotherapy.* In *Collected Papers*, Vol. I.

14. ———. *On Narcissism: An Introduction.* In *Collected Papers*, Vol. IV.

15. FROMM-REICHMANN, FRIEDA. "Psychoanalytic Psychotherapy with Psychotics," *Psychiatry*, VI (1943), 277–79.

16. ———. "Recent Advances in Psychoanalytic Therapy," *ibid.*, IV (1941), 161–64.

17. ———. "Transference Problems in Schizophrenics," *Psychoanalyt. Quart.*, VIII (1939), 412–26.

18. ———. "A Preliminary Note on the Emotional Significance of Stereotypies in Schizophrenics," *Bull. Forest Sanitarium*, I (1942), 17–21.

19. HEMPHILL, ROBERT. "The Aims and Practice of Recreational Therapy," *Bull. Menninger Clin.*, I (1937), 117–22.

20. KEMPF, E. J. *Psychopathology.* St. Louis: C. V. Mosby Co., 1920.

21. KNIGHT, ROBERT P. "The Place of Psychoanalytic Therapy in the Mental Hospital." In GLUECK, BERNARD (ed.), *Current Therapies of Personality Disorders*, pp. 59–69. New York: Grune & Stratton, 1946.

22. ———. "Psychoanalysis of Hospitalized Patients," *Bull. Menninger Clin.*, I (1937), 158–67.

23. ———. "The Use of Psychoanalytic Principles in the Therapeutic Management of an Acute Psychosis," *ibid.*, IX (1945), 145–54.

24. McKIMENS, DOROTHY. "Psychiatric Nursing: The Viewpoint of a Nurse," *Bull. Menninger Clin.*, II (1938), 40–46.

25. MEDD, MARIAN. "Individualized Occupational Therapy," *Occupational Therapy*, XIV (1935), 47–51.

26. MENNINGER, KARL A. "Psychoanalytic Psychiatry: Theory and Practice," *Bull. Menninger Clin.*, IV (1940), 105–23.

27. MENNINGER, WILLIAM C. "Individualization in the Prescriptions for Nursing Care of the Psychiatric Patient," *J.A.M.A.*, CVI (1936), 756–61.

28. ———. "Individualization of Psychiatric Hospital Treatment," *Wisc. M. J.*, XXXVII (1938), 1086–88.

29. ———. "Psychiatric Hospital Therapy Designed To Meet Unconscious Needs," *Am. J. Psychiat.*, XCIII (1936), 347–60.

30. ———. "Psychoanalytic Interpretations of Patients' Reactions in Occupational Therapy, Recreational Therapy, and Physiotherapy," *Bull. Menninger Clin.*, I (1937), 148–57.

31. ———. "Psychoanalytic Principles Applied to the Treatment of Hospitalized Patients," *ibid.*, I (1936), 35–43.

32. ———. "Therapeutic Methods in a Psychiatric Hospital," *J.A.M.A.*, XCIX (1932), 538–42.

33. MENNINGER, WILLIAM C., and McCOLL, L. "Recreational Therapy as Applied in a Modern Psychiatric Hospital," *Occupational Therapy*, XVI (1937), 15–24.

34. MORSE, R. T., and NOBLE, T. D. "Joint Endeavors of Administrative Physician and Psychotherapist," *Psychiat. Quart.*, XVI (1942), 578–85.

35. NOBLE, DOUGLAS. "Some Factors in the Treatment of Schizophrenia," *Psychiatry*, IV (1941), 25–30.

36. REIDER, NORMAN. "Hospital Care of Patients Undergoing Psychoanalysis," *Bull. Menninger Clin.*, I (1937), 168–75.

37. SIMMEL, ERNST. "Die psychoanalytische Behandlung in der Klinik," *Internat. Ztschr. Psychoanal.*, XIV (1928), 352–70. Translation in *Internat. J. Psychoanal.*, X (1929), 70–89.

38. ———. "The Psychoanalytic Sanitarium and the Psychoanalytic Movement," *Bull. Menninger Clin.*, I (1937), 133–43.

39. SULLIVAN, HARRY STACK. "Environmental Factors in Etiology and Course under Treatment of Schizophrenia," *M. J. & Rec.*, CXXXIII (1931), 19–22.

40. ———. "Affective Experience in Early Schizophrenia," *Am. J. Psychiat.*, VI (1927), 468–83.

41. ———. "A Note on Formulating the Relationship of the Individual and the Group," *Am. J. Sociol.*, XLIV (1939), 932–37.

42. ———. "Psychiatric Training as a Prerequisite to Psychoanalytic Practice," *Am. J. Psychiat.*, XCI (1935), 1117–26.

43. ———. "Socio-psychiatric Research: Its Implications for the Schizophrenia Problem and for Mental Hygiene," *ibid.*, X (1931), 977–91.

44. ———. "Conceptions of Modern Psychiatry," *Psychiatry*, III (1940), 1–117.

45. TIDD, CHARLES W. "An Examination of the Recovery Process in Three Cases of Schizophrenia," *Bull. Menninger Clin.*, I (1936), 53–60.

46. WEININGER, BENJAMIN I. "Psychotherapy during Convalescence from Psychosis," *Psychiatry*, I (1938), 257–64.

47. WHITE, WILLIAM ALANSON. Outlines of Psychiatry. New York: Nervous and Mental Disease Pub. Co., 1935.

48. ZILBOORG, GREGORY. "Affective Reintegration in the Schizophrenias," *Arch. Neurol. & Psychiat.*, XXIV (1930), 335–47.

49. ———. "Ambulatory Schizophrenias," *Psychiatry*, IV (1941), 149–55.

(13)

NOTES ON THE DEVELOPMENT OF TREATMENT
OF SCHIZOPHRENICS BY PSYCHOANALYTIC
PSYCHOTHERAPY

In the preanalytic phases of psychiatric development, psychotherapists considered schizophrenic states non-treatable. There seemed to be no medium in which the disturbed schizophrenic and the psychiatrist could communicate with each other. The thought processes, feelings, communications, and other manifestations of the disturbed schizophrenic seemed nonsensical and without meaning as to origin, dynamics, and actual contents.

Psychoanalysts know that <u>all manifestations of the human mind are potentially meaningful.</u> This refers equally to the psychotic manifestations of the disturbed schizophrenic while awake and to the transitory psychotic productions of the mentally healthy dreamer while asleep. Schizophrenic thought processes and means of expression have been successfully studied by Betz, Bleuler, Cameron, Goldstein, Hanfmann, Kasanin, Storch, Sullivan, Vigotsky, and others.[1] Their parallelism with

Reprinted from *Psychiatry: Journal of the Biology and Pathology of Interpersonal Relations*, Vol. XI, No. 3 (August, 1948). Copyright by The William Alanson White Psychiatric Foundation, Inc.

1. Barbara J. Betz, "A Study of Tactics for Resolving the Autistic Barrier in the Psychotherapy of the Schizophrenic Personality," *Am. J. Psychiat.*, CIV (1947), 267–73.

P. E. Bleuler, "Dementia praecox oder Gruppe der Schizophrenien," in *Handbuch d. Psychiatrie*, ed. G. Aschaffenburg (Leipzig and Vienna: Franz Deuticke, 1911).

Norman Cameron, "Reasoning, Regression, and Communication in Schizophrenics," *Psychol. Mono.*, No. 221 (1938).

T. M. French and J. S. Kasanin, "A Psychodynamic Study of the Recovery of Two Schizophrenic Cases," *Psychoanalyt. Quart.*, X (1941), 1–22.

Kurt Goldstein, "Methodological Approach to the Study of Schizophrenic Thought Disorder," in *Language and Thought in Schizophrenia: Collected Papers*, ed. J. S. Kasanin (Berkeley: University of California Press, 1944), pp. 17–40; "The Significance of Special Mental Tests for Diagnosis and Prognosis in Schizophrenia," *Am. J. Psychiat.*, XCVI (1939), 575–88; "The Significance of Psychological Research in Schizophrenia," *J. Nerv. & Ment. Dis.*, XCVII (1943), 261–79.

E. Hanfmann, "Analysis of Thinking Disorder in a Case of Schizophrenia," *Arch. Neurol. & Psychiat.*, XLI (1939), 568–79.

E. Hanfmann and J. S. Kasanin, "An Experimental Study of Concept Formation in Schizophrenia," *Am. J. Psychiat.*, XCV (1938), 35–52; *Conceptual Thinking in Schizophrenia* (Mono. No. 67 [New York: Nervous and Mental Disease Pub. Co., 1942]).

J. S. Kasanin, "The Disturbance of Conceptual Thinking in Schizophrenia," in *Language* dream processes has been constructively emphasized by Freud, Jung, Sullivan, Federn, and the writer.[2] It is now generally recognized that the communications of the schizophrenic are practically always meaningful to him and potentially intelligible and not infrequently actually understandable to the trained psychoanalyst. It was not the nature of the schizophrenic communication, therefore, that constituted an obstacle to psychoanalytic psychotherapy with schizophrenics.

The reluctance to apply psychoanalytic knowledge and technique to the psychoses stems from Freud's paper on narcissism.[3] This concept of the narcissistic origin and the regressive character of schizophrenic disorders excluded, according to him, the possibility of establishing a workable relationship between the schizophrenic and the psychoanalyst.

Subsequent revisions have led to changes in Freud's concept. It is true that the schizophrenic is hit by initial traumatic warp and thwarting experiences at a very early period of life, when he has not yet developed a marked and stable degree of relatedness to other people. It is also true that the final outbreak of schizophrenic disorder will be characterized by regressive tendencies in the direction of this original early period of schizophrenogenic traumatization. One of the means of defense against warp from the outside and hostile reaction against it from within in the pre-schizophrenic as well as in the schizophrenic personality is the withdrawal of interest from the outside world and from other people.

As was pointed out early in psychoanalytic research by Fenichel and

and Thought in Schizophrenia: Collected Papers, ed. J. S. Kasanin, pp. 41–49.

Nolan D. C. Lewis, *Research in Dementia Praecox* (New York: National Committee for Mental Hygiene, 1936).

A. Storch, "The Primitive Archaic Forms of Inner Experiences and Thought in Schizophrenia," *J. Nerv. & Ment. Dis.* (Mono. No. 36 [1924]).

Harry Stack Sullivan, "The Language of Schizophrenia," in *Language and Thought in Schizophrenia: Collected Papers*, ed. J. S. Kasanin, pp. 4–16; *Conceptions of Modern Psychiatry* (Washington, D.C.: The William Alanson White Psychiatric Foundation, 1947).

L. S. Vigotsky, "Thought in Schizophrenia," *Arch. Neurol. & Psychiat.*, XXXI (1934), 1063–77.

2. Paul Federn, "Psychoanalysis of Psychoses," *Psychiat. Quart.*, XVII (1943), 3–19, 246–57, 470–87.

Frieda Fromm-Reichmann, "Psychoanalytic Psychotherapy with Psychotics," *Psychiatry*, VI (1943), 277–79; "Remarks on the Philosophy of Mental Disorder," *ibid.*, IX (1946), 293–308.

C. J. Jung, *The Psychology of Dementia Praecox* (Mono. No. 3 [New York: Nervous and Mental Disease Pub. Co., 1936]).

Sullivan, "Affective Experience in Early Schizophrenia," *Am. J. Psychiat.*, VI (1927), 467–83; "Environmental Factors in Etiology and Course under Treatment of Schizophrenia," *M. J. & Rec.*, CXXXIII (1931), 19–22.

3. Sigmund Freud, "On Narcissism: An Introduction" (1941), in *Collected Papers* (London: Hogarth Press, 1925), IV, 30–59; see also section on "The Interpretation of Dreams," in *The Basic Writings of Sigmund Freud* (New York: Modern Library, 1938).

Abraham,[4] the withdrawal is not a complete one, nor is the early developmental phase to which the schizophrenic regresses one in which he is "narcissistic" to the exclusion of his relatedness to other people.

Sullivan[5] teaches that there is no developmental period when the human exists outside the realm of interpersonal relatedness. From the very early postnatal stage, at which time the infant first learns to sense approval and disapproval of the mothering person by empathy, some degree of interpersonal relatedness is maintained throughout life by everyone, regardless of his state of mental health; therefore, its disruption in the schizophrenic is only partial.

Fairbairn[6] has offered another significant revision of Freud's concept. Psychoanalytic theory attributes a two-sided significance to the early phases of psychosexual development. The oral and anal preoccupations of the child or of an adult in a regressive state are first understood in terms of the feelings of lust obtainable from these bodily zones and from their functions and, second, in terms of their use for the expression of one's relatedness to significant people. According to Fairbairn, the latter is what counts for the developmental understanding of schizophrenic psychopathology. In his investigation of schizophrenic oral preoccupation from the viewpoint of its interpersonal significance rather than as a source of autoerotic gratification, Fairbairn also made it evident that schizophrenics do not ever totally relinquish their ability to relate themselves to others, even in the most regressive withdrawal states with marked oral preoccupation.

Moreover, the schizophrenic patient has lived and developed personal relationships in his premorbid days—that is, prior to being actually disturbed and given to marked withdrawal and regression. Here is an additional reason for the psychoanalyst's always being able to find traces of previous interpersonal developments in the schizophrenic. No matter how tenuous they may be, they are sufficient for the establishment of a new relationship, the doctor-patient relationship. This experience has been verified by all those who have done psychoanalytic psychotherapy with schizophrenics. In addition to the above-mentioned authors, it has received verification especially by Federn[7] and recently by Rosen.[8]

4. Karl Abraham, "Short Study of the Development of the Libido Viewed in the Light of Mental Disorders" (1924), in *Selected Papers of Karl Abraham*, ed. Ernest Jones (London: Hogarth Press, 1927), pp. 418–501; Otto Fenichel, *Outline of Clinical Psychoanalysis* (New York: W. W. Norton & Co., 1934).

5. Sullivan, *Conceptions of Modern Psychiatry*.

6. W. R. D. Fairbairn, "Endopsychic Structure Considered in Terms of Object-Relationships," *Internat. J. Psychoanal.*, XXV (1944), 70–93; "Object-Relationships and Dynamic Structure," *ibid.*, XXVII (1946), 30–37.

7. Paul Federn, "Principles of Psychotherapy in Latent Schizophrenia," *Am. J. Psychotherapy*, I (1947), 129–44; and "Psychoanalysis of Psychoses."

8. John N. Rosen, "A Method of Resolving Acute Catatonic Excitement," *Psychiat. Quart.*, XX (1946), 183–98; "The Treatment of Schizophrenic Psychosis by Direct Analytic Therapy," *ibid.*, XXI (1947), 3–37, 117–19.

Several authors—for instance, Hinsie[9]—found, as this writer[10] did, that the schizophrenic's expectancy and tendency toward resuming interpersonal contacts were sometimes equally as strong as his original motivation for withdrawal. This seemingly paradoxical attitude can be easily understood, since the schizophrenic has not resigned from interpersonal dealings freely or of his own design but is motivated by dire, defensive necessity. Because of this, he is frequently very willing to break through his self-imposed withdrawal if the analyst has been successful in overcoming the schizophrenic's well-founded suspicions, not only of the significant people because of whose malevolence he originally withdrew, but later of the members of the human race at large, including himself and the psychoanalyst.

It appeared, then, that it was possible to regard schizophrenic communication as meaningful and potentially understandable and to establish workable relationships between the psychoanalyst and the schizophrenic. So the road was open to follow the hope and suggestion expressed by Freud in his paper "On Psychotherapy" that analytic technique might be modified for application to the psychotic.[11] This has been done during the two last decades by authors quoted elsewhere in this paper and by Bak, Ernst, Hollos, LaForgue, MacBrunswick, and Silverberg[12] and by the psychoanalysts connected with the psychoanalytically oriented mental hospitals.[13]

I had the privilege of reporting upon this work at two previous meetings of the American Psychoanalytic Association. In this paper I wish to describe the changes in technique as they have been developed in the Washington-Baltimore area since my last presentation in 1945. Also I wish to elaborate on the personal problems arising for the psychiatrist who undertakes to do psychoanalytic psychotherapy with disturbed schizophrenics. Before proceeding, I wish to sum up briefly those basic schizophrenic dynamics which have guided the psychoanalysts in developing and changing the psychotherapeutic approach to schizophrenia. The schizophrenic is painfully distrustful and resentful of other people, because of the severe early warp and rejection that he has encountered in important people of his infancy and childhood, as a rule mainly in a

9. Leland E. Hinsie, "Schizophrenias," in *Psychoanalysis Today*, ed. Sandor Lorand (New York: International Universities Press, 1944), pp. 274–86.

10. Frieda Fromm-Reichmann, "Transference Problems in Schizophrenics," *Psychoanalyt. Quart.*, VIII (1939), 412–26.

11. Freud, "On Psychotherapy" (1904), in *Collected Papers*, I, 249–63.

12. M. G. Ernst, "A Psychotherapeutic Approach in Schizophrenia," *J. Ment. Sc.*, LXXXVI (1940), 688–74; J. Hollos, *Hinter der gelben Mauer* ("Bücher des Werdenden") [Bern: Huber]) ; René LaForgue, "A Contribution to the Study of Schizophrenia," *Internat. J. Psychoanal.*, Vol. XVIII (1936), Part 2; W. V. Silverberg, "The Schizoid Maneuver," *Psychiatry*, X (1947), 383–93; Gregory Zilboorg, "Ambulatory Schizophrenias," *Psychiatry*, IV (1941), 149–55.

13. Chestnut Lodge, Forest Sanitarium, The Haven, The Menninger Clinic, Dr. Boss's Psychoanalytic Hospital, Zurich, Switzerland.

schizophrenogenic mother. During his early fight for emotional survival, he begins to develop the great interpersonal sensitivity which remains his for the rest of his life. His initial pathogenic experiences are actually, or by virtue of his interpretation, the pattern for a never ending succession of subsequent similar ones. Finally, he transgresses the threshold of endurance. Because of his sensitivity and his never satisfied lonely need for benevolent contacts, this threshold is all too easily reached. The schizophrenic's partial emotional regression and his withdrawal from the outside world into an autistic private world, with its specific thought processes and modes of feeling and expression, are motivated by his fear of repetitional rejection, his distrust of others, and equally so by his own retaliative hostility, which he abhors, as well as the deep anxiety promoted by this hatred.

Changes in the technique of psychoanalytic treatment during recent years are in regard to both the establishment of the doctor-patient relationship and the approach to the contents of psychotic communication.

Psychoanalysts used to approach the schizophrenic with the utmost sensitive care and caution. We assumed this to be the only way of making it possible for him to overcome his deep-rooted, suspicious reluctance to reassume and accept any personal contacts, including those with the psychoanalyst. This was especially true for the initial establishment of the relationship. I have described the work during these years of apprenticeship in my paper, "Transference Problems in Schizophrenics."[14]

I still believe that it was ultimately helpful to start out that way. Retrospectively, it seems to have been the only way for the psychoanalyst to overcome, first, his anxiety in coping with the schizophrenic's aloofness and, later, his amazement at the possibility of breaking through the schizophrenic's state of withdrawal. It paved the way toward enabling us to convince the patient as well as ourselves and our colleagues of the schizophrenic's and the psychoanalyst's ability to establish workable contacts with each other.

Once a relationship with the patient was established, treatment was continued with as much acceptance, permissiveness, and as little rejection as could possibly be administered without damage to the institution and to personnel and other patients. Nothing short of actually destructive or suicidal action was prohibited.

Previously, Sullivan had begun to do most successful and instructive research work along similar lines on his schizophrenic ward at the Sheppard and Enoch Pratt Hospital.[15] Kempf and Hadley did similar work at St. Elizabeths.[16]

14. See n. 10.

15. Sullivan, "Affective Experience in Early Schizophrenia," and "Environmental Factors in Etiology and Course under Treatment of Schizophrenia."

16. E. J. Kempf, *Psychopathology* (St. Louis: C. V. Mosby Co., 1920).

Non-professional closeness, pretense of personal friendship, and violation of the schizophrenic's fear of closeness, with its concomitant fear of his own hostility, were, of course, avoided. Also omitted were such signs of acceptance and permissive gestures as would go beyond the psychiatrist's endurance to sustain or repeat over a prolonged period of time. This had to be seriously considered, lest what appeared to be therapeutic acceptance would ultimately be reversed into a new case of rejection.

In spite of this background of basic permissiveness, treatment was not just effective by virtue of the "love" offered, as Kurt Eissler[17] has intimated. What has been described here is the interpersonal background, not the contents of the treatment.

The psychoanalysts of this area have subsequently learned that this was not the only, or even the best, way of establishing an effective interpersonal treatment background. One reason is that this type of doctor-patient relationship addresses itself too much to the rejected child in the schizophrenic and too little to the grownup person before regressing. Something in every non-deteriorated adult schizophrenic senses, at least dimly, that his disaster cannot be solved by one person's offering him a type of acceptance otherwise not mutually obtainable in adult society. Therefore, the psychoanalyst also should address himself to the patient on the level of his present chronological age. There is the danger that unmitigated acceptance may be experienced by the sensitive adult schizophrenic as condescension or at least as lack of respect on the part of the psychoanalyst. There is the further danger that oversolicitousness in playing up to the patient's sensitivities will be interpreted by the patient as —and may actually be—a sign of anxiety on the part of the therapist. Such anxiety and other countertransference phenomena and the role of the therapist's personality in general need serious consideration in the psychoanalytic work with schizophrenics; they will be discussed in the second part of this paper.

As for the approach to the patient, it holds true for the psychotic as well as for the neurotic that the damage done to him in early life cannot be undone by therapeutically manufactured unlimited acceptance in later life but only by understanding of and insight into the nature of the early trauma.

For all these reasons, the psychoanalyst learned to change his generalized attitude of permissiveness and acceptance into one of acceptance of and permissiveness toward the regressive infant as part of the patient's personality, blended, however, with one of respect and understanding in keeping with the patient's chronological age. This holds true for the initial period of establishing contact and throughout the treatment period.

For example, when a patient has had to be induced to accept treat-

17. Kurt R. Eissler, "Limitations to the Psychotherapy of Schizophrenia," *Psychiatry*, VI (1943), 381–91.

ment by three months of waiting outside his door,[18] initial contact with the patient should be tried while he is in a pack or continuous bath until he has overcome the period of violent opposition. The reasons for this procedure should be frankly discussed with him.

After the initial contacts with the patient have led to the establishment of a workable doctor-patient relationship, the attempt is made with the articulate schizophrenic to establish a consensus about the need for treatment and its reasons. The patient will then be guided with the psychoanalyst as participant-observer into collaborative efforts at understanding, working through, and gaining insight into the genesis and dynamics of his mental disturbance, until constructive, lasting, and therapeutically valid insight becomes his. In other words, the goal of treatment is the same as it is with neurotics. The method is different until manifest psychotic symptomatology has disappeared.

The investigation of the doctor-patient relationship and its distortions will be included in the therapeutic process. I do not agree with Abraham and Federn,[19] who suggest the fostering of positive transference phenomena with the schizophrenic and that one refrain from analyzing them. Those elements of the schizophrenic's relationship with the psychoanalyst the transference character of which is obvious should be used for analytic clarification. Only those elements which are an expression of the real, positive interrelatedness between patient and analyst need not be touched by the psychoanalyst. Sooner or later the articulate schizophrenic will take care of their discussion by himself.

The psychoanalytic knowledge of the potential meaningfulness of most schizophrenic productions plays an important role as presupposition for a therapeutically valid interpersonal exchange between patient and analyst. However, in recent years the actual role of the therapeutic use of the contents of the schizophrenic's manifestations has undergone considerable change. Formerly, the greatest possible attention was paid to the contents per se of all the psychotic's utterances, no matter how bizarre, cryptic, and, at times, seemingly unintelligible.

If the analyst understood the content of the patient's communications, he evidenced his understanding by his responses and further questions. Such mutual agreement on the understanding of content was designed to help break through the self-imposed isolation of the patient in his private world. It was also considered an aid in creating a desirable background for collaborative therapeutic endeavor. However, the analyst would not try to "interpret" content.[20] "Interpretation" in psychoanalytic terminology means to translate the manifestations of that which is barred from awareness into the language of consciousness. That is what the psycho-

18. Fromm-Reichmann, "Transference Problems in Schizophrenics."
19. Federn, references in n. 7.
20. Fromm-Reichmann, references in nn. 2 and 10.

analyst has to do for the neurotic, in order to help him to become aware of and to understand repressed thought and feeling.

The schizophrenic's problem is not so much that thought or feeling is barred from awareness as that he is swamped by, from the observer's viewpoint, unconscious material which breaks through the barriers of dissociation. The neurotic and the healthy person have succeeded in keeping this material dissociated. Most of the time this material is within the schizophrenic's awareness. He knows the meaning of his psychotic productions, as far as their contents are concerned. It was the psychoanalyst's knowledge of the schizophrenic's awareness of the meaning of his communications that made it seem inadvisable, if not most of the time redundant, to interpret the contents of his productions. I did not refrain from doing so "for the purpose of promoting a type of introjection of the analyst as a good object, which avoided a splitting of the ego," as Sylvia Payne suggested in her paper on "Theory and Practice of Psychoanalytical Technique."[21]

This does not mean that I would advocate exclusion of formulations of vague, indirect schizophrenic communications. They frequently become therapeutically more meaningful to the patient as he hears them clearly and directly reformulated in the rational language of the therapist.

As far as actual interpretive help goes, it is needed by the schizophrenic when it promotes understanding of and insight into the *genetics* and *dynamics* of his disturbance. Grotjahn has recently stressed the same point.[22] The analyst has, of course, continued to pay attention to the contents of the schizophrenic's communications so that the analyst may know, if possible, what the patient wishes to convey, but its therapeutic importance is no longer overestimated. The importance of the psychoanalyst's misunderstanding and misinterpretation of the schizophrenic's production has also been overestimated. The patient's therapeutic contact with the analyst and his progress, by and large, will not be interfered with by a miscarriage in understanding on the part of the psychoanalyst, if it happens in the spirit of therapeutic humility and not in the spirit of any type of overbearing, personal therapeutic ambition. Lack of spontaneity or overcaution may be more detrimental than faulty directness, as long as the latter is serious and sincere in purpose. Clear directness is a necessary device in dealing with disturbed schizophrenics. Their one-track thought processes and lack of reality testing and foresight make it greatly desirable for the psychoanalyst to offer his therapeutic suggestions in terms of one-sided, meaningful, concrete, concise questions and

21. Sylvia M. Payne, "Notes on Developments in the Theory and Practice of Psychoanalytical Technique," *Internat. J. Psychoanal.*, XXVII (1946), 12–19.

22. Martin Grotjahn, "Emotional Reeducation in Supportive Therapy," in *Psychoanalytic Therapy*, ed. Franz Alexander and T. M. French (New York: Ronald Press Co., 1946), pp. 165–72.

statements. Questioning in terms of "either/or" tends to be confusing, therefore anxiety-producing, to the insecure, indecisive schizophrenic.

John Rosen has recently re-established the therapeutic use of interpretation of the content of schizophrenic manifestations in a new setting.[23] I hope that the evaluation of Rosen's material will help to explain the reasons for the therapeutic moves in opposite directions.

Some analysts have misevaluated the significance of the meaningfulness of schizophrenic communications by operating on the faulty conclusion that they can argue on a rational level with the patient about the rationality of his communications and that they can, for example, try to "talk" the patient "out" of a delusional system.

Although this obviously does not work, another similar approach has proved to be therapeutically valid. That method is to respond, for example, to hallucinatory or delusional manifestations in terms of registering disagreement, without, however, arguing about them—for instance, by stating, "I do not hear or see what you hear or see. Let us investigate the reasons for the difference in our experience." The analyst may react similarly to psychotic behavior by remarking: "Your hair-pulling, spitting, and so on, do not convey any meaning to me. Maybe you can verbalize what you want to convey rather than act it out."

Incidentally, discouraging irrational behavior by professing lack of understanding of its meaning is not tantamount to advising in principle to "cut it out," the way the analyst does in his dealings with a neurotic. At times "acting out" is the only way of communication available to the inarticulate schizophrenic.[24] The *irrationality* of his "acts" should then be approached therapeutically. The acting out, per se, has to be accepted until it yields to therapeutic efforts and is replaced by the patient's regained ability to use verbalized communication.

Only in cases where sustained efforts to reach the patient on a verbalized rational level have consistently proved to be unsuccessful over a period of time has it seemed necessary to enter into the schizophrenic's psychotic world temporarily. In such cases the analyst participates for the time being in the patient's delusional experiences until he gets ready to investigate their dynamics with the psychoanalyst.

Here again our present method in this area differs from Rosen's, and we hope to get an answer to the validity of both approaches upon future investigation.

Now, as to the changes tried in this area after the therapeutic approach in terms of overemphasis of contents was discarded: Mainly promoted by Sullivan,[25] it was replaced in recent years by developing a technique of

23. Rosen, references in n. 8.

24. Fromm-Reichmann, references in n. 2.

25. Sullivan, references in n. 2; see also his "Therapeutic Investigations in Schizophrenia," *Psychiatry*, X (1947), 121–25; "Notes on Investigation, Therapy, and Education in

focusing therapeutic attention upon the genesis and dynamics which determine the contents of the schizophrenic production. As a way of accomplishing this, close attention is paid to, and careful investigation done about, the following: present timing and circumstances, the original setting, precipitating factors, and bodily and emotional symptoms preceding or concomitant with a psychotic manifestation. The patient is trained, if he is in contact, to join the psychoanalyst in his endeavor to find those connections. We have been gratified by the disappearance of psychotic manifestations subsequent to their consistent, repetitive, generic, and dynamic scrutiny. Once accepted by the introspectively gifted schizophrenic, this procedure leads automatically toward the investigation and understanding of neighboring symptomatology which has been linked with the manifestations originally under scrutiny. Staveren has given an illustrative example of this technique in his paper on "Suggested Specificity of Certain Dynamisms in a Case of Schizophrenia."[26] For other illustrative examples of the above-described method see Tower and Cohen.[27]

When the patient is too disturbed to participate actively in this generic and dynamic scrutiny, it still has proved ultimately helpful if the analyst directs his therapeutic attention in this direction and tries to communicate this effort to the patient until such time as the patient emerges sufficiently from his psychotic state to follow suit.

There has been much discussion about the timing of the analyst's active therapeutic endeavor with the schizophrenic. In my opinion, much valuable time has been lost by waiting too cautiously until the patient was "ready" to accept one or another active therapeutic intervention. Once a workable doctor-patient relationship has been established, the patient is "ready" to be approached with active therapeutic moves. The fact that he may not be able to accept them immediately is not necessarily a sign that the approach is contraindicated. It may have to be repeated and "worked through" innumerable times, but that is no reason not to get started.

There are only two reasons for being cautious in one's timing of active therapeutic moves. One reason is the slowed-down and narrowed concrete thought processes of many schizophrenics. These make it necessary to offer only one therapeutic suggestion at a time and not to offer a second one before there is evidence that the first one has been heard, even though not yet necessarily worked through and integrated.

Psychiatry and Their Relations to Schizophrenia," pp. 271–80; "The Meaning of Anxiety in Psychiatry and in Life," *ibid.*, XI (1948), 1–13.

26. *Psychiatry*, X (1947), 127–35.

27. Robert A. Cohen, "The Management of Anxiety in a Case of Paranoid Schizophrenia," *Psychiatry*, X (1947), 143–57; Sarah S. Tower, "Management of Paranoid Trends in Treatment of a Post-psychotic Obsessional Condition," *Psychiatry*, X (1947), 137–41.

The second reason is the schizophrenic's anxiety and tendency to go into panic. Therapeutic moves which are liable to produce manifest anxiety have to be offered in such dosage that anxiety does not turn into panic. Also they should be offered at a time when the psychoanalyst will be available, if needed, to help the patient cope with his anxiety.

In recent years, Sullivan has succeeded in giving more specific direction and content to the therapeutic scrutiny of the schizophrenic's communications and symptomatology. According to him, the psychodynamics of mental illness, including the schizophrenic manifestations, can be understood as a result and an expression of unbearable anxiety and, at the same time, as an attempt at warding off this anxiety and keeping it from awareness. Full-fledged anxiety is to be considered the most uncomfortable and disconcerting experience to which a person can be subjected. Remembering this, the analyst will not be surprised to find that the most bizarre and, as to contents per se, unintelligible, irrational, time-, thought-, and energy-consuming communications and symptoms may be used as security operations in the presence of threatening anxiety.[28]

"Anxiety," in Sullivan's definition, is the discomfort which the child learns to feel in the presence of the disapproval of the significant adult who first uses the arousal of this discomfort as a tool while training the child to abide by the basic requirements of acculturation. With great variations as to the ultimate threshold of endurance, anxiety remains effective throughout people's lives in response to disapproval from important people which interferes with the individual's security and prestige.[29]

In Freud's later formulation, as given in *The Problem of Anxiety*, anxiety is the fear of the dangers which threaten people from within, that is, regarding their culturally unacceptable inner strivings.[30]

I will not enter into a discussion of the variations in concepts of anxiety offered by other authors, such as Goldstein[31] and Horney,[32] but refer to it in terms of the above-given definitions.

The therapeutic validity of a consistent dynamic approach to schizophrenic symptomatology as a manifestation of the patient's underlying anxiety and his operational efforts to evade its rise and awareness has proved to be most useful and effective with many schizophrenics.

Other suggestions as to setup and technique in psychoanalytic work with schizophrenics are still valid as previously given.[33] The classical set-

28. Sullivan, *Conceptions of Modern Psychiatry*, and references in n. 25.

29. Sullivan, *Conceptions of Modern Psychiatry*.

30. Freud, *The Problem of Anxiety* (New York: W. W. Norton & Co., 1936).

31. Kurt Goldstein, *Human Nature in the Light of Psychopathology* (Cambridge, Mass.: Harvard University Press, 1940).

32. Karen Horney, *The Neurotic Personality of Our Time* (New York: W. W. Norton & Co., 1937) ; *New Ways in Psychoanalysis* (New York: W. W. Norton & Co., 1939).

33. Fromm-Reichmann, references in nn. 2 and 10; see also "A Preliminary Note on the Emotional Significance of Stereotypies in Schizophrenics," *Bull. Forest Sanitarium*, I, 17–21; "Problems of Therapeutic Management in a Psychoanalytic Hospital," *Psychoanalyt. Quart.*, XVI (1947), 325–56.

up of the psychoanalyst sitting behind the patient who lies on the couch is contraindicated. This arrangement interferes with the re-establishment of the patient's ability for reality testing and of the psychoanalyst's use of visual observations which are especially helpful in the case of inarticulate schizophrenics.

Equally contraindicated are rigidly scheduled one-hour interviews. Flexible schedules which allow for either cancellation of sessions, sessions of several hours, or non-scheduled extra interviews are indispensable in psychoanalytic work with disturbed psychotics.

Unlike Schilder[34] and Glover,[35] I recommend, with Sullivan,[36] Weininger,[37] and Rosen,[38] that the schizophrenic be seen by the analyst through all prolonged states of psychotic disturbance, regardless of the visible and immediate gain of insight from interviews during such periods. Usually one sees later on that there has been some gain in insight, even though it could not be acknowledged or verbalized at the time. Also, the maintenance of therapeutic contact through periods of disturbance is useful for the sake of later therapeutic reference. Incidentally, my experience with reviewing these disturbed periods with the patient following his recovery has also been a gratifying one—in contrast to some other therapists who warn against it.[39]

The use of the technique of free association constitutes a definite mistake in psychoanalytic therapy with schizophrenics. The thinking and expression of the disturbed schizophrenic are frequently disorganized or in danger of disorganization. The psychoanalyst certainly does not wish to increase the loosening-up and disorganization of psychotic thought and expression by the artifact of free associations for alleged therapeutic purposes. The only time when the analyst may ask the psychotic to express himself in terms of associative thinking will be in regard to a specific problem, its origin and timing, and so on, if direct questioning does not lead to the desired results.

In this connection the problem of dream interpretation with schizophrenics should be discussed. Because of the above-mentioned similarity between the dynamics of thought processes in dreams and schizophrenic thought processes in awakened states, psychoanalysts used to consider it contraindicated to work on dreams with schizophrenics, and we discouraged the recital of dreams. In recent times, however, three treatment histories of paranoid schizophrenics were brought to my knowledge (Drs.

34. Paul Schilder, *Psychotherapy* (New York: W. W. Norton & Co., 1938).

35. Edward Glover and Marjorie Brierley, *An Investigation of the Technique of Psychoanalysis* (London: Baillière, Tindall & Cox, 1940).

36. Sullivan, references in nn. 1, 2, and 5.

37. Benjamin I. Weininger, "Psychotherapy during Convalescence from Psychosis," *Psychiatry*, I (1938), 257–64.

38. Rosen, references in n. 8.

39. Fromm-Reichmann, references in nn. 2, 10, 33.

M. Spottswood, J. Hartz, and T. Lidz in Baltimore) which encouraged reconsideration of our viewpoint. Each of the patients anticipated in a significant dream marked improvement which he subsequently accomplished upon recital and collaborative interpretation of the dream with the psychoanalyst.

While the analyst does not wish to induce associative thinking but prefers to direct the patient's productions, he must keep in mind that there are many schizophrenics whose verbalized productions are so scarce that he cannot direct their communications. Then he must use what productions he can obtain for meaningful therapeutic work, regardless of the seeming remoteness of such communications from the immediate therapeutic aim. If the analyst is sufficiently flexible he will be able to use in his therapeutic plan, sooner or later, any manifestation which he elicits from an inarticulate patient.

This approach is somewhat similar to play technique with children. It will be well in this context to keep Federn's remark in mind: "When we treat a schizophrenic, we treat several children of different ages."[40] Yet the truth of the matter is, as mentioned before, that the psychoanalyst, as he works with a disturbed schizophrenic, is not only treating a child at different ages but also, and at the same time, an adult person of the chronological age at which he comes into treatment. This is one of the main reasons for the difficulties in psychoanalytic work with schizophrenics. All analysts, in their dealings with schizophrenics, seem to struggle with it as they try to develop the technique of treatment most suitable to their own and to the patients' personalities. Psychiatrists who are not sufficiently flexible may find it difficult to address themselves simultaneously to both sides of the schizophrenic personality. They may behave like rigid parents who refuse to realize that their children have grown up. The undesirable results of the psychiatrist's reluctance to communicate with the adult part in the patient's personality and his addressing himself only to the regressive parts in the patient have been discussed before.

If, on the other hand, the psychotherapist addresses himself to the adult patient only, out of an erroneous identification with the patient, he renounces comprehension of and alertness to crucial parts of the schizophrenic psychopathology.

The intricacies in the handling of this situation point toward the discussion of the role that the personality of the therapist plays in the treatment of schizophrenics.

The results of psychotherapeutic endeavors with disturbed schizophrenics, so far, are not too discouraging. However, cures have not been to the psychoanalysts' satisfaction as to number or durability. Some of the failures are not because of the therapeutic techniques used but be-

40. Federn, references in n. 7.

cause of personal problems of the psychotherapist in his dealings with schizophrenics and because of the personality of the therapist.

Every psychotherapist, especially one who works with schizophrenics, should be clear about his role in the psychotherapeutic process. He should know that he is not called upon to fulfil any noble, magic mission. More skeptical of all types of would-be and as-if attitudes than the rest of us, the schizophrenic will definitely react unfavorably to a therapist with alleged missionary and similar Godlike attitudes. They are usually designed to make the therapist feel good as a self-inflationary measure, but they fail to make the therapist alert to the patient's needs, and they certainly fail to impress the schizophrenic.

The job of the psychotherapist is to be the participating observer in the interpersonal process between himself and the psychiatric patient. He must know how to listen and how to elicit the data from the patient. By these means he can guide the patient toward the therapeutically valid generic and dynamic understanding of and insight into his illness that are the goal of psychoanalytic psychotherapy.

In the course of this process, without becoming involved himself, the psychotherapist must be able to allow the patient to repeat and, by doing so, to resolve old pathogenic interpersonal patterns with him as a person and as a distorted shadow of other important people of the patient's previous life.

One more reason for the specific difficulty in doing psychotherapy with the schizophrenic springs from the schizophrenic's aloofness. The active, eager psychotherapist is liable to interpret this general aloofness, which long antedates the patient's contact with the psychiatrist, as a sign of personal resistance directed against him. He may be liable, then, to allow himself to be hurt or paralyzed by the patient's state of withdrawal.

Another feature of schizophrenic psychopathology which seems to be taxing to many psychiatrists is that many schizophrenic communications, while meaningful to the patient, will not be intelligible to the therapist. Many psychiatrists find it difficult to accept the fact that they, supposedly being of sound mind, cannot make out what the disturbed schizophrenic, who is allegedly "out of his mind," communicates and understands. This experience threatens some psychiatrists' security, and it arouses the resentment of others against the patient, by whom they feel humiliated. Either outcome will interfere with the doctor's therapeutic usefulness.

A fourth personal difficulty springs from the resentment and at times rage or fury harbored by the schizophrenic in response to his early traumatic experiences and of which the patient himself is afraid. Without any artificial encouragement, every schizophrenic will, at times, give vent to this hostility in front of the therapist, thus learning to face and to integrate it, or to overcome part of it. I do not believe, as many classical psychoanalysts do, that man is born to be hostile. However, the personal hostility which is engendered by the early pathogenic warp, rejection, and malevolence he has encountered is among the serious psychopathological problems of the schizophrenic. Nevertheless, encouragement of hostile expression in the schizophrenic for alleged therapeutic purposes is not to be advocated. Nor should the psychiatrist expose himself to hostile action or violence on the part of the patient. Schizophrenic violence is seldom malevolent, but it should not be endured by the psychiatrist with the erroneous rationalization of therapeutic heroism. Avoidance, if possible, is recommended not only for reasons of the doctor's self-protection but also to protect the patient's self-respect. In retrospect, recall of violence constitutes a serious blow to the self-respect of many schizophrenics.

Each time the psychiatrist undertakes one of the therapeutically important frontal attacks against the schizophrenic's defenses in his avoidance of the rise and awareness of anxiety, he ought to make sure that his own state of mind is one of stability and serenity. Otherwise his own counterhostility, fear, or anxiety may blind him in the therapeutic evaluation of the patient's experience. Also, they will, in turn, make the patient more hostile and anxious. The psychiatrist's anxiety is a threat to the insecure schizophrenic, and it causes an empathic increase in his anxiety. It is a measuring rod for the degree of disapproval and rejection which the patient expects from his fellow men for the anxiety-provoking, negative impulses which he suffers and which he himself abhors.[41]

Another possible unfortunate outcome of the therapist's anxiety is his need to give uncalled-for reassurance to the anxious schizophrenic, thus killing the patient's attempts at bringing his anxiety into the open and verbalizing it. Constructive reassurance is encouraging the patient to express and face adequate amounts of hostility and anxiety and their causes. Attempts at mitigation by patting the patient on the back, as it were, are discouraging. The patient senses the therapist's own anxiety or lack of understanding that underlies such a nontherapeutic performance. For all these reasons it should be evident that it will constitute a serious handicap to ultimately successful therapy if the schizophrenic succeeds in evoking the psychiatrist's anxiety.

The schizophrenic's ability to eavesdrop, as it were, on the doctor creates another special personal problem for some psychiatrists. The schizophrenic, since his childhood days, has been suspiciously aware of the fact that words are used not only to convey but also to veil actual communications. Consequently, he has learned to gather information about people in general, therefore also about the psychiatrist, from his inadvertent communications through changes in gesture, attitude and posture, inflections of voice, or expressive movements. Observation of all these intangibles is one way of survival for the anxious schizophrenic in the presence

41. Fromm-Reichmann, references in nn. 2, 10, 33.

of threatening malevolent interpersonal performances which he is always expecting. Therefore, the schizophrenic may sense and comment upon some of the psychotherapist's assets and—-what is more frightening—his liabilities, which had been beyond the limit of the psychiatrist's own realization prior to his contact with the schizophrenic patient. An insecure psychiatrist will be made anxious by being exposed to the schizophrenic's empathic capacity for this type of eavesdropping and so become preoccupied with his own defenses.

Perhaps the greatest threat to a favorable outcome of psychotherapy with schizophrenics that is directly attributable to the therapist is the conventional attitude of many psychotherapists toward the question of the so-called social adjustment of their schizophrenic patients. The recovery of many schizophrenics depends upon the psychotherapist's freedom from conventional attitudes and prejudices. These patients cannot, and should not be asked to, accept guidance toward a conventional adjustment to the customary requirements of our culture, much less to what the individual therapist personally considers these requirements to be. The therapist should feel that his role in treating schizophrenics is accomplished if these people are able to find for themselves, without injury to their neighbors, their own sources of satisfaction and security, irrespective of the approval of their neighbors, of their families, and of public opinion. This attitude is required because, as a rule, a schizophrenic's recovery will not include the change of his premorbid schizoid personality to another personality type. Schizophrenia, in this sense, is not an illness but a specific state of personality with its own ways of living.[42]

I am convinced that many schizophrenics who remain ill could recover if the goal of treatment were seen in the light of the needs of a schizoid personality, not according to the needs of the non-schizophrenic, conforming, good-citizen psychiatrist.

In conclusion, I wish to recommend that the therapist be trained in recognizing and controlling his own dissociated feelings and motivations and in overcoming his own insecurity, previous to working with schizophrenic patients. Many failures in the treatment of schizophrenics due to the therapist's failure in handling his and the patient's mutual interpersonal problems adequately could then be avoided.

42. Fromm-Reichmann, references in n. 2; Sullivan, references in nn. 1 and 25.

(14)

SOME ASPECTS OF PSYCHOANALYTIC PSYCHO-
THERAPY WITH SCHIZOPHRENICS

Most psychiatrists are familiar with the basic philosophy underlying the psychoanalytic treatment of neurotic personality disorders. Many of them have practiced it for a long time. The same cannot be said with regard to psychoanalytic psychotherapy with psychotics, and particularly with that predominant group of the mentally disordered—the schizophrenics. In fact, many psychotherapists are still refraining from treating schizophrenics psychoanalytically. What are the reasons for this reluctance and this delay? Two factors seem to be responsible for psychiatrists' having delayed so long before undertaking directed, intensive, psychoanalytically oriented psychotherapy with schizophrenics.

The first of these factors stems from the teachings of classical psychiatry, according to which the verbal communications of the disturbed schizophrenic could not be understood. His interpersonal manifestations, evidenced by attitudes, gestures, and actions, were considered to be even less intelligible to the psychiatrist than his verbalized communications.

The second factor is derived from the older teachings of classical psychoanalysis. According to these precepts, the infantile, "narcissistic" self-engulfment of the schizophrenic made it impossible for the psychoanalyst to establish a workable doctor-patient relationship with him. Those who promoted this line of reasoning, thereby opposing attempts to treat schizophrenics psychoanalytically, were guilty of overlooking Freud's statement in which he expressed the hope for future modifications of psychoanalytic techniques which would make it possible to do intensive psychoanalytically oriented psychotherapy with schizophrenics.

What, then, has finally happened in psychiatry to open the road to the promotion of psychoanalytically oriented intensive psychotherapy with schizophrenics?

Indoctrinated by Freud's teachings, psychiatrists have learned about the working of the unconscious and its manifestations in the everyday life of the mentally healthy and the mentally disturbed. In the last twenty-five or thirty years, psychiatrists have learned also that the

Reprinted from *Psychotherapy with Schizophrenics* (New York: International Universities Press, Inc., 1952).

dreams of the mentally healthy resemble psychotic states undergone while asleep and that the productions of the psychotic are like permanent dreams in a waking state. Following this, psychiatrists learned that, in word and action, psychotic productions are potentially as understandable to the listener as are dreams and that, even if they are not understood by the listener, they may still be meaningful, most of the time, to the schizophrenic patient himself.

Subsequently, motivated by their recently stimulated curiosity as therapists and in research efforts, psychoanalysts discovered that the schizophrenic could easily be encouraged partly to abandon his state of only seemingly self-sufficient withdrawal. This could be accomplished if he was approached by a psychiatrist who knew that the patient's longing for interpersonal contact was just as intense as his fear of it, which had originally driven him into a state of regression and withdrawal. That is, an intensively charged relationship could be established between the schizophrenic patient and the psychiatrist.

These two discoveries marked the beginning of psychoanalytically oriented psychotherapy with schizophrenics. But the excitement and elation of psychiatrists over their discoveries also delayed the development of an intelligently directed, systematic psychoanalytic psychotherapy with these patients. A whole decade elapsed during which great emphasis was placed upon understanding and interpreting schizophrenic communications, and this procedure was unduly made the center of the psychiatrist's psychotherapeutic attention. Furthermore, an entire decade passed during which the establishment of a workable doctor-patient relationship was considered to be a therapeutic accomplishment in its own right, instead of becoming what it actually is, the matter-of-fact presupposition for psychoanalytic psychotherapy with schizophrenics. This writer is among those responsible for this delay.

A representative follow-up of the trials and tribulations which we psychiatrists had to undergo before we began to learn how to do meaningful intensive psychoanalytically oriented psychotherapy with schizophrenics may be found in my two papers, "Transference Problems in Schizophrenics" (6) and "Notes on the Development of Treatment of Schizophrenics by Psychoanalytic Psychotherapy" (8) and in the literature reviewed in both papers. You will also read there that we are fully aware of the fact that there is still a great deal to be learned about the treatment of schizophrenics. Let us see what we know about it thus far.

As I mentioned before, psychiatrists can take it for granted now that, in principle, a workable doctor-patient relationship can be established with the schizophrenic patient. If and when this seems impossible, it is due to the doctor's personality difficulties, not to the patient's psychopathology. Elaboration on this theme is, for two reasons, a most important part of any discussion of psychoanalytic psychotherapy with schizophrenics. First, the investigation of the vicissitudes of the doctor-patient relationship in both participants, the patient and the doctor, is an even more central issue in psychoanalytic psychotherapy with schizophrenics than it is with neurotics. This holds true for transference and counter-transference and, above all, for conscious defense maneuvers and for unconscious manifestations of resistance on the part of the patient as well as of the psychiatrist. The schizophrenic who emerges from a state of acute disturbance and/or withdrawal of interest from the outside world and its population is in need of a therapist who is fit to act as a reliable bridge to reality. The schizophrenic submits the significant people of his environment and among them, more than anybody else, his psychotherapist to a serious test before he actually attempts to relinquish interpersonal aloofness and isolation. The patient's emergence and the eventual recovery may depend on the psychiatrist's availability at this point as someone who is free from emotional preoccupation and capable of establishing and accepting a mutual, reasonably spontaneous, relationship with the patient. That is, the psychiatrist should feel himself free to meet the patient in the spirit and with the expression of simple, meaningful spontaneity and frankness. Another requirement for the psychoanalyst's therapeutic usefulness to the schizophrenic is the doctor's ability to carry adequately the patient's outbursts of transferred and personal hostility.

For these two reasons, work with psychotics is obviously much more taxing for most psychiatrists than is therapy with neurotics. For example, the psychiatrist may be afraid of the schizophrenic's actual or potential violence, in word or action, which he encounters as one of the manifestations of these patients' anxiety. Or his own security may be threatened by the content of the patient's anxiety, thus arousing problems which may possibly strike too close to home. Some psychiatrists may be frightened by the schizophrenic's ability to sense and seek out their weak points and to comment on them, or play upon them without words. In any of these instances the psychiatrist may become too preoccupied with his own need for safety, security, and prestige—hence too defensive and argumentative—to relate himself successfully to schizophrenic patients and vice versa. Again, a psychiatrist may try to counteract his own anxiety by giving uncalled-for reassurance to the patient, which is, in reality, designed to reassure the doctor. Thus he may jeopardize the patient's capacity to relate himself to the doctor, and, in addition, he may, more often than not, becloud the issues under psychotherapeutic investigation. Things are made no easier for the doctor by the fact that frequently these manifestations of the psychiatrist's anxiety are empathically sensed, or actually observed, by the schizophrenic.

The worst interference with the establishment of a therapeutically meaningful doctor-patient relationship comes from the attempts of anxious psychiatrists to counteract their anxiety by trying to placate an anxious schizophrenic. Such manipulations can work only as antitherapeutic substance for the schizophrenic's reluctance to trust, and to relate himself to, another person. This evolves from the schizophrenic's immanent suspicion, an ever present sensitive scar, engendered by the nature of his pathogenic early childhood experiences and by their repetition in his adult life, either in reality or by virtue of his interpretations.

Another great difficulty in handling schizophrenics is constituted for many psychiatrists by the schizophrenic's negativism in all its manifold manifestations. As we know, negativism is the historically determined attempt of the schizophrenic to survive and to maintain his identity in the face of actual or alleged threats of being overruled, effaced, or neglected. If this negativism is misinterpreted and dealt with as conscious stubbornness or lack of collaboration, treatment is doomed to failure. Dr. Florence Powdermaker has reported about important research in this field (13). She has tried to eliminate schizophrenic negativism by confronting her patients consistently with their need to maintain faulty ancient perceptions, for fear of submitting to the correct, conventional perceptions of their environment.

The enumeration of the psychiatrist's potential difficulties in establishing and maintaining a workable relationship with the schizophrenic implies that treatment of schizophrenics must be accompanied, more than the analytic treatment of milder personality disorders, by a consistent scrutiny of, and alertness to, the vicissitudes of the state of relatedness to the patient in which the psychoanalyst is involved. As a matter of fact, at a recent meeting held by the Committee on Treatment of Schizophrenia of the Group for the Advancement of Psychiatry, the investigation of the psychiatrist's countertransference reactions was established as the crucial part of all psychoanalytic psychotherapy with schizophrenics. This holds true all the more because the psychiatrist's anxiety can become a constructive adjunct to psychoanalytic psychotherapy with schizophrenics if he is able to recognize and accept it without burdening the patient with his ill-advised security operations. The doctor's anxiety in relation to the patient may then become a means of spotting the patient's hidden anxieties and their causes, to which the doctor responds with anxiety in his turn (9).

This enumeration of the psychiatrist's potential difficulties in establishing a workable relationship with the schizophrenic does not imply that a psychiatrist who cannot overcome these barriers in his own personality should worry guiltily about responsibilities not adequately met. Guilt feelings are an unconstructive, paralyzing luxury, which should be discouraged in doctors as well as in their patients. Instead, the psychiatrist should admit to himself that—in his present state of personality development—he is not equal to coping with schizophrenics, if there is the danger of his burdening them with his anxieties and their manifestations, in addition to their own anxieties. He may succeed in effecting change within himself by searching out and working through the hidden roots of his anxieties and thus become able to eliminate their operation on the psychotherapeutic scene. Or he may discover that he cannot overcome or adequately cope with his personal discomfort in the presence of a schizophrenic patient. If so, then he should decide to direct his psychotherapeutic endeavors to other types of mental patients. Generally speaking, every psychotherapist should go through an analytic inventory of his own personality, regardless of whether or not he suffers these difficulties. Also, it should be one of the goals of the science of psychotherapy to increase our ability to determine the types of personalities and the types of mental patients who are best suited to engage in psychotherapeutic work with each other. Research on this problem is being planned by the Chestnut Lodge Sanitarium and by the Washington School of Psychiatry.

The preceding elaboration of the therapeutic difficulties of psychiatrists who are made anxious by schizophrenic patients does not imply, either, that physicians are required to submit themselves passively to all the patient's hostile outbursts. The contrary is true. Violence in action should be prohibited, and verbalized hostile outbursts should be first listened to and then responded to with a therapeutic investigation of their causes. Silent acceptance of violence in word or action is inadvisable, not only in self-defense, but also in pursuit of the respect due to patients and in protection of their self-respect. Retrospectively, schizophrenic patients loathe themselves for their hostile outbursts and do not respect the therapist who lets them get away with it.

Let us now turn to the discussion of psychiatrists' initial overestimation of the significance of understanding the contents of schizophrenic communication. This has tended to delay psychotherapeutic progress even more than uncritical elation about the possibility of establishing a meaningful relationship with the schizophrenic.

Abandoning the myth of the meaninglessness of schizophrenic manifestation as such was, of course, of the greatest consequence in promoting psychotherapy with these patients. Where there is no potentially meaningful communication between people in general and between doctor and patient in particular, there is no possibility of establishing contact, hence no hope of accomplishing meaningful psychotherapeutic interchange. Therefore, the discovery that schizophrenic manifestations have meaning and that they are potentially intelligible and understandable brought about a feeling of great encouragement to all psychotherapeutically minded psychiatrists. Nevertheless, much too much time has been spent by psychiatrists on efforts actually to understand the content meaning per se of schizophrenic manifestations and more time wasted in interpreting to the patient the content meaning of his communications.

As you know, the general trend in psychoanalytic psychotherapy points increasingly away from content interpretation. I will refer to this statement later. With the schizophrenic, unqualified thriftiness in content interpretation is indicated even more than with other patients, because, unlike the neurotic, he is many times aware himself of the content meaning of his communications.[1]

At present, psychiatrists consider it wise to try to understand the meaning of the content of schizophrenic communications while listening and, if they *do*, to indicate it by asking pertinent questions which open up new therapeutic avenues of approach. Perhaps it is redundant to add that the psychiatrist should never pretend to understand. As will be demonstrated later, the schizophrenic needs help in understanding the genetics and dynamics of his communications, not their content. In the rare cases when interpretive approach to content is indicated, however, the patient should be encouraged to find his interpretations himself. It is only very seldom that interpretation of content by the doctor may be helpful, either for therapeutic clarification or as one of the ways for the psychiatrist to convey his own understanding to the patient. These interpretations should preferably be implicit in the psychiatrist's reaction to a patient's manifestation rather than given in so many words.

Translating a cryptic schizophrenic communication was done, for example, with at least temporary success in the case of a formerly meticulously well-dressed woman who was seen on the disturbed ward with her clothes reduced to rags, her hair hanging untidily over her face. This patient suddenly shouted at the psychiatrist: "Best, best, best! Why do you always have the best?" etc. The doctor noticed the patient's quick glance at Best's label on the coat which she had put down. Since Best's was a good women's apparel store, the psychiatrist grasped the meaning of the patient's envious hostile outburst. She therefore expressed the hope that the time was not too remote when the patient could go into Garfinckel's again, to buy attractive clothes for herself. (Garfinckel's was a department store in town considered to be superior to Best's.) Immediately after that, the patient quieted down. During the following few weeks, the patient was freer from manifestations of acute hostility and anxiety than she had been for a long time. These weeks could be utilized for successful psychotherapeutic scrutiny of the roots of her anxiety. Then she had another psychotic episode, which was precipitated by an experience of hostile competition with one of the nurses. Ancient unsuccessful competition with a younger sister, better endowed than the patient, was discovered to be at the root of this pattern.

This example, as well as several of the following ones, have been quoted in my book (9). Because of their particularly illustrative validity, I take the liberty of repeating them here.

1. Hanna Segal has recently disagreed with this viewpoint (21).

FRIEDA FROMM-REICHMANN

The suggestion that the psychiatrist show the schizophrenic if and when he understands his communications and that he not pretend to understand implies that there are many times when it is not possible for the psychiatrist to understand schizophrenic communication. Sometimes this is caused by the patient's expressing himself in an ambiguous way on purpose, in an effort to mitigate the burden of the anticipated possibility of being misunderstood. In other cases, failure to understand a patient should not be looked upon as a result of unfamiliarity with the schizophrenic's means of communication per se. Their means of communication is different from that used by the non-schizophrenic psychiatrist, because of the different psychological frame of reference in which it is conceived. It is just as futile to expect to be able to understand every schizophrenic communication, however secretly meaningful one may consider it to be, as it is to expect to be able always to understand the latent contents of every dream, from merely listening to the language in which a person communicates its manifest contents. The dreamer and the psychotic live in a world which is psychologically different from the rational world of the healthy in their waking states. The schizophrenic uses all the means of communication, well known as subjectively meaningful, but frequently non-intelligible to those of you who are familiar with dream language and dream interpretation. This being so, the psychiatrist should learn to accept the fact of the potential meaningfulness of schizophrenic communication and resign himself to the fact that his ability to catch on to it is limited.

To illustrate, would any non-schizophrenic psychiatrist be able to disentangle the meaning of the following schizophrenic communication without the patient's help? This patient suffered from bed- and pants-wetting when a child. The parental answer to this behavior was thorough humiliation and discrimination against her, especially on the part of her father. When she was five years old, organic causes for her predicament were discovered, and an operation was successfully performed. Her parents did not offer the girl a word of apology.

Another item from her history was that she came from a family in which the women were disposed to become overweight, and avoidance of overweight was made a religion. In defiance, the patient developed into an obese, compulsive eater. "Pants-wetting and overweight belong together," she volunteered one day during a psychoanalytic interview, "and not only because both are connected with defiance and resentment against my parents and with the anxiety connected with these feelings." There followed a pause. Then she went on, "*Wet* and *weight* belong together, but I don't know how." Eventually a childhood memory followed: the patient was in the dressing cabin at the swimming pool of a camp which she attended upon parental dictum and against her own wishes. She shared this cabin with another girl. While alone there in the nude, she had to urinate, and she wet her large turkish towel. When the patient heard the other girl coming into the cabin,

[182]

she tried to wring the wet towel, and she remembered how hard it was to do this when she was only a little girl. "It was 'the *weight*' of the '*wet*' towel which made it so hard," she stated. "There you are, 'weight and wet.' 'Wet' has to do with my resentment against my father, 'weight' with my defiance against mother, and I hated them both for forcing me to go to that camp. So they might not love me any more. . . . So I was frightened. . . . There you have my whole hostility and meanness, and my whole anxiety. 'Wet' and 'weight' are father and mother, and the camp stands for both of them."

So you see, the patient took over where I was not able to do so. My not understanding her was no obstacle to useful psychotherapeutic interchange, as long as she realized that I was listening alertly, expecting her to make sense. Incidentally, after one and a half years of treatment, this patient developed a wholesome friendly relationship with both parents.

Two undesirable therapeutic aspects of overemphasis on content interpretation should be added. First, misinterpretations or partial interpretations were given all too frequently and, as such, obstructed further communication and meaningful therapeutic investigation.

This was the case with one of my patients who refused to be bathed, combed or manicured, and who eliminated outside the toilet most of the time, and preferably on the ground, in the presence of the psychiatrist. The doctor interpreted this behavior as perhaps being designed to erect an isolating wall of dirt, actually and symbolically, between the patient and her environment. From all appearances this interpretation was accepted most readily at the time it was given, only to be completely rejected and corrected two years later. At that time the patient confessed to great anxiety about her being of part Negro descent. The person bathing her or manicuring her hands would see the bluish moons of her nails and thus find out about her Negro blood.

Now I wish to give an example of the delaying effect which an incomplete interpretation may produce. I have learned about that from a number of patients, but especially in the following case:

This patient, while in the middle of psychotherapeutic endeavors which she herself recognized and labeled promising, stubbornly insisted on being dismissed from the hospital. Fear of getting well and returning to her home environment, unwillingness to grant the psychiatrist the feather in her cap which the patient's recovery might mean, lack of insight into the remaining unresolved elements of her psychopathology were each considered to be the right explanations when given, and seemingly accepted, yet with no therapeutic benefit. Change in the patient's attitude toward hospital treatment was finally effected when she herself, at long last, volunteered the interpretation that she was afraid to prolong her stay in the hospital lest she commit suicide as her father had done some years ago while hospitalized. The patient held herself responsible for his suicide, because she had not been available as a traveling companion to her father prior to his hospitalization. After the therapeutic working through of this material was completed, the patient felt free to remain in the hospital until the rational medical need for hospitalization subsided.

In both these cases much precious time could have been saved had the patients not been kept from producing conclusive interpretive material by the psychiatrist's untimely, incorrect, or partial interpretations. Some of you, no doubt, are thinking that such misinterpretations or offerings of partial truths also happen in the psychoanalyst's work with patients other than schizophrenic and that, as a rule, we do not consider this too detrimental to the general course of treatment, if it does not happen too frequently. Indeed, this is true. The reason that misinterpretations are more harmful in the case of the schizophrenic is that his inclination is to acquiesce compliantly to misinterpretation, out of a sense of futility and discouragement, inwardly expressed by "Oh, what's the use?" Outwardly, the schizophrenic may express his disagreement by a change in posture and facial expression, which will be caught only by a very alert and sensitive observer of non-verbal communication. Furthermore, a markedly withdrawn—say, hebephrenic—patient, who expects no benefit from human contact anyway, may be reluctant or unable to object to faulty interpretations, because nothing matters to him but to be left alone.

The neurotic patient who spots misinterpretations, however, may be able to speak up or to respond with verbal or non-verbal resistance. The investigation of the neurotic's corrections of wrong interpretations and/or the resistance aroused by them can then be utilized in psychotherapeutic collaboration with a non-defensive psychiatrist.

John Rosen's experience with his method of "direct interpretations" of psychotic material, in what he calls "deteriorated" schizophrenic states, should be discussed in this connection (16). I believe that many of his interpretations are arbitrary, if not incorrect. Yet they work, according to Rosen's reports and evaluation of his therapeutic results. I am in accord with Eissler,[2] who says that Rosen's patients emerge from "their states of acute psychotic disturbance" because of the convincing, consistent intentness of purpose, attitude, speech, and tone of voice with which he relates himself to them. His shocking random interpretations are one of his effective emotional tools. They are effective, irrespective of their truth or faultiness. However, what Rosen does with his method is not to cure schizophrenics but to help them to emerge quickly from acute psychotic episodes, and I wish to add that he helps his patients to emerge more rapidly from acute psychotic states than I and my associates do. That in itself is important enough, as long as the therapist realizes what he is doing. But another problem of treatment

2. *Psychotherapy with Schizophrenics*, pp. 130–67.

begins in the postpsychotic state and with the treatment of the schizoid personality. Rosen turns his patients over to another psychoanalyst at this point. It is only recently, so Dr. Rosen informs me, that he has begun to treat his patients himself beyond this point.

What, then, is the present method of choice as suggested by this author and her associates of the Chestnut Lodge Sanitarium, when doing intensive psychoanalytically oriented psychotherapy with schizophrenics in acutely psychotic and non-psychotic states?

All mental patients—in fact, all human beings—have one experience in common: that is that, temporarily or consistently, to a greater or lesser degree, everyone suffers from the most painful, ubiquitous experience there is—anxiety.[3] The degree of anxiety from which a person suffers, its various modes of expression, and the varying types of defenses which people utilize against it constitute a means of differential diagnosis between healthy and mentally sick people and form a reliable background for a new classification of mental disturbances. As Freud demonstrated most convincingly in *The Problem of Anxiety*, mental symptoms can be understood in their bipolarity as, *uno acto*, an expression of anxiety and as a means of warding it off (5).

This being so, modern trends in the intensive psychoanalytically oriented treatment of mental disturbances have been to put the investigation of the unknown and the known genetic and dynamic causes of a patient's anxieties into the center of psychotherapeutic endeavor. His ways of expressing anxiety and of warding it off by his symptomatology at large are scrutinized and, among them, especially his security operations with and his defenses against the psychiatrist, who undertakes to bring the patient's anxieties to the fore. Through the scrutiny of a patient's security operations with the psychiatrist, his defenses against the other people of his present and previous environment can also be spotted. This therapeutic approach has been strongly promoted with neurotics by Anna Freud (4), by Reich (14), and by Hartmann, Kris, and Loewenstein (10). Sullivan (25, 26), and, recently, Pious (12) also developed it most conclusively in his work with obsessionals and schizophrenics. The investigation of these defenses against the rise of anxiety, in turn, permits clarification of the unknown causes of patients' anxieties. Eventually, patients should learn to spot their anxieties and to recognize the irrationality of these anxieties by virtue of this therapeutic procedure, and they should learn to understand their pathological manifestations for what they are: manifestations of anxiety and of their attempts to ward it off. Thus patients should learn to relinquish as much of their anxieties as human beings are able to give up. They should be able to become sufficiently aware of the remaining anxiety as it may temporarily

3. Dr. Rollo May presented us recently with a comprehensive study of this subject in his significant book (15).

arise in anyone's life, and, by virtue of this awareness, they should be able to handle it adequately. Thus they should become free from symptoms, since symptoms are, as we may say more correctly now, an expression of, and a defense against, unrecognized excess anxiety.

This is the basic philosophy underlying our intensive psychoanalytically oriented psychotherapy with all types of mental patients, neurotics and psychotics. Certain variations in its application are indicated, of course, depending upon the type of patient and also, to a certain degree, upon the personality of the psychiatrist.

What about its application to the schizophrenic? The schizophrenic, to express it in the language of the late Paul Federn (3), is, more than any other mental patient, simultaneously a regressed infant and child and the person of his present chronological age. He is bewildered about his regressive trends and about their underlying anxiety. His primary problem is not his anxiety about others but fear of his own hostile, destructive tendencies, which he acquired in response to repetitive, early interpersonal traumata and which he abhors as much as and more than his associates do (11). Reduced to the basic dynamics which they have in common and for the purpose of our therapeutic philosophy, delusions, hallucinations, catatonic stupor and excitement, persecutory ideas, impulses of homicide, suicide, and self-mutilation, refusal to eat and to eliminate, and the whole gamut of schizophrenic symptomatology may be studied as an outcome of the patient's problems in this frame of reference.

In our therapeutic endeavors we try to address ourselves, if it is at all feasible, to the adult part of the patient's personality, regardless of how disturbed he is, and to guide him gradually to look at the manifestations of his illness—that is, his interpersonal difficulties with the psychoanalyst and other people and other symptoms—as the outcome of his anxieties and his defenses against them.[4]

Treatment begins by establishing some introductory facts about the doctor's and the patient's mutual relationship. Included among these facts will be the need for medical intervention. The doctor's medical role with the patient in his own right should be established. This should include a consensus between patient and doctor to the effect that the doctor is not an emissary of relatives or friends or any third person who may have been instrumental in, or responsible for, a patient's seeking the help of the psychiatrist or of a mental hospital. The doctor should suggest his willingness to assume this role and offer it for acceptance

4. This is in marked contrast to the technique suggested by Paul Federn (2), who recommends encouragement of the schizophrenic's positive transference experiences only and the avoidance of the analysis of his negative reactions to the psychoanalyst. We believe that these suggestions are an expression of Federn's basic skepticism regarding the possibilities of actual cures of schizophrenics by psychoanalytic psychotherapy versus symptomatic recoveries.

to the patient without ever attempting to becloud the fact that doctor and patient are personal strangers.

Trying to initiate or facilitate treatment of a schizophrenic by making friends with him or by other attempts at turning the strictly professional relationship into a pseudo-social one may, according to our experience, turn into a serious threat to successful psychotherapeutic procedure. As we know from psychoanalytic work with neurotics, such attempts are unacceptable there. They may destroy the central core of psychoanalytic psychotherapy, which is to utilize the vicissitudes of the doctor-patient relationship as a mirror of patients' patterns of interpersonal relationships at large, hence as the most informative therapeutic means of investigating and understanding their psychopathological aspects. In the case of schizophrenics, there are several additional serious difficulties connected with any falsification of the professional character of the doctor-patient relationship. This must be definitely kept in mind in the presence of the temptation to try to reach a very disturbed psychotic schizophrenic by offering closeness, friendship, or love. Moreover, the psychoanalyst who feels tempted to do so should ask himself whether he may not be motivated by his own anxiety rather than by an alleged concern for the patient's welfare.[5]

To continue with the description of what has proved to be the most valuable approach to psychoanalytic psychotherapy with schizophrenics to this writer—my suggestion of elimination of non-professional contacts in psychoanalytic treatment is not intended to imply a repudiation of all the very valuable attempts to create an atmosphere of acceptance, comfort, understanding, or elimination of anxiety-arousing factors from these patients' environment. Such efforts are most commendable as means of speeding patients' emergence from acute psychotic states and, if administered by persons other than the psychoanalyst, as most useful adjuncts to the psychoanalytic treatment proper (1). Eissler's report about his interesting cases of rapid emergence from acute psychotic disturbance in soldiers is very much to the point (1). They were given treatment of unconditional loving acceptance for their psychotic symptomatology, under the pressure of the necessities of military medical routine. Stanton and Schwartz will soon publish their research on the influence of the mental hospital ward-as-a-whole on schizophrenic patients.[6] I have discussed this question in my paper, "Problems of Thera-

5. These recommendations are in contrast to the work presented by Milton Wexler in *Psychotherapy with Schizophrenics* (p. 179) and the paper which he recently read before the American Psychiatric Association (27). The same holds true for the work of Mme Sechehaye, which came to my attention after this paper was completed and which will be evaluated at some later time (20). All this proves how much treatment in each case is, at the present time, codetermined by the specificity of the personality of the therapist and of the doctor-patient relationship.

6. Cf. the following papers which came from this research work (19, 22–24).

peutic Management in a Psychoanalytic Hospital" (7). These attempts, however, should be basically differentiated from the specific psycho-therapeutic work of the psychoanalyst with his schizophrenic patient. This holds true especially for the technique we are suggesting. *It is designed to be one and the same throughout the whole course of treatment, irrespective of the degree of the patient's disturbance at any time during its course.*

Incidentally, with some of the patients who are treated with the technique which I will presently describe, it may very well occur that the duration of the acute disturbance will be longer than, say, with Rosen's technique. So far, we are inclined to take this possibility in stride. We believe it to be for the benefit of the patient's ultimate, that is, not only symptomatic, recovery.

Now to return to the discussion of the specific reasons for our warning against offering non-professional warmth to a schizophrenic patient in the setting of psychoanalytic treatment—first, the schizophrenic is afraid of any offer of closeness. Closeness in the present entails the danger of rebuff in the future to the early-traumatized schizophrenic. Also, he will not be able to hide his "ugliness," his "meanness," his hostile and destructive impulses, from a person who comes close to him.

"I warned you against becoming friendly with me," said one schizophrenic after a painful display of hostility. "I told you you'd find out that I am an unbearably hostile person. Do you think it pleases me to behave that way? I assure you it does not. Why then do you trespass that way by forcing me to let you see what I'd rather not see myself, much less share the knowledge with someone else?"

Again, closeness increases the schizophrenic's ever existing fear of having lost or of losing his identity, of losing the sense of the boundaries between himself and the outside world.

There is one last reason which makes me warn against the attempt to start psychotherapy with a schizophrenic on the basis of any relationship other than the realistic professional one, and that is his alert sensitivity to and rejection of any feigned emotional experience. As one patient bluntly expressed herself upon being offered friendship in an initial interview by a young psychoanalyst, "How can you say we are friends? We hardly know each other."

The next preliminary step in the course of psychoanalytic treatment is to elicit information about the patient's complaints and about the basic data of his present personal life. In the case of a very disturbed or an inarticulate patient, from whom these data cannot be secured and who gives no sign of understanding, the psychiatrist will realize later that in most cases his initial approach has gone on record for future reference, no matter how little evidence of it can be secured for the time being.

Once this initial work is done, all the patient's manifestations are approached along the lines of the general philosophy of modern psychoanalytic psychotherapy, as outlined. Collecting the known data and the lost memories of the patients' histories is, of course, part of the therapeutic procedure. Without knowing them, the psychiatrist cannot investigate with his patients the genetic roots of their anxieties. Acquaintance with the peculiarities of the indirect, symbolic language and the double-talk of the schizophrenic will be helpful. The doctor's ever present realization of the great sensitivity and subtlety in sizing up interpersonal situations which he will encounter in these patients will be indispensable for this type of psychotherapeutic intervention. The doctor must remember that this sensitized subtlety is theirs as a result of their early fight for survival in the midst of the hostile interpersonal integrations of their childhood.[7] This does not mean, however, that we recommend treatment of the patient by indirectness and "sweetness." This would be highly suspect to any schizophrenic. It means, rather, the recommendation that the patient be spoken to as one speaks to someone highly interpersonally sensitized, who perceives his environment through a wealth of sensory and extrasensory channels. These qualities should not be ignored but mobilized in the patient's collaborative efforts to find out about the genetic and dynamic roots of his anxieties and about the symptoms, blind spots, and defenses which it produces.

Incidentally, we have repeatedly referred to the schizophrenic as a person who has suffered early interpersonal traumatization, the investigation of which helps the psychiatrist and the patient to obtain genetic understanding of his psychopathology. However, the genetic understanding of the significance of these early environmental traumata should not be mistakenly used as an excuse for the patient's interpersonal difficulties. This holds true for psychotics as well as for neurotics. It follows that the interpersonal approach which psychoanalysis suggests, that the repeated discussion and understanding of what was done to the patient in his early years, must sooner or later be followed up by the investigation of what, in his turn, the patient has done to his environment. This is especially important in the case of the schizophrenic, whose retaliative, anxiety-arousing hostility plays so much of a basic part in his symptomatology.

Dr. Mary Julian White, of Chestnut Lodge, is in the process of developing a more active therapeutic approach to schizophrenics, especially paranoid patients, by using the technique of an early frontal attack on the patients' malevolent trends of thought and action against the parents of their childhood in their own right and in its implications with other people, including the psychoanalyst. At the same time, these

7. See also Rosen (18).

patients learn to recognize this malevolence as one aspect of their—potentially corrigible—general misery, helplessness, and emptiness.

The work of Dr. Rose Spiegel, of New York, should also be mentioned in this connection. She has recently tried to treat young schizophrenic patients indirectly, as it were, especially if they refused contact with a psychiatrist in their own right. She has seen one or both of the patient's parents in weekly therapeutic sessions and has investigated and evaluated with them what went traumatically wrong in the parents' mutual relationships with and in their attitudes toward the patient, and vice versa.[8]

Now, to illustrate the therapeutic approach in terms of scrutiny along the lines of the patient's anxiety, its various manifestations, and his defenses against it, as I have outlined it in this and previous papers:

A patient shouted at the psychiatrist during their first visit, "I know what you will do now! You'll take my gut-pains, and my trance, and my withdrawal states away from me! And where will I be then?" The psychiatrist first asked for a description of the three pathological states, the loss of which the patient allegedly feared. The patient's answer made it possible for the psychiatrist to demonstrate to her the attempt at escaping anxiety, which all three of the states had in common. Subsequently, her anxiety regarding the psychiatrist's role as a foe rather than as a co-worker was labeled as such, and the historical roots for this interpersonal attitude and expectation could be scrutinized. After that the patient was told that her symptoms would not be taken away from her but that, in all likelihood, she herself would wish to dispose of them when she learned to understand enough about her anxiety to make it decrease. Also the patient's attention was drawn to the fact that she had made her symptoms known immediately to the psychiatrist. It was suggested that this seemed to indicate that, perhaps without realizing it, she was just as desirous of losing her symptoms as she was anxious, within her awareness, at the prospect of being deprived of them. Thus psychiatrist and patient were in the middle of a therapeutic discussion of various aspects of the patient's anxiety right at the beginning of her treatment.

Later on, the treatment history of this patient was characterized by a pattern of relapsing into disturbed states of withdrawal and self-mutilation and of resorting to painful hallucinations and delusions which she had previously relinquished. This occurred whenever another new symptom was resolved or whenever she gave away another telling secret from her private world. The hostility against the analyst and the family and the anxiety aroused by this hostility could be seen by the patient, and its repetitive connection with the previous similar situations in camp, school, and family could be investigated.

Another example is taken from the history of a patient who made a suicidal attempt by slashing his wrist without cutting arteries or tendons. He was first given evidence of the psychoanalyst's realization that the patient must have felt quite bad when prompted to make a suicidal attempt. Then his interest

8. I am indebted to Drs. White and Spiegel for their personal information about this work. Reports have not been published to date.

was engaged in investigating the motivating powers—more specifically, the anxiety behind his action. It appeared that he was consumed with the fear that both the psychotherapist and his brother, who had brought him to the hospital, would not know how really miserable he was. He had kept part of his symptoms (hallucinations, etc.) a secret. The psychiatrist would be angry about his withholding information and would become hesitant to work with him under these circumstances and so would not object to the patient's dismissal. Yet the patient wished to stay in the hospital. (The motivation for this wish was not discussed with him at this time.) The brother would also wish to remove the patient from the hospital, so the patient argued, because of his dissatisfaction with the psychiatrist's failure to extract the patient's withheld secrets. The psychiatrist, however, would believe that this was not his fault but solely the patient's. This alleged disagreement between the two significant people in the patient's life was another source of the rise of resentment and anxiety. Subsequently, the bipolarity of the patient's anxieties could be brought into the open: he had withheld the information about his hallucinations for fear of being considered too disturbed. At the same time, he was afraid that he was not considered to be as disturbed as he actually felt, because of this withheld information. Hence he felt driven to make a suicidal attempt, so as to bring the degree of his disturbance to the doctor's and to his brother's attention.

As to the method of the suicidal attempt, the patient's professed main interest was focused on the fact that he had barely missed cutting his tendons and paralyzing his hand. He threatened to "try it again"—"and this time I'll slash the tendons, and paralyze the future use of my hand for good." Therapeutic investigation of this aspect of the suicidal attempt revealed that there was a need to put his hand out of action for fear he might hit his brother and/or the psychiatrist: "and if he hit, he would hit hard. They had it coming to them. Why hadn't they forced him to talk more frankly about his predicament?"

Also he was filled with anxiety lest he hit his (prudish) family morally by masturbating publicly, using the hand which therefore had better be paralyzed. "What else could one expect from a person confined in a mental hospital?" The patient assumed that the psychoanalyst would not like his masturbating in public, either. That would be another reason for disliking the patient and wanting to get rid of him. "And how I hate you both for this," he continued.

Subsequently he learned to understand the psychopathological chain of keeping secrets, hatred of self for doing it, hatred of people who did not guess his secrets, anticipated hatred from those whom he deceived, expression of his hatred and defiance in his fantasy of masturbating in public, anticipated hatred from others for that, and therefore anxiety and fantasies of self-punishment.

These two examples are designed to demonstrate the leading principle of the psychotherapist's approach to the schizophrenic, in terms of investigating his total symptomatology and especially the vicissitudes of his relationship with the psychiatrist as expressions of, and as defenses against, the patient's underlying anxiety. The approach is applicable to schizoid personalities in the later part of treatment as well as to the severely disturbed psychotic in the beginning of treatment. The latter will be facilitated if the psychoanalyst is somewhat familiar with and adaptable to the specific thought processes, feelings, and modes of expression which are used by a disturbed schizophrenic.

Working time and again through these experiences until their understanding turns into real insight is, of course, as much an integral part of intensive psychotherapy with schizophrenics as it is in the psychoanalysis of neurotics.

This outline of psychotherapy with schizophrenics is, of necessity, a spotty and incomplete one. But I hope that the readers are somewhat familiar with part of the literature on the subject, so that this contribution gains meaning in the context of the short history of intensive psychoanalytically oriented psychotherapy with schizophrenics.

References

1. EISSLER, K. R. "Psychiatric Ward Management of Acute Schizophrenic Patients," *J. Nerv. & Ment. Dis.*, CV (1947), 307.
2. FEDERN, P. "Psychoanalysis of Psychoses. I. Errors and How To Avoid Them. II. Transference," *Psychiat. Quart.*, XVII (1943), 3 and 246.
3. ———. "Principles of Psychotherapy in Latent Schizophrenia," *Am. J. Psychotherapy*, I (1947), 129.
4. FREUD, A. *The Ego and the Mechanisms of Defense.* New York: International Universities Press, Inc., 1946.
5. FREUD, S. *The Problem of Anxiety.* New York: W. W. Norton & Co., 1936.
6. FROMM-REICHMANN, F. "Transference Problems in Schizophrenics," *Psychoanalyt. Quart.*, VIII (1939), 412.
7. ———. "Problems of Therapeutic Management in a Psychoanalytic Hospital," *ibid.*, XVI (1947), 325.
8. ———. "Notes on the Development of Treatment of Schizophrenics by Psychoanalytic Psychotherapy," *Psychiatry*, XI (1948), 263.
9. ———. *Principles of Intensive Psychotherapy.* Chicago: University of Chicago Press, 1950.
10. HARTMANN, H., KRIS, E., and LOEWENSTEIN, R. M. "Comments on the Formation of Psychic Structure." In *The Psychoanalytic Study of the Child*, Vol. II. New York: International Universities Press, Inc., 1946.
11. Panel Discussion: "Provocation and Manifestations of Anxiety in Schizophrenia." American Psychoanalytic Association, April 29, 1950. Abstracted in *Bull. Am. Psychoanal. A.*, VI (1950), 37.
12. PIOUS, W. L. "Obsessive-compulsive Symptoms in an Incipient Schizophrenic," *Psychoanalyt. Quart.*, XIX (1950), 327.
13. POWDERMAKER, F. "Considerations in the Psychotherapy of Schizoid Patients." Read before the American Psychiatric Association, Cincinnati, May 8, 1951.

14. REICH, W. *Character Analysis.* New York: Orgone Institute Press, 1949.
15. MAY, R. *The Meaning of Anxiety.* New York: Ronald Press Co., 1950.
16. ROSEN, J. N. "A Method of Resolving Acute Catatonic Excitement," *Psychiat. Quart.,* XX (1946), 183.
17. ———. "The Treatment of Schizophrenic Psychosis by Direct Analytic Therapy," *ibid.,* XXI (1947), 3 and 117.
18. ———. "The Survival Function of Schizophrenia," *Bull. Menninger Clin.,* XIV (1950), 81.
19. SCHWARTZ, M. S., and STANTON, A. H. "A Social Psychological Study of Incontinence," *Psychiatry,* XIII (1950), 399.
20. SECHEHAYE, M. A. *Symbolic Realization: A New Method of Psychotherapy Applied to a Case of Schizophrenia.* New York: International Universities Press, Inc., 1951.
21. SEGAL, H. "Some Aspects of the Analysis of a Schizophrenic," *Internat. J. Psychoanal.,* XXXI (1950), 1.
22. STANTON, A. H., and SCHWARTZ, M. S. "The Management of a Type of Institutional Participation in Mental Illness," *Psychiatry,* XII (1949), 13.
23. ———. "Medical Opinion and Social Context in the Mental Hospital," *ibid.,* p. 243.
24. ———. "Observations on Dissociation as Social Participation," *ibid.,* p. 339.
25. SULLIVAN, H. S. *Conceptions of Modern Psychiatry.* Washington: William Alanson White Psychiatric Foundation, 1947.
26. ———. "The Theory of Anxiety and the Nature of Psychotherapy," *Am. J. Psychiat.,* XII (1949), 3.
27. WEXLER, M. "Distance as a Factor in the Treatment of a Schizophrenic Patient." Read before the American Psychiatric Association, Cincinnati, May 8, 1951.

(15)

PSYCHOTHERAPY OF SCHIZOPHRENIA

When I received the invitation to talk to you about the psychotherapy of schizophrenia, I gave a good deal of thought to the question of how you might like me to approach the topic. Finally, I felt it might be most appropriate to report the development in the understanding and the technique of our clinical work since 1948, when I had the privilege of talking to you about it at the schizophrenia symposium during the annual meeting in Washington. [See Paper 13, p. 160.]

The goal of psychotherapy with schizophrenics was seen then, as it is now, as helping them, by a consistent dynamically oriented psychotherapeutic exchange, to gain awareness of the unconscious motivations for and curative insight into the genetics and dynamics of their disorder.

As a result of the continued research which is inherent in dynamic psychotherapy, I have gained some further insight into the dynamics of schizophrenic symptomatology from which have evolved some variations in the details of the treatment. Briefly, they are as follows:

1. The old hypothesis according to which the schizophrenic's early experiences of warp and rejection were of over-all significance for the interpretive understanding and treatment has been somewhat revised.

2. The conflict-provoking dependent needs of schizophrenic patients have been seen more clearly.

3. The devastating influence of schizophrenic hostility on the patients themselves has been understood more clearly in connection with their states of autism and partial regression (weak ego—autistic self-depreciation).

4. This has led to a therapeutically helpful reformulation of the anxiety of schizophrenic patients as an outcome of the universal human conflict between dependency and hostility which is overwhelmingly magnified in schizophrenia.

5. The multiple meaning of some schizophrenic communications and its influence on the psychiatrist's interpretive endeavors have been clarified.

Before I begin to elaborate these topics, I have to ask you to forgive me for lack of reference to publications of other workers in the field.

The Academic Lecture read at the hundred and tenth annual meeting of the American Psychiatric Association, St. Louis, Missouri, May 3–7, 1954.

Reprinted from *American Journal of Psychiatry*, Vol. III, No. 6 (December, 1954).

There is unfortunately not time enough to comment on the published work of our colleagues, to indicate what I owe to them, and also to develop my own conceptions. So I felt that I ought to decide to do the latter.

I would like to begin by stating that my discussion will comprise the treatment of hospitalized disturbed psychotics as well as that of manifestly less disturbed ambulatory patients whom we treat in the same way through all phases and all manifestations of their illness. This position is not new, but it has recently become more controversial because of opposite techniques which other authors have propagated.

From a social and behavioral standpoint and from the viewpoint of the special care which manifestly psychotic patients may need in order to be protected from harming themselves and others, the difference between these two types of patients may seem tremendous. Psychodynamically speaking, I see no difference between the symptomatology of actively psychotic and more conformative schizophrenics.

All schizophrenic patients live in a state of partial regression to early phases of their personal development, the disturbed ones more severely regressed than the conformative ones. All are also living simultaneously on the level of their present chronological age, the conformative ones more obviously so than the severely disturbed ones. Irrespective of the degree of regression and disturbance, we try to reach the regressed portion of their personalities by addressing the adult portion, rudimentary as this may appear in some severely disturbed patients. Also, the general psychodynamic conception that anxiety plays a central role in all mental illnesses and that mental symptoms in general may be understood simultaneously as an expression of and as a defense against anxiety and its underlying conflicts holds, regardless of the severity of the picture of illness and regardless of its more or less dramatic character. Hence we make the exploration of the dynamic roots of the schizophrenic's anxieties our potential goal through all phases of illness.

Lack of immediate communicative responses to treatment in acutely disturbed patients is no measuring rod for their actual awareness of and for their inner response to our psychotherapeutic approach. This old experience has been further corroborated in more recent dealings with several recovered patients. They did refer to various aspects of our psychotherapeutic contacts, after their emergence, while we were working through the dynamics of their problems, or later, while we were reviewing treatment and illness during the recovery period.

While symptomatic psychotherapy of acute psychotic manifestations may be necessary with some patients for situational reasons, many of us consider it not too important to be overconcerned with the duration of the acutely disturbed states of patients while they are under psychotherapy.

My experience during the last twenty years has been mainly with schizophrenic patients who came to our hospital in a state of severe psychotic disturbance, from which the majority emerged sooner or later under intensive dynamic psychotherapy. After their emergence, they continued treatment with the same psychiatrist through the years of their outwardly more quiet state of illness, with the aim of ultimate recovery with insight. During both phases the patients were seen for four to six regularly scheduled interviews per week, lasting one hour or longer. Sometimes relapses occurred. Such relapses were due to failure in therapeutic skill and evaluation of the extent of the patient's endurance for psychotherapy, to unrecognized difficulties in the doctor-patient relationship, or to responses to intercurrent events beyond the psychiatrist's control. As a rule, these relapses could be handled successfully if the psychiatrist himself did not become too frightened, too discouraged, or too narcissistically hurt by their occurrence.

From the experience with these patients we learned about one more reason for advocating the same type of psychotherapeutic approach through all phases of the illness: part of the work which a patient has to accomplish during treatment and at the time of his recovery is, in my judgment, to learn to accept and to integrate the fact that he has gone through a psychotic illness and that there is a "continuity," as one patient called it, between the person as he manifested himself in the psychosis and the one he is after his recovery. The discussion of the history of patients' illness and treatment after their recovery serves, of course, the same purpose. This is in contrast to the therapeutic attitude of some psychiatrists who hold that recovering patients should learn to detest and eject their psychotic symptomatology, like a foreign body, from their memory.

The difficult task of integrating the psychotic past, which we advocate, will be greatly facilitated if it can be done on the basis of the patient's confidence in a psychiatrist who has maintained the same type of psychotherapeutic relationship with him throughout the course of treatment. Changes in the doctor's therapeutic approach may easily become a mirror of the lack of continuity in the patient's personality and, incidentally, may become an inducement for the patient to dwell in one or another phase of his illness, depending upon his preference for this or another type of therapeutic relationship.

The following experience with a patient illustrates the difficulties of integrating the experience of a past psychosis:

This patient emerged from a severe schizophrenic disturbance of many years' duration, for which she was finally hospitalized for two years at Chestnut Lodge and then treated as an ambulatory patient for another two years. Eventually she became free of her psychotic symptomatology except for the maintenance of one manifest symptom: she would hold on to the habit of pulling the skin off her heels to the point of habitually producing open wounds. No attempt at understanding the dynamics of this residual symptom clicked, until the patient developed one day an acute anxiety state in one of our psychotherapeutic interviews in response to my commenting on favorable "changes" that had taken place in her. After that, the main dynamic significance of the skin-pulling became suddenly clear to her and to me. "I am still surprised and sometimes a little anxious about the change which I have undergone," she said, "and about finding and maintaining the continuity and the identity between the girl who used to be so frightfully mixed up that she had to stay locked up on the disturbed ward of Chestnut Lodge, and the popular and academically successful college girl of today." The skin-pulling as a symptom similar to another self-mutilating act of burning herself, which she repeatedly committed while acutely ill, helped her to maintain her continuity. It made it possible to be ill and well at the same time, because it was only she who knew about the symptom which could be hidden from everybody else with whom she came in contact as a healthy person. After this discovery, the symptom eventually disappeared.

Incidentally, important as the understanding of this one dynamic aspect of the patient's symptom was for therapeutic reasons, this does not mean that it constituted its only significance.

It was stated that mental symptoms in general can be understood as a means of expressing and of warding off anxiety and the central conflicts which are at the root of this anxiety and that the exploration of this anxiety is most important in psychotherapy with schizophrenics. If this is true, we have to ask for a specific psychodynamic formulation of the causal interrelatedness between schizophrenic symptomatology and the conflicts underlying the anxiety in schizophrenic patients. A correct workable conception of the psychodynamic correlation between anxiety and schizophrenic symptom formation is a prerequisite for the development of a valid method of dynamic psychotherapy with schizophrenic patients.

We know the historically determined deadly fear of schizophrenics of being neglected, rejected, or abandoned and their inability to ask for the acceptance and attention they want. Consequently, most psychiatrists who did psychotherapy with schizophrenics in the early days suggested treating them with utter caution, as I did, or with unending maternal love, permissiveness, and understanding, as did Schwing and, more recently, Sechehaye. While doing so, psychiatrists faced another dynamically significant problem of the schizophrenic—the unconscious struggle between his intense dependent needs and his recoil from them. These we learned to understand genetically as the correlate to the patients' experience of neglect by the "bad mother" at a time when her attention was indispensable for the infant's and the child's survival.

We also know about the resentment, anger, hostility, fury, or violence, with which the infant and child—the "bad me," as Sullivan called it—

who later becomes the schizophrenic patient responds to the early damaging influences of the "bad mother," as he experienced her.

In order to understand the devastating significance of this hostility for schizophrenic patients, we have to realize the following developmental facts of their lives. As we first learned from Freud and Bleuler, schizophrenics are people who have responded to their early misery in interpersonal contacts not only with anger and hostility but also with a partial regression into an early state of ego development and of autistic self-concern and self-preoccupation. This early traumatization and the partial regression make for a weak organization of the schizophrenic's ego. Consequently, he feels more threatened than other people by all strong emotional experiences and, above all, by the realization of his own hostile impulses.

Another reason for the specific hardship which schizophrenic hostility creates for the patients is that their autistic self-preoccupation makes them painfully concerned with their own "bad me," with their own hostility and fury, or their fantasies of violence and destruction against themselves and others.

Besides, their grandiose concept of power in these states of regression to an early state of interpersonal development makes for their preoccupation with themselves as more or less dangerous people.

Where other types of patients are mainly concerned with the fear of disapproval, of the withdrawal of love which they may elicit in other people by their hostile impulses or other emanations of their "bad me," schizophrenic patients are more concerned with their own status as dangerously hostile people, with the damage which may be done to others who associate with them, and with their impulses of punitive self-mutilation.

Yet neither the fearful and grandiose preoccupation with his dangerous hostility nor the threat of the primary abandonment by mother nor the resulting dependent needs from which the patient simultaneously recoils nor the secondary rejection he may have elicited in the mother and other significant persons in his environment because of his "badness" is in itself potent enough to elicit schizophrenic anxiety.

Schizophrenics suffer, as all people in our culture do, even though to a much lesser degree, from the tension between dependent needs and longing for freedom, between tendencies of clinging dependence and those of hostility. For the above-mentioned reasons, the degree of the schizophrenic's need for dependency, the extent to which he simultaneously recoils from it, and the color and degree of his hostile tendencies and fantasies toward himself and others are much more intense than in other people. As a result, the general tension engendered by the clash of these powerful emotional elements becomes completely overwhelming. In other words, the quantitative difference between the schizophrenic's anxiety and similarly motivated tensions in people who have not been emotionally traumatized as early in life as the schizophrenic and who could therefore develop a stronger ego organization is so great that it acquires a totally different quality. It is this tremendous volume of the schizophrenic's anxiety that makes it unbearable in the long run. It then has to be discharged by symptom formation; i.e., schizophrenic symptomatology is seen as the expression of and defense against schizophrenic anxiety, engendered by the tremendous tension between his great dependent needs, his fear of giving them up, his recoil from them, his hostility, and his fantasies of destructiveness against himself and others.

In delineating the dynamic interrelatedness between schizophrenic anxiety and symptomatology, I do not claim, of course, to solve the total problem of schizophrenic symptomatology. I am referring only to such portions of the dynamics as seem necessary for the clarification of my therapeutic conceptions. Our treatment of many schizophrenic manifestations has been corrected or markedly improved in the light of the hypothesis offered.

Take, for example, the meaning of the schizophrenic's "fear of closeness," a formulation which, incidentally, has been much abused. In the early years of psychotherapy with schizophrenics we used to understand this fear of intimacy as an expression of anxiety that all closeness, much as it was simultaneously desired, might be followed by subsequent rejection; then we learned that this fear of closeness seemed also strongly determined by the fear which the partially regressed schizophrenic, with his weak ego organization, felt, that closeness might endanger his identity, might destroy the boundaries between his own ego and that of the other person.

In the meantime, I learned from my work with quite a number of further patients that their fear of closeness is tied up with their anxiety regarding the discovery of their secret hostility or violence against persons for whom they also feel attachment and dependence. They give a mitigated, non-dangerous expression to this hostility and try simultaneously to hide it as a secret by staying away from people.

Let me mention, in this context, an experience which I had repeatedly with patients whom I saw in an office connected with my home: they became tense and anxious when we met after my secretary and maid had left the house. The patients commented on the lack of protection against their hostile impulses.

One young paranoid patient formulated this outrightly, by asking, "Do you realize that I can knock you down in no time?" Unfortunately, I became preoccupied with my role of demonstrating the lack of fear which at the time was luckily mine. Thus I failed to notice how frightened the patient felt by the realization of his potential violence against a woman-doctor, with whom he had established at the same time a dependent relationship. Later on I realized that he was warning me against and asking for protection from future acts of violence, by which he felt we were both threatened. Subsequently, such threats against me or other doctors whom he accidentally saw in my house, against the house itself, and against the attendants who came to take care of him were the unfortunate result. All these assaultive acts were accompanied by marked signs of anxiety.

I continued seeing the patient in a wet pack, until he agreed to abstain from all violent actions and to express his hostile feelings verbally. This he did for some time, alternately with verbal expressions of his dependent attachment and with non-verbal signs of anxiety, until he developed a marked manifest psychotic symptomatology. After that, it became more difficult to have the patient face his dependent needs and his hostility or the anxiety engendered by both. Had I caught on immediately to the patient's anxiety regarding his own hostility, he might have been spared the necessity of transforming it into overt psychotic symptomatology.

Let us now take a look at states of catatonic stupor in the light of our hypothesis. I believe it is of interest to state that many clinicians have been accustomed to describe stuporous states as a result of the schizophrenic's withdrawal of interest from outward reality. Hence the oversimplification of interpreting them only as a response to catatonic fear of rejection becomes quite understandable.

Actually, a patient in stupor has not withdrawn his interest from the environment. As we know from reports about the experiences while in stupor, which these patients furnish after their emergence, they are, more frequently than not, keen observers of what is going on in their environment. Withdrawal of the ability for interpersonal communication is what characterizes the condition of the patient in stupor, not withdrawal of interest in the environment per se. As we know now, this comes about not only in response to the threat of rejection by others but much more for fear of the patient's own hostility or violence in response to actual or assumed acts of rejection from other people.

I remember in this connection the catatonic patient previously reported who became stuporous when she did not receive my message that I had to postpone a scheduled interview. Upon discovering this unfortunate omission, I painstakingly explained the situation to the patient. When she heard and understood me, she emerged from the stuporous state, and psychotherapeutic contact could be resumed.

Incidentally, while telling you about my therapeutic approach to this or other patients, I have to fight off a temptation to dramatize—this, in spite of the fact that dramatization certainly is not in accord with what I would consider good taste in delivering a scientific paper. Upon asking myself about the reason for this temptation, I discovered that actually it is not so illegitimate as it appears to be. It is promoted by the fact that I feel inclined to duplicate tone and inflections of the patient's and my voices, the concomitant gestures, changes in facial expression, etc. This comes about because the doctor's non-verbal concomitants of the psychotherapeutic exchange with schizophrenic patients, in and outside manifestly psychotic episodes, are equally, if not at times more, important than the verbal contents of our therapeutic communication.

The particular emotional stimulus to which a stuporous schizophrenic will respond, which instigated this digression, must be much stronger than one that can be produced by the content per se of what is said. An academic type of delivery to the patient will not do the trick.

Of course, to a certain extent non-verbal elements play a great role in all interpersonal communications, but the degree of expressive skill with which the patient himself uses means of non-verbal communication and his specific sensitivity to the meaning of its use by the psychotherapist are such that, for all practical purposes, the difference in quantity, here again, turns actually into one of quality.

This great perceptive sensitivity of schizophrenic patients was one of the reasons for my overcautious approach to them in bygone times. We used to look at the sensitiveness of these patients in a merely descriptive way and labeled it as one of their admirable characteristics. If we investigate it psychodynamically, we realize that it develops actually in response to their anxiety as a means of orientation in a dangerous world, and we can use it as a signpost on our road toward the psychodynamic investigation of schizophrenic anxiety. Also we should not overlook the possibility that many of the initially correct results of the schizophrenic's perceptive sensitivity may be subsequently subject to distorted psychotic interpretation and misevaluation.

To return to our discussion of the psychodynamics of states of catatonic stupor, I too used to interpret them as a sign only of the patients' having withdrawn because of the lack of consideration or rejection of them. I believe now that this is neither the primary nor the only cause and that withdrawal into stupor is more strongly motivated by the anxiety of patients who realize the danger of their own hostile responses to such neglect by people on whom they depend and to whom they are attached. Several patients corroborated the validity of this hypothesis by spontaneous comments after their recovery.

The symptoms that patients in stupor show concomitant with their withdrawal of interest from communication furnish another proof. Stuporous patients regress to a period of life when they used food intake and elimination as an expression of their hostility against and of their wish to exert control over their environment.

The hostile meaning of disturbances in elimination can also be demonstrated outside stuporous states. I had impressive proof of it in my dealings with a schizophrenic woman patient, who is also mentioned in the

FRIEDA FROMM-REICHMANN

Stanton and Schwartz paper, "A Social Psychological Study of Incontinence."

One day, this patient urinated, before I came to see her, on the seat of the
chair on which I was supposed to be seated during our interview. I did not
see that the chair was wet. The patient did not warn me, and I sat down. I
became aware of the situation only after the dampness had penetrated my
clothing. I thereupon expressed my disgust in no uncertain terms. Then I
stated that I had to go home. The patient asked anxiously about my coming
back, which I refused with the explanation that the time allotted to our interview would be over by the time I had taken a bath and attended to my soiled
clothes.

Obviously, the patient's wetting my chair was an expression of hostile aspects in her dependent relationship with me. However, I did not say so in so
many words, because I felt that the verbalization of this insight should come
from the patient. In subsequent discussions of the event, she responded first
with symptom formation and non-verbal communication, wavering back and
forth from expressions of hostility against me to expressions of attachment
and dependence, until she was finally able to reveal that this had been a
planned expression of resentment against me. The patient wished to punish me
for what she had experienced as excessive therapeutic pressure during an interview preceding the chair-wetting.

Certain symptoms of several hebephrenic patients of our observation
could also be psychodynamically understood and therapeutically approached as an expression of the anxiety connected with their hostility
toward people on whom they likewise felt extremely dependent. These
patients withdrew their interest from their interpersonal environment except for a kind of tolerant and peaceful, if incomprehensible, give-and-
take with some of their fellow patients, until it was all suddenly interrupted by an outburst of hostility against these patients or against the
personnel. As far as their dealings with me went, they did what hebephrenic patients will do at times, as we all know: a kind of mischievous
smile or laughter accompanied or interrupted their scarce communications or was in itself the only sign of their being in some kind of contact
with me. Two patients stated, after they were ready to resume verbal contacts with me, that their laughter was a correlate of hostile derogatory
ideas against and fantasies about me. As they at last established a close
relationship of utter dependence upon me, this was accompanied by a
marked increase in intensity and duration of these spells of derogatory,
tense laughter. The anxiety connected with the establishment of a dependent relationship expressed itself and was warded off by the increased
derogatory laughter. The laughter subsided eventually, in response to the
psychotherapeutic investigation and the working through of the various
aspects of the patients' relationship with me.

With regard to paranoid patients, one of their dynamisms is, as we

[202]

know, that they project onto others the blame for what they consider blameworthy in themselves. Upon investigation of the contents of their blameworthy experiences, we always discover that they are extremely hostile in nature. The suspiciousness of these people points in the same direction.

Again, their suspicion and hostility increase parallel with the realization of their friendly dependent relationship with the psychiatrist. This showed quite impressively in the above-mentioned violent man-patient. The fact that the office where we initially met was part of my home became to him, to use Mme Sechehaye's expression, a "symbolic realization" of his wish to be my friend and houseguest. As he fantasied that I shared his wishes and hallucinated that he heard me say so, he became more and more hostile and anxious.

If our hypothesis about the interrelatedness between craving for and recoiling from dependency, dangerous hostility and violence against themselves and others, overwhelming anxiety, and schizophrenic symptomatology is correct, we must ask how the therapeutic approaches of consistent love and permissive care, as they used to be given to schizophrenic patients by some therapists, including myself, could be helpful. We used to think that they were successful (1) because they gave a patient the love and interest he had missed since childhood and throughout life; (2) because his hostility could subside in the absence of the warp which had originated it; and (3) because the patient was helped to reevaluate his distorted patterns of interpersonal attitudes toward the reality of other people.

We now realize that what we have long known to be true for neurotic patients also holds true for schizophrenics. The suffering from lack of love in early life cannot be made up for by giving the adult what the infant has missed. It will not have the same validity now that it would have had earlier in life. Patients have to learn to integrate the early loss and to understand their own part in their interpersonal difficulties with the significant people of their childhood.

I also know now, and can corroborate this with spontaneous statements of recovered patients, that the love and consideration given to them is therapeutically more significant because they interpret it as proof that they are not so bad, so hostile, in the eyes of the therapist, as they feel themselves to be.

The few fragments of therapeutic exchange with patients quoted so far may serve as examples of the change in our psychotherapeutic attitude, part of which I have already elaborated in my contribution to the 1950 Yale Symposium on Psychotherapy with Schizophrenics.

Of course, we give our schizophrenic patients all the signs of empathic consideration that they need because they suffer. If possible, we prefer to do so by implication or in non-verbalized innuendoes. Too marked sympathetic statements may enhance fear of intimacy and may unnecessarily increase patients' dependence on the therapist, putting into motion the psychopathological chain of dependent attachment, resentment, anxiety, symptom formation.

However, we no longer treat the patients with the utter caution of bygone days. They are sensitive but not frail. If we approach them too cautiously or if we do not expect them to be potentially able to discriminate between right and wrong, we do not render them a therapeutically valid service. We contribute to their low self-evaluation, instead of helping them to develop a healthier attitude toward themselves and others.

Also, if there was lack of parental interest in infancy, this entails lack of guidance in childhood. This fact deserves more therapeutic consideration than it has been given so far. There are therapeutically valid variations of the guidance needed and missed in early childhood, which can be usefully included in psychotherapy with schizophrenics in adulthood.

One exuberant young patient, the daughter of indiscriminately "encouraging" parents, was warned against expecting life to become a garden of roses after her recovery. Treatment, she was told, should make her capable of handling the vicissitudes of life which were bound to occur, as well as to enjoy the gardens of roses which life would offer her at other times. When we reviewed her treatment history after her recovery, she volunteered that this statement had helped her a great deal, "not because I believed for a moment that you were right, Doctor, but because it was such a great sign of your confidence in me and your respect for me, that you thought you could say such a serious thing to me and that I would be able to take it."

In line with our attempts at raising patients' low opinions of themselves, we replace offers of interpretation by the therapist, if possible, by attempts at encouraging patients to find and formulate their interpretations themselves, as demonstrated in my exchange with the patient who wet the chair.

So far we have discussed the psychodynamics of schizophrenics' symptom formation in general as a response to their anxiety. Let us now consider the double and multiple meaning that is inherent in many of the schizophrenic's cryptic and distorted manifestations. Many of them elude the psychiatrist's understanding, but they may yield indirectly to therapeutic endeavors in other areas. Insight into their dynamics may thus be gained in subsequent discussions.

Others, such as hallucinations and delusions, I found frequently accessible to a direct psychotherapeutic approach. They would be successfully examined with the patient as they occurred in his experience and in terms of his own formulations. I stated, however, explicitly to the patient that I did not share his hallucinatory or delusional experience.

There is one more access to understanding schizophrenic communications which has not yet been mentioned. Schizophrenics are able to refer in their productions simultaneously to experiences from the area of their early childhood, from their present living in general, and, if they are under treatment, from their relationship with the therapist, as dreamers do in their dreams. Sometimes we are able to understand the meaning of and their reference to various chronological levels of experience, sometimes not.

At any rate, it is most important for the psychiatrist to realize this multiple meaning of many schizophrenic symptoms and communications. This realization should make us replace the old therapeutic attitude that therapists ought to be able to find and offer to the patient the only correct meaning of a symptom or communication by the suggestion that they should train themselves to become able to feel which of several meanings of a schizophrenic symptom or communication (if they catch on to several of them) is the therapeutically most significant one at a given time. This ability of the psychiatrist to select sensitively when and what to present to the patient is most desirable, because of the narrowed ways of the schizophrenic's thinking and his short span of attention, which limits his capacity to listen.

The insights into the possibilities and the limitations of understanding schizophrenic communications should do away with the endless discussion that used to go on between various members of groups of psychotherapists as to whether a patient's communication in word or action meant only what Dr. A heard or exclusively what Dr. B heard. Depending upon the scope of personal and clinical experience and the personality of the therapist and on his ability to understand patients' communications via identification, each among several psychotherapists may catch on to one of the different meanings of a patient's communication.

The insight into the manifold meanings of patients' symptoms or other manifestations may also do away with the continuing discussions in our literature of the question whether or not schizophrenic patients understand their own communications. I believe it should be stated that they sometimes do and sometimes do not. Sometimes they may, above all, be aware of the descriptive content of their communication but not of its dynamic significance. While this whole question holds great theoretical interest, I believe now that its solution is not too important for therapeutic purposes. This holds true all the more, since the main trends in treatment no longer go in terms of translating the descriptive meaning of the content of any single symptom.

There are two facts that have led us more and more away from working with patients in terms of interpreting their various symptoms and other cryptic communications. One is negative and is determined by the fact that most isolated interpretations of the content of a single symptom or other communication will not cover all its meanings in a therapeutically significant way. The other is an important positive one: it follows from the knowledge of the psychodynamic fact that schizophrenic patients, like any other mental patients under treatment, repeat with the therapist the interpersonal experiences which they have undergone during a lifetime.

Hence we have moved increasingly in the direction which I have already elaborated in previous papers: we make the therapeutic exploration and clarification of schizophrenic anxiety and symptomatology, as they manifest themselves in the patient-doctor relationship, as integral a part of psychotherapy with schizophrenics as it is with neurotic patients. Some modifications are, of course, required in view of the difference between schizophrenic and neurotic modes of relatedness with the psychiatrist and with other people. But in both cases our therapeutic attention is focused on the dynamic investigation and clarification of the conscious and the unconscious aspects of the patient-doctor relationship in its own right and in its transference aspects. Special attention is paid to the exploration of the anxiety aroused by the therapist's probing into the patients' problems and to their security operations against it.

Here is an example from the treatment history of the patient who pulled the skin off her heels, which illustrates both the multiple meaning of schizophrenic symptoms on various experiential levels and our approach to its basic dynamic significance in terms of investigating its manifestations in the patient-doctor relationship:

We are already familiar with the dynamic validity of the skin-pulling as a way for the patient to establish her "continuity." As we learned in the course of its further investigation, the localization of this symptom was determined by mischievously ridiculing memories of her mother's coming home from outings to prepare a meal for the family, going into the kitchen, removing shoes and stockings but not coat and hat, and walking around the kitchen on bare feet.

The self-mutilating character of the symptom proved to be elicited by the patient's resentment against me. In her judgment, I misevaluated the other act of self-mutilation from which she suffered during her psychotic episodes, the compulsion to burn her skin. The patient thought of it as a means of relieving unbearable tension, whereas she felt that I thought of it only as a serious expression of tension. In maintaining the skin-pulling, while otherwise nearly recovered, she meant to demonstrate to me that skin injuring was not a severe sign of illness.

During the treatment period after the dismissal from the hospital, the patient tried for quite a while to avoid the recognition of her hostility against me and the realization of her dependent attachment to me, which she resented, by trying to cut me out of her everyday life. She did so, repeating an old pattern of living in two worlds, the world which she shared with me during our therapeutic interviews and her life outside the interviews, during which she excluded me completely from her thinking. Previously, the patient had established this pattern with her parents by living for eleven years in an imaginary kingdom which she populated by people of her own making and by the spiritual representations of others whom she actually knew. They all shared a language, literature, and religion of her own creation. Therapeutic investigation taught us that the patient erected this private world as a means of excluding her prying parents from an integral part of her life. It was her way of fighting her dependence on them and of demonstrating how different she was from them in all areas where she disliked and resented them.

The patient recognized the significance of the dichotomy in her dealings with me as a means of escape from her resentment against and dependence on me, only after going twice through a sudden outburst of hostility and anxiety which led to brief periods of readmission to the hospital, where she regressed to her old symptom of burning herself.

After a few stormy therapeutic interviews, she understood the dynamic significance of her need for readmission; she felt so dependent on me and so hostile against me that she had to come back to live in the hospital and to burn her skin.

During the ambulatory treatment periods which followed, the patient learned eventually to recognize that her excluding me from one part of her life was a repetition of the exclusion of her parents from her private kingdom. After that, she saw, too, that her resentment against me was also a revival of an old gripe against her parents; they had a marked tendency to make her out to be dumb, as I tried to do, in her judgment, by inflicting upon her my misevaluation of the skin burning. They kept her for many years in a state of overdependence, as I had done, too, by virtue of our therapeutic relationship.

All these transference facets of the patient's relationship with me, as well as the problems of the doctor-patient relationship in their own right, had to be worked through several times before the patient could ultimately become free from her interpersonal difficulties with me, with her parents, and with other people and from the anxiety which they engendered.

While we consider the suggestions about psychotherapy with schizophrenics, which we have offered, to be psychodynamically valid and helpful rules, we believe, on the other hand, that the ways and means to go about using them will inevitably be subject to many variations, depending on the specific assets and liabilities of the personality of the therapist and hence on the specific coloring of his interaction with his patient.

Psychotherapy with schizophrenics is hard and exacting work for both patients and therapists. Every psychiatrist must find his own style in his psychotherapeutic approach to schizophrenic patients. About technical details such as seeing patients only in the office, walking around with them, seeing them for non-scheduled interviews I used to have strong feelings and meanings. Now I consider them unimportant, as long as the psychotherapist is aware of and alert to the dynamic significance of what he and the patient are doing and what is going on between them. What matters is that he conduct treatment on the basis of his correct appraisal and exploration of the psychodynamics of the patient's psychopathology and its manifestations in the doctor-patient relationship. Successful histories of treatment with the principles suggested, but conducted in various and sundry interpersonal and environmental settings, are living proof of the validity of my present corrected attitude.

Since the work with schizophrenics makes great and specific demands on the psychiatrist's skill and endurance, no discussion of psychotherapy with schizophrenics is satisfactory as long as the consideration of the specific personal problems of the therapist is omitted. In view of the extensive previous discussions of this topic by others and by myself, I shall only briefly enumerate the specific problems and requirements which ought to be met and solved by psychiatrists who wish to work with schizophrenics: they should be able to realize and constructively handle unexpected emotional responses, such as fears or anxieties, at times inevitably aroused in each of them by anxious, violent, overdependent, or lonely schizophrenic patients.

There is one special point I might add. Psychotherapists who share the fear of loneliness, which is the fate of men in our time, must watch out specifically lest their need to counteract their own loneliness make them incapable of enduring the inevitable loneliness and separation that their schizophrenic patients may bring home to them in their isolating cryptic communications. An undesirable urge to translate cryptic schizophrenic communications prematurely may interfere in such therapists with the more sound tendency to wait paitently and listen to the patient's own explanations of their communications.

In summary, the goal of dynamic psychotherapy with schizophrenics is the same as that of intensive psychotherapy with other mental disturbances, i.e., to help both ambulatory and hospitalized patients gain awareness of and curative insight into the history and unknown dynamic causes responsible for their disorder.

The same type of psychotherapeutic approach to schizophrenic patients during all phases and manifestations of the disorder and discussions of illness and treatment after their recovery are recommended for the purpose of helping such patients to integrate their recovery with their psychotic past.

An attempt is made to understand schizophrenic symptomatology and to approach it therapeutically as an expression of and a defense against anxiety. The hypothesis is offered that the universal human experience of tension between dependency, fear of relinquishing it, recoil from it, and interpersonal hostility becomes, in the case of schizophrenic persons, so highly magnified and so overwhelming that it leads to unbearable degrees of anxiety and then to discharge in symptom formation.

The multiple meaning of many schizophrenic symptoms, communications, and other manifestations has been discussed. The need for understanding and translating them descriptively for therapeutic reasons has been questioned, and the significance of non-verbal communications with schizophrenic patients has been stressed.

Psychodynamic investigation and clarification of schizophrenic anxiety and symptomatology in its conscious and unconscious manifestations in the patient-psychiatrist relationship is presented as being equally crucial for psychotherapy with schizophrenics as for other mental patients.

(16)

BASIC PROBLEMS IN THE PSYCHOTHERAPY

OF SCHIZOPHRENIA

Psychoanalytically oriented psychotherapy with schizophrenic patients is currently undertaken in many places. I use the term *psychoanalytically oriented psychotherapy* advisedly, and not simply *psychoanalysis*, because modifications of the classical psychoanalytic technique are necessary in the treatment of the psychotic person. I consider the differences between the psychotic and the neurotic—or the healthy, for that matter— to be much more differences of degree than of kind. Yet, since these differences have genetic and dynamic aspects, modifications in the therapeutic approach to the psychotic patient are warranted. The necessary therapeutic modifications will be described in the following discussion of psychoanalytically oriented dynamic psychotherapy as applied to the schizophrenic reaction.

The particular difficulties of intensive psychotherapy with the schizophrenic patient have two main sources. They stem from the dynamics of the schizophrenic patients and from the kinds of countertransference reactions which these patients arouse in their psychotherapists. These groups of difficulties are, of course, closely interrelated. I shall discuss first the specific difficulties stemming from the psychodynamics of schizophrenia.

As a result of narcissistic regression, the schizophrenic person is self-engulfed and withdrawn. He also shows another characteristic sign of early narcissistic developmental phases: he overrates his positive skills and his negative powers. One of the great problems of all schizophrenic patients is, of course, their difficulty in dealing with their hatred and their potential violence, both engendered by the severe warp inflicted upon them by significant environmental figures of their early infancy—in this culture, primarily by the mothering one. Because of the narcissistic, infantile elements in the schizophrenic's self-appraisal, he overrates the effectiveness of his hostility and of his actual and fantasied violence.

This paper was posthumously presented to the Second International Congress for Psychiatry, Zurich, Switzerland, September, 1957. It was read in English by Otto Allen Will, Jr., and in German by Margaret J. Rioch.

Reprinted from *Psychiatry: Journal of the Biology and Pathology of Interpersonal Relations*, Vol XXI, No. 1 (February, 1958). Copyright by The William Alanson White Psychiatric Foundation, Inc.

Therefore, he feels an exaggerated guilt about both. This, I believe, is doubly true because of his poor discrimination between thought and action and because of the magic elements inherent in his narcissistic approach to reality. His narcissistic conception of himself makes him judge his negative character trends as more unforgivable than they would appear to be to a less narcissistic person.

The average neurotic person represses his hatred and his assaultive fantasies for fear of retributive loss of love and of punishment on the part of the significant people in his past and present environments. The narcissistic schizophrenic person is his own most severe judge. He may be so afraid of his own hostile impulses that he flees into a self-imposed state of physical and emotional paralysis—catalepsy, stupor, muteness— in order to counteract outbursts of his own hostility.

Many writers have described instances in which stupor followed actual or imagined neglect by the psychotherapist. When the resentment so engendered could become openly expressed and the doctor-patient relationship clarified, stupor disappeared. In hospitals in which psychiatrists and nursing personnel are able to establish and maintain meaningful interpersonal contacts, few cases of catalepsy are to be observed.[1]

One of the prominent symptoms of the schizophrenic patient—his fear of closeness—can be understood as a response to the anxiety centering around his own hostility. I learned this first from a patient with whom I thought a satisfactorily close relationship had been established. Suddenly he became very angry in response to a remark of mine which he disliked. After quieting down, the patient, who was quite sophisticated, surprised me with the telling statement: "I warned you against becoming friendly with me. I told you that you'd find out that I am an unbearably hostile person. Do you think it pleases me to behave this way? I assure you that it does not. Why do you trespass, and make me let you see what I'd rather not see myself, much less share with you?"

Since then, similar feelings have been expressed by many more of my patients. For instance, as I reported in an early paper on the treatment of schizophrenia, a patient ran away from me "for fear of another rebuke," as he said. This happened at the height of what I experienced at the time as a warm and trustful relationship between us. As I understand it now, he told me only a half-truth. The full truth would have been: "I run for fear of another rebuke, which might arouse uncontrollable hostile impulses which are frightening to me."

For the schizophrenic, this disapproval of himself and this fear of his own feelings of hostility are reinforced and made more complex by their close interlinkage with his dependency needs. As do most people, the

1. This statement is based upon personal communications from Ross McLure Chapman, late superintendent of the Sheppard and Enoch Pratt Hospital, Towson, Maryland, and upon the experience of my colleagues and myself at Chestnut Lodge Sanitarium, Rockville, Maryland.

schizophrenic patient feels the need to be guided by one or more dependable persons. This need has been only partially fulfilled in his infancy and childhood, and he resents or hates those who were responsible for this neglect. The eternally unfulfilled hunger for guidance and love is at the same time counteracted by the wish for independence. He resents and hates himself even more for hating those whose guidance and love he craves.

The eternal conflict between hatred and dependency constitutes .a universal human experience. As such, it is not pathogenic or pathognomonic. Its close emotional connection with implacable self-hatred, however, is a characteristically schizophrenic experience and is not necessarily a part of the experience of the healthy person. Moreover, in the schizophrenic person the total experience is, because of the specific warp of his longing for guidance and dependence in early childhood, overwhelmingly fierce and intense, so that the quantitative difference between the general human conflict and the dependency-hostility problem of the schizophrenic becomes a qualitative one.

In offering the patient's fear of his own hostility as an explanation for his fear of closeness, I do not mean to overlook other interpretations of this phenomenon. In my own experience with schizophrenic patients, I have found Bak's interpretation true in many cases—namely, that the schizophrenic patient, with his weak ego organization, feels his ego boundaries threatened if he comes too close to another person.[2] I have also found confirmation of the older interpretation that the patient's fear of closeness indicates his inability to give and receive love because of lack of early learning experience in this area.

This threefold interpretation raises another problem in the treatment of the schizophrenic patient. Schizophrenic symptoms, as well as neurotic ones, have multiple meanings. They are determined and overdetermined, as are elements of the dream. The old psychoanalytic rule of delaying interpretation until the psychotherapist is sure that he has found the one and only meaning of a patient's communication is therefore incorrect in the treatment of schizophrenia. It may also be incorrect in the treatment of the neuroses.

How should this affect the psychotherapist's technique? I believe that he should be resigned to the multiplicity of meanings inherent in most schizophrenic communications and to the inevitable fact that he is lucky if he grasps *one* aspect of a cryptic schizophrenic verbalization. If he does, he may offer his interpretation whenever he thinks it will be helpful to the patient. But he should be mindful of the fact that either he or the patient will eventually find further interpretations of the communica-

2. [*Editor's note:* Dr. Fromm-Reichmann was apparently referring to the discussion by Dr. Robert C. Bak of her paper, "Modified Psychoanalytic Methods in Psychotherapy of Schizophrenia," at the American Psychoanalytic Association meeting in Detroit, Michigan, May, 1943.]

tion or symptom in question. One is just as little likely to understand the meaning of all facets of a patient's symptoms and communications as to understand all the elements of a dream.

An experience with a patient which I have previously reported[3] may be repeated here as an illustrative example from which I have learned a great deal:

A patient who had recovered from a severe schizophrenic illness of many years' duration held on to one symptom—namely, pulling the skin off her heels. Eventually, we discovered the meaning of this symptom—or so we thought at the time. By holding on to this reminder of her sick years while giving the appearance of health, the patient established an inner continuity between her life during her illness and her life after her recovery. Naturally, we were both pleased with this interpretation. Some weeks later a different interpretation came to the patient's mind. During the height of her illness, she had resented the seriousness with which I took another self-mutilating act— that of burning her skin. By continuing to mutilate herself while she seemed otherwise recovered, she wished to demonstrate how much the therapist had overrated the pathology of this and other self-mutilating acts. After a few more weeks, another memory appeared which shed further light on this symptom. Her mother's feet had been a source of ridicule in the family. Now the patient's feet were being used to ridicule the therapist. Each of these three interpretations appeared to be correct, and none of them excluded the validity of the others. The patient's symptom was determined and overdetermined, as are most schizophrenic manifestations.

This example also illustrates the difficulty of deciding when to make an interpretation. Often it may be desirable to give the patient the opportunity to find his own answers rather than to serve him these answers ready-made on a silver platter. Thus delaying therapeutic intervention, which is frequently indicated in psychotherapy with the neurotic person, is even more significant in work with the schizophrenic patient. It must be remembered that the schizophrenic patient suffers from a seriously warped self-appraisal because of the lack of acceptance which he originally experienced in his infancy and childhood and because of the self-rejection engendered by his hostility and possible violence. This schizophrenic low self-esteem can be favorably influenced if the psychotherapist, by being slow to speak, encourages the patient to make his own interpretation. I emphasize this because sometimes the schizophrenic patient may be well aware of the meaning of a communication which seems obscure to the doctor. Parenthetically, the reason for expressing himself cryptically may be his wish to test whether the psychiatrist is able to grasp the meaning of the communication and whether he will frankly admit it if he does not. The following experience with a paranoid schizophrenic patient may illustrate this point:

3. In the Academic Lecture given at the annual meeting of the American Psychiatric Association, Chicago, May, 1954; published as "The Psychotherapy of Schizophrenia," *Am. J. Psychiat.*, CXI (1954), 410–19.

The patient was seen four times weekly, through severely disturbed periods and clinically quiet periods. Over many months, he would repeatedly tell me that he thought I was afraid of losing my job. While I sensed that this was not what he actually thought, I did not grasp the hidden meaning of his statement for a long time. Finally it dawned on me, and I exclaimed: "Oh, you poor fool. You cannot accept the idea that I come to see you, rain or shine, four times a week, because I'd like to see you come to the point of living a happier and more creative life! I just come for fear of losing my job, don't I?" "Doctor, you have a remarkably intuitive perspicacity," was the response of this very hostile patient, who usually did not speak with such clarity. I pooh-poohed this would-be compliment by stating that, after all, it had taken me about a year to catch on. After this exchange the patient began to improve. I believe that the reason for his beginning progress was not the "perspicacity" of my interpretation but rather my perspicacity in catching on to the derogatory nuance of his "compliment."

These last two examples may also serve to illustrate another aspect of interpretive intervention. As a rule, the schizophrenic patient will not resent the psychiatrist's failure to understand or his offering of an incorrect interpretation, so long as he senses that the doctor uses interpretations in an attempt to be helpful rather than as a means of impressing the patient or other staff members—if he works in a hospital—with his therapeutic brilliance. There are, however, situations in which a doctor's ill-considered comment may hit a sore spot in a patient's past or present life. The patient may then not be able to endure the therapist's blunder without reacting to it. An inarticulate patient, who cannot blame the blundering therapist in so many words, may get even with him by acting out his resentment, as in the following situation:

The patient, before being admitted to Chestnut Lodge Sanitarium, had spent several years in other mental hospitals, where she had been known for her assaultiveness. I later learned that in another hospital there had been a sign on the door of her room warning the staff of her unpredictable acts of violence—a sign which she could not help seeing each time she left her room. Upon her admission to Chestnut Lodge, however, I went to meet her without first securing any information about her. I began the interview by asking her about her previous stays in other hospitals. Her immediate response was to strike me in the face with a cup from which she was drinking. In retrospect, I consider this act of violence wholly justified from the patient's point of view. She had every reason to interpret my question as an implied reference to her assaultiveness; it made me another of those people who labeled her a violent person.

Here, then, was one of the allegedly "unpredictable" schizophrenic reactions which made psychotherapy with these patients inadvisable in the eyes of previous generations of psychiatrists. But if the patient's action was unpredictable from *my* viewpoint, this was the result of my not having read her history before seeing her.

To continue the discussion about interpretive technique, it should be mentioned here that in recent years the interest of psychotherapists in interpreting the content of schizophrenic manifestations has lessened. This is part of the general change in therapeutic technique furthered by recent developments in the understanding of the psychodynamics of anxiety and of ego psychology. Having learned to understand the patient's symptomatology as an expression of his anxiety and, at the same time, of his defense against it, the therapist is able to scrutinize these symptom formations profitably in *statu nascendi* as they recur and as they are handled in the doctor-patient relationship. Hence it has become the central psychotherapeutic task in modern psychoanalysis to investigate the patient's anxieties and defense mechanisms as they reappear in his relationship with the therapist. This applies not only to therapy with the psychotic patient but to psychoanalytic therapy in general.

To return to the question of timing in making interpretations, the most important criterion is one's estimate of the patient's relationship to the doctor and his capacity to assimilate an interpretation. The patient's preoccupation with his inner experiences, which can be delusional, hallucinatory, or real, may render the doctor's interpretation ineffective. The degree of anxiety aroused in the patient by an interpretation must be considered in gauging the most useful time at which to offer the interpretive comment.

Now I will turn to the second group of difficulties occurring in the psychotherapy of schizophrenia—namely, the countertransference problems of the therapist. These are greater and of more consequence in working with the schizophrenic patient than they are in work with neurotic patients. Moreover, these problems deserve special attention in the case of schizophrenic patients for the following reason: In work with the psychotic, the psychiatrist is not only a participant-observer and a therapeutic agent, as he is in the treatment of the neurotic, but he is also to a greater degree a representative of, and a bridge to, a better reality, the experiencing of which has been previously denied to the patient.

What are the specific countertransference difficulties arising in psychotherapeutic work with the schizophrenic patient? First, I should like to consider the negative countertransference reactions. Severe anxiety states of the patient may be contagious to some psychotherapists. Schizophrenic loneliness, as evidenced by the mute, stuporous catatonic or the withdrawn hebephrenic, may arouse severe anxiety in other therapists. Some may become quite anxious in the face of marked schizophrenic dependency needs, and, for almost all psychotherapists, schizophrenic hatred and threatened or actual violence constitute a source of anxiety. Negative countertransference may also occur if the patient does not show marked signs of improvement after the therapist has invested much interest and effort.

Another difficulty for the therapist may be created by the great anxiety which drives many schizophrenics into a state of continuous vigilance, so that they become highly efficient "eavesdroppers," as it were, who may, without being told, know or sense character traits or emotional problems in their doctor which he would not voluntarily discuss with them. Sometimes these patients may even surprise the doctor by pointing out personality characteristics of which he himself is unaware. These "eavesdroppers" may evoke therapeutically undesirable responses of narcissistic hurt or self-consciousness in sensitive, pompous, or humorless psychiatrists.

Another difficulty may be created by the schizophrenic distrust of the doctor's verbal communications. The schizophrenic person has learned all too early in life that while words may serve the purpose of meaningful communication, they are also used to veil the truth, and hence he distrusts words. The psychotherapist's communications are not exempt from this distrust; therefore, he should be prepared to have his veracity tested and retested in the interchange with the schizophrenic patient. These testing maneuvers may arouse irritation, impatience, and self-righteous withdrawal in some therapists.

Another characteristic of many hospitalized patients is that they have lived in semiseclusion, or even isolation, for so long that they have ceased to make use of the conventional rationalizations and the polite forms of social interchange. Thus they may speak with brutal frankness, making devastatingly uncomplimentary remarks to the therapist. This proves troublesome if one is not able to respond simply, factually, and without conventional prejudice.

Psychotherapy with the schizophrenic patient is also a hotbed for positive countertransference difficulties. The great investment in time and the intense effort which the psychiatrist puts into the work make him more liable to become emotionally involved than he is with the neurotic patient. Such involvement may be a therapeutically undesirable overattachment, and the therapist may be seduced into sharing the patient's delusions, antipathies, and prejudices. He may even enter into a secret pact with the patient in his fight against institutions or significant figures in the environment.

What can the psychiatrist do to overcome his countertransference difficulties with the schizophrenic patient? Much will be gained if he succeeds in becoming aware of, and alert to, their occurrence. If he does, he may try to overcome them by self-analysis or by discussions with colleagues experienced in psychoanalytic psychotherapy with psychotic patients. If he is incapable of overcoming his anxiety, then it is best to discuss the matter frankly with the patient. This should be done, of course, not in the spirit of burdening the patient with the problems of the therapist, but with the single goal of clearing the therapeutic atmosphere. If the therapist is anxious because of the patient's potential assaultiveness, he may decide to see him in the presence of a third person or with the patient in a wet pack. He should then frankly admit to the patient that he does so for the purpose of counteracting his own anxiety, so that he will be free from this interference while listening.

From all this it follows that the psychiatrist who wishes to learn to do psychotherapy with schizophrenic patients should be a person who knows that "we are all more simply human than otherwise."[4] He should be endowed with a fine sensitivity to the overt and covert meanings of human communication and at the same time have a humble realization of its limitations.

In noting how the psychiatrist may diminish his anxieties in treating schizophrenic patients, one should not overlook the important fact that *mild* degrees of anxiety may be an asset in helping him to recognize the problems of the patient which arouse this anxiety. If the doctor's anxiety is more marked, however, patients frequently look upon its appearance as a measuring rod of their own liabilities, whereas the doctor's relative freedom from anxiety connotes to them encouragement and trust in their own potentialities. The following experience illustrates this statement:

For a long time, because of her assaultiveness, a patient was kept in a wet pack during our interviews. One day she asked me to unpack her. After a short period of hesitation, I complied with her request. Later, when I reviewed the significant events which had occurred during her illness, I asked what she thought had contributed to her recovery. She responded with: "Don't you know that without asking? Of course, my recovery began the day you unpacked me. You were not too afraid to do so. That meant to me that I was not so bad that one had to be afraid of me when I was out of a pack. Therefore, your unpacking me made a dent in my discouragement. If I was no longer considered dangerous, I could get well."

Incidentally, many psychiatrists, including myself, routinely review the history of the illness and the treatment with patients who are soon to be discharged. I consider this procedure to be a way of facilitating the integration of the patient's sick past with his current, more healthy state. It also adds to the therapist's own psychiatric education.

Much more has yet to be learned about psychotherapy with schizophrenic patients. In addition to continued psychiatric investigation, further sociological studies of significant environmental factors are needed. Analyses of recorded interviews and sound movies with the help of linguists and motion-picture technicians are desirable and are already under way at some places. Semantics and communication theory may also have something to offer. Growing clinical experience with the psychotherapy of psychotic people holds promise for the attainment of further progress in the understanding of human behavior and of that aspect of it known as schizophrenia.

4. Harry Stack Sullivan, *Conceptions of Modern Psychiatry* (New York: W. W. Norton & Co., 1953), p. 16.

IV

On Manic-Depressive Psychosis

(17)

INTENSIVE PSYCHOTHERAPY OF
MANIC-DEPRESSIVES

Prior to the 1920's, classical psychiatrists had assumed that intensive psychotherapy could not be used with disturbed psychotics because they believed their communications to be unintelligible and without meaning. Later, psychiatrists learned from Freud's teachings that, in principle, psychotic productions are meaningful and potentially understandable, just as is all human expression, whether openly expressed or veiled as in dreams, legends, and folklore. Concurrently, psychoanalysts believed and taught during these years that, because of the regressive self-engulfment ("narcissism") of disturbed psychotics, a workable doctor-patient relationship (transference) could not be established, thus making it impossible to do intensive psychotherapy with these people. They later revised this concept.

As a consequence of these changes in insight, pioneers in psychiatry over the last thirty years, chiefly those in this country, have been developing a method and technique of intensive dynamic psychotherapy with disturbed psychotics.[1]

During these informative years the majority of dynamic psychiatrists worked with that largest group of hospitalized psychotics in this country, the schizophrenics, and published their experiences in intensive psychotherapy with this group.

Subsequently, an attempt was made along the same therapeutic lines to approach the other large group of psychotics, the manic-depressives. Whereas it appeared to work with the schizophrenic, it was not generally successful with the manic-depressive.

For three years, 1944–47, the Washington School of Psychiatry ran a research seminar on manic-depressive states.[2] The purpose of the seminar

"Confinia Neurologica" ("Borderland of Neurology"), reprinted from *Grenzgebiete der Neurologie*, Separtum Vol. IX, Fasc. 3/4 (1949).

1. For literature on intensive psychoanalytic psychotherapy with schizophrenics see bibliographies in my papers, "Transference Problems in Schizophrenics," *Psychoanalyt. Quart.*, VIII (1939), 412–26, and "Problems of Psychotherapeutic Management in a Psychoanalytic Hospital," *ibid.*, XVI (1947), 325–56.

2. Participants whom I want to thank for their contributions were Drs. Grace Baker, Mabel Cohen, Robert Cohen, Robert Morse, David Rioch, Olive C. Smith, Alfred Stanton, Herbert Staveren, Sarah Tower, Benjamin Weininger, and Mary J. White.

was to investigate their psychopathology and to find ways of modifying and improving the psychotherapeutic technique. In the seminar of 30 three-hour sessions, nine cases were studied which had been or still were under treatment with one of the participants. The discussions were recorded, the total material is still being studied and evaluated[3] and is not as yet ready for publication.* At this point, however, we can offer some contributions to the specific developmental history and pathology of the interpersonal processes of the people who suffer from manic-depressive mood swings. They are suggestive of certain modifications in psychotherapeutic technique with manic-depressives as compared with the methods applied to schizophrenics.

The technique of any type of intensive psychotherapy, of course, must be adapted to the specificities of the personality and psychopathology of the patient being treated. What, then, are the specific criteria of the people whose picture of illness is characterized by manic-depressive mood swings in contrast to mental patients who use different symptoms as an expression of their disorder and as a means of warding off their anxiety?

As a result of our investigation I can offer the following suggestions: As a rule, people who suffer predominantly from manic-depressive mood swings seem to come from large families with multiple parental figures who share the responsibility for the guidance of the infant and child. There is no single significant adult who carries full responsibility for the child and to whom the child can relate himself meaningfully. Moreover, there is usually no one who is interested in the welfare of the child in its own right. The relatedness of the grownups to the child is determined by the purpose for which the child is needed and by the role into which it is cast according to the needs of the family. The needs of the families of these future manic-depressives are usually determined by the fact that these families belong to isolated minority groups to whom it seems very necessary to maintain given standards or to fight for survival. They accomplish these necessities by eagerly cultivating their part in a closely knit group unity.

Frequently the family saga holds the child responsible for this or that disaster which either the family as a whole or individual family members have previously undergone. Examples of this about which we learned in the research seminar were such instances as the death of a mother sometime after delivery or a parent getting sore feet while working as a traveling salesman to support the family after the arrival of the newcomer. The child accepts the responsibility cast upon him, no matter how irrational it may be to burden him with it. He feels guilty and hates those who make him feel guilty. But there is also rebellion, as a result of which he learns at an early age to falsify data in order to be able

3. By Drs. Robert Cohen, Sarah Tower, and the writer.
* [For the report on these nine cases, plus three others, see Paper 18, which follows.—ED.]

to shift the blame from himself to others, in an attempt to justify himself.

As a result of lack of personal guidance, the future manic-depressive, as a rule, grows up with an amazing lack of information about the important items of living, among them sex information.

This type of background is not one which makes it possible for a child to learn to relate himself meaningfully to another person, to gain experience in looking introspectively at interpersonal processes, or to gather and report correct, meaningful data.

The schizophrenic is able to do this, although he too, as we know, has great interpersonal difficulties in infancy and childhood. He may have suffered serious warp and damaging frustration from a hostile mother. But, hostile as the schizophrenic mother may be, she is, as a rule, closely related to the child, so that even hostile integration builds a significant interrelatedness and the child is important to her in his own right. The future schizophrenic is not lacking in early interpersonal experience. As a young child, he tries to evaluate and assimilate it and to protect himself against its damaging effects by introspection. Also there are usually introspectively gifted adults in his family, and the family is more concerned with the personal role of its members and less with the role of the group as a whole than is the family of the future manic-depressive.

That the manic-depressive has been subjected to multiple guidance in infancy and childhood and usually by non-introspectively interested grownups, that there is not one significant person responsibly related to the child, and that the child is not really important to anyone in its own right create a great and specifically colored insecurity for him. The manic-depressive considers himself ineffective, he feels defenseless, and if he tries to defend himself, he considers his self-defense ineffective also. He does not cease to look for a significant person to whom he can be important, and he clings to him when he believes that he has found someone. In later years, when a patient, the relationship to his therapist will be characterized by this clinging type of dependence. This may perhaps constitute one of the reasons for the disinclination of many dynamic psychiatrists to become the psychotherapist of a patient suffering from manic-depressive mood swings.

The manic-depressive's need for the glorification of his family, or at least for certain figures of his ancestry, seems to be related to his insecurity. "If I am no good, I may at least bask in the glory of my ancestors or try to convince the listener of their grandeur." This attitude constitutes another therapeutically important difference between a patient suffering from manic-depressive mood swings and the classical schizophrenic. The schizophrenic is in a state of revolt. He is a skeptic in regard to traditional morals, social conventionalities, and family customs. To him these are all problems. The manic-depressive relies upon his ancestry, which he considers superior to those who do not belong, be they select or minority. As a matter of fact, the family members are the only ones toward whom the manic-depressive appears to feel a certain amount of real intenseness of emotion. Their conventional values are his.

Schizophrenics can be treated successfully only if the therapist respects their need for a certain degree of isolation from, skepticism about, and independence of conventional values. Manic-depressives can be treated successfully only if the therapist is able to help them break through their clinging dependence upon the family and its substitutes and to revaluate the family conventions.

A child who is not important to anyone, whose life in many ways is not his own, and who carries the burden of an alleged responsibility for unhappy events in the family group inevitably develops, as we have previously mentioned, intense feelings of hatred. Since there is not one specific significant person in the life of the future manic-depressive patient to whom he can relate these feelings of hatred, his hate and hostility appear to be diffuse and anonymous as compared with the schizophrenic's hostility, which is directed toward specific people of the past or against their present substitutes. In addition, manic-depressives appear to be more interested, more clever, and more successful than schizophrenics in actually finding the vulnerable spots of those people whom they happen to make the target of their hostility.

Further investigation of the specific coloring of the manic-depressive's feelings and expressions of hostility in contrast to the feelings and expressions of schizophrenic hatred may bring one more answer to the present unresolved question that we have previously mentioned. That is, why is it that most dynamic psychiatrists, who are greatly interested in psychotherapeutic work with disturbed schizophrenics, are very reluctant to undertake psychotherapy with manic-depressives?

As a result of their lack of any close interpersonal relatedness, the reports of manic-depressive patients are peculiarly stereotyped, diagrammatic, and limited. There is a lack of subtlety, alertness for implications and refinement, and a tendency toward indiscriminate oversimplification in their reports. They profess little interest in refined insight into their interpersonal experiences with people of their previous or present life. The contents of the diagrammatic reports and the scarce data given during manic episodes are stereotypically identical with those which these patients give while depressed. It may be of interest to note that the data given by their introspectively uninterested relatives show, as a rule, the same peculiar characteristics. In view of their lack of ability to report pertinent data, to develop subtle introspective insight, along with their lack of experience in relating themselves to another person and in looking introspectively at interpersonal experiences, it may be more discerning not to see these people for daily psychotherapeutic interviews but to see them, as a rule, not more than two or three times a week. One of the participants of the seminar reported marked improvement in the course of treatment and in a patient's state of health after following this schedule with a patient who had previously been seen in daily interviews.

Although stereotyped, diagrammatic, and limited, the information these people are able to give is of a peculiar frankness and intenseness. This is equally as true for their symptomatological complaints as for those about personality difficulties. Frequently, they convey the impression that interpersonal experiences about which they are able to report have been very dramatic and vehement, if not characterized by actual violence. The close study of the nine cases under scrutiny in our group research project led us to the conclusion that this intensity and the reports of violence were due to the manic-depressive's lack of complexity and subtlety. We learned that they are not due to an actual talent for increased aliveness or freedom in expression.

In some cases, reports on the same subject or event were colored and changed in accordance with the various and sundry roles in which these patients experienced themselves as they talked about themselves and the person whose part they played at that particular time. This tendency to be identified with a role which the patient feels called upon to play may lead to certain changes and distortions of their otherwise monotonous, repetitive reports.

Other variations spring from the manic-depressive's need to gear his reports to the known or assumed attitude of the listening physician, to whom he clings in great dependence. If he avoids the tendency to color the contents for the benefit of the listener, he will at least gear the evaluation and interpretation of his data to the actual or assumed attitude of the psychotherapist. It appears that this will be done partly to impress the therapist and partly in an attempt to manipulate him.

More often than not, this appraisal of the psychiatrist's personality and his attitudes will be erroneous. The manic-depressive seemingly has the ability to become acquainted immediately with everyone with whom he comes in contact. As a result, he may, for example, know the name, the pet name, the age and social background, as well as bits of the history of every patient on the ward, literally within a few minutes after admission to the ward. Yet this uncanny ability to establish quick, superficial contacts is not accompanied with a real interest in the other person. It appears to be the manic-depressive's way of coping with and reassuring himself in a fight against his insecurity and sense of rejection.

In concluding this preliminary report, I wish to explain my reason for having referred to these people as patients suffering from manic-depressive mood swings rather than simply speaking of them as manic-depressives. Our investigation led us to question the justification of Kraepelin's classification of the manic-depressive disorder as a specific clinical entity of its own. Further studies of the case histories which formed the basis of our research, of more patients suffering from manic-depressive mood swings, and of treatment histories available in the literature should point up whether or not these mood swings may constitute a syndrome which may occur in connection with, or on the basis of, other mental disorders, especially schizophrenia, or whether there is actually a clinical and nosological entity of manic-depressive disorders.

The developmental data and personality trends mentioned in this report could be equally responsible for a nosological entity of manic-depressive disorders as they could be characteristic of the rise of manic-depressive reactions in people basically suffering from other kinds of mental disorder.

I feel that one more concluding remark is called for, to explain the reason for my repeatedly comparing manic-depressive people with classical schizophrenics. The impression could be created that I consider the schizophrenias to be the measuring rod of all personality disorders. I would not like to give such an erroneous impression. The schizophrenias have been used as a frame of reference because there is a great body of psychotherapeutic experience with schizophrenics and very little experience with research in dynamic psychotherapy of manic-depressives.

This paper is a preliminary report on the proceedings of a research seminar of the Washington School of Psychiatry on the psychopathology and therapy of manic-depressive states.

The difference between schizophrenics as we know them and people who suffer predominantly from manic-depressive mood swings is investigated in regard to their developmental histories, dynamics, present personalities, and psychotherapeutic prospects. It is recommended that the methods of psychoanalytic psychotherapy which have been developed during the last twenty years in psychiatric work with schizophrenics be modified according to the specific requirements and personalities of people who suffer from manic-depressive mood swings.

(18)

AN INTENSIVE STUDY OF TWELVE CASES OF
MANIC-DEPRESSIVE PSYCHOSIS

The purpose of this study is to examine the manic-depressive character by means of the intensive psychoanalytic psychotherapy of a number of patients. We feel this to be potentially useful, since the newer understanding of interpersonal processes and of problems of anxiety has not hitherto been brought to bear on this group of patients. The older psychoanalytic studies of the psychopathology of the manic-depressive have largely described the intrapsychic state of the patient and left unexplained the question of how the particular pattern of maladjustive behavior has arisen. Thus, to use a simple example, the manic-depressive is said to have an oral character. However, the question of how or why he developed an oral character is left unconsidered, except that such factors as a constitutional overintensity of oral drives or overindulgence or frustration during the oral phase are mentioned. Our purpose is to delineate as far as possible the experiences with significant people which made it necessary for the prospective manic-depressive to develop the particular patterns of interaction which comprise his character and his illness. To this end, neither constitutional factors nor single traumata are stressed in this report, although we do not deny their significance. Rather, we have directed our attention to the interpersonal environment from birth on, assuming that it has interacted with the constitutional endowment in such a way as to eventuate in the development of a manic-depressive character in the child. In other words, the personality of the parents, the quality of their handling of the child, and the quality of the child's response to this handling have played an important part in the development of a characteristic pattern of relating to others and reacting to anxiety-arousing situations which we consider typical of the manic-depressive character.

Such a study has many implications for the improvement of the therapeutic approach to the patient. We follow the basic premise of psychoanalytic theory—that in the transference relationship with the therapist the patient will repeat the patterns of behavior which he has developed

Written with Mabel Blake Cohen, Grace Baker, Robert A. Cohen, and Edith V. Weigert.
Reprinted from *Psychiatry: Journal of the Biology and Pathology of Interpersonal Relations*, Vol. XVII, No. 2 (May, 1954). Copyright by The William Alanson White Psychiatric Foundation, Inc.

with significant figures earlier in his life. By studying the transference, we can make inferences about earlier experiences; conversely, by understanding the patient historically, we can make inferences about the transference relationship. As our grasp of the patient's part of the pattern of interaction with his therapist improves, we can gain some concept of what goals of satisfaction he is pursuing, as well as what sort of anxieties he is striving to cope with. We may then intervene through our part in the interaction to assist him more successfully to achieve his goals of satisfaction and to resolve some of the conflicts which are at the source of his anxiety.

In this research project, a total of twelve cases was studied. All were treated by intensive psychoanalytic psychotherapy for periods ranging from one to five years. Nine of the cases were presented and discussed in the original research seminar from 1944 to 1947. During 1952 and 1953, the present research group studied three additional cases in great detail; the members of the group met in three-hour sessions twice monthly during that period. All twelve of the cases are referred to in brief throughout the report, and extracts are used from the last three cases (namely, Miss G, Mr. R, and Mr. H) to illustrate various points.

SURVEY OF THE LITERATURE

At the end of the last century, Kraepelin[1] attempted to classify the psychiatric syndromes, including the manic-depressive or circular psychosis, as nosological entities. While his classification, in general, brought some order into the existing confusion, he was unable to establish a pathological substratum or a specific etiological factor for either dementia praecox or the manic-depressive psychosis, and this situation still exists. Nevertheless, typical cases of manic-depressive psychosis, as Kraepelin first described it, do exist as well as a great number of atypical cases.

Manic or depressive syndromes have been found in exogenous psychoses, general paresis, brain injuries, and involutional and epileptic illnesses, as well as in hysteric and obsessional neuroses. It is particularly difficult to make a differentiation between schizophrenia and manic-depressive psychosis, and this has frequently become a controversial issue between different psychiatric schools. Lewis and Hubbard and P. Hoch and Rachlin[2] have all noted that a certain number of patients originally diagnosed as manic-depressives have later had to be reclassified as schizophrenics. More infrequent is a reversal of the diagnosis of schizophrenia into that of manic-depressive psychosis.

The apparent lack of specificity of etiological factors in manic-de-

---

1. E. Kraepelin, *Psychiatrie* (7th ed.; Leipzig: Barth, 1904).

2. N. D. C. Lewis and L. D. Hubbard, "The Mechanisms and Prognostic Aspects of the Manic-depressive–Schizophrenic Combinations," *Proc. A. Res. Nerv. & Ment. Dis.*, XI (1931), 539–608; P. Hoch and H. L. Rachlin, "An Evaluation of Manic-depressive Psychosis in the Light of Follow-Up Studies," *Am. J. Psychiat.*, XCVII (1941), 831–43.

pressive psychosis stimulated Bellak[3] to propose a "multiple factor psychosomatic theory of manic-depressive psychosis"; he felt that anatomical, endocrine, genetic, infectious, neurophysiological, and psychological *PHYSICAL* factors might contribute to the provocation of manic and depressive syndromes. Sullivan[4] has also subscribed to this general approach to manic-depressive psychosis, stressing the importance of physical factors; this is particularly interesting because he has stressed dynamic psychogenic factors in the schizophrenic. The importance of genetic factors in the determination of the ego strength[5] of the manic-depressive has been rather generally recognized and studied. For example, studies have been made of the high incidence of manic-depressive illness in the same family, which cannot be explained entirely in terms of environmental influences;[6] other studies have been made to validate E. Kretschmer's[7] thesis of the relation between what he terms the "pyknic" body shape and the manic-depressive type; and there has been some research done on identical twins who have manic-depressive psychoses.

In our study we have been particularly interested in pursuing the part that psychodynamic factors play in bringing about the manic-depressive illness. But we agree with Rado[8] that the multiplicity of etiological factors calls for the close collaboration of the pathologist, the neurophysiologist, the endocrinologist, the geneticist, the psychiatrist, and the psychoanalyst. In the long run, better teamwork by all these specialists may improve the method of therapy, which at present varies from custodial care with sedation to prolonged narcosis,[9] different forms of shock therapy, lobotomy, and occasionally various forms of psychotherapy. The prevailing ignorance about the etiology of manic-depressive psychosis is

3. L. Bellak, *Manic-depressive Psychosis and Allied Conditions* (New York: Grune & Stratton, 1952).

4. Harry Stack Sullivan, unpublished lectures given at Chestnut Lodge, Rockville, Maryland, in 1944; see also his *Conceptions of Modern Psychiatry* (Washington D.C.: William Alanson White Psychiatric Foundation, 1947), p. 51.

5. Bellak has pointed out that the quality of an illness depends on the quantity of the integrating forces (ego strength) in relation to the disintegrating forces from within and without (*op. cit.*). In addition, as Freud has noted, "we have no reason to dispute the existence and importance of primal, congenital ego variations" (see "Analysis Terminable and Interminable" in *Collected Papers*, V [London: Hogarth Press, 1925], 316–57).

6. There has accumulated a considerable body of evidence suggesting that constitutional factors may play a larger role in the manic-depressive than in the schizophrenic, such as Kallman's studies on familial incidence. See, for instance, F. J. Kallman, "The Genetic Theory of Personality," *Am. J. Psychiat.*, CIII (1946), 309–22.

7. E. Kretschmer, "Heredity and Constitution in Aetiology of Psychic Disorders," *Brit. M. J.*, II (1937), 403–6.

8. S. Rado, "Recent Advances of Psychoanalytic Therapy," *Proc. A. Res. Nerv. & Ment. Dis.*, XXXI (1953), 42–57; "Psychosomatics of Depression from the Etiologic Point of View," *Psychosom. Med.*, XIII (1951), 51–55.

9. J. Klaesi, "Über die therapeutische Anwendung der 'Dauernarkose' mittels Somnifen bei Schizophrenen," *Ztschr. ges. Psychiat. u. Neurol.*, LXXIV (1922), 557.

reflected in the haphazard application of shock therapy and lobotomy, the effects of which still remain in the realm of speculation. There are many speculative elements in the psychotherapeutic approach, too, as evidenced in this study. But psychotherapeutic experimentation abides, or tries to abide, by the medical standard of "nihil nocere."

Psychoanalytic Research

Abraham, in 1911,[10] was the first systematically to apply the psycho-analytic method to the treatment of the circular psychoses. He concluded that manic and depressive phases are dominated by the same complexes, the depressive being defeated by them, the manic ignoring and denying them. Some of his ideas on depression might be summarized as follows: the regression to the oral level of libido development brings out the characterological features of impatience and envy, increased egocentricity, and intense ambivalence; the capacity to love is paralyzed by hate, and this inability to love leads to feelings of impoverishment; and the depressive stupor represents a form of dying. Abraham thought that the indecision of ambivalence is close to the doubts of the compulsive neurotic and that, in the free interval, the manic-depressive is an obsessional neurotic. He recommended psychoanalysis in the free interval, since, in the acute phases of the psychosis, it is very difficult to establish rapport.

In 1921, Dooley continued Abraham's experiment in this country by studying, psychoanalytically, five manic-depressive patients in St. Eliza-beths Hospital.[11] Like Abraham, she found considerable resistance in her patients' extroverted egocentricity, for which she accepted White's concept of "flight into reality."[12] According to White, this tendency toward extroversion of libido makes the prognosis of manic-depressive psychosis more favorable, in terms of spontaneous recovery, than that of schizo-phrenia. He felt that, because of the dominance of his egocentric wishes, the manic-depressive patient can make "use of every object in range of his senses." But Dooley found that the resistances of the manic-depressive against analysis are even stronger than those of schizophrenics. Dooley suggested that the manic attack is a defense against the realization of failure. The patient cannot look at himself in the mirror of psychoanaly-sis; he cannot hear the truth. "Patients who manifest frequent manic attacks are likely to be headstrong, self-sufficient, know-it-all types of person, who will get the upper hand of the analyst. . . . The analyst is

10. K. Abraham, *Selected Papers on Psychoanalysis* (New York: Basic Books, 1953) ; see the following articles: "Notes on the Psycho-analytical Investigation and Treatment of Manic-depressive Insanity and Allied Conditions" (1911), "The Influence of Oral Erotism on Character-Formation" (1924), "A Short Study of the Development of the Libido" (1924).

11. L. Dooley, "A Psychoanalytic Study of Manic-depressive Psychosis," *Psychoanalyt. Rev.*, VIII (1921), 37–72, 144–67.

12. W. A. White, "Personality, Psychogenesis, and Psychoses," *J. Nerv. & Ment. Dis.*, LXXXIII (1936), 645–60.

really only an appendage to a greatly inflated ego." Since the life-conditions of the manic-depressive are often no more unsatisfactory than those of many a normal person, there must be a lack of integration which keeps the manic-depressive from achieving the sublimations of which he is potentially capable. Dooley came to the conclusion that the manic and depressive episodes are due to deep regressions to the sadomasochistic level of the child. "Autoerotic wishes were satisfied by hypochondriacal complaints." In a much later paper on "The Relation of Humor to Masochism,"[13] Dooley mentioned a manic-depressive patient who began to develop humor in the analysis as she became aware that she "could neither hurt me, nor wrangle me into loving her." Dooley considered this kind of insightful humor to be a milestone in the healing process of the excessive mood swings; it indicates that the superego is losing its tragically condemning cruelty and is permitting laughter at the overweening, pestering child-ego.

In 1916–17, Freud compared melancholia to normal mourning[14] as follows: The loss of a love object elicits the labor of mourning, which is a struggle between libido attachment and detachment—love and hate. In normal mourning this struggle of ambivalence under the pressure of confrontation with reality leads to gradual rechannelization of the libido toward new objects. In the case of melancholia, the loss, which may take the form of separation, disappointment, or frustration, remains unconscious, and the reorientation exacted by reality elicits strong resistances, since the narcissistic character of the disturbed relation does not permit detachment. In this way, an intensified identification with the frustrating love object in the unconscious results. "The shadow of the object has fallen on the Ego." The whole struggle of ambivalence is internalized in a battle with the conscience. The exaggerated self-accusations are reproaches against the internalized object of love and hate; the self-torture is a form of revenge and, simultaneously, an attempt at reconciliation with the internalized partner. The narcissistic, ambivalent character of the relation to the lost love object either is the result of transitory regression or is constitutionally conditioned. Thus the loss of self-esteem and the intense self-hate in the melancholic become understandable.

In 1921, Freud added some statements about mania to his earlier interpretation of depression.[15] He suggested that the mood swings of normal and neurotic persons are caused by the tensions between ego and ego ideal. These mood swings are excessive in the case of manic-depressive

13. L. Dooley, "The Relation of Humor to Masochism," *Psychoanalyt. Rev.*, XXVIII (1941), 37–47.

14. S. Freud, "Mourning and Melancholia," in *Collected Papers*, IV, 152–70; Kretschmer, *op. cit.*

15. S. Freud, *Group Psychology and the Analysis of the Ego* (London: Hogarth Press, 1922).

illness because, after the frustrating or lost object has been re-established by identification in the ego, it is then tormented by the cruel severity of the ego ideal, against which, in turn, the ego rebels. According to Freud, the manic phase represents a triumphant reunion between ego and ego ideal, in the sense of expansive self-inflation but not in the sense of a stabilized equilibrium.

Abraham, in 1924,[16] pursued his interest in biological development and tried to find specific fixation points for mental illnesses in different phases of libido development. He interpreted character traits as being highly symbolized derivatives of pregenital instinctual impulses that were, in the case of the mentally ill person, hampered in their normal development by frustration or overindulgence. Because of Abraham's influence, psychoanalytic research in ego development has for a long time been dependent on highly schematized concepts of libido development and its symbolizations. Abraham located the fixation to which the manic-depressive periodically regresses as being at the end of the second biting oral phase and the beginning of the first expelling anal phase. This assumption could explain the frequent preoccupation of the manic-depressive with cannibalistic fantasies as well as his fantasies of incorporation in the form of coprophagia; his character trends of impatience, envy, and exploitiveness, dominating possessiveness, and exaggerated optimism or pessimism; his intense ambivalence; and his explosive riddance reactions. The object loss that precedes the onset of a depression is mostly not conscious but, according to Abraham, repeats a primal depression, a frustration at the time of transition from the oral to the anal phase, when the child was disappointed in the mother. The oral dependence may be constitutionally overemphasized in the manic-depressive, Abraham suggested.

In 1927 Rado[17] went a step further in the theory of identification. Freud's and Abraham's theories imply an incorporation of the lost or frustrating object, in both the tormented ego and the punishing ego ideal or superego. This double incorporation, Rado postulated, corresponds to an ambivalent splitting into a "good"—that is, gratifying—object, and a "bad" or frustrating object; at an early stage of development, when the synthetic function of the ego is still weak, both of these are the mother. The good parent by whom the child wants to be loved is incorporated in the superego, endowed with the privilege of punishing the bad parent, who is incorporated in the ego. This bad object in the ego may be punished to the point of total destruction (suicide). But the ultimate goal of

16. K. Abraham, "A Short Study of the Development of the Libido," and *Selected Papers on Psychoanalysis.*

17. S. Rado, "Das Problem der Melancholie," *Internat. Ztschr. Psychoanal.,* XIII (1927), 439-55.

this raging orgy of self-torture is expiation, reconciliation, synthesis.[18] Rado described the manic phase as an unstable reconciliation reached on the basis of denial of guilt. The automatized cycle of guilt, expiation, and reconciliation is patterned after the sequence of infantile oral experience: rage, hunger, drinking. The drinking, which resembles the state of re-union or reconciliation, culminates in a satiated pleasure experience, which Rado called the "alimentary orgasm." In a paper published in 1933,[19] Rado described the way in which the drug addict, in the artifi-cially produced intoxication, expresses the same yearning for reconcilia-tion and blissful reunion with the gratifying mother.

In the same year, 1933, Deutsch[20] illustrated the theory of manic-de-pressive psychoses, as developed up to that time, by several abbreviated case presentations. She agreed with Rado that the melancholic phase is sometimes introduced by a phase of rebellion of the ego against the cruel superego. After the ego succumbs to the superego's punishment with the unconscious intention of bribing the superego and of gaining forgiveness by such submission, the ego may rescue itself from the dangerous intro-jection by projecting the threatening enemy onto the outside world; ag-gression can then be directed against the projected superego, which has become an external persecutor. Another form of escape from the melan-cholic predicament is the denial of any narcissistic deprivation—be it the loss of mother's breast or the absence of a penis—in a glorious triumph of manic or hypomanic excitement. Deutsch regarded mania and para-noia as alternative defenses against the intense danger to survival of an ego oppressed by melancholia. In the hypomanic patient, the underlying depression has to be lifted into consciousness if therapy is to be success-ful. In 1938, Jacob[21] made a similar observation on a periodically manic patient.

Gero illustrated "The Construction of Depression" (1936)[22] by two case presentations. One was of a woman patient with an obsessional char-acter structure built up as a defense against the painful ambivalence in her family relations. Only after these character defenses yielded to analy-sis could this patient see avenues of realistic satisfactions and therewith surmount her depressions. The other case was a male patient who had

18. Alexander has elaborated on this idea in his discussion of the bribing of the superego by self-punishment (see F. Alexander, *Psychoanalysis of the Total Personality* [New York: Nervous and Mental Disease Pub. Co., 1935]).

19. S. Rado, "The Psychoanalysis of Pharmacothymia (Drug Addiction)," *Psychiat. Quart.*, II (1933), 1–23.

20. H. Deutsch, "Zur Psychologie der manisch-depressiven Zustände, insbesondere der chronischen Hypomanie," *Internat. Ztschr. Psychoanal.*, Vol. XIX (1933).

21. Gertrud Jacob, "Notes on a Manic-depressive," lecture given before the Washington-Baltimore Psychoanalytic Society, 1938.

22. G. Gero, "The Construction of Depression," *Internat. J. Psychoanal.*, XVII (1936), 423–61.

identified with an overambitious, overexacting father and a rejecting mother and had repressed the rage against both frustrating parents by withdrawal into an apathetic regression, punishing therewith the internalized objects of his hate and rage. After his father's death, he himself became a sick old man. The liberation of rage and hate in the transference freed the genital aggressiveness from the odium and guilt of sadomasochistic distortions. In both cases the analyst succeeded in winning the patients back from a hopeless negativism to a hopeful confirmation of life.

Jacobson described in 1943[23] a severely depressed patient, with strong suicidal urges, intense experiences of depersonalization, and "Weltuntergang" fantasies—a case on the border line between manic-depressive psychosis and schizophrenia. Jacobson was able to uncover a primal depression in this patient at the age of three and a half, when the birth of a brother coincided with a disruption of the parental marital relation. Turning from mother to father and back to mother left the patient empty. Threatened by complete loss of objects, she maintained a masochistic dependence on her mother. As substitutes for the disappointing parents, she built up fantasies of idealized, perfect parents who endowed her superego with cruel severity, so that she lived in constant danger of complete desertion and in horror of punishment.

Weiss in 1944[24] took a slightly different approach. He postulated that melancholic episodes are a reaction to the realization of antisocial, dishonest, or egotistical aspects of the personality. The inability of the patient to reach an integration between his antisocial wishes and his moral standards causes a tension in his "ego feeling," so that the patient hates himself. The exaggerated guilt reaction maintains the split between persecuting and persecuted "introjects." Identifications with hated objects may make the task of ego integration very difficult indeed. In the manic phase, the passive objectionable introject is projected, and the ego assumes the active role of the persecuting superego against objects of condemnation in the outside world. Weiss points out that in paranoia the ego does not cling strongly to the superego, and the *persecuting* introject, the superego, is projected; in mania, however, the *persecuted* introject is projected. The paranoic, by this projection, succeeds in preserving his narcissistic position, while the melancholic fails; the result of his inner persecution may be self-destruction.

To turn to more recent material, Bibring[25] has summed up all the features that different kinds of depression have in common, including not only the depressions of circular psychosis but also the reactive depressions and depressions in the course of physical illness and in states of fatigue or

23. Edith Jacobson, "Depression, the Oedipus Complex in the Development of Depressive Mechanisms," *Psychiat. Quart.*, XII (1943), 541-60.

24. E. Weiss, "Clinical Aspects of Depression," *Psychoanalyt. Quart.*, XIII (1944), 445-61.

25. E. Bibring, "Das Problem der Depression," *Psyche* (Stuttgart), V (1952), 81-101.

exhaustion. A common factor is the lowering of self-esteem, the loss of self-love, which, in melancholia, is intensified into self-hate. Bibring compares depression with states of depersonalization and boredom. In the mildly depressed person, there is not so much hate turned against the self as there is an exhaustion of the narcissistic supply of self-love. The mildly depressed person is less inclined to kill himself than to let himself die.

Frank in a lecture on "The Defensive Aspects of Depression"[26] follows a line of thought similar to Bibring's. He compares unspecific depressions to the hibernation of animals—a defensive response to frustrating life-conditions. Depression as a defense tunes down the desires and expectations to a lower key, so that the shock of unavoidable frustration is reduced to a minimum.

The manic aspect of the manic-depressive psychosis has, on the whole, elicited less attention on the part of psychoanalysts than has the depressed aspect, probably because the manic patient does not so frequently seek therapeutic help. B. Lewin, in a monograph on *The Psychoanalysis of Elation*,[27] regards elation as a defense of denial against depression. During the analytic process, Lewin suggests, normal mourning increases insight into the self and may terminate in a sense of heightened well-being, increased sexual potency, and capacity for work and sublimation. But elation and depression resist the testing of reality; they produce negative therapeutic reactions in the face of insight that cannot at the time be emotionally assimilated. The depressed and the elated ego are not trying to separate the true from the false, but the good from the bad; reality-testing is replaced by morality-testing. Lewin compares mania to sleep: in sleep the ego disappears; in mania the superego vanishes. Sleep stems from oral satisfaction—the infant drops asleep when he is satiated with nursing at the mother's breast. But the manic patient is a notoriously poor sleeper, and he is haunted by "the triad of oral wishes,"—to devour, to be devoured, and to sleep. The wish-fear to be devoured transforms the wish to sleep into a fear of dying. The yearning for the gratifying maternal breast —the wish to sleep—may be transmuted into a desire for union with the superego. In the artist this union is accomplished, as a result of the inspiration and the actualization of this inspiration in the creative process, which satisfies both the superego and the world of the artist's contemporaries.

In several papers on suicide,[28] Zilboorg emphasizes that suicide is frequent in manic-depressive psychoses. "A number of suicides occur when

26. R. Frank, "The Defensive Aspects of Depression," lecture given before the American Psychopathological Association, 1952.

27. New York: W. W. Norton & Co., 1950.

28. G. Zilboorg, "Differential Diagnostic Types of Suicide," *Arch. Neurol. & Psychiat.*, XXXV (1936), 270–91; "Suicide among Civilized and Primitive Races," *Am. J. Psychiat.*, XCII (1936), 1347–69; "Considerations on Suicide, with Particular Reference to That of the Young," *Am. J. Orthopsychiat.*, VII (1937), 15–31.

the depressed person appears to be convalescing and all but recovered from his depressed state." In pathologic depressions the patient is identified with a person toward whom his feelings have been highly ambivalent. Zilboorg says of such a patient: "He feels detached from reality and therefore experiences a sense of poverty of the Ego. The unconscious sadism originally directed against the object, reinforced by a sense of guilt, produces the singular phenomenon of the person becoming sadistic toward himself." Frequently, the identification with a close relative who died at the time when the patient went through the Oedipus conflict or puberty contributes to the suicidal tendency in later years. Zilboorg stresses the observation that suicide may occur in a variety of other psychopathologic conditions on the basis of different motivations, such as spite and fear.

Early Parent-Child Relationships

Since all authors who have studied depressive and manic syndromes point to a primal depression or serious disturbances in the early parent-child relation, we have been interested in learning what the child psychoanalysts have to say. Two of Spitz's[29] papers are interesting in this connection. Spitz defines anaclitic depression as the state of dullness, unresponsiveness, and arrest of emotional development that can be observed in a baby removed from his mother's care and left in a hospital, so that the baby's dependency relation with his mother is interrupted. In this state, Spitz observed that the baby showed tension, anxieties, excitement, increased autoerotic activities, and increased demandingness toward the environment. When the deprivation does not last more than three months, Spitz notes that the baby recovers, once his emotional needs are again met. When the deprivation lasts longer, however, irreversible changes take place, and permanent physical and psychological damage occurs; the adaptation breaks down; there is arrest of appetite and sleep, loss of weight, morbidity, decreased motility, and facial rigidity; excitement changes into depression; learning is arrested; and autoerotic activities disappear. Social responsiveness—demandingness toward the environment—is the last of the compensatory efforts to disappear, Spitz observes; indeed, the life of the baby who suffers from hospital marasmus is seriously endangered.

Melanie Klein's[30] contribution to the understanding of the psychoses is

29. R. Spitz, "Anaclitic Depression," in *The Psychoanalytic Study of the Child* (New York: International Universities Press, 1946), Vol. II; "Depression—a Psychological Disturbance of the General Adaptation Syndrome," lecture given before the American Psychopathological Association, 1952.

30. Melanie Klein, *Contributions to Psycho-analysis, 1921–1945* (London: Hogarth Press, 1950), esp. "A Contribution to the Psychogenesis of Manic-depressive States," pp. 282–310, and "Mourning and Its Relation to Manic-depressive States," pp. 311–38; *The Psychoanalysis of Children* (London: Hogarth Press, 1932).

based on her observaton of babies in the preverbal stage and by her empathic understanding of children, with whom she has worked therapeutically in the early verbal stages. In this paper we shall be concerned with examining only that part of her thinking which is contributory to an interpretation of manic-depressive psychosis. In approaching Klein's work, it is well to keep in mind that her theories place a great deal of emphasis on the theory of the death instinct. Although Freud in his last formulation of the instinct theory postulated the death instinct, many psychoanalysts have maintained a certain reserve in relation to this concept. Freud himself, with a certain caution, has called the instinct theory "our mythology," and the instincts "mythical beings, superb in their indefiniteness."[31]

In contrast to Freud, Klein assumes that the infant from birth on is never merely autoerotically or narcissistically oriented and that, from the start of the extrauterine existence, there are object relations of an introjective, projective type, although the ego boundaries are still very fluid. The ego is built up on early introjection, according to Klein; but, since the synthetic function of the ego is still weak, the infant is endangered by disruptive projections and disintegration, indicated by his readiness for the alarm reaction of anxiety. According to Klein, these early months of labile integration contain the fixation points to which the psychotic individual regresses under stress and strain. Constitutional weakness in the synthetic function of the ego permits such regression even under lesser degrees of stress. Klein calls these fixation points the "paranoid" and the "depressive position." She means by this not that the infant passes through the major psychoses but that the potentialities of psychotic disintegration are implied in the early ego weakness.

The paranoid position develops first, Klein says, as automatic defense against pain or displeasure in the form of projection. In the earliest phase, when the infant's behavior is centered around the oral zone and swallowing and spitting are his main life-preserving activities, he learns a reflexive discrimination between pleasure and displeasure. The pleasurable object is automatically incorporated, the unpleasurable spat out or eliminated. The infantile organism tends to maintain automatically a "purified pleasure ego" by splitting pleasure and pain; Sullivan[32] has referred to this phenomenon as "me" and "not-me," since pleasure is incorporated as me and displeasure ejected as not-me. The not-me—the strange, the unfamiliar, and the uncanny—elicits in the infant the response of dread even in the first weeks of life. Klein has defined the ejected not-me as "bad," the persecutor, and has called the infant's dread-reaction, "persecutory anxiety."

31. S. Freud, *New Introductory Lectures on Psycho-analysis* (New York: W. W. Norton & Co., 1933), p. 131.

32. H. S. Sullivan, *The Interpersonal Theory of Psychiatry* (New York: W. W. Norton & Co., 1953).

The depressive position which develops at about the time of weaning—around the first half-year of life—is the second fixation point in Klein's theory. It is at this time that the mother is first recognized as one person, whether she is at the moment gratifying or depriving, "good" or "bad." This marks the beginnings of recall and foresight in the baby. Even if the mother is absent at a given moment or does not feed or care for the child satisfactorily, there is no longer the desperate quality of "never again" or complete desertion; that is, there is some hope and trust in her return. This hope and trust are based, according to Klein, on the internalization of good experience, "internal good objects." But the beginning durability of the ego and its relation to the object are constantly endangered by the automatic splitting processes "good mother—bad mother" and "good me —bad me." Only the gratifying, good mother elicits good feelings of fulfilment, and the good internal object makes the gratified child feel good himself. But an excess of bad experience with a frustrating mother makes the child hateful, enraged, bad, and fills him with bad emotional content that he tries to get rid of by elimination or denial. The bad internal object threatens the good internal object with destruction. In this inner conflict, which characterizes the depressive position, Klein sees the first guilt feelings arise as predecessors of what is subsequently conscience or superego formation. Because of the synthetic function of the ego, the dependence on the mother as a whole person so needed for survival and the guilty anxiety prompt the child into repair actions, magically designed to transform the bad mother into a good mother, to protect the good inner object against the onslaught of the bad one. One is here reminded of the words of Orestes after he had murdered his mother: "Save me, ye Gods, and save your image in my soul."[33] The guilty anxiety uses the magic of self-punishment, excessive crying spells, and rage directed against the child's own body.

According to Klein, this depressive position is constantly in danger of being reversed into the earlier "paranoid position," in which the infant was dominated solely by the urge to rid himself of bad inner and outer objects by projection or by manic denial and usurpation of self-sufficient omnipotence. Thus the depressive position is still dominated by the all-or-none principle. The good mother on whom the child depends for survival is idealized into perfection without blemish; and the bad mother appears disproportionately dreadful because of the child's helpless dependency. Only gradually are these contrasts melted into the unity of one realistic mother. Warm consistency on the part of both parents supports this natural process of integration. But parental incompetence, overindulgence, or excessive deprivations, as well as the child's constitutional oversensitivity or intensity of drives, his physical illness, and external pressures—such as a new pregnancy or hostile envy on the part of older sib-

33. See Goethe's *Iphigenie auf Tauris*.

lings—might interfere with the secure harmony which guarantees the optimum in the child's integration with the family. Disrupting, disintegrating experiences are, according to Klein, accompanied by psychotic fears of fantastic proportions, since the lack of grasp on reality in the young child delivers him as a helpless victim to uncanny powers; this is reflected in his early nightmares and later in his fairy tales, his animal and other phobias.

According to Klein, paranoic and depressive anxieties in early childhood are closely related. The more primitive persecutory anxiety is centered solely around the preservation of the ego and the object remains a partial object, incorporated as far as it is "good" or gratifying; but the object is eliminated, projected, and therewith experienced as persecutor as far as it is frustrating or "bad." The later depressive anxiety is centered around the need to preserve the good object as a whole person, and it indicates a broadening of the child's horizon. The badness of his love object in this position spells to the child his own badness on the basis of introjection. The depressive anxiety is a guilty anxiety, coupled with the need to preserve the good object, with the tendency to make amends, to achieve magic repair. This tendency to repair, to make amends, stands in the service of the synthetic function of the ego. When separation anxieties can be surmounted, when repair succeeds, it contributes to a broadening integration of the child's ego and to a more realistic cementing of his labile object relations. Successful repair actions are the basis of sublimation—of all those creative activities by which the growing person maintains his own wholeness and his hopeful, trusting, integrative relations with his objects. One can say that, without the stimulus of depressive anxieties, the child would never outgrow his early egocentricity, his fearful withdrawal, and his tendencies toward hostile projections. But an excess of depressive anxieties without successful experience of repair produces a fixation to the depressive position. It is this position to which the adult regresses whenever frustrating life-experiences tax his integrative functions to such a degree that a creative conflict solution appears impossible. The manic reaction presents itself in this context as a pseudo-repair action, since a reconciliation with frustrating objects or goals is manipulated by the manic with the inadequate means of primitive defense—the splitting of good and bad, the fantastic idealization of the goal or object to be reached, and the hasty incorporation and contemptuous denial of the negative, frustrating aspect of the object or goal.

Many psychoanalysts have expressed doubts about Klein's observation that the child has Oedipus experiences in the first year of life. But there is much agreement with Klein's theory that there is no period of narcissistic self-sufficiency, that the infant is object-related from the start by introjection and projection, and that his claim for exclusive appropriation of his love object which guarantees his security in a world of unknown dangers makes him intensely anxious when he witnesses any intimacy between the parents that excludes him. Such intimacies jeopardize his equilibrium and elicit rage reactions, which, in turn, are intensely alarming to the child because of his anxious cannibalistic destructiveness. In such early stages of Oedipus conflict as Klein sees it, the destructive possessiveness and not the incestuous wishes give rise to guilty anxiety.

Although Klein's theories are partially deviant from psychoanalytic theory and may even sound fantastic to the psychiatrist who is reluctant to engage in any speculation on what is going on in the preverbal child, one cannot dismiss her empathic understanding of infantile emotions, impulses, and fantasies, which in the child's early verbal phase are expressed symbolically in his play. Her intuitive understanding is at least a working hypothesis for explaining the similarities between infantile and psychotic states of mind. The latter may seem enigmatic because of this very regression to early patterns of unsuccessful integration.

Rado,[34] too, sees depression as a process of miscarried repair in his more recent work on manic-depressive psychoses. The depressive phase, he says, has a hidden pattern of meaning, and the observer must penetrate into the "unconscious"—the "non-reporting" parts of the patient's experience. The depressive spell is a desperate cry for love, precipitated by loss of emotional or material security, an expiatory process of self-punishment, to reconcile and regain the image of the gratifying mother's breast. The intended repair miscarries, Rado believes, because the dominant motivation of repentance is complicated by strong resentment. The depressed person wants to force his object to love him. The love-hungry patient's coercive rage has oral, biting, and devouring features. Fasting—the earliest and most enduring form of expiation—springs from the fear of having destroyed mother forever. Rado thinks that coercive rage increases self-esteem and pride but that repentance makes the ego feel weak. Thus merciless rage, turned against the self, complicates repentance, since the absurdity of self-reproaches betrays the rage against the lost object. The patient is torn between coercive rage and submissive fear. If rage dominates, the patient has an agitated depression; if fear and guilt prevail, the patient experiences a retarded depression. These opposite tensions compete for discharge; and the phenomenon of "discharge-interference" leads to an interminable struggle. In therapy the physician may be inclined to treat the patient with overwhelming kindness in order to meet the patient's craving for affection. But when guilty fear and retroflexed rage are alarming in the sense of the danger of suicide, harsh treatment may provoke a relieving outburst of rage.

In general, Rado's work shows a commendable disinclination to engage in speculation. In addition, he strives to make psychoanalytic terminology understandable to scientists in related disciplines, and we agree that this

34. S. Rado, "Psychosomatics of Depression from the Etiologic Point of View."

kind of collaboration is needed if the goal of improved therapy is to be reached.

To summarize, the literature seems to show a wide divergence of opinion on the etiology of the manic-depressive psychosis. In surveying it, we have laid particular stress on the development of the psychoanalytic literature because it is this approach that represents the area of our interest. We have discussed at some length the work of Melanie Klein because it is her approach which has proved to be closest to our own thinking.

FAMILY BACKGROUND AND CHARACTER STRUCTURE

For all twelve patients studied, a consistent finding appeared in regard to the family's position in its social environment. Each family was set apart from the surrounding milieu by some factor which singled it out as "different." This factor varied widely. In many instances it was membership in a minority group such as the Jews, as in the case of Mr. H. In others it was economic; for example, one patient's family had lost its money and was in a deteriorating social position, and in Mr. R's case, the father's illness and alcoholism had put the family in poor economic circumstances and in an anomalous social position. In another case, the difference resulted from the mother's being hospitalized for schizophrenia. In every case the patient's family had felt the social difference keenly and had reacted to it with intense concern and with an effort, first, to improve its acceptability in the community by fitting in with "what the neighbors think" and, second, to improve its social prestige by raising the economic level of the family or by winning some position of honor or accomplishment. In both these patterns of striving for a better social position, the children of the family played important roles; they were expected to conform to a high standard of good behavior, the standard being based largely on the parents' concept of what the neighbors expected. Thus Mr. R's mother was greatly overconcerned that he not walk in front of company in the living room, and Mr. H's mother threatened him with severe punishment when he misbehaved while out on the street with her. One mother described her early attitudes toward her child as follows:

I was always an independently minded person, not very demonstrative; so therefore most affection I may have had for anyone wasn't exactly worn on my sleeve. Kay I always loved, and there was nothing I didn't try to get for her. My first thought, in most all my selfish material gains, was to get her things I had wanted or didn't have; to go places that I always longed to go to. Hasn't she ever told you of all the good times she has had? College proms, high-school parties, dances, rides, silly girl incidents? I can remember so many she has had. Those were the things I had worked for her to have, and believe me, I had to fight to get them. . . . If you could have just an inkling of the unhappiness I have had trying to give her the material things I thought she wanted, for she never showed any love to me, perhaps you would understand my part. I always tried to protect her from the hurts that I had. . . .

These attitudes on the part of the parents—chiefly the mother—inculcated in the child a strict and conventional concept of good behavior and also one which was derived from an impersonal authority—"they." The concept seemed to carry with it the connotation of parents whose own standards were but feebly held and poorly conceptualized but who would be very severe if the child offended "them."

In addition to the depersonalization of authority, the use of the child as an instrument for improving the family's social position again acted as a force devaluing the child as a person in his own right. Not "who you are" but "what you do" became important for parental approval. Getting good grades in school, winning the approval of teachers and other authorities, receiving medals of honor, winning competitions, and being spoken of as a credit to the parents were the values sought by the parents from the child. In a few cases the family's isolation seemed to stem from the fact that they were "too good" for the neighboring families, because they had more money or greater prestige. But here, too, the child's role was seen as being in the service of the family's reputation.

In a number of cases the child who was later to develop a manic-depressive psychosis was selected as the chief carrier of the burden of winning prestige for the family. This could be because the child was the brightest, the best looking, in some other way the most gifted, or because he was the oldest, the youngest, or the only son or only daughter.

The necessity for winning prestige was quite frequently inculcated most vigorously by the mother. She was usually the stronger and more determined parent, whereas the father was usually the weakling, the failure who was responsible for the family's poor fortunes. This was not invariably the case; thus one patient's mother had been hospitalized with schizophrenia from the patient's babyhood on. However, in the more typical cases, the mother was an intensely ambitious person, sometimes directly aggressive, at other times concealing her drive beneath a show of martyrdom. She tended to devalue the father and to blame his weakness, lack of ambition, or other fault for the family's ill fortune. The mother of the patient referred to as Kay wrote in the following terms:

About Kay's father, I'm afraid I can't tell you too much about him, because I was away a good deal, and didn't see too much of him. But as I remember him, I guess he was sort of a pathetic person, or at least I always had a feeling of pity. He had no real home; no immediate family; no decent jobs, at least in my opinion, and no real character.

This blaming of the father for the family's lack of position is, in all likelihood, due to the fact that in this culture the father is customarily the carrier of prestige, as well as being due to the peculiarities of the mother's relationship with him. The mother was usually thought of by the child as the moral authority in the family, and his attitude toward her was usu-

[242]

ally cold and unloving, but fearful and desirous of approval. Blame was also leveled at the mothers by the fathers for their coldness and contemptuousness. It seemed that the consistent use of blaming attitudes was of importance in establishing the child's patterns of self-evaluation.

The fathers in the cases studied were thought of by their children as weak but lovable. Two fathers were unsuccessful doctors, one an unsuccessful lawyer, one an unsuccessful tailor, another simply a ne'er-do-well, and so on. By and large, they earned some kind of living for their families and did not desert them, but they were considered failures because of their *comparative* lack of success in relation to the standard that the family *should* have achieved. The fathers usually were dependent on their wives, although they sometimes engaged in rather futile rebellious gestures against the pressures put on them—as when Mr. H's father spent the evenings playing pool and gambling with his men friends instead of at home listening to his wife's nagging. But, on the whole, they apparently accepted the blame visited upon them and thus implied to their children, "Do not be like me." Each patient, in general, loved his father much more warmly than his mother and often attempted to defend and justify the father for his lack of success; but in the very defense of the father the patient demonstrated his acceptance of his mother's standards. This pattern appeared, regardless of the patient's sex.

Another important contrast in the child's attitude toward his parents was that in his eyes the mother was the reliable one. Thus the child faced the dilemma of finding the unreliable and more or less contemptible parent the lovable one, and the reliable, strong parent the disliked one. This pattern also was quite consistent in most of the families of these patients, whether the patient was a boy or a girl. The attitude of the mother toward the father served, in addition, as a dramatic example of what might happen to the child, should he fail to achieve the high goals set by the mother.

Early Development of the Child

Present-day concepts of the development of personality in infancy and early childhood no longer assume that the infant lacks relationships with the people around him until he has reached the age of a year or so. Rather, it is believed that object relations develop from birth on, although it is obvious that early relationships must be quite different in quality from those experienced later on. Much evidence on infantile development in the early postnatal period[35] demonstrates that the infant reacts selectively to various attitudes in the mothering one. He thrives in an atmosphere of warmth, relaxation, and tenderness, while he experiences digestive disorders, shows a variety of tension disorders, and may even die of marasmus in an atmosphere of tension, anxiety, and physical coldness. Un-

35. See particularly Margaret Ribble, *The Rights of Infants* (New York: Columbia University Press, 1943) ; see also references in n. 29.

der these circumstances, a vague, chaotic, and somewhat cosmic concept of another person—the mothering one—very soon begins to develop, and to this person the infant attributes his feelings of well-being or ill-being; this person is experienced as being extremely powerful.

We have compared the reports of the inner experiences of manic-depressives with those given by schizophrenic patients in regard to the times of greatest anxiety in each. While it is manifestly impossible to make specific constructions on the basis of such accounts, it is nevertheless our impression that they support the conception that the major unresolved anxiety-provoking experiences of the manic-depressive patient occur at a later stage in the development of interpersonal relationships than is the case with the schizophrenic. In the schizophrenic, a conception of self clearly differentiated from the surrounding world does not seem to have been developed, and the patient in panic believes that others are completely aware of his feelings and that their actions are undertaken with this knowledge. The manic-depressive seems not to experience this breaking-down of the distinction between himself and others in times of intense anxiety; rather, he mobilizes defenses which preserve the awareness of self as distinct from others. This formulation has much in common with that of Melanie Klein.[36]

The common experience of therapists with the two disorders is to find the manic-depressive much more irritating but much less frightening to work with than the schizophrenic. This may be related to the different concepts of self and others that the two groups of patients have.[37]

Figure 1 is intended to show pictorially the difference in interpersonal closeness and object relations between the schizophrenic and the manic-depressive characters.

Points A, B, and C represent successive stages in development. At and soon after birth (A), other persons—chiefly the mother—are hardly recognized as such; interpersonal closeness is great but is based upon the intense dependence of the infant upon his mother. As relationships develop, the primary closeness based upon identification diminishes (B). Later, a more mature closeness begins to develop (C), in which the self is at last perceived as distinct and separate from other persons. It is evident that a critical phase in development (B) occurs when the closeness with the mother based upon identification has begun to disappear, but the more mature type of relationship based on recognition of others as whole, separate persons has not as yet developed to any great degree.

We conceive of the major unresolved anxiety-provoking experiences of the schizophrenic patient as occurring at point A. At this phase of personality development, closeness is based upon identification, and relation-

36. See references in n. 30.

37. For further discussion of this point see a later section of this paper on "Differential Diagnosis of the Manic-depressive."

ships are partial in character. In the manic-depressive patient, these experiences would occur at point *B*, at a time when identification is less frequently used but when the ability to relate to others as individuals distinct from oneself is in the earliest stage of development. Consequently, although relationships at point *B* are more mature than at point *A*, the individual in another sense is in a more isolated position, since he no longer employs the mechanism of identification to the degree that he did in earlier infancy but has yet to develop the capacity for a higher level of interpersonal relatedness. At this time, therefore, the developing child could be expected to feel peculiarly alone and consequently vulnerable to any threat of abandonment. We would conceive of the neurotic individual as

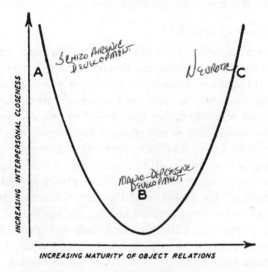

FIG. 1

having experienced his major unresolved anxiety experiences at point *C*, when interpersonal relatedness is more advanced than at *B*.

While reliable data about infancy are extremely difficult to gather, our series of manic-depressive patients shows a preponderance of normal infancies with one major exception, Mr. R, who was a feeding problem and was malnourished and fretful for the first several months of his life. The mothers of these patients appear to have found the child more acceptable and lovable as infants than as children, when the manifold problems of training and acculturation became important. Our impression is that it was the utter dependence of the infant that was pleasurable to the mother and that the growing independence and rebelliousness of the early stage of childhood were threatening to her. Unconforming or unconventional behavior on the part of the child was labeled "bad" by the mother, and she exerted great pressure to stamp it out. Thus the heretofore loving and tender mother would rather abruptly change into a harsh and punishing figure, at about the end of the first year. The child, under the stress of anxiety, would have difficulty integrating the early good mother and the later bad mother into a whole human being, now good, now bad. While a similar difficulty in integration may face all children, this split in attitude toward authority is eventually resolved in the more fortunate as the personality matures; but it remains with the manic-depressive for the rest of his life unless interrupted by life-experience or therapy. An important authority is regarded as the source of all good things, provided that he is pleased; but he is thought of as a tyrannical and punishing figure unless he is placated by good behavior. These early experiences probably lay the groundwork for the manic-depressive's later ambivalence.

Later Development of the Child

In later childhood, when the child's personality traits and role in the family have begun to crystallize, the manic-depressive may be likened to Joseph in the Bible story. Joseph was his father's favorite son. The envy of his eleven brothers was aroused by his father's giving him a multicolored coat and was increased after they heard of two of Joseph's dreams. The first dream was about eleven sheaves bent down, and one standing upright; everybody knew that this represented Joseph, with his eleven brothers bowing to him. In the other dream, eleven stars, the sun, and the moon were bowing to the twelfth star, and everybody agreed that this represented the mother, the father, and the eleven brothers bowing before Joseph. His envious brothers decided to kill him, but one of them, finding himself unable to agree to killing his own flesh and blood, influenced the others to throw him into a pit in the wilderness and finally to sell him to a passing merchant from a foreign land. After his separation from his family and his arrival in the foreign land, Joseph immediately grew in stature and quickly rose to the position of the Pharaoh's first adviser. By his skill and foresight, he averted the evil effects of a threatening famine, not only in Egypt, but also in the neighboring countries.

This story can be used to illustrate some aspects of the manic-depressive's relationship to his family. Many of these patients are the best-endowed members of their families, excelling in some cases in specific creative abilities over their siblings and over one or both of their parents. Some of them have a special place in the family as a result of their own ambitious strivings, as, for example, Mr. H. Others are the favorites of one or both parents for other reasons, sometimes because they are the only one of their sex among the siblings, as in one of our patients. All this makes for their enviously guarding their special position in the family group, despite their being burdened with great responsibilities in connection with their special position. It also subjects them to the envy of their siblings and, quite often, to the competition of one or both parents. Neither the patients themselves nor the family members are, generally speaking, aware of their mutual envy and competition. Mr. H's difficulties with envy were particularly acute. His therapist reported as follows:

Mr. H suffers from extreme feelings of envy toward his male contemporaries who have been more successful than he. The envy is so acute and painful that it is for the most part kept out of awareness. It occasionally forces itself upon his attention, particularly at times when some one of his contemporaries has received a promotion or other sign of success. The patient always feels that he deserves the promotion more than the other person and believes that his illnesses are the stumbling block in the way of his receiving it or, at times, that the lack of recognition is due to anti-Semitism. While he is an extremely intelligent and able person who does his work adequately, except in periods of emotional disturbance, he does not visualize himself as succeeding on the basis of his productivity, and he makes little effort to succeed on the basis of doing a better job than his competitors. His efforts toward success are directed toward getting to be the friend of the boss, becoming a companion of the boss in sports or games, or going to the races with the boss. By getting the boss to like him especially or find him pleasant and agreeable to be with, he hopes to interest the boss in promoting his future. During his psychotic episodes this pattern increases in its scope and becomes a grandiose fantasy in which he is being groomed for the Presidency of the United States or in which the eye of some mysterious person is watching over him. He once said, for instance, "There is an organization, the FBI, which is set up to find the bad people and put them where they can't do any harm. Why should there not be a similar organization which has been set up to find the good people and see to it that they are put in a position of importance?"

As mentioned previously, manic-depressives usually come from families who are in minority groups because of their social, economic, ethnic, or religious status. The family members in these minority groups cling together in group-conscious mutual love and acceptance and in the wish and need to maintain and raise their family prestige in their groups and their group prestige before an adverse outer world. There is little room for, or concern with, problems of interpersonal relatedness. Under the all-important requirement of seeking and maintaining high prestige, it seldom occurs to any member of these groups to think in terms other than "we belong together." This, then, is a background in which neither the active nor the passive participants in developments of envy and competition are aware of these developments. Yet, without being aware of it, the best-endowed children will spend quite a bit of energy to counteract the envy of the siblings, of which they are unconsciously afraid. Often the children are brought up, not only by their parents, but also by the joint endeavor of several other important older members of the clan. In spite of all this supervision, there is rarely an individual on whom a child can rely with confidence in a one-to-one relationship. In fact, it is frequently the case that the family group has a number of authority figures in it—grandparents, uncles, aunts, and so on—so that the child's experiences of authority are with multiple parent-figures. In this setting, the manic-depressive in very early childhood is frequently burdened with the family's expectation that he will do better than his parents in the service of the prestige of the family and the clan; consequently, he may feel, or be made to feel, responsible for whatever hardship or failure occurs in the family. For example, one of our patients was held responsible by her sisters for her mother's death when the patient was eighteen months old—"Mother would still be here, had you not been born"; for the failure of her father's second marriage, which had been made to provide a mother for the patient; and for her father's "ruined" feet, the result of tramping the streets as a salesman after his position of considerable prominence had ended in bankruptcy. Another patient at the age of three felt that he had to take over certain responsibilities toward the clan, sensing that his parents had failed in the fulfilment of them.

The special role in the family group which these patients hold is accentuated by the fact that they are, as a rule, pushed very early into unusual responsibility or else themselves assume this role. As a result, their image of the significant people in the family usually differs considerably from that of the other siblings. With their different appraisal of one or both of their parents, from early childhood they are extremely lonely, in spite of growing up in the group-conscious atmosphere which we have described, where there is little feeling for privacy and where the little-differentiated experiences of the various family members are considered in the light of the common good of the whole family or the whole clan. In many cases these people are unaware of their loneliness, as long as they are well, because the sentiment of "we belong together" is fostered by their family.

As these people grow up, they remain extremely sensitive to envy and competition. They know what it is like to harbor it themselves and to be its target. One means of counteracting this envy, which early becomes an unconscious pattern, is to undersell themselves to hide the full extent of their qualifications. Another pattern which many of these patients develop to counteract feelings of envying and being envied is to be exceptionally helpful to their siblings, to other members of the early group, and, later on, to other people with whom they come in contact in various ways. They often use their talents for promoting other persons and their abilities. The price they unconsciously demand for this is complete acceptance and preference by the others. These traits are repeated in the transference situation during treatment.

For instance, a patient was brought to the hospital against her will, without any insight into her mental disturbance. Much to everybody's surprise, she most willingly entered treatment with one member of our group. Everything seemed to run in a smooth and promising way until suddenly, after about two weeks, the patient declared vehemently that she would continue treatment no longer. When she was asked for her reasons, she said that she had been under the impression that she might help her doctor, who was an immigrant, to establish herself professionally in the new country by allowing the doctor to treat her successfully. But during the two weeks she had been at the hospital, she had found that the doctor had already succeeded in establishing herself, and therefore the patient's incentive for treatment was gone.

THE ADULT CHARACTER

As adults, persons with cyclothymic personalities continue to manifest many of the same traits that they exhibited in childhood. During the "healthy" intervals between attacks, they appear from a superficial point of view to be relatively well adjusted and at ease with other people. A certain social facility is typical of the hypomanic, although it is not seen so clearly in the depressive person in his "healthy" intervals. For instance, the hypomanic typically has innumerable acquaintances with whom he appears to be on most cordial terms. On closer scrutiny of these relationships, however, it becomes apparent that they cannot be considered to be in any sense friendships or intimacies. The appearance of closeness is provided by the hypomanic's liveliness, talkativeness, wittiness, and social aggressiveness. Actually, there is little or no communicative exchange between the hypomanic and any one of his so-called friends. He is carrying out a relatively stereotyped social performance, which takes little or no account of the other person's traits and characteristics, while the other person, quite commonly, is allowing himself to be entertained and manipulated.

Both the hypomanic and the depressive share in their tendency to have one or a very few extremely dependent relationships. In the hypomanic this dependency is concealed under all his hearty good humor and apparent busyness, but it is quite clear in the depressive. The hypomanic or the depressive is extremely demanding toward the person with whom he has a dependent relationship, basing his claim for love and attention upon his need of the other, and making it a *quid pro quo* for his self-sacrifice. Demands are made for love, attention, service, and possessions. The concept of reciprocity is missing; the needs of the other for similar experiences are not recognized.[38] Yet the failure to recognize the needs of the other does elicit unconscious guilt, which may be manifested by the manic-depressive's consciously thinking of himself as having given a great deal. What the giving seems to amount to is a process of underselling himself. In the relationship the devaluation and underselling also indicate to the partner the person's great need of him and serve

38. This formulation is similar to that made by O. Spurgeon English, who states: "Closely tied up with the matter of love is the patient's self-esteem or love of himself. The manic-depressive does not seem to have much feeling of love to give, and what he has he is afraid to give" ("Observation of Trends in Manic-depressive Psychosis." *Psychiatry*, XII [1949], 125–33, esp. 129).

to counteract the old, unconscious, fearful expectation of competition and envy from the important person. The cyclothymic person's own envy and competition, too, are hidden from his awareness and take the form of feelings of inferiority and great need. The person conceives of himself as reaching success, satisfaction, or glory through the success of the other rather than by efforts of his own. Thus Mr. H made himself the stooge of the president of the class in high school, receiving as his reward the political plums that the president was able to hand out and failing to recognize that what he actually wanted was to be class president himself. He continued this kind of relationship with some important figure—usually male—in every free period afterward, while in his psychotic attacks the wish to be president himself came to consciousness, and he made futile efforts to achieve it.

Thus the process of underselling themselves, both for the sake of denying envy and in order to become the recipient of gifts from the other, often reaches the point where these persons actually paralyze the use of their own endowments and creative abilities. They themselves frequently believe that they have lost their assets or that they never had any. The process of underselling themselves, especially in depressives, may also convince other people in their environment of their lack of ability. At this point, they begin to hate these other people for being the cause of the vicious circle in which they are caught; and they hate themselves because they sense the fraudulence of their behavior in not having expressed openly all their inner feelings.

One patient said time and again during his depression, "I'm a fraud, I'm a fraud; I don't know why, but I'm a fraud." When he was asked why he felt fraudulent, he would produce any number of rationalizations, but at last it was found that the thing he felt to be fraudulent was his underselling of himself. This same patient got so far in his fraudulent attempt at denying his total endowment that he was on the verge of giving up a successful career—which, while he was well, held a good deal of security and satisfaction for him—in order to regain the love of an envious friend, which he felt he was in danger of losing because of his own greater success.

We see, then, in the adult cyclothymic a person who is apparently well adjusted between attacks, although he may show minor mood swings or be chronically overactive or chronically mildly depressed. He is conventionally well behaved and frequently successful, and he is hardworking and conscientious; indeed, at times his overconscientiousness and scrupulousness lead to his being called obsessional. He is typically involved in one or more relationships of extreme dependence, in which, however, he does not show the obsessional's typical need to control the other person for the sake of power but, instead, seeks to control the other person in the sense of swallowing him up. His inner feeling, when he allows himself to notice it, is one of emptiness and need. He is extremely stereotyped in his attitudes and opinions, tending to take over the opinions of the person in his environment whom he regards as an important authority. Again this contrasts with the outward conformity but subtle rebellion of the obsessional. It should be emphasized that the dependency feelings are largely out of awareness in states of well-being and also in the manic phase; in fact, these people frequently take pride in being independent.

His principal source of anxiety is the fear of abandonment. He is afraid to be alone and seeks the presence of other people. Abandonment is such a great threat because his relationships with others are based upon utilizing them as possessions or pieces of property. If he offends them, by differing with them or outcompeting them, and they withdraw, he is left inwardly empty, having no conception of inner resources to fall back on. Also, if they offend him and he is compelled to withdraw, this leaves him similarly alone. In this situation of potential abandonment, the anxiety is handled by overlooking the emotional give-and-take between himself and others, so that he is unaware of the other person's feelings toward himself or of his feelings toward the other. This is clearly seen in the well-known difficulty which therapists have in terminating an hour with a depressive. Regardless of what has gone on during the hour, at the end of it the depressive stands in the doorway, plaintively seeking reassurance by some such question as "Am I making any progress, Doctor?" An attempt to answer the question only leads to another or to a repetition of the same one, for the patient is not seeking an answer—or, rather, does not actually believe there is an answer—but instead is striving to prolong his contact with the doctor. In carrying out this piece of stereotyped behavior, he is unaware of the doctor's mounting impatience and irritation and overlooks its consequence— namely, that, instead of there being increasing closeness between patient and doctor, a situation has now been set up in which the distance between them is rapidly increasing.

This character structure can be seen to have a clear-cut relationship to the infantile development which we have hypothesized for the manic-depressive. According to this hypothesis, interpersonal relations have been arrested in their development at the point where the child recognizes himself as being separate from others but does not yet see others as being full-sized human beings; rather, he sees them as entities who are now good, now bad, and must be manipulated. If this is the case, then the adult's poorness of discrimination about others is understandable. His life and welfare depend upon the other's goodness, as he sees it, and he is unable to recognize that one and the same person may be accepting today, rejecting tomorrow, and then accepting again on the following day. Nor can he recognize that certain aspects of his behavior may be acceptable while others are not; instead, he sees relationships as all-or-none propositions. The lack of interest in and ability to deal with interpersonal subtleties are probably also due to the fact that the important persons in the child's environment themselves deal in conventional stereotypes. The child, therefore, has little opportunity at home to acquire skill in this form of communication.

We have said little in this report about the manic-depressive's hostility. We feel that it has been considerably overstressed as a dynamic factor in the illness. Certainly, a great deal of the patient's behavior leaves a hostile impression upon those around him, but we feel that the driving motivation in the patient is the one we have stressed—the feeling of need and emptiness. The hostility we would relegate to a secondary position: we see hostile feelings arising in the patient as the result of frustration of his manipulative and exploitive needs. We conceive of such subsequent behavior—demandingness toward the other or self-injury—as being an attempt to restore the previous dependent situation. Of course, the demandingness and exploitiveness are exceedingly annoying and anger-provoking to those around the patient—the more so because of the failure of the patient to recognize what sort of people he is dealing with. But we feel that much of the hostility that has been imputed to the patient has been the result of his annoying impact upon others rather than of a primary motivation to do injury to them.

The Psychotic Attack

The precipitation of the depressive attack by a loss is well known. However, there have been many cases in which attacks have occurred where there has been no loss. In some it has seemed that a depression occurred at the time of a promotion in job or some other improvement in circumstances. On scrutiny, it can be seen that, in those patients in whom a depression has occurred without an apparent change in circumstances of living, the actual change has been in the patient's appraisal of the situation. The patient incessantly hopes and strives for a dependency relationship in which all his needs are met by the other. This hope and the actions taken to achieve it are, for the most part, out of awareness, since recognition of them would subject the person to feelings of guilt and anxiety. After every depressive attack, he sets forth upon this quest anew. In the course of time, it becomes apparent to him that his object is not fulfilling his needs. He then gets into a vicious circle: he uses depressive techniques—complaining or whining—to elicit the gratifications he requires. These grow offensive to the other, who becomes even less gratifying; therefore, the patient redoubles his efforts and receives still less. Finally, he loses hope and enters into the psychotic state in which the pattern of emptiness and need is repeated over and over again in the absence of any specific object.

As to the person who becomes depressed after a gain rather than a loss, we interpret this as being experienced by the patient himself as a loss, regardless of how it is evaluated by the outside world. Thus a promotion may remove the patient from a relatively stable dependency relationship with his co-workers or with his boss and may call upon him to function at a level of self-sufficiency which is impossible for him. Also, being promoted may involve him in a situation of severe anxiety because of the envious feelings which he thinks it will elicit in others, the fear occurring as the result of his unresolved childhood pattern of envying those more successful than himself and, in return, expecting and fearing the envy of others at his success. Having made them envious, he may believe that he can no longer rely on them to meet his needs, whereupon he is again abandoned and alone. For example, an episode from Mr. R's life was described by his analyst as follows:

After about a year of treatment it was suggested to the patient by one of his fellow officers that he ought to apply for a medal for his part in the war, and he found the idea very tempting. When this was discussed with me, I attempted to discourage it, without coming out directly with a strong effort to interfere, and the discouraging words I said were unheard by the patient. He went ahead with a series of manipulative acts designed to win the medal, and it was awarded to him. No sooner had he received it than he became acutely anxious and tense. He began to suspect his compeers of envying him and plotting to injure him in order to punish him for having taken advantage of them by getting a medal for himself, and he thought that his superior officers were contemptuous of him for his greediness. His life became a nightmare of anxiety in which he misinterpreted the smiles, glances, gestures, hellos, and other superficial behavior of his fellow officers as signifying their hatred and disapproval of him.

The manic attack is similar to the depressive in following a precipitating incident which carries the meaning of a loss of love. It often happens that there is a transient depression before the outbreak of manic behavior. For instance, Mr. H was mildly depressed at Christmas time; his behavior from then on showed increasing evidence of irrationality, which, however, was not striking enough to cause alarm until June, when he developed a full-blown manic attack. We believe, from our experience with patients who have had repeated attacks, that the presence of depressive feelings prior to the onset of the manic phase is very common, and perhaps the rule.

It is well known that many manic patients report feelings of depression during their manic phase. As one of our patients put it, while apparently manic:

I am crying underneath the laughter. . . . Blues all day long—feelings not properly expressed. Cover up for it, gay front while all the time I am crying. Laughing too much and loud hurts more. Not able to cry it complete and full of hell. All pinned up inside, but the misery and hatred are greater than the need to cry. Praying for tears to feel human. Wishing for pain in hopes that there is something left. Fright is almost indescribable.

We agree with Freud, Lewin, and others that, dynamically, the manic behavior can best be understood as a defensive structure utilized by the patient to avoid recognizing and experiencing in awareness his feelings of depression. The timing of the manic behavior varies widely; it may either precede the depression, in which case it can be understood as a defense which has eventually failed to protect the patient from his depression; or it may follow the depressive attack, when it represents an escape from the unbearable depressive state into something more tolerable. Subjectively, the state of being depressed is one of more intolerable discomfort than the state of being manic, since the patient in effect is threatened with loss of identity of his self.

There are personalities who are able to lead a life of permanent hypomania, with no psychotic episodes. Of course, many chronic hypomanics do have psychotic episodes, but there are some who never have to be hospitalized. Such a patient was Mr. R, who had a very narrow escape from hospitalization when he became agitatedly depressed at a time when several severely anxiety-producing blows occurred in rapid succession. On the whole, however, he maintained what appeared to be an excellent reality adjustment. Subjectively, he was usually constrained to avoid thinking of himself and his feelings by keeping busy, but when he did turn his attention inward, then intense feelings of being in an isolated, unloved, and threatened position would arise.

We have noted in our private practices a trend in recent years for an increased number of persons who utilize rather typical hypomanic defense patterns to enter into analytic therapy. These people tend in general to be quite successful in a material sense and to conceal their sense of inward emptiness and isolation both from themselves and from others. Probably their entering analysis in increasing numbers has some correlation with the popular success achieved by psychoanalysis in recent years in this country. Once committed to treatment, these so-called extraverts rapidly reveal their extreme dependency needs, and, on the whole, our impression has been that psychoanalysis has proved decidedly beneficial to them.

In the light of the foregoing discussion of the manic and depressive attacks, we have come to the conclusion that they need to be differentiated psychodynamically chiefly on the score of what makes the manic defense available to some patients while it is not so usable by others. Some investigators postulate a constitutional or metabolic factor here, but in our opinion adherence to this hypothesis is unjustified in the present state of our knowledge. We feel that further investigation of the manic defense is indicated before a reliable hypothesis can be set up.

We feel that the basic psychotic pattern is the depressive one. The onset of a depression seems understandable enough in the light of the patient's typical object-relation pattern described earlier. That is, becoming sick, grief-stricken, and helpless is only an exaggeration and intensification of the type of appeal which the manic-depressive makes to the important figures in his life in the healthy intervals. When this type of appeal brings rejection, as it usually does when carried beyond a certain degree of intensity, then the vicious circle mentioned earlier can be supposed to set in, with each cycle representing a further descent on the spiral. At the end, the patient is left with his severely depressed feelings and with no feeling of support or relatedness from the people on whom he formerly relied. At this point, where the feelings of depression and emptiness are acute, the patient may follow one of three courses: he may remain depressed; he may commit suicide; or he may regress still further to a schizophrenic state.

If he remains depressed, he carries on a chronic, largely fantastic acting out of the pattern of dependency. There is no longer a suitable object. The members of the family who have hospitalized him are now present only in fantasy. The patient does, however, continue to address his complaints and appeals to them as though they were still present and powerful. In addition, he rather indiscriminately addresses the same appeal to all those around him in the hospital. The appeal may be mute, acted out by his despair, sleeplessness, and inability to eat, or it may be highly vociferous and addressed verbally to all who come in contact with him, in the form of statements about his bowels being blocked up, his insides being empty, his family having been bankrupted or killed, and so on. The same pattern is developed with his therapist: instead of a therapeutic relationship in which he strives to make use of the doctor's skill with some confidence and notion of getting somewhere, the same empty pattern of mourning and hopelessness is set up, in which he strives to gain help by a display of his misery and to receive reassurance by repeatedly requesting it. It is notable and significant that his ability to work on or examine the nature of his relationships is non-existent; that difficulties with others are denied and self-blame is substituted. The major therapeutic problem with the depressive is actually the establishment of a working relationship in which problems are examined and discussed. Conversely, the major system of defenses which have to be overcome in order to establish such a working relationship lies in the substitution of the stereotyped complaint or self-accusation for a more meaningful kind of self-awareness. There seems to be a sort of clinging to the hope that the repetition of the pattern will eventually bring fulfilment. Relinquishing the pattern seems to bring with it the danger of suicide, on the one hand, or disintegration, on the other. It is our opinion that, in the situation in which the patient has given up his habitual depressive pattern of integration and has as yet not developed a substitute pattern which brings some security and satisfaction, he is in danger of suicide. The suicide, as has been well demonstrated by previous workers, has the meaning of a further, highly irrational attempt at relatedness. It can be thought of as the final appeal of helplessness. "When they see how unhappy I really am, they will do something." This fits in with the almost universal fantasy indulged in by most people in moments of frustration and depression of what "they" will say and do when I am dead. Along with this magical use of death to gain one's dependent ends goes a fantasy of recapturing the early relationship by dying and being born again.

For instance, Miss G took an overdose of barbiturates as a last resort after her failure to persuade her father to accede to a request by other means. It appeared that in this case there was little intent to die but that the action was resorted to because lesser means of convincing him had failed. Probably in this instance of a conscious suicidal gesture the manipulative goal is much more apparent and more clearly in awareness than with the majority of cases. On the other hand, self-destruction also has a more rational element; that is, it is the final expression of the feeling that all hope is lost, and the wish to get rid of the present pain. We are inclined to believe that the element of hopelessness in the act of suicide has not been given sufficient weight in previous studies.

Sullivan, at the end of a great many years of studying the obsessional neurotic, came to the conclusion that many of the more severely ill cases were potentially schizophrenic in situations where their habitual and trusted obsessional defenses proved inadequate to deal with anxiety. This statement also applies to the depressive: if the defensive aspects of the depression become ineffectual, then a collapse of the personality structure can occur, with an ensuing reintegration on the basis of a schizophrenic way of life rather than a depressive one.

Guilt and the Superego

We have avoided using the term "superego" in this report and have not involved the cruel, punishing superego in our attempted explanation of the depression. It is our opinion that utilization of the term "superego" in this way merely conceals the problem rather than explains it. There are several basic questions regarding the problems of conscience and guilt in the manic-depressive. First, what influences account for the severe and hypermoral standards of these people? And, second, what is the dynamic function of the self-punishing acts and attitudes which are engaged in during the periods of illness?

The overcritical standards of manic-depressives are not explicable as a direct taking-over of the standards of the parents, since these patients in childhood have usually been treated with rather exceptional overindulgence. However, in the section on "Family Background and Character Structure" we have mentioned the peculiar combination of lack of conviction of worth and a standard of behavior in the family coupled with an intense devotion to conventional morality and to what other people think. It is logical that a child raised by an inconsistent mother who is at times grossly overindulgent and at others severely rejecting would be unable to build up a reasonable code of conduct for himself and that his code—focused around what an impersonal authority is supposed to expect of him and based on no concept of parental reliability or strength —would be both oversevere and frightening in its impersonality. In all probability, much of his moral code is based on the struggle to acquire those qualities of strength and virtue which he finds missing in his parents. Later in this report we shall return to the problem of authority in the manic-depressive. Suffice it to say here that, in dealing with authority, this type of patient shows a rigid preconception of what authority expects of him, as well as a persistent conviction that he must fit in with these expectations, which are beyond the reach of reason or experience. The authority appears, in our experience, at times as an incorporated superego and at other times as a projected, impersonal, but tyrannical force. Or, rather, every significant person in the patient's social field is invested with the quality of authority.

In this relationship with authority, the self-punitive acts and experiencing of guilt can be understood as devices for placating the impersonal tyrant. The guilt expressed by the depressive does not carry on to any genuine feeling of regret or effort to change behavior. It is, rather, a means to an end. Merely suffering feelings of guilt is expected to suffice for regaining approval. On the other hand, it may also be seen that achieving a permanent, secure, human relationship with authority is regarded as hopeless. Therefore, no effort to change relationships or to integrate on a better level of behavior is undertaken, and the patient merely resorts to the magic of uttering guilty cries to placate authority.

DIFFERENTIAL DIAGNOSIS OF THE MANIC-DEPRESSIVE

Some observers have stated that in the intervals between attacks the manic-depressive has a character structure similar to that of the obsessional neurotic.[39] It has also been asserted that in the psychotic phase the manic-depressive illness is essentially schizophrenic. This latter statement is supported by the fact that many manic-depressives do, in the course of time, evolve into chronic schizophrenic psychoses, usually paranoid in character, and that there are many persecutory ideas present both in the manic attack and in the depression. In general, there has always been much uncertainty as to who should be diagnosed manic-depressive—an uncertainty which is reflected in the widely differing pro-

39. See Abraham, *Selected Papers on Psychoanalysis.*

portions of manic-depressives and schizophrenics diagnosed in different mental hospitals.

What, then, is the point of singling out a diagnostic category called "manic-depressive"? In our opinion, the manic-depressive syndrome does represent a fairly clear-cut system of defenses which are sufficiently unique and of sufficient theoretical interest to deserve special study. We feel that equating the manic-depressive character with the obsessional character overlooks the distinguishing differences between the two. The obsessional, while bearing many resemblances to the manic-depressive, uses substitutive processes as his chief defense. The manic, on the other hand, uses the previously mentioned lack of interpersonal awareness as his chief defense, together with the defensive processes which are represented by the manic and the depressive symptoms themselves. The object relations of the obsessional are more stable and well developed than those of the manic-depressive. While the obsessional's relations are usually integrations in which there is an intense degree of hostility, control, and envy, they do take into consideration the other person as a person. The manic-depressive, on the other hand, develops an intensely dependent, demanding, oral type of relationship which overlooks the particular characteristics and qualities of the other.

According to Sullivan's conceptualization of the schizophrenic process, the psychosis is introduced typically by a state of panic, in which there is an acute break with reality resulting from the upsurge of dissociated drives and motivations which are absolutely unacceptable and invested with unbearable anxiety. Following this acute break, a variety of unsuccessful recovery or defensive processes ensues which we call "paranoid," "catatonic," "hebephrenic." These represent attempts of the personality to deal with the conflicts which brought about the panic: the paranoid by projection; the catatonic by rigid control; the hebephrenic by focusing on bodily impulses. According to this conception, the manic-depressive can be differentiated from the schizophrenic by the fact that he does not exhibit the acute break with reality that is seen in the schizophrenic panic. On the other hand, his psychotic processes of depression or of mania can be thought of as serving a defensive function against the still greater personality disintegration that is represented by the schizophrenic state. Thus in persons whose conflicts and anxiety are too severe to be handled by depressive or manic defenses, a schizophrenic breakdown may be the end result.

Contrasting the schizophrenic and the manic-depressive from the point of view of their early relationships, we see that the schizophrenic has accepted the bad mother as his fate, and his relation to reality is therefore attenuated. He is inclined to withdraw into detachment. He is hypercritical of family and cultural values. He is sensitive and subtle in his criticisms, original but disillusioned. He is disinclined to rely on others and is capable of enduring considerable degrees of loneliness. His reluctance to make demands on the therapist causes the therapist to feel more sympathetic, and therefore the therapist is frequently more effective. In addition, the schizophrenic patient is more effective in his aggression; he can take the risk of attacking, for he is less afraid of loneliness. He is more sensitively aware of the emotions of the therapist, since the boundaries between ego and environment are more fluid. The schizophrenic is not inclined to pretend and is not easily fooled by other people's pretenses. Dream and fantasy life are nearer to awareness, and guilt feelings are also more conscious than unconscious.

The typical manic-depressive, on the other hand, has not accepted the "bad mother" as his fate. He vacillates between phases in which he fights with the bad mother and phases in which he feels reunited with the good mother. In the manic phase, his relationship with reality is more tenuous; he shows a lack of respect for other people, and all reality considerations are dismissed for the sake of magic manipulation to make the bad mother over into a good mother. The manic-depressive is, therefore, mostly a good manipulator, a salesman, a bargaining personality. He is undercritical instead of being hypercritical. He easily sells out his convictions and his originality in order to force others to love him, deriving from this a borrowed esteem. In the depressive phase, he sacrifices himself to gain a good mother or to transform the bad mother into a good one. In order to do this, he calls himself bad and suffers to expiate his sins. But these guilt feelings are, in a sense, artificial or expedient, utilized in order to manipulate the bad mother into becoming a good mother. The depressive does not come to terms with realistic guilt feelings. Instead, he uses his self-accusations, which frequently sound hypocritical, to convince the mother or a substitute that his need to be loved has absolute urgency. He denies his originality because he is terribly afraid of aloneness. He is more of a follower than a leader. He is dependent on prestige and is quite unable to see through the pretense of his own or other people's conventionalities. He shows a high degree of anxiety when his manipulations fail. His denial of originality leads to feelings of emptiness and envy. His lack of subtlety in interpersonal relationships is due to his overruling preoccupation with exploiting the other person in order to fill his emptiness. This operates as a vicious circle: he has to maintain his claims for the good, fulfilling mother, but his search for fulness via manipulation of another makes him feel helpless and empty. This incorporation of another person for the purpose of filling an inward emptiness, of acquiring a borrowed self-esteem, is very different from the lack of ego boundaries in the schizophrenic. The schizophrenic is in danger of losing his ego, and he expresses this danger in fantasies of world catastrophe. The manic-depressive is threatened by object loss, since he habitually uses the object to patch up his ego weakness. Object relations in the manic-depressive are, therefore, clouded by illusions, but even when he wails, demands, and blames the frustrating object, he is—by this very agitated activity in behalf of his own salvation, ineffective as it may be—defended against the loss of the ego. When the manic-depressive becomes schizophrenic, this defense breaks down.

It should be noted that the infantile dependency and manipulative exploitiveness seen in the manic-depressive are not unique to this type of disorder. They occur, in fact, in many forms of severe mental illness. The hysteric, for instance, exemplifies infantile dependency and exploitiveness as dramatically as the manic-depressive, and in *la belle indifference* one may see a resemblance to the euphoria of the manic or the hypomanic. However, the combination of the dependent and exploitive traits with the other outstanding characteristics of the cyclothymic personality—particularly the communicative defect and the accompanying inability to recognize other persons as anything but good-bad stereotypes and the conventional but hypermoralistic values—does become sufficiently distinct and unique to distinguish these patients characterologically from other types.

PROBLEMS IN THERAPY

Transference

The diagnosis of manic-depressive character has, in the past, been made largely on the basis of the patient's exhibiting the classic manic and depressive symptomatology. It can, however, be as validly made on the basis of the transference-countertransference pattern, which is set up between the patient and the therapist. The transference pattern is particularly characteristic; the countertransference pattern would, of course, vary considerably according to the personality of the therapist, although it, too, shows a number of quite typical features.

The transference pattern shows two outstanding characteristics which could be labeled (1) the exploitive, clinging dependency and (2) the stereotyped approach to other persons, who are not seen as personalities in their own right.

(1.) *The dependency.*—Other workers in the field of the study of manic-depressive illnesses have amply documented the deep-seated dependency of this type of person (Abraham, Freud, Rado, Klein). The dependency attitudes toward the object are highly ambivalent. Gratification is demanded[40] but is not accepted or experienced as such, and the patient feels that attention, care, and tenderness must be forced from the other person.

40. We use the term "demand" to denote unrealistic and inappropriate requests as distinguished from those requests which are appropriate in the treatment situation. The "demand" type of request seems to spring from a need which is essentially unfulfilable. That is, there is no realistic action that the therapist can take which will make the patient feel satisfied. When the things asked for—such as exra time, reassurance, and so on—are granted, they do not lead to a feeling of satisfaction on the patient's part.

The force applied is that of demonstrating to the other person how miserable he is making one, how much the depressed one needs the other, and how responsible and culpable the other is if he fails to meet the depressive's needs. The demands are not directly verbalized but rather consist of a wordless exploitation; the reactive hostility is not experienced as such but, instead, is experienced as depression.

In the depths of the depression, it seems impossible to satisfy the patient's dependency needs. As one therapist put it, the patient seems to be saying, "I am starving, and I won't get what I need." The amount of time and attention the patient receives does not suffice to give him a sense of satisfaction. He remains depressed, crying out for more. We have not tried the experiment of spending the major portion of each day with a depressive person. Certainly, 24-hour-a-day nursing does not suffice to give the patient a sense of gratification. Whether unlimited time from a therapist would have more effect is debatable in the light of our experience with Mr. R, which will be discussed in more detail in the section on "Therapeutic Techniques." This type of demandingness is typical of the depressive aspects of the illness. When the patient is in a period of relative mental health, these needs are less apparent. This raises the question of what becomes of these needs during such periods: Are they not present and only stirred up again when some unusual deprivation or threat to security occurs, or are they successfully kept in repression during the healthy phases? We have commented on this question in the section on "The Adult Character."

In the manic phase, the demandingness is much more open but is seen by the patient as demanding his rights rather than as asking for favors. Rejection of the demands is met with overt hostility rather than with a depressive response. The manic, of course, shows, in addition to the demandingness, the tendency to take what he needs by force, if necessary, and he will use direct aggression—in contrast to the depressive, who uses reproaches against the other person as a forcing maneuver.

2. The stereotyped response.—The manic-depressive personality shows a highly characteristic tendency to look upon others as stereotyped repetitions of parental figures. This has been described elsewhere in this report as "a lack of interpersonal sensitivity." The therapist is regarded (a) as an object to be manipulated for purposes of getting sympathy and reassurance, (b) as a moral authority who can be manipulated into giving approval, and (c) as, in actuality, a critical and rejecting authority figure who will not give real approval but can be counted on only for token approval, which can be achieved by proper behavior or manipulation. This uncritical categorization of the therapist results in the patient's inability to use the therapist to provide himself with a fresh point of view. Everything that the therapist says is reworked into the old pattern of concealed disapproval covered over with the sugar of artificial reassur-

ance. This impenetrability to the reception of new ideas from the therapist represents one of the great obstacles in therapy with this type of patient, who will give lip service to the role of the therapist as a noncritical authority without a feeling of conviction that this is so. However, the lip service itself then becomes incorporated into the set of manipulative acts which will receive approval and adds another bulwark to the defense.

Early in the study of these patients, it was felt that the lack of ability to appraise the therapist as a person represented a real learning defect in the patient and that one of the therapeutic tasks, therefore, was a somewhat educational one of showing the patient how one person could be different from another. On further study we have come to the conclusion that the defect is not an educational one, evidence for this being that, as the anxiety diminishes in an interpersonal relation, the sensitivity increases. Mr. R is an excellent illustration of this point. His therapist spoke of him as follows:

When the patient first entered treatment, I would have described him as being without the ability to empathize with another. During the subsequent years of treatment, it became apparent that the patient was acutely sensitive to nuances in the attitude of others to him, but that his interpretation of these attitudes was extremely static and stereotyped. Finally, at the end of treatment, he retained much of his sensitivity but had also gained in his ability to respond with accuracy in interpersonal situations.

Mr. R's sensitivity is illustrated by the following incident:

The patient wished to make a change in his Army assignment. The therapist was, he believed, in a position to use her influence to get him the new assignment. He did not ask the therapist to use her influence except by implication; that is, he wrote a letter stating what his plans were about getting the new assignment, and, reading between the lines, it became apparent to the therapist that she was expected to offer to use what influence she had to bring this about. This indirect request was answered indirectly by the therapist with an encouraging letter in which no offer was made to intervene on the patient's behalf. The patient became depressed in a matter of weeks, and when he next saw the therapist, his statement was that the therapist obviously did not approve of his new plans and believed him to be incapable of the change of job which he had wished for. The interpretation was promptly made that these were projections which had been precipitated by his unverbalized request and his unconscious resentment when his request was not met. The patient accepted the interpretation without hesitation, and the projected hostile belittling attitudes attributed to the therapist were immediately dropped and the patient's further discussion continued on a more realistic basis.

Another therapist expressed her experience with a patient in the following way:

The discontinuity between what she thinks and how she acts and the impression of routinization or mimicry in both seem to come from deficiency in the function of empathy from the rest of her activity, so that the rest of her activity, both thinking and acting, is without a dimension which seems to give it depth, at least in communicating about it. . . . The schizophrenic, in contrast, seems to have adequate development of the function of empathy. He has had his experiences in that medium and has utilized them, and the patient-physician communication in that medium is much as with any so-called normal person, except for the patient's abnormal sensitivity and his misinterpretations. . . . I extend myself actively to engage empathically with these [manic-depressive] patients. I keep in mind that I am talking to the patients not so much verbally as preverbally. I use the verbal communication as a means of carrying inflection and an accompaniment of facial expression and postural components. And with such patients at the end of an hour I often find I have the greatest difficulty recollecting what the verbal exchanges as such have been, because my concentration has been so much on the empathic component.

In this discussion, the therapist is using the term "empathic exchange" to signify an essentially non-verbal communication of affect or meaning. We have used a variety of descriptive phrases, including "a lack of interpersonal sensitivity" and "the stereotyped response." These two terms attempt to describe the same phenomenon as the therapist is describing in terms of a maldevelopment of the empathic function. The phenomenon is observed by a multitude of therapists but is not yet satisfactorily understood, as witness the multiplicity of descriptive phrases. We feel that it is closely related dynamically to the difficulty in object relationships mentioned in the section on "Early Development of the Child." There the developmental defect in the child who will later become a manic-depressive is described as a failure to integrate the early part-objects into wholes and instead the retention of the concept of a separate good and bad mother. Approaching the problem from the point of view of present-day relationships, we suggest that it is anxiety-arousing for the manic-depressive to recognize others as persons, as well as to conceive of himself as a person in his own right. It is probable that the intolerable aspect of this is the recognizing of good and bad traits in one and the same person; this requires a certain amount of independence—that is, the ability to deal with the good and put up with the bad. The manic-depressive's recognition of bad or unacceptable traits in another person would interfere with his dependency on him; it would be necessary for him to abandon the other person for his badness, and this would then leave him alone. In order to avoid this anxiety, the manic-depressive avoids the recognition and identification of the medley of attractive and unpleasant traits in others and thereby avoids the exchange of a variety of complex feelings. Thus, as is so often true in psychopathology, what begins as a developmental defect ends up as an anxiety-avoiding defense.

Technical Problems

There are two major technical problems in dealing with the manic-depressive patient which derive logically from the transference picture as developed above. These are the technical problems related to meeting the dependency needs and the technical problems related to breaking through the stereotyped characterization of the therapist. The dilemma with regard to dependency can be stated as follows: Attempts to meet the dependency needs and to permit the type of manipulation that the patient characteristically engages in merely support the present way of relating. Our experience has shown us that the assumption of the classical passive and accepting role of the therapist tends to imply to the patient that his dependency needs are being met or will be met. There is, of course, considerable frustration for the patient in the therapist's non-intervention in any active way in the direction of meeting the patient's needs when the classical psychoanalytic technique is used. However, this does not seem to suffice to interfere with the patient's fantasy that the therapist will be, or can be induced to be, the sort of giving parental figure that the patient is looking for; it therefore seems that something more active is needed in terms of a denial by the therapist that he will play the role that the patient wishes him to play. The opposite tactic of actively rejecting the patient's demands is equally, or even more, undesirable, since this then reinforces the patient's belief that he is bad and tends to push him in the direction of redoubling his efforts to please the harsh authority and thereby receive the blessings of approval, and so on. Furthermore, in both these types of therapeutic approach, the threat of suicide is an ever present, although perhaps not verbalized, obstacle. In our experience suicide during therapy frequently occurs under the following conditions: The patient establishes his characteristic dependency relationship and enters into his characteristic fantasies of gratification. He then experiences something in the relationship which he interprets as a rejection. Following this, he becomes hopeless about achieving his goal, and then he becomes suicidal. In other words, as long as the patient hopes that he can get the gratification from the object, the danger of suicide is less. Consequently, any therapeutic situation which implicitly promises to the patient that he can get his need gratified is running the risk of the patient's finally discovering the hopelessness of this search and becoming suicidal.

Following these considerations a step further, it seems logical to suppose that a relatively active denial of the role in which the patient casts the therapist must be present from the beginning of treatment. This is extremely difficult to achieve. One of the countertransference difficulties, which will be discussed later, is the fact that the therapist unconsciously frequently falls into a variety of ways of meeting the patient's demands without being fully aware of the fact that he has been manipulated.

The second major technical difficulty—that of breaking through the patient's stereotyped response sufficiently to introduce new concepts to the patient and to free his own feelings—is not, of course, unique to the treatment of the manic-depressive, although it does represent quantitatively a greater obstacle with these patients. It has become a truism of psychotherapy that a patient with a distorted attitude toward others tends to relate himself to new persons in such a way as to perpetuate his own problem. This process has been named *selective inattention* by Sullivan. Thus one who believes in his own unlovability will observe and react only to the rejecting elements in the attitude of the people around him, utilizing his observations continually to confirm the "fact" that people don't like him. The rigidity with which such a point of view is maintained varies with the severity of the illness and the strength of the anxiety and is much more difficult to deal with in the psychoses than in the neuroses. However, in the manic-depressive, the problem is reinforced by the stereotyped defense mentioned earlier. This is in contrast to the schizophrenic, who notices nuances of expression and inflection, frequently in clear awareness, and then distorts their meaning. Thus a schizophrenic patient will note his therapist's tension as manifested, perhaps, by his swinging his leg during the interview. Having noticed it as tension, he will then attach a meaning to it which is inappropriate. For instance, he may interpret it as meaning that the therapist is sexually attracted to him. The manic or depressed patient will not take note of the tension phenomenon in the therapist; there may be a subliminal noticing of what goes on, but it is not sufficiently in awareness to be given a meaning. If the patient has such an occurrence called to his attention and is asked to put a meaning to it, the interpretation will fall into the category of the therapist's expressing boredom or disapproval of him. With the schizophrenic, therefore, the problem boils down to correcting a misinterpretation of an observed event; with the manic-depressive, both the observation and the interpretation are awry. Once the awareness of signals from other persons is more accessible to the manic-depressive, the misinterpretation is more easily corrected than in the schizophrenic.

Countertransference

While countertransference problems in the treatment of manic-depressives must necessarily vary with the personality of the therapist, there are a number of quite general responses generated in therapists which are deserving of notice. Perhaps the most striking one of these is the fact that, of those psychoanalysts who are working with psychotics, the large majority prefer working with schizoid and schizophrenic patients and tend to avoid those in the manic-depressive category. This preference has been thought by us to relate to the type of character structure found in the therapists. Such persons are usually schizoid or obsessional in character themselves and, as such, are rather subtle, introverted persons who are interested in the observation of their own and others' reactions. The extraverted, apparently unsubtle, manic-depressive is a threat to such therapists in several ways. In the first place, communicative efforts are a strain because of the lack of response. Second, the so-called healthy extra-verted approach to reality is likely to fill the more sensitive, introspective person with self-doubts as to the possibility that he makes mountains out of molehills, reads meanings in where none were meant, and so forth; one of our therapists had particular difficulty in speaking of feelings with a manic patient, on the basis that the patient would regard all that as fool-ishness. Third, the therapist tends to dislike this sort of person and to think of him as "shallow." And, finally, the patient's difficulty in recog-nizing or discussing his or another's feelings or meanings throws the therapist into a situation of helplessness, since these things are the coin in which he deals. An interpretation which is highly meaningful to the therapist and which he would expect to have a tremendous impact on one of his obsessional or schizoid patients is hardly noticed by his manic-depressive patient. One therapist describes this difficulty with a patient as follows:

The outstanding therapeutic problem during this period was that of getting the patient to think in terms of "psychic causality," that is, to recognize that there was a connection between what he experienced in his dealings with oth-ers and the way he felt. He was unable to recognize, for instance, that when someone did something to slight him, this would lead to his having hurt feel-ings. His feeling-response to the happenings of his life was out of awareness. This can be illustrated by an incident: He was doing some part-time teaching in a night law school, and at Christmas time the students gave presents to the various members of the faculty. Since the patient had been a faculty member for only a very short time, he received a small present, a necktie, while some of the other teachers received much more magnificent ones. Following this event, the patient came to his hour and complained of not feeling well. As he went through his account of the happenings of his life during the previous few days, the fact that he had received a Christmas present was mentioned. He did not, however, mention any comparison between the size of his gift and that of others or any feeling of being wounded that he had not received a finer gift. Largely by chance, I inquired in more detail about the Christmas giving at this school, and when I did so, I heard the full story. It was still not apparent to the patient that he had felt hurt and did not become apparent to him until I asked him whether he had felt hurt. When I asked the question, he then real-ized that he had been hurt. He was then able to go on and see that his feeling of depression had been initiated by this episode. However, without actually hav-ing his feeling experience identified for him and named by me, he was unable spontaneously to recognize it.

We have wondered whether, on the basis of these facts, a more appro-priate choice of therapist for the manic-depressive could not be made from among the psychiatrists who have, character-wise, something in common with them. Our data on this point are largely impressionistic, but among the therapists who have participated in this seminar there has seemed to be some tendency for greater success and greater preference for this type of patient among those with characters more nearly approaching the manic-depressive than the schizoid. It should also be noted, however, that, as our familiarity with the problems of the manic-depressive person increased and some, however vague, conceptions of how to meet them came into being, the general feeling of dislike or distaste diminished and was replaced by interest.

Many of the therapists had countertransference difficulties with the patients' demandingness. This is illustrated by the therapeutic difficulties with the patients Mr. H and Mr. R, both of whom were treated by the same therapist. In the initial stage of treatment, the therapist tended to permit herself to be manipulated into meeting or promising to meet the demands of the patient. This is a rather characteristic personal problem of the therapist, who is somewhat overinvolved in playing a benign and powerful role with patients. The second phase of the difficulty occurred when the therapist became aware of how she had been manipulated and then became overhostile and overrejecting. With both these patients, the whole treatment process was affected by these countertransference difficulties. The process in both patients shows a similar course, in that treatment for the first year, or year and a half, was relatively smooth but relatively unproductive of improvement. During this time the "honeymoon" was going on, and the therapist was permitting herself to be manipulated in a variety of ways into fulfilling or seeming to fulfil the patient's needs. Following this phase in both patients there occurred a crisis in which, on the one hand, the patients' symptoms became more severe and, on the other hand, the therapist became consciously hostile and rejecting toward the patients. These crises came about through a recognition on the part of the therapist of the lack of progress in the patients, a recognition of the manipulative aspects of the relationships, and an increasing resentment of being so manipulated. This led to a fairly abrupt and unkind rejection of the patients. Following the crises, during which the therapist worked through some of her resentful attitudes toward the patients, therapy in one case went on to a much more productive relationship, with consequent improvement and insight developing in the patient. In the other more severely sick patient, the improvement was missing.

Another therapist consciously set the goal of meeting the patient in empathic communication. The patient was severely depressed, and the therapist undertook the exhausting task of providing such a bridge between them. The approach proved very useful during the patient's depression; indeed, it was sufficiently successful to remove the necessity for hospitalizing the patient, a step which had been necessary in previous depressions. However, after the depression lifted and the patient became hypomanic, the treatment was disrupted. The patient became hostile and dismissed the therapist. At this time the therapist commented:

She had developed a type of behavior which actually got under my skin—the telephone calls. When she first talked about the transference [the patient accused the doctor of "throwing the transference out of the window"], I think that she was talking about the hostility and frustration in me when I wasn't able to protect my own life. A further element was the change in my attitude as I watched her move from depression into elation, the change in my evaluation of potentialities in this person. During the depression the sense of depth that attends this affect leads one to feel that there must be considerable to this character. When the depression lifted and, in the period prior to the elation, I began to see the range of her interests and the smallness of the grip that her interests had on her, my feeling about her changed. I came to question the notion that I had had about what treatment would amount to. I believe that she had reacted to my hopes for the treatment and to a process going on in me of giving them up.

Another therapist found herself protected in refusing to meet the patient's dependency demands by the reflection that, since it was commonly accepted that no one knew how to treat manic-depressives successfully, her professional prestige would not be threatened if she failed with the patient. Apparently this point gave her sufficient security to deny the patient's demands without experiencing too much uneasiness. She did, however, show some vulnerability to the patient's demanding attitude, in that on one occasion she felt that the patient was justified in being angry at her for an unavoidable tardiness. And on several other occasions when the therapist had to be away from town for a day, she made the probably meaningful arrangement of making up the missed hour with the patient *in advance*. We concluded that, even though the therapist was relatively secure in the face of the patient's demandingness, a certain degree of apprehensiveness remained of which she was unaware.

Therapeutic Techniques

Many of the topics covered throughout this report carry therapeutic implications, since rational therapy must be based primarily upon an understanding of the patient's dynamics and specifically upon an understanding of the transference and countertransference patterns.

All the members of the seminar agreed that the first step in therapy with these patients should be the establishment of a communicative relationship, in the ordinary sense of the term, in which thoughts, feelings, and meanings are noticed and talked about. A variety of maneuvers were suggested for the accomplishment of this goal: (1) One suggestion was that the emphasis in communication with the manic-depressive be non-verbal, chiefly using tone of voice and gesture rather than emphasis on the intellectual content of the exchange, with a view toward development of more facility for noticing non-verbal experiences. This was done by one therapist largely by assuming this sort of role herself. (2) Another therapist felt that the usual technique, applied with more patience and

more intenseness, would suffice, with the addition that it would be necessary for the therapist to realize that the patient's seemingly good contact
and ability to tell a great deal about himself should not deceive the therapist into assuming that meaningful communication exists when it does
not. A further point made by this therapist is that the presence of strong
feelings of envy and competitiveness with the therapist keeps the patient
focused on "who is better" and prevents him from working on his problems. She would use this interpretation quite consistently in the early
stages of treatment. (3) Another suggested maneuver was to press the
patient in an insistent manner to look for and give the emotionally meaningful material, on the basis of the assumption that the material is present and available if the therapist demands it. This would involve treating
the stereotypy of the patient as a defense from the outset. (4) Another
approach suggested was summed up under the name "relationship therapy," by which is meant the substitution of action for words. This would
include the non-verbal technique mentioned above, and it could also include the various shock or startle experiences which have seemed to help
in shaking the stereotypy defense of these patients. This latter has been
explained as being effective because it was sufficiently intense and spontaneous to loosen the defensive armor of the patient momentarily and involve him in a more genuine emotional interchange. It is, of course,
highly speculative whether such a sudden, spontaneous eruption of the
therapist could be fashioned into a planned technical approach. However,
the point remains that the conventionalized verbal psychoanalytic approach may be quite an undesirable one for the conventionalized manic-
depressive patient. As one member of the seminar expressed it: "Words
become very easily stereotyped, whether you use Freudian language or
Sullivanian language; whatever language you use, it becomes stereotyped
and doesn't convey any feeling. When you want to get at the feeling, there
has to be some startle reaction."

The consensus of the seminar was that the *first and foremost problem
is that of getting beyond the conventionalized barrier into the area of
emotional exchange.* The variety of methods suggested for approaching
this goal is a reflection of the variety of personalities in the seminar
group. In addition to the various approaches suggested, however, there
appeared to be general agreement that looking at the stereotyped or conventional behavior as a defense against anxiety and making interpretations of it as such constitute a therapeutically fruitful approach.

A second point of general agreement in the treatment of these patients
had to do with the handling of the demands. From the material in the
section on countertransference it can be seen that there are dangerous
pitfalls in this aspect of the relationship, especially since too great or impossible demands on the part of the patient are likely to mobilize countertransference anxieties in the therapist. While numerous speculations

were entered into as to the feasibility of meeting some or all of the patient's demands, the experience of the years seemed to indicate that it is more desirable to *take a firm and consistent attitude of refusing to attempt to meet irrational demands from the beginning.* To this must be added a certain watchfulness, lest one be outmaneuvered by the patient and, while saying "no" to one demand, be simultaneously trapped into meeting another. This seemed to be the case with the therapist who was impelled to make up missed hours in advance. And, of course, this is an area where the manipulative ingenuity of the patient is particularly spectacular. We also agreed that, since the manipulative aspects of the relationship are prone to involve the therapist in various degrees of unspoken or even unrecognized resentment, great care and alertness should be exercised (*a*) to get the demandingness out into the open and (*b*) to resolve the tensions which come into the relationship by a full discussion of the reactions of both patient and therapist.

Another therapeutic difficulty which is closely related to the demandingness is the problem of acting out. In the manic, this takes the form either of ill-advised acts which do the patient's reputation or economic security real damage or of making decisions at a time of poor judgment which seriously alter the course of life. In the depressive, the acting out takes the form either of failure in job or life-situation due to apathy and hopelessness or of suicide. These dangers seem to imply the need for firmness and guidance in dealing with both the manic and the depressive aspects of the illness. However, as soon as the therapist begins to play a guiding role with the patient, he seems to meet one of the patient's most basic demands and opens himself up to receiving more and more demands which are presented as necessary to prevent injurious acting out. The therapist is soon in a situation in which the patient is able to re-enact with him his old pattern of dependency, and the therapist does not know where or how to draw the line. Numerous almost humorous tales are told by psychiatrists about how they have handled suicidal threats from patients. One psychiatrist, in response to a suicidal threat, told the patient, "Well, please don't do it on my doorstep." Another, when telephoned by a patient who threatened to kill himself, said, "Well, what did you wake me up to tell me that for?" A third therapist told the patient that it was against the rules for him to commit suicide, and, if he did so, she would discontinue the treatment! Laughable as these illustrations are, their effectiveness in reducing the danger of suicide nonetheless makes a point regarding the dynamics of the patient. On the one hand, a denial of responsibility for the continued existence of the patient seems vitally necessary in order to prevent the use of suicide as a weapon to enforce the patient's dependency demands. However, implicit in each statement is the doctor's admission to the patient that he is meaningful or important to him; this aspect of the problem has been referred to before. We feel that an air of blandness or indifference is quite undesirable in dealing with these patients; that a condition of involvement of the patients with their therapists, and vice versa, is necessary for their progress and even survival. The patient seems to need recognition of his importance from the therapist in order to attain even a minimal degree of security in the therapeutic relationship. This is usually sought for in terms of dependency— the patient endeavors to see the therapist as dependent on him—for his reputation, if for nothing else. This often leads the patient to use suicidal threats as a means of testing the therapist's dependency. It seems probable that the patient's underlying fear is that he will be unable to keep the therapist's interest and therefore that the therapeutic relationship will dissolve unless the therapist needs him. This fear can often be modified if the therapist can make the distinction to the patient that the patient can be important to him as a person without the therapist's necessarily having to be dependent on him.

This problem is illustrated in the management of Mr. R's acute depression. In order to avoid the necessity of hospitalizing him, the therapist was seeing him six or seven times a week. In addition, the patient was referred to an internist for help with his insomnia and saw him about twice a week. And, beyond this, a psychiatrist friend of the patient made himself available and spent an evening or two a week listening to the patient's complaints. All this attention was ineffective; the patient's tension continued to rise, and his suicidal threats increased in number. It was not until his therapist grew angry and scolded him thoroughly that the patient's tension began to subside. On reconsideration of this episode we concluded that it was the fact that the therapist cared enough to grow angry that made the episode significant to the patient. Her anger startled the patient sufficiently to push his stereotyped defense aside for a moment and permit a real exchange of feeling to occur. It seems to have been the first time that the therapist ever appeared to be a human being to him, and, following this first experience, later recognition of her humanness became more easily achieved.

In dealing not only with the depressive but also with the manic it is manifestly impossible for the therapist's denial of the patient's dependency demands to go to the length of passive indifference. In treating a manic, either within or outside a hospital, restrictions on his activity are necessary to prevent both his destructive impact on his environment and his destroying himself. Such restrictions are also necessary for the sake of the therapist. That is, exploitation beyond the particular level of tolerance of any individual therapist will inevitably lead to non-therapeutic resentment, and the manic will characteristically attempt to find the limits and then go beyond them.

We have concluded, on the basis of these considerations, that the manic-depressive can best be treated in a situation where certain rules are laid down for him in an active, vigorous, and "involved" way by the therapist. We feel that his irrational demands should be recognized, labeled, and refused. We feel that the therapist should not make decisions for the patient or attempt to give him advice on how to behave; in fact, the therapist's pressure should be in the opposite direction—that of the patient's working through his conflicts to the point of being able to make his own decisions. The rules should be laid down in terms of setting up a structure or frame of reference within which the patient would then be responsible for working out his own personal choices and decisions. We conceive of the making of rules or setting of limitations as conveying to the patient not only guidance but also a sense of his own importance. To illustrate: In dealing with a depressive who was unable to eat or dress, the therapist would convey much more a sense of the patient's importance by setting up a rule that the patient must eat a certain minimum number of meals a day than by allowing the patient to starve or undernourish himself until he "worked out his conflict" about eating.

The patient's sense of his own meaningfulness to the therapist is, we believe, also promoted by the therapist's continuous attempt to convey to the patient some sense of the therapist's own feeling attitudes. Thus we would advocate the expression of resentment to a manic or depressive patient when it was genuinely and warmly felt. In the treatment of Mr. R, after the initial change for the better occurred, his therapist found that his stereotyped defenses would be dropped if she *complained* that she did not know what he was talking about. This can be considered to be an interpretation that he was now using a defensive maneuver, plus an expression of feeling—annoyance—about it.

As in any other analysis, the working through of the transference and countertransference with the manic-depressive constitutes the most important part of the analysis. The particular defenses in this kind of illness make these problems unusually acute and probably contribute to the feeling among many therapists that manic-depressive patients are the most difficult of all patients to treat. We feel that the difficulty in communication resulting from the stereotyped response of these patients is by all odds the greatest technical problem to be solved in their therapy.

SUMMARY AND CONCLUSIONS

An intensive study of twelve manic-depressive patients was made, in order to reformulate and further develop the dynamics of the character structure of these patients in terms of their patterns of interpersonal relationships. In addition to developing further our knowledge of their psychodynamics, we hoped to arrive at therapeutic procedures which would prove more useful in interrupting the course of this kind of illness.

A comprehensive survey of the literature was made, to determine the present state of development of psychopathological theory in regard to manic-depressive states.

The manic-depressive character was investigated from the point of view of (1) the patterns of interaction between parents and child and between family and community; (2) the ways in which these patterns influenced the character structure of the child and affected his experiencing of other people in his subsequent life; and (3) the way in which these patterns are repeated in therapy and can be altered by the processes of therapy.

Psychopathology

Among the significant parent-child interactions, we found that the family is usually in a low-prestige situation in the community or socially isolated in some other way and that the chief interest in the child is in his potential usefulness in improving the family's position or meeting the parents' prestige needs. A serious problem with envy also grows out of the importance of material success and high prestige. We also found that the child is usually caught between one parent who is thought of as a failure and blamed for the family's plight (frequently the father) and the other parent who is aggressively striving, largely through the instrumentality of the child, to remedy the situation. And, finally, the serious disturbance in the child's later value system (superego) is in part attributable to the lack of a secure and consistent authority in the home and to the tremendous overconcern of the parents about what "they" think.

A study of the major unresolved anxiety-provoking experiences of the manic-depressive indicates that the crucial disturbance in his interpersonal relationship occurs at a time in his development when his closeness (identification) with his mother has diminished but his ability to recognize others as whole, separate persons has not yet developed. This accounts for the perpetuation of his response to important figures in his later life as either good or bad, black or white, and his inability to distinguish shades of gray.

Therapy

As a result of our study of these patients, we found that our ability to intervene successfully in the psychosis improved. While all the factors which contributed to successful therapy with these patients are by no means understood, we concluded that certain areas could be isolated, as follows:

Communication.—The primary problem in therapy is establishing a communicative relationship, which is, of course, a reflection of the patient's basic life-difficulty. The most characteristic aspect of the manic-depressive's defenses is his ability to avoid anxiety by erecting conventional barriers to emotional interchange. We have learned to interpret this as a defense rather than a defect in the patient's experience, and we have found that when it is interpreted as a defense, he responds by developing a greater ability to communicate his feelings and to establish empathic relationships.

(2)   *Dependency.*—A second major problem is that of handling the patient's dependency needs, which are largely gratified by successful manipulation of others. Since the manic-depressive's relationships with others are integrated chiefly on the basis of dependency, the therapist is in a dilemma between the dangers of allowing himself to fit into the previous pattern of the dependency gratification patterns of the patient and of forbidding dependency *in toto*. Furthermore, the therapeutic relationship in itself is a dependent relationship. The therapist must be alert to the manipulative tendencies of the patient and must continually bring these into open discussion rather than permit them to go on out of awareness.

(3)   *Transference-countertransference.*—The most significant part of treatment is, as always, the working through of the transference and countertransference problems. The patient's main difficulties with the therapist are those of dealing with him as a stereotype and as a highly conventionalized authority figure, who is either to be placated or manipulated and by whom all his dependency needs are to be met. The main difficulties of the therapist are in the frustrations and helplessness of trying to communicate with the patient through his defensive barriers and the strain of constantly being the target for the manipulative tendencies. These problems inevitably involve the therapist in a variety of feelings of resentment and discouragement which must be worked through. We have found that a recognition of the ways in which transference-countertransference patterns manifest themselves and vary from the patterns found with other types of patients makes the working through of this problem possible.

(4)   *Problem of authority and defining limits.*—One of the great risks in therapy with the manic-depressive is the danger of suicide when he is depressed or of the patient's damaging his economic and social security when he is in a manic phase. Much of the success in handling this destructive element must, of course, depend on successful therapy. However, we have found that a careful definition of limits and an appropriate expression of disapproval when the limits are violated are helpful.

Further Areas for Study

We feel that the conclusions derived from our intensive study of twelve patients require confirmation by further investigation of a larger series. A thorough statistical study of the families of manic-depressives is desirable in order to confirm and elaborate the picture of the family patterns as we have developed it. And, finally, a more intensive study of psychotherapeutic interviews with manic-depressive patients is needed in order to define more clearly the characteristic patterns of communication and interaction between patient and therapist and to contrast these with the interactions in other conditions. This is a logical next step in advancing our knowledge of the psychopathology of all mental disorders.

V

On General Psychiatric Problems

PSYCHOANALYTIC REMARKS ON THE CLINICAL
SIGNIFICANCE OF HOSTILITY

In a paper on "The Psychopathological Significance of Hostility," Dr. Hadley has discussed the enormous influence that hostility has on every human being's biological and emotional life, be he sick or healthy. As to its clinical significance, hostility gives rise to many pathological conflicts. Let us see why.

Modern social life is, on the one hand, more or less unconsciously based on general competitive hostility. On the other hand, modern people's consciences are consciously oriented on the commandments of Christian morality demanding general charity toward everybody. Thus we live through a constant conflict between our hostile tendencies against an inimical environment or even toward simultaneously beloved persons, on the one side, and between our conscience's demands of loving our neighbors as ourselves, on the other. In addition, people's ill-will against their neighbor makes them feel insecure because of fear of hostile retaliation.

These conflicts start in early childhood when children first have to deal with hostility and competition in their family environment and when they have to stand their beloved parents' training efforts, which show as antagonism toward their infantile longing for exclusive pleasure; they will answer it by feeling resentful toward their parents while still continuing to love them. Thus "ambivalence" (that is to say, the capability of simultaneously liking and disliking persons and things and the disability of exclusively loving them) rises as a general feature of human emotional life. It is developed most decidedly in early childhood and later on decreases but never disappears.

If the tension between the hostility and the commandments of charity, between love and hatred, that one adult person feels toward another becomes, for some reason or other, so intense that he cannot stand the constant conflict which is raised by this antagonism, hostility will be repressed. Very often this repression will not be successful. In this case the person may escape from a reality in which he is constantly submitted to the conflict between his hostility and his blaming conscience and to the

Read before the Section on Neurology and Psychiatry of the Maryland Psychiatric Society, November 7, 1935.

Reprinted from *Medical Annals of the District of Columbia*, Vol. V, No. 9 (September, 1936).

fear of retaliation into the unreality of sickness (psychoneurosis or psychosis), and he may express his incompletely repressed hostility by psychogenic physical or psychic symptoms. By these means, repressed hostility and ambivalence give rise to many nervous and mental diseases.

Let me give one clinical example of its etiologic significance from the group of organ neuroses, namely, migraine; one from the group of psychoneuroses, namely, agoraphobia; and one from the group of psychoses, namely, melancholia.

Experience with eight cases of migraine (each of which I treated and studied an hour a day for a year or longer) has given me the following impression: they all were persons who, because of their hypersensitive consciences, their fixation on very cultured and somewhat conventional old families with a particularly strong family moral standard, or the intense destructiveness of their hostile tendencies, could not stand their ambivalence and therefore tried to repress their hostility. This repression was not totally successful, and therefore the hostility expressed itself by the physical symptoms of migraine.

In order to understand our patients' ability to express emotions by their body, I should like to recall our experience with healthy persons' equal psychophysical mechanism. Little children, for example, express their troubles and their wishes, before they are developed enough to talk, by shouting, crying, vomiting, etc. Healthy adults sometimes also express, as we know, emotions, wishes, and feelings by bodily changes, e.g., by blushing, heartbeating, diarrhea, etc. Neurotic and psychotic patients are using the same mechanism if they do not succeed in totally repressing forbidden emotions and wishes, thus building psychogenic physical symptoms, so-called "conversion symptoms."

Coming back to the symptoms of migraine, they are, as we know, unilateral headache, scintillating scotomata or other visual disturbances, nausea, retching and vomiting, intestinal disturbances—namely, spastic constipation, sometimes ending in diarrhea—urine retention, and attacks of chilliness and pallor which may be unilateral. Strikingly enough, all these different symptoms are produced by the same functional mechanism, that is, by spasmodic muscular contractions of involuntary smooth muscles. The headache, the visual disturbances, nausea and vomiting, and urine retention are caused (because of sympathetic irritation) by spasmodic contractions of the smooth musculature of cerebral blood vessels, which cause, in turn, ischemia and edema, irritating the brain as a whole and its centers. In addition to the central muscular spasms, the chilliness and the pallor of the skin are caused by local vascular spasms; constipation and diarrhea (due to vagus irritation) by the activities of the smooth muscles of the bowels; retching and vomiting by cramplike contractions of the muscular system of the diaphragm and of the pylorus; urine retention by spasms of the muscular system of the bladder.

In order to make us understand this mechanism as an expression of unconscious hostility, I want to recall the fact that conscious hostility is also
physically expressed by our skeletal muscular system. Does not the man
who feels enraged against his enemy wish to assault him? And, since this
real physical aggression is usually forbidden within our culture, does he
not at least contract those muscles by the activity of which he could hurt
his adversary? Indeed he does! He clenches his fist, gnashes his teeth,
kicks at the hated person, etc., i.e., he contracts the respective voluntary
striped muscles.

Thus the migraine patient's repressed hostility toward a beloved person is expressed by spasmodic contractions of his involuntary muscular
system, which obeys only unconscious impulses, on the same principle as
an average healthy person's hostility is expressed by contractions of his
voluntary skeletal muscular system that obeys conscious impulses.

(By the way, we may note in this connection the muscular cramps and
convulsions in epilepsy and its close relationship to migraine. Psychoanalysis considers these epileptic convulsions also to be an expression of the
epileptic's hostility.)

In describing this psychogenic mechanism of migraine and its main
symptom, headache, I do not mean to overlook the well-known fact that
common headache very often also arises as a conversion symptom expressing anger, rage, or hatred.

However, although nearly every neurotic, as well as a so-called healthy
person, may occasionally express an attack of anger or hatred which is
more or less temporarily or more or less superficially repressed or even
only suppressed, by producing an attack of common headache, I have the
impression that migraine always seems to be one specific expression of
deeply repressed continuous hostility against beloved persons, that is to
say, the specific expression of unresolved ambivalence. AGORAPHOBIA

Let us now see about the etiologic significance of unconscious hostility
in a psychoneurosis, namely, agoraphobia. The patients suffering from
agoraphobia are, as we know, fearful and therefore unable to walk alone
in streets and open places. They are capable of doing this only if somebody is with them.

Formerly we tried to understand this anxiety as a result of the patients'
fear of the sexual "dangers of the street." Recently, however, psychoanalysis has shown that this interpretation does not suffice but that agora
phobic patients also suffer from intense unconscious hostility toward a
person whom they consciously love or whom they are at least supposed
not to dislike. The agoraphobic symptoms, however, are not so much a
direct expression of the patient's hostility as the migraine symptoms are;
according to my experience, they are secondarily caused by the agoraphobic's fear of retaliation and punishment for his hostility. Because of
this hostility in fantasy he wishes to injure or even to kill the beloved and

hated person. According to the magic way of unconscious mentation, the patient does not feel any difference between the thoughts and wishes he has in his unconscious mind and their real fulfilment. So he unconsciously believes that his evil wishes will be fulfilled. Wishing evil, he fears retaliation. Therefore, he is afraid to walk alone and to deal by himself with the real dangers of the street, which may turn against him for punishment and retaliation, and he feels secure and protected from its dangers only if somebody is with him. When accompanied, therefore, he succeeds in crossing the dangerous streets and places.

One of my patients, the daughter of a psychotic mother whom she hated, wished secretly to kill her. Naturally this hatred and this wish were very deeply repressed and unconscious until analysis revealed them.

"If I leave mother," she reported after this unconscious experience became conscious to her, "mother will die because of my wishes. On the other hand, I cannot wish mother's death, first, because you are not allowed to hate your mother and you are certainly not allowed to kill her; then because father would punish me by wanting me to die, too; and his death wishes would certainly kill me."

When the agoraphobia of this patient began, the only way of getting her across a street was for her father to accompany her. Later on, she was also able to walk if a substitute accompanied her. After the disclosure of her emotional conflicts the patient recovered.

Deutsch and other psychoanalytic authors add another explanation. According to their theory, the agoraphobics can cross streets only when somebody else is with them because they take the companion as a substitute for the person toward whom their evil wishes are directed. Having this person himself or his substitute unhurt with them, the patients feel the reassurance that their injuring wishes against him are not fulfilled, thus being at the same time relieved from feelings of guilt and fear of retaliation.

Now let us consider an example of the etiologic significance of hostility in psychoses, namely, melancholia. The symptoms of melancholia are, as we know, the patients' deeply depressive mood, lack of self-confidence and strong self-reproaches, sleeplessness, refusal to eat, fear of impoverishment, and suicidal tendencies.

What do these symptoms mean? As we know from our analytic experience, the melancholics are persons whose love life remained undeveloped or who, because of a strong emotional conflict which is primarily responsible for their depressive and mournful mood, started again to react according to the laws that were active in their early instinctual development. This emotional conflict may be represented by the loss of a beloved person, by the real or imagined loss of his love, or by any experience that made them face their own loving disability.

Because of their regressive instinctual life, the melancholics also feel extremely ambivalent, not only toward other persons, like the neurotic and psychoneurotic cases we discussed before, but also and very decidedly toward themselves. They symbolically demonstrate their suffering from this poor love life by complaining about their fear of impoverishment, meaning consciously their material impoverishment and unconsciously their fear of being bare of active and passive love in regard to themselves and to other persons.

As to their hatred against themselves, which shows by their conscience's constant disapproval of themselves, it finds its main expression in their intense self-accusations and their tendency to deprive themselves of basic life-necessities like sleep and nourishment.

At the same time these symptoms serve the unconscious purpose of ruling over and getting attention from the patients' associates, which they expect to comfort them continually, to talk them out of their self-reproaches, and to take care of their neglected physical requirements. Thus their self-reproaches have the additional real content of reprimanding themselves for their sadistic tendencies toward other people.

The early and primitive state of the melancholics' emotional life has still another consequence. Instead of loving or hating other persons as such, the melancholics deal with their feelings toward these persons—to say it in psychologic terms—by identifying with them, which means, biologically, by introjecting them or by swallowing these persons in fantasy. (In order to understand this unconscious mechanism, we may think of primitive people who really swallow a person's body or parts of it if they want to incorporate beloved or hated persons' character qualities. They eat, e.g., a brave chief's heart, thus incorporating, as they believe, the dead chief's bravery.)

Since the melancholics, by these means, feel identical with the swallowed persons, their self-accusations have the secret additional contents of blaming on the incorporated persons everything they consciously accuse themselves of.

The same mechanism holds for the melancholic's suicidal impulses. On the one hand, they are the final conscious expression of his ambivalence against himself; on the other hand, they unconsciously mean, at the same time, murdering impulses against the incorporated person, who, being identical with him, is supposed to be killed with him if he commits suicide. Since homicidal tendencies are mostly forbidden, even more than suicide, they remain unconscious, and the melancholic consciously knows only about his suicidal impulses.

One analyst's patient responded to this insight that he had gained in the course of his analytical treatment by bringing a knife into his analytic hour and attempting to kill the analyst rather than himself.

Other melancholics in fantasy murder their friends, relatives, or physi-

FRIEDA FROMM-REICHMANN

cians, as it were, by commiting suicide, because they hope to make them feel guilty and miserable forever.

"I thought of killing myself," said one of my patients, "but I did not feel sure enough that you would mind it."

I realize that this short description of the very complicated unconscious mechanism in melancholia as verified by psychoanalytic research work done on many cases (Fenichel) may not appeal especially to those colleagues who usually will not deal with psychoanalysis. I hope, however, that I have at least succeeded in showing, in principle, how unconscious hostility becomes the reason for developing this psychosis, just the same as it does in a great number of psychoneuroses, as in our paradigm agoraphobia and in many organ neuroses, such as migraine.

[282]

(20)

CONTRIBUTION TO THE PSYCHOGENESIS
OF MIGRAINE

Experience with eight cases of migraine (two men and six women) has given me the impression that they were all patients suffering from unresolved ambivalence; they could not stand to be aware of their hostility against beloved persons; therefore, they unconsciously tried to keep this hostility repressed and finally expressed it by the physical symptoms of migraine.

I had the good fortune to have this brought home to me by one of my patients who used to develop and stop migraine attacks in the course of her analytical hour. She expressed her original ambivalence, which she recognized later to be the reason for her migraine attacks, most appropriately: "When I was a child," she said, "I did not always totally agree with my beloved mother's ideas and resented one or another decision she made. Each time I felt very bad and guilty of treason, and finally I got this bad headache." During her analysis the patient went through a similar experience in the transference, feeling that she had betrayed the analyst whenever she felt any criticism about analysis or analyst. Consequently, she repressed for a long time all antagonism toward the analyst. As a result, she would often develop a migraine attack during her analytical hour. On becoming conscious of her hostility to the analyst, her migraine symptoms would immediately, to quote her own words, "melt away."

In order to understand why the organism should choose, as it were, the symptoms of migraine as a means of expressing repressed hostility, we may remind ourselves what its classical and occasional symptoms are. As we know, they are, above all, the attacks of one-sided headache and variably scintillating scotomata or other visual disturbances, nausea, retching and vomiting, intestinal disturbances—namely, spastic constipation and finally diarrhea—urine retention, and attacks of general, sometimes one-sided, chilliness and paleness.

How are these symptoms produced? The neuropathologists have, as

Read at the midwinter meeting of the American Psychoanalytic Association, Boston, Massachusetts, December, 1935.

Reprinted from the *Psychoanalytic Review*, Vol. XXIV, No. 1 (January, 1937), by arrangement with the copyright owner, *Psychoanalysis and the Psychoanalytic Review*, National Psychological Association for Psychoanalysis, Inc., 66 Fifth Avenue, New York 11, New York.

we know, tried to answer this question by a great number of hypotheses. I will not discuss them within this psychoanalytical paper. They were recently collected by Riley in the *Bulletin of the Neurological Institute of New York* (1932). The most plausible and experimentally demonstrable theory runs as follows: Migraine is (because of sympathetic irritation) produced by spasmodic contraction of the smooth musculature of the cerebral blood vessels. According to Gordon and Stone, these angiospasms in turn cause ischemia and edema, which irritate the brain as a whole and its centers and produce by these means the headache, the visual disturbances, the nausea and vomiting, and the urine retention.

In addition to the central muscular spasms, the local symptoms are caused by peripheral muscular spasms: namely, the chilliness and paleness of the skin by local blood vessel spasms; constipation and diarrhea (due to vagus irritation) by the activities of the smooth muscles of the bowels; retching and vomiting by cramplike contractions of the muscular system of the diaphragm and of the pylorus; urine retention by spasms of the muscular system of the bladder.

If this is true, it means that the migraine symptoms are all, strikingly enough, produced by the same functional mechanism, though their final appearance and their localization may be ever so different—namely, by spasmodic muscular contractions of involuntary smooth muscles.

What is the significance of this fact for the hypothesis that migraine is a physical expression of unconscious hostility against consciously beloved persons? I believe we may be able to answer this question if we remember that conscious hostility is also physically expressed by our muscular system.

Does not the man who feels enraged against his enemy wish to assault him? And, since this real physical aggression is usually forbidden within our culture, does he not at least contract those muscles by the activity of which he could hurt his adversary? Indeed he does! He clenches his fist, gnashes his teeth, kicks at the hated person, etc., thus contracting the respective voluntary striped muscles. Ancient poets—Homer, for instance—who wanted to describe, and sculptors and artists who want to show, the hostile tension of a hero going to fight represent the skeletal muscles of his face, body, and limbs as strongly contracted; for both artist and public realize that these contracted muscles are an outstanding sign of hostility.

If we remember our well-known analytic experience that the organism is able to give unconscious utterance to repressed feelings by involuntary movements, then we understand that a patient suffering from migraine—that is, from the results of unconscious spasmodic contractions of the involuntary muscular system—is unconsciously expressing his repressed hostility against a beloved person on the same principle as another would express his conscious hatred.

The average person, feeling conscious hatred against an adversary, uses contractions of his voluntary skeletal muscles, which obey conscious impulses, as a normal conscious means of expressing his hostility. The migraine patient, who represses his hostility against consciously beloved persons, produces, as his unconscious expression of this repressed hatred, spasmodic contractions of involuntary smooth muscles, which obey unconscious impulses.

By the way, we may note in this connection the muscular cramps and convulsions in epilepsy and the close relationship of epilepsy to migraine. These epileptic convulsions are also known as an outstanding expression of the epileptic's hostility.

Coming back to our presentation of angiospastic migraine attacks, we may state that it refers to the classical and widespread picture of migraine as observed in all my patients. As to its angioparetic variations, namely, relaxation of the smooth muscles and their clinical consequences, which some authors describe, I had no opportunity to observe them as independent pictures of illness by themselves. They frequently showed, however, in one way or another at the termination of the spastic migraine attacks, and I wonder whether this angioparetic symptom complex could be explained as the final phase of a mild preceding spastic migraine attack that went unobserved.

If this is true, it belongs together with the well-known terminal symptoms in classical migraine we described before, namely, diarrhea, often following spastic constipation, or abundant final voiding, frequently following spastic urine retention; terminal crying; and warmth and flushing of the skin, sometimes following chilliness and paleness. These terminal symptoms prove to be the subjective and objective signs of local and general physical and psychic relaxation that follows the preceding general tenseness and spasticity of the migraine patients. They evidently indicate the suspension of their present attack of hostility, just as the relaxation of the clenched fist or jaws shows the solution of unrepressed conscious hostility.

This is the reason why the above-mentioned patient, for instance, felt as I said at the end of her attacks of transference hostility that her hatred had "melted away" and, to quote her once more, that the crying that each time ended her attacks was "like a relaxing urine flood coming from her eyes instead of her urethra."

Other patients describe their postmigraine relaxed condition in a comparable way: "You feel at that time good and tender and totally relaxed. It feels as if you won a serious fight," said one of them, the "at that time" referring to the moment when diarrhea took the place of spastic constipation and when the headache simultaneously stopped.

Coming back to the primary signs of migraine and its main symptom, headache, we do not mean to overlook the well-known fact that common headaches very often will arise as a conversion symptom expressing anger, rage, or hatred.

Although nearly every neurotic, as well as the so-called healthy person, may occasionally express an attack of anger or hatred which is more or less temporarily or more or less superficially repressed or even only suppressed, by producing an attack of common headache, I have the impression that migraine always seems to be one specific expression of deeply repressed continuous hostility against beloved persons, that is to say, the specific expression of unresolved ambivalence.

Steckel[1] explains migraine as a neurotic expression of the struggle between the moral ego and the drive-ego, but he does not investigate what the specific variations of this general neurotic conflict are in migraine patients.

In order to find out about this fundamental pathogenic problem we have to look for the answer to two questions:

First: What are the reasons for the intensity of our migraine patients' ambivalence? That is to say, why do they feel it so decidedly necessary to repress their negative feelings toward consciously beloved persons?

Second: Why do they chiefly use their head to express it?

As to the question why migraine patients cannot endure facing their ambivalent feelings, I have the following impression: All my migraine patients came from very cultured and somewhat conventional old families with a particularly strong solidarity within the family and a highly developed family pride. Within groups like these, aggression against one another is, as we know, extremely taboo. If one member of these families should dare to express hostility against another, he would be punished by exclusion, that is to say, by losing the protection of his family background, which means being abandoned in the struggle of life. This fear of punishment by being deprived of the family's protection was rather decidedly the fundamental reason for repressing hostility in all my migraine patients.

One of them described the moment when her older sister announced to her parents that she had voted for a different political party from the rest of the family as the most frightening life-experience she ever had— this was in Europe! "I thought the world would perish if one of us thought differently from the rest," she commented.

We may imagine the amount of hostility that persons living within such an environment must suppress and repress and what intense guilt feeling they must develop if they fail in repressing their antagonism.

Another patient said: "We were raised with the law: We family members belong together and love each other, as if that was the eleventh commandment, and when a child I consciously obeyed this law very strictly. However, as I know today, I secretly hated my mother with all my heart because of her enor-

1. In his *Anxiety-States* (1912). In the later editions the article on migraine is omitted.

mous family pride and especially because of one fundamental proof of it that she gave me: she would not take care of me when I was ill, because her family vanity made her imagine that no family member ought to be ill at any time. But she heartily enjoyed taking care of invalid persons who were not family members. We children had to help her at that job. Consciously I admired mother's procedure very much; however, I became secretly furious whenever I had to pay a visit to one of her protégés, and I regularly came home with a migraine attack."

Four of my patients, who had, as far as consciousness goes, personalities refined beyond the average, had still another reason for keeping their hostility hidden from themselves, namely, that their hatred of the beloved persons had such tremendously destructive unconscious aims that their sensitive consciences could not bear to realize it. They secretly wanted to destroy their beloved enemies, either morally in following the famous pattern as given in the Bible by Joseph, who dreamed of making his parents and siblings his slaves, or physically, as illustrated, for example, by the vivid childhood memory one of my patients recalled from her fourth year: she was sitting on a couch; one of her younger sisters with whom she had an intense rivalry looked for something on the floor under the couch. The patient in fantasy pushed the couch vigorously down with her buttocks, thus smashing her sister's head. This childhood experience, by the way, codetermined the patient's choice of migraine as a conversion symptom in regard to its main localization in the head, although it certainly was not the only reason for it.

As to our second etiological question of why the other patients utilized the head as a means of expressing hostility, it can be answered by looking at the content of their hostility. This was that they were rivals of their beloved adversaries or felt resentful in regard to their intellectuality, which they unconsciously wanted to destroy or at least to feel superior to.

One of them, e.g., was married to a very brilliant and clever, but sexually impotent, man who would boast of his intelligence, urge the patient to accomplish her intellectual education, and make fun of her lack of brilliancy. "To hell with him and all his intelligence, why isn't he potent and sexually satisfactory," she finally dared to say after one year of analysis. Every morning that followed a night during which her husband had tried in vain to have intercourse with her and very often when he boasted of his brilliancy or blamed her for her lack of it, she got an attack of migraine. She finally got rid of her symptoms after her husband's death—by the way, without starting at that time another sexual relationship, so that I could not verify Gutheil's experience[2] that a lack of heterosexual satisfaction and the Oedipus complex or other general neurotic mechanisms in themselves may cause migraine attacks.

Another patient, being a scientist like her husband, would consciously make every effort to help him to do his work. She would neglect her own work,

2. *Psychoanalyt. Rev.*, Vol. XXI, No. 3 (1934).

which she ostensibly considered less important than the husband's. However, unconsciously, she was a most intense rival of his and could not stand his superiority. So she produced migraine attacks as an expression of her secret rivalry with the consciously admired husband until she succeeded in becoming aware of her secret antagonism and gained analytic insight into and worked through her conversion mechanism.

This general mechanism is that migraine patients primarily want to destroy their partners' intelligence and brilliancy, that is to say, their brains and heads, as the concrete representative of their mental capacity. This mental castration of another person is not allowed and therefore, according to the analytically well-known unconscious mechanism, is turned back toward the patient himself; he does to himself by these means what he wanted to do to his partner, thus punishing himself for his forbidden tendencies.

It is, however, understood that this destruction of brain and head very often proves an active castration tendency displaced from below to above because of its specific mental aims and contents.

This mechanism showed most distinctly in two of my cases, two unknown physicians, A and B, who hardly earned their living by their small practices. Both of them suffered from migraine as an expression of their repressed rivalry and resentful feelings against an admired older brother, A's brother being a successful psychoanalyst, B's a well-known lawyer. Both patients' dreams, fantasies, and symptomatic actions showed open or disguised active castration tendencies against the secretly resented and consciously admired rivals.

Coming back to the statement that the migraine patients turn their hostile activity from other persons against themselves, we have, of course, to realize that it is a mere descriptive one. Dynamically seen, it means, as we especially know from our analytic experiences with melancholia, mourning, etc., that the patients introject the beloved and hated person, so that injuring themselves means at the same time hurting the introjected person, and vice versa.

If we keep this in mind, we understand that the different symptoms of ejection, as described before as to their relaxation significance, may have the unconscious contents that the patients overcome their hatred and the introjected beloved and hated persons by ejecting them, as in one case which a colleague told me personally, who, because of his repressed hostility against his mother, suffered for at least a couple of years from severe migraine attacks without ever being nauseated and without vomiting. He finally had one hard attack accompanied by nausea and regurgitation and then lost his migraine altogether. He spontaneously commented that he had thrown out his mother and his hatred against her by this final migraine attack.

I think we are justified in these deductions as to the psychogenesis of migraine from our observations on eight patients. There are still other very fascinating migraine problems, like the bisexuality of migraine patients which Gutheil emphasizes or the left- or right-sided localization of headache. However, I did not succeed in finding out enough about these questions to be able to give a satisfactory account of them.

Allow me to add a short remark about the analytic therapy of migraine. Five of my patients became practically cured, two got decided relief as to the number and intensity of their attacks, one remained practically uninfluenced. Her instinctual organization and, even more, her life-situation made it necessary for her to develop a greater amount of destructive hostility than she ever could consciously admit to herself.

(21)

NOTES ON THE MOTHER ROLE
IN THE FAMILY GROUP

The problem of the mother role in the family group may be approached from a biological angle, by discussing the problems of pregnancy, delivery, nursing period, etc., or from a psychological and sociological angle. In this paper we deal with its psychological aspects and discuss the following three questions: (1) What is the mother's actual psychological function in the family group? (2) Are there maternal instincts or drives? (3) What is the psychological concept of the ideal role of the mother in the family group of our culture?

The actual mother role in the family is dependent on the general role of women in the family group according to the cultural structure of the individual family and of the society to which that family belongs. Let us, for example, compare the role of the woman in European society and the maternal function in European families with women's position in the social and family group of this country.

In the countries of western Europe the social structure is distinctly patriarchal. The family structure in middle-class groups and among the working and farmer classes is patriarchal to the extent that the husband and father is undoubtedly the unanimously acknowledged head of the family, who rules over wife and children. He earns their living; therefore, he is allowed to run, or to make his wife run, the whole home and family life according to his personal wishes and necessities and to use or abuse his home as an outlet for every kind of emotional reaction which he may have to suppress on the outside. His wife and children have to bear his good and his bad moods. His wife has to wait on him and obey him, and she must provide every kind of accommodation for him at her own emotional and physical expense. And while the father and husband rules over wife and children, they, in turn, are very close to each other by virtue of their common fear of the father.

This family structure puts the mother decidedly in the role of the children's confidante, friend, and helper. It is she to whom they talk

This paper was prepared for a mental hygiene and social workers' meeting in Washington, D.C., and subsequently read at a joint meeting of the Topeka Psychoanalytic Society and the staff seminar of the Menninger Clinic in Topeka, Kansas, on January 3, 1940.

Reprinted from the *Bulletin of the Menninger Clinic*, Vol. IV, No. 5 (1940).

about their troubles and secrets; it is she who gives them relief from their fear of father. Mother will give them comfort and affection, father will rule over them and punish them.

The International Institute for Social Research, now connected with Columbia University, did some interesting research work in Europe in regard to this problem.[1] The institute sent one group of some five hundred questionnaires pertaining to problems of authority and family to experts on psychological research work on children and to experienced teachers, social workers, and others in Switzerland, Belgium, France, and Austria, and another group of questionnaires directly to several thousands of Swiss, French, and British adolescents. One of the questions was: "To whom do children turn with their troubles and secrets?" According to an overwhelming majority of experts (82.6 per cent in one of the groups), children were considered to confide their troubles to the mother alone.

Among a group of 508 Swiss adolescents who were asked directly, 24 per cent answered "To mother only," and only 7 per cent "To father only"; that is, the mother was confided in three times as often as the father. The opposite question: "Who punishes the children?" was answered by the great majority of experts and adolescents: "Father."

We all know how different things are in this country. Women's rights and privileges in social life are more like men's than in Europe. Most jobs and professions are open to women. And especially important along the line of our question is the fact that the number of women who teach school is proportionately much larger than in Europe.

In the family group, American women are very often the leaders, and men wait on them as wives wait on their husbands in European families. And even though this may not be so as a rule, there is certainly a fundamental difference between the atmosphere of the American family and that of the European family, and the basic fact holds true that American women are not afraid of men, as European women are, and that the average American wife does not fear her husband. Consequently, the wife and mother is often the bearer of authority in the family group (as recently pointed out by the American ethnologist Margaret Mead).[2] The children may, therefore, be afraid of her as they are in Europe of the father; the more so, since the teacher, the bearer of the school authority, is more often than not a woman. The American father, on the other hand, is more of a confidant and friend to his children. It is he who will share their troubles and their secrets, and it is he who plays

1. *Autorität und Familie* ("Studien a.d. Institut f. Sozialforschung," ed. M. Horkheimer [Paris: Librairie Félix Alcan, 1936]) (with English and French abstracts).

2. Margaret Mead, "On the Institutionalized Role of Woman and Character Formation," *Ztschr. Sozialforsch.*, Vol. V, No. 1 (1936).

with them and helps them solve their problems with their mechanical toys.[3]

If it is true that in Europe the authoritative father is the main psychological problem of the family, because of the European social and family structure, it holds that the corresponding family problem of this country is the child's fear of his domineering mother.

Why do we call this the *main* family problem? Because through psychoanalysis it has been found that the individual's whole development is decisively influenced by his conscious and unconscious emotional childhood experiences. Because of the relatively long period of the biological and psychological helplessness of every human infant and the long period of social dependency that children have to undergo within this culture,[4] this question is paramount: Do they feel security in the kindness, friendliness, and love of the persons on whom they are dependent? If these persons are domineering—like the father in the European patriarchal culture or like the mother in the family structure of this country—then they will arouse *feelings of insecurity, anxiety, and hatred* in the mind of the dependent child which he may often not overcome for the rest of his life.

During the infant's early life the influence of maternal domination may even be more disastrous for the child's emotional development than the influence of an overauthoritative father. But at all ages the child will consciously or unconsciously sense any kind of domination, be it overt and verbalized or indirect and subtle.

As a consequence of the lack of affection that the child meets (or interprets) in an imperious mother, he may early start to develop a *compulsive need for everybody's affection* which may remain with him for his whole life, making him insecure and overdependent on other people. Because of constant skepticism about the affection of mother in childhood, he may become doubtful and skeptical of nearly everything and everybody in later life. He may even unconsciously use skepticism as a snobbish mask to hide his insecurity.

Consistent fear of an oversevere maternal authority will prevent the child from developing according to his potentialities. He will try to model himself on the domineering parent's wishes and drives, in order to avoid further domination and punishment and to keep the affection of his parents, on whom he feels dependent. At the same time, conscious or unconscious feelings of hatred will be aroused against the parent who is restricting his *drive toward growth and perfection*. Fear of retribution

3. A poll among the audience of the Topeka meeting did not bear out the above. Approximately 40 per cent of the audience claimed to have confided their secrets preferably or exclusively to their mothers in childhood, 40 per cent to their fathers, approximately 20 per cent to neither.

4. S. Freud, *The Problem of Anxiety* (New York: W. W. Norton & Co., 1936).

for this hatred will intensify his primary anxiety, for there are few things in life that children resent more than frustration in their efforts at self-realization and self-accomplishment.

It seems to be this drive for self-achievement of which Freud is thinking when he mentions the individual's need to develop his secondary self-love by gaining the approval of his own conscience, of his "superego." We believe, however, that Freud does not put enough stress on the individual's basic legitimate urge to live up to the requirements of his ideals and to his potentialities and therefore undervalues the conflicts engendered if a person is kept from achievement. Hence he underestimates the child's resentment and hatred of the oversevere authority of his parents, who hinder his growth and development.[5]

Freud describes the child's hatred of the imperious parent, but not as such. He considers the hatred and anxiety toward the parent of the same sex to be one aspect of the Oedipus constellation arising from its other aspect, the feelings of sexual attraction toward the parent of the other sex. However, even though it is undoubtedly true that phases of unconscious erotic attraction on an infantile level between the child and the parent of the other sex may develop for a certain time, modern research workers show that the choice of persons between whom competitive hatred will develop is altogether dependent on the society and family structure and that this hatred toward the parent of the same sex is not necessarily due to sexual competition.

The ethnologist Malinowski shows in his study *The Sexual Life of Savages in North Western Melanesia*[6] that the boys of the Trobriand Islands, who live within a matriarchal family structure, develop no hatred whatsoever against their father, who has no authoritative power within the family group but is just his boys' friend and playmate and their mother's sex partner. The boys' whole hostility turns, however, against the mother's brother, who is the holder of the family authority and in charge of the family estate and who has the social functions of the father in a patriarchal family.[7] In some other primitive matriarchal societies this hatred against the authoritative powerful uncle is considered to be so great that the boys are allowed to destroy their uncle's orchard once or twice a year in order to get rid of their suppressed hostility toward him.

These data indicate that the boys' hatred of their father need not be

5. See E. Fromm, "Selfishness and Self-Love," *Psychiatry*, Vol. II, No. 4 (1939).

6. London: Routledge & Sons, 1932.

7. Margaret Mead, *Growing Up in New Guinea* (New York: W. Morrow Co., 1930); see also B. Malinowski, "Mutterrechtliche Familie und Oedipuscomplex," *Imago*, Vol. X (1924), reviewed in *Internat. J. Psychoanal.* (1925); F. Boehm, "Zur Geschichte des Oedipuscomplexes," and O. Fenichel, "Spezialformen des Oedipuscomplexes," *Internat. Ztschr. Psychoanal.*, Vol. XVII, No. 1 (1931), reviewed in *Internat. J. Psychoanal.*, Vol. XII (1931).

directed toward the father as the boys' sexual rival but may be against the domination of a father who is the boys' rival and adversary by virtue of the power and authority that the European patriarchal society grants him.

In *this* country the boy may develop the same kind of competitive fear and hatred of his domineering mother (in spite of their mutual sexual attraction, which may meantime develop, or try to develop, concomitantly). The fact that he thus finds himself hating a person whom he simultaneously loves and is supposed to love reinforces his guilt feelings, his tendencies to suppress his emotions, and therefore his unsteadiness and insecurity.

As to the *child's sexual attraction toward the parent of the other sex,* I believe from my experience that it is, as a rule, less of a problem, the more secure a child feels about his parents' and especially his mother's love and kindness and the freer from general anxiety he is. The more the little boy feels that he can count on his mother's steady maternal acceptance, no matter what happens and no matter who else is around, the less intense and compulsive is his craving for other proofs of mother's love in the form of sexual wishes and fantasies with regard to her.

(Incidentally, we find the same mechanisms in the working out of positive transference experiences of our neurotic patients in analysis. If the therapist succeeds in giving them the security of a consistent and steady good will, friendliness, and acceptance, no matter what comes up during the treatment hour, the role of the sexual aspect in the patient's transference relationship with the analyst will be considerably minimized. Indulging in sexual fantasies and wishes can frequently be interpreted as the only expression that insecure patients know for their general longing to be liked and accepted. On the other hand, sexuality is frequently used merely as a means of resistance and defense.)

This means, in regard to the child-parent relationship, that the less cause for a defensive attitude the child's parents (mainly the mother) give, the less inclined will he be to develop defensive attitudes toward them, among which the craving for sex along the line of the Oedipus complex may be one.

So much for the question of the actual psychological function of the mother in the family group.

Now as to our second problem: To what extent is the mother's psychological role determined by maternal instincts and drives? A survey of the investigations of this problem shows that there is marked divergence of opinion.[8] The American psychologists from James to McDougall have built up a general instinct theory which to them accounts for emotional reactions. Hence they consider the mother's psychological role

---

8. See E. Fromm, "Die socialpsychologische Bedeutung der Mutterrechtstheorie," *Ztschr. Sozialforsch.*, Vol. III, No. 2 (1934) (with English abstract).

and functions to be the expression of a specific maternal instinct in women. On the other hand, the present generation of American psychologists does not believe in the existence of an original maternal instinct in women, or even in instincts in general.

Psychoanalysis has not yet dealt adequately with this problem. The only ideas that Freud gives about it are that the woman's drive to have a child is due to her primary wish to have male genital organs, her desire for pregnancy and a baby being the substitute for this basic female wish. I believe that this hypothesis must be understood as the consequence of Freud's patriarchal European tradition, culture, and thinking. Because of this background, he has created a negative concept of female psychosexuality, women being to him just castrated men and the female genitalia being merely rudimentary male organs; he has succeeded in doing so by thinking of the clitoris only and seemingly forgetting the existence of the vagina, the uterus, and the ovaries.

Another reason for Freud's androphilic concept may be that his experiences are primarily taken from his neurotic patients, in whom the envy of men and of the male organ is indeed frequently found as a neurotic symptom. Many healthy little girls, however, discover and proudly accept the clitoris, some of them also the vagina, as their specific female organs. Most healthy girls believe that they have inner female organs which are not inferior to the boys' visible organs, as soon as they have the opportunity to observe another pregnancy of their mother's,[9] especially if the mother enlightens them about it in a proper and candid way. They will develop then and later, after the baby's birth, maternal emotions and wishes of their own in identifying with their mothers.

Other girls understand their female and mother role as soon as menstruation gives them, so to speak, a natural enlightening message of the build and functions of their body. Neurotic girls may regard menstruation as a repetition of the passive castration fantasies of their childhood. Depressive moods during menstruation in emotionally healthy girls are usually due to disappointment over the egg that leaves the body unimpregnated, not to the memory-fantasy of a lost penis.[10] Moreover, modern psychoanalytic experience has shown that there are men who envy women for their ability to have children, just as there are

9. See Melanie Klein's concept of the fantasies of male and female children about the precious contents of the abdomen (*Psychoanalysis of Children* [London: Hogarth Press and Institute of Psychoanalysis, 1932]).

10. Karen Horney, "On the Genesis of the Castration Complex," *Internat. J. Psychoanal.*, Vol. V, No. 1 (1924); "Die menstruellen Verstimmungen," *Ztschr. psychoanalyt. Pädagogik*, Vol. V, Nos. 5/6 (1931); *New Ways in Psychoanalysis* (New York: W. W. Norton & Co., 1939); Sylvia M. Payne, "A Conception of Femininity," *Brit. J. M. Psychol.*, Vol. XV, Part I (1935) (contains also survey of additional literature); Lucile Dooley, "The Genesis of Psychological Sex Differences," *Psychiatry*, Vol. I, No. 2 (1938).

women who envy men for their possession of the penis. It seems to us that either attitude is frequently due not so much to the wish to exchange the psychosexual characteristics of their own sex for those of the envied sex, as it is to the desire to taste all the possibilities that life has to offer.

Among men analysts it is mainly Groddeck, who, quite contrary to Freud, believed in the specificity of female and maternal psychosexual characteristics. "You women conceal from men your knowledge of your instincts and drives," he used to say, "as you do your bodily organs. Why don't you tell us men more about them?"[11] I am afraid the women must answer that it is because they know less about them than Groddeck suspected.

While I believe with Groddeck that there are specific psychosexual characteristics in women, modern psychoanalytic investigation has still to elaborate scientifically the question of female and maternal drives and instincts and conscious or unconscious psychological attitudes in emotionally healthy women.[12] The difficulty that these investigations meet with is that it is very hard to decide which part of the maternal attitude that a woman actually shows is original and which part is due to social order and tradition. While discussing the difference between the female attitude in the American and in the European family, we have seen how important this influence may be.

Ethnologists like Morgan[13] in his study on ancient society and like the Swiss ethnologist and psychologist Bachofen[14] in his book on matriarchal society claim that, before mankind developed the present patriarchal culture, men lived in a matriarchal society. In contrast to the patriarchal concept requiring the fulfilment of one's duties, the wish for success, and the fear of failure as the purpose of life, Morgan and Bachofen hold that this matriarchal society was characterized by a state of love and of freedom, with the opportunity to be happy, to develop according to one's own wishes, and to enjoy life, as the result of the mothers' specific maternal instincts and attitudes.

The concept of the British author Briffault[15] follows that of Morgan

11. At the annual meeting of the psychoanalysts of southwestern Germany and Switzerland at Heidelberg, 1932.

12. The research work done by Therese Benedek and Boris B. Rubenstein represents a step in this direction ("The Correlations between Ovarian Activity and Psychodynamic Processes," *Psychosom. Med.*, Vol. I, No. 2 [1939]).

13. Lewis Henry Morgan, *Ancient Society or Researches in the Lines of Human Progress from Savagery, through Barbarism to Civilization* (New York: Henry Holt & Co., 1877).

14. Johann Jakob Bachofen, *Das Mutterrecht: Eine Untersuchung über die Gynaikokratie der alten Welt nach ihrer religiösen und rechtlichen Natur* (Stuttgart: Kraiss & Hoffmann, 1861).

15. R. Briffault, *The Mothers: A Study of the Origins of Sentiments and Institutions* (New York: Macmillan Co.) ; see also E. Fromm, "Robert Briffault's Werk über das Mutterrecht," *Ztschr. Sozialforsch.*, Vol. II, No. 3 (1933).

and Bachofen. He describes the maternal attitude as mainly characterized by the tendency to take care of helpless children (not only one's own children), and he maintains that all kinds of social feelings, including real love, arise from the maternal instinct. This real love, which to him is basically different from "sexual appetite," concerns itself with the beloved person's needs and with his desire for self-realization.

Other authors differ and even totally oppose one another, according to their cultures. The French authors of the Enlightenment period of the seventeenth and eighteenth centuries, e.g., who wrote during a period which fought for women's emancipation, believed in no psychological difference whatsoever between men and women. The Romanticists, who taught during the following reactionary period which did not believe in women's freedom, talked about a fundamental natural and eternal psychological difference between men and women as qualities found both in organic nature and in the whole spiritual and psychic world.

All this shows how much the viewpoints of an author depends on the age, culture, and society into which he was born.

We psychoanalysts do not feel competent yet to decide about *the border line between the cultural and the biological causes for the female and maternal attitudes of our age and culture,* either. Bachofen's, Morgan's, and Briffault's ideas about the existence of a *fundamental, loving, maternal attitude* which grants freedom and happiness for the children's growth may, however, guide us while we discuss the third problem of this paper: the ideal, desirable functions and role of the mother in the modern family group.

Before we begin this question, I wish to give some examples of the dangerous influence of the *undesirable domineering mother* on the development of her children from my analytic experience:

A woman patient had three siblings, two brothers and one sister. Besides herself, one brother and the sister suffered from serious neurotic symptoms and were extremely insecure and inhibited in handling their own affairs; only one brother was healthy and able to manage his life reasonably according to his wishes and capabilities. The three neurotic siblings were brought up by an extremely domineering mother; the healthy boy lived for most of his childhood years in the family of an aunt who was able to give him all the maternal love that his mother failed to give to the other children.

Another example: a twenty-year-old boy whom I treated for stammering lost this symptom when he found out that he unconsciously wanted to call his mother bad names, to curse and shout at her, because she had managed his whole life for him, never allowing him to make any decision of his own and punishing him by declining to talk with him whenever he disobeyed.

A third instructive example comes from a young engineer who suffered from an inability to show affection to anyone and from the fear of being disparaged and disliked. In spite of an excellent knowledge of his science, he became panic-stricken as soon as he was supposed to give a speech before his colleagues. He had lost his loving mother to whom he had felt very close when he was five years old. After that he was brought up by his grandmother, a mother substitute who resented having to take care of the child and therefore made him constantly feel unloved. Analysis showed that this lack of the security of maternal love in his childhood was the reason for his symptoms, which disappeared at the end of the treatment.

In these examples we find support for Bachofen's, Morgan's, and Briffault's concept of the function of maternal love. The mother ought to create an atmosphere of encouragement and security of love which makes it unnecessary for the children to develop any anxiety or fear of maternal aggression and domination. She is supposed to be free enough from the authoritative restrictions and conventionalities that modern society inflicts on its members to meet her small social group, the family and the children, without any unnecessary display of authority.[16]

In stating that this kind of maternal love ought to be the leading principle for the mother's attitude toward the children, we do not, however, mean to say that the child should be submitted to any kind of hypertenderness or oversolicitude, which quite frequently represents nothing but a hidden form of domination.[17] Every child has to learn that the opportunities for his own growth and happiness have their barriers when and where they interfere with his neighbor's necessities. It is up to the parents to teach the child to adjust to social life and social requirements, sometimes even at the expense of his own actual pleasure. That is to say, he needs training, has to learn to accept restrictions and refusals, and may need sometimes to be punished. But all restrictions, refusals, and punishments have to be given without depriving the child of the security of the mother's love. Maternal love is not supposed to be dependent on the child's behavior and by no means supposed to be a premium for his obedience. The child must be able to rely on it, no matter how he may behave. Once the mother succeeds in creating and maintaining this basic maternal attitude, it does not make much difference what methods of training and what means of punishment she chooses. Given the fundamental security of love, even the methods and time of weaning and of the training for cleanliness are not so important for the infantile development as the classical psychoanalytic literature has assumed. I should not be surprised if further analytic experience showed that the time of initiating training and the methods, as such, have no traumatic influence on the child as long as

16. This suggestion as to the desirable maternal attitude holds just as true for pedagogues and psychotherapists who want their students and patients to gain independence, freedom of growth, and the ability to enjoy and master life. See Karl Menninger, "Parents against Children," *Atlantic Monthly*, August, 1939.

17. David M. Levy, "Maternal Overprotection," *Psychiatry*, Vol. II, Nos. 2, 3, 4 (1939).

ON GENERAL PSYCHIATRIC PROBLEMS

they are not the expression of a general atmosphere of unkindness or love deprivation or of an attitude of domineering or hostile superiority.

The danger of showing aggressive superiority toward a child may especially arise within our modern culture, where everybody has to face the secret hostility and competition of his neighbor, yet does not dare express his counterhostility for fear of retribution. The infant and the little child are the only helpless beings on whom, because of their dependence on her, the mother may dare to vent her hostile tendencies without fear. For it is just this dependence of the child which makes it so disastrous for his development if his mother uses the necessity to train and to punish him as an outlet for her hostility and aggression. Other dangers to be avoided by the mother when punishing her child are that she may take her own needs as the needs of the child whom she is training and that she may try to train him to make up for her own frustrations and punish him for her own sense of guilt.

To illustrate: a patient was the eldest of three brothers from an impoverished family. The father was resigned to mediocrity and had given up hope of a profession which would satisfy his wife's and his own ambitions. The mother resented poverty and marriage to an unsuccessful husband. The oldest son was supposed to make up for all this. At the mother's instigation, the whole family gave every penny they could spare to this son for his education. None of the boys was allowed to spend any money on pleasure, and the oldest son was never allowed to have any recreation whatsoever. He had to study, study, study. Never was he asked whether or not he wanted to. The mother took it for granted that the son had to make up for the failures of her own life, and the boy was so intimidated by the whole performance, which was forced on him under the veil of maternal love, that he did not even dare to admit to himself how he hated it, until he finally became psychotic. His illness started with a period of elation. This made him unable to continue studying for the time being and allowed him to express his inhibited resentment and to curse his mother to his heart's content.

A patient of this kind can, of course, get well only if his psychotherapist succeeds in making up for his mother's domineering selfishness, proving to him that he will care for him no matter how he behaves and no matter whether he decides to continue or discontinue college.

We realize that it is rather difficult (if not impossible) for any mother to follow constantly our concept of the ideal and desirable mother, for three reasons: first, because of the counteracting influences of her own authoritative, if not hostile, environment, as mentioned earlier; second, because maternal love, like all human love, is influenced by waves of ambivalence—no mother will constantly succeed in exclusively loving and enjoying her child; and, third, because there will be actual conscious reasons for her ambivalence, for instance, jealousy of her child, who represents to her youth and the future while she is getting older,

[299]

or resentment of the child, who makes his own contacts and enjoys them independently of her. However, the more a mother dares to admit her ambivalence to herself without feeling guilty for it, even though it is so different from conventional ideas about mother love, the more she will be able to reduce to a minimum this interference with an ideal maternal attitude.

Another difficulty which may interfere with a consistent attitude of maternal acceptance may arise from the mother's possible sexual feelings for the child. The more frankly she recognizes them whenever they may come up, the better she will be able to handle them. Only as long as the mother does not deny her own sexual attraction to the child if and when it arises, will she be able to keep from interfering harmfully with the child's natural sexual drives.

These statements touch one of the hardest maternal tasks: The mother carries the child for nine months; she is delivered of it with danger to her life; she nurses and rears it and grants it a constant security of love; and yet fate asks her to give up her claim on her child as soon as the child is ready to become independent. This fate could be considered unbearable were it not for the fact that mothers derive direct satisfaction from pregnancy, birth, nursing, and the rearing of their children.

We may still raise the question: How much should the mother sacrifice her own life for the child? We know from psychoanalysis that there are few sacrifices made without resentment. Therefore, we do not think that a mother should give up her own happiness for the sake of her child. The happier the mother can be, the more she will be able to secure happiness and freedom of growth for her child; the more happiness she sacrifices for the sake of her child, the more she will resent the child for whom she did so, thus diminishing her capability to deal with him, without hostility and resentment.

In the case of unhappy marriages, when the mother resents her husband, it does not usually benefit the children for her to stay with him. She will very likely transfer the antagonism or hatred she feels toward the husband onto the child. She will resent the characteristics that the child has in common with the unloved husband and be unable to give the security of her maternal love.

To illustrate, a mother asked my advice about her "unattractive, awkward, and mannish daughter, who simply would not get well or be successful in life." As a matter of fact, the daughter was a most attractive, charming, young girl, gifted and socially talented, and quite capable of being a success if she could overcome the paralyzing influence of her mother's hatred. This hatred which warped the mother's judgment was due to the fact that she was disappointed in her marriage and therefore blamed the child for all of the father's shortcomings.

To conclude and summarize: The psychological and social role of the mother in the family is not fixed but changes according to various historical periods, countries, and cultures. We do not know yet to what extent the mothers' attitudes are biologically founded and to what extent they are due to culture. Therefore, our suggestions as to an ideal and desirable maternal attitude are in their turn also not specific suggestions as to the mothers' attitude but rather suggestions as to a *maternal principle*. This maternal principle ought to replace any kind of parental domination and grant the children the security of love which is the fundamental psychological requisite for their normal growth and their development to later freedom and independence. This should be the ideal parental attitude, no matter whether it is father or mother who is its more able representative within the culture.

DISCUSSION

DR. ROBERT P. KNIGHT: I think this is a very fine paper and I want to congratulate Dr. Fromm-Reichmann for its splendid content. The idea that female psychology has characteristics of its own and has to be explained from the standpoint of female development and female specific psychology rather than from the made-over psychology of man is one that the women analysts have been proposing for some time and one in which they are being more and more joined by some male analysts.

I was especially pleased with the part of the paper which deals with mental hygiene and prophylactic psychology, because I feel that many parents are looking to the analysts for specific guideposts, and we are inclined, I think, to clutter up our advice with many trivialities, such as whether to start the toilet training before the child is weaned (which is, after all, not trivial in itself, but which is certainly to be very much subordinated to the main attitude of affection from the parents).

DR. HENRY A. MURRAY: Was the questionnaire you spoke of Dr. Fromm's?

DR. FROMM-REICHMANN: It was a collective research project done by the Institute of Social Research, directed by Professor Max Horkheimer. Dr. Fromm was one of its members at that time.

DR. MURRAY: Was it used in America?

DR. FROMM-REICHMANN: No, they have not continued it here; they have published the results of their European studies in *Autorität und Familie*.

DR. MURRAY: I think that what you said about the chief difference between European and American mothers is very true, but I think that it is more a difference of degree than a difference in kind. You say that in America the mother is dominant, in Europe the father. We have examined about 120 Harvard students and found the same condition as you describe in Europe; that is, the father is more apt to be the disciplinarian, but not to the same extent as in Europe. Of course, we cannot generalize on the basis of so few cases.

DR. FROMM-REICHMANN: I am very surprised to hear you say so, because from my own analytic experience in both countries (four and three-quarters years in America), I have definitely gained the impression which I described, and so have my German analyst-friends with whom I have discussed the problem. Of course, it is probably just as wrong as all generalizations. Has your work been published?

DR. MURRAY: A part of it has been, in connection with an experimental study of cheating and guilt. I think that the study covers only sixty of the cases. It was found that the boys who did not cheat, or felt guilty if they did, were the ones who, on the whole, had preferred their fathers, had formed alliances with them, and had had mostly verbal punishments from them. Those who cheated, on the other hand, were those who had been hostile to their fathers, feared them, and had been allied to their mothers; they had been excused by their mothers and not kept up to such rigid standards. In this study it came out that there were more punishments from the father and that he was, on the whole, more domineering than the mother—perhaps in 65 per cent of the cases. I can see how you, coming from Europe, would notice the difference. Perhaps it is different in different parts of the country; maybe New England has something to do with it; maybe it is different in the Middle West and in the South.

DR. SYLVIA ALLEN: I want to express appreciation for the paper; I think it was excellent. I would like to ask a question in regard to technique. Suppose the analyst is capable of giving this type of love you describe and the patient has no actual reasons to be hostile toward him; then hostility is expressed toward either parent but is not directly aimed at the analyst; does it have the same value that it would have if the patient could feel that the hostility was directed against the analyst?

DR. FROMM-REICHMANN: I think that, even if we could be lucky enough to succeed in giving no actual reason for the patient to be hostile to us (which never happens), we would certainly expect that he would still use us as the father or mother whom he hated, on account of the transference mechanism. Because of the working rules of the unconscious, the patient uses us as the repetition of father and mother without our having to behave like them. Freud says that we should be as neutral as possible, so that the patient can use us as a record on which he can project his feelings. You surely have had patients who said that you were black-haired and blue-eyed like their mother, because at that moment you were the mother. I had one patient who saw me with a black beard like his father's, one who talked about the wallpaper in my office which he thought had big yellow flowers in it like his grandmother's living room, which it did not. I should think that these childhood situations could be repeated better during the analysis, the more we were able to create an atmosphere of steady friendliness, because that helps the patient to relax; the more relaxed he is, the less he will control his associations and the closer to the unconscious his experience during the analytic interview will lead him.

DR. JOACHIM HAENEL: I want to express my appreciation for this paper, particularly the second part. Maybe I can add one point: Dr. Fromm-Reichmann spoke about the identification which takes place in the mother who is living in a particular marriage—that she identifies the child with her husband—and of the special consequences which can arise from this. I have found in almost all cases that the child will identify himself with the non-aggressive partner in the marriage. If the father is domineering, the child will be inclined to identify himself with the mother; and vice versa. So the aggression of a mother against her husband and of a father against the mother has a special effect, in this way.

I think a word should be said in favor of the inclination of the child to identify with the parent of the other sex. I understood you to say that the hatred of the child is always directed toward the dominating partner in the marriage. I am very interested in what you have in mind there. I think that this hatred against the domineering parent comes a little later than the sexual attraction of the child toward the parent of the other sex.

DR. FROMM-REICHMANN: According to the research done by Malinowski, Boehm, Mead, and others, it seems that the time of the sex attraction to the parent of the other sex arises at the same time that the resentment of the authority of the person of the same sex sets in. The point I meant to make is *not* that sex attraction does not exist but that I don't think it plays the ubiquitous role that Freud attributes to it. I think the hatred toward the parent of the same sex, which comes up at the same time as the sex attraction toward the parent of the opposite sex, is not generally due to sex competition but seems to be more largely due to competition with the person's authoritative power. That certainly does not mean to say that it is *never* a sexual jealousy. I think, however, that we are likely to overlook things if we do not always keep in mind that there are other reasons for resenting the person of the same sex, besides sex competition.

DR. MURRAY: I should like to ask Dr. Fromm-Reichmann whether I understood her correctly, and, if so, I should say that it is a particularly important point: that is, that maternal love, as she describes it, as well as other kinds of love, can be taken as an independent factor, as a constitutional, instinctive factor, which may be treated separately, though it may often be fused with a purely sexual factor.

DR. FROMM-REICHMANN: I definitely believe so. I think this is something still to be worked out in psychoanalysis. Freud really did not work out the psychological concept of non-sexual love. I do not think that we can explain every kind of love as a sexual phenomenon. I think that this is one of the things in regard to which we psychoanalysts are trained incorrectly.

DR. MURRAY: I heartily agree with you. The next problem I am interested in is the reason for the development (in American culture) of the relative dominance of women. It is about 120 years old, having come in with the Romantic movement in America.

DR. FROMM-REICHMANN: I don't know enough about that; the sociologists must answer this question.

DR. MURRAY: Two observations I should like to make. It seems to me that dominance in women is most exaggerated in cases where the husbands are inadequate as lovers and the women have not been satisfied sexually; they have, as it were, a grudge against life. The other point is that the increase in woman's authority came at a time when they began to develop diverse cultural interests and became integral parts of the larger social structure. Therefore, to a certain extent they have had to support the culture because of their participation in it, whereas in Europe it is the men almost solely who must sustain the culture. Do you agree?

DR. FROMM-REICHMANN: Yes, I was very interested in your first point, because that leads to something which it would be worthwhile to discuss: that the attitude toward sex and the role that sex plays are definitely different here than in Europe.

DR. MURRAY: You compared the European mother with the American mother and went on to suggest what the ideal mother might be—more loving, like the European mother; but you have left out the American father. Would you want him to be more dominating or more affectionate toward his children?

DR. FROMM-REICHMANN: I could evade that issue very easily and say that the paper deals only with women.

DR. HAENEL: In the psychoanalytic background of the paper there are quite surprising statements, I think, especially in regard to Freud's conception of penis envy. I think it must be a reality factor that penis envy is stronger than birth envy, because the penis is an organ that is always there and a little child can see it, while a birth is something which happens once in a great while. You might compare the vagina with the penis, but the penis is a positive organ and the vagina a negative one.

I do not agree with you about the menstrual period because we find the castration complex in other than neurotic persons. In analysis we always find that what the child experiences in his childhood (regarding differences in sex) is more prominent than any feelings which he may have about the womb or the menstrual period. I think when you find the normal female regretting that her womb is not fertilized, it has the meaning of castration.

DR. FROMM-REICHMANN: To begin with the question of penis envy: I do agree with the statement that in a patriarchal society where preference is given to the little boy, it may occur quite frequently that the little girl envies the boy's penis, because she cannot see any other reason why the male child should be preferred to her except that he has something visible (his genital) which she does not have. Like quite a number of women analysts, however, I do not believe what Freud maintains, that there is a female envy of the male organs due to the girl's conception of the biological inferiority of her genital organs as compared with the boy's. I have tried to get information on this question from biologists. They do not assume that any living creature could develop biological inferiority feelings per se. I do not see why the female human being should be an exception to this general experience of natural scientists. The only thing I do believe is that the early penis envy is an expression of the search for the visible reason for the preference given the boy in patriarchal society.

As to the other point: menstruation and castration: Interpreting a woman's regret about not being fertilized means either that one uses the term "castration" symbolically and not for its actual biological significance or else that one interprets a specific female experience in specifically male concepts. As to the depression which sometimes goes with menstruation, I think that this is a psychological experience which is one of the basic things that maternal women are likely to feel.

DR. ERNEST LEWY: I think another word could be said in favor of the biological aspects. Dr. Fromm-Reichmann pointed out that it does not make much difference when the child is trained in toilet habits, if the home atmosphere contains the necessary security. I think it does make some difference if the child is not ready; there must be definite damage and a feeling of insecurity created.

DR. FROMM-REICHMANN: If there is a basic atmosphere of maternal love, the mother will certainly not train the child at the wrong time. I did not mean to say that it made no difference when it is done. I meant to say that the importance of this question as an isolated phenomenon is overemphasized in our literature.

(22)

PSYCHIATRIC ASPECTS OF ANXIETY

The most unpleasant and at the same time the most universal experience except loneliness is anxiety. We observe both healthy and mentally disturbed people doing everything possible to ward off anxiety or to keep it from awareness.

Mentally disturbed people try to dispel anxiety by developing mental symptoms. In fact as first stated by Freud (9), mental symptoms are at the same time both the expression of unbearable anxiety and the means of warding it off. In other words mental symptoms and mental illness can be understood simultaneously as the outcome of anxiety and as a defense against it. Mental illness can be understood as a person's response to unbearable anxiety. Therefore, anxiety constitutes an essential problem in psychotherapy.

This holds true, even though we consider anxiety to be an experience by no means limited to the mentally disturbed. As initially stated, we realize that anxiety in its milder forms is a universal human phenomenon. Philosophers and psychologists have known and advanced this knowledge for a long time. In their eagerness to be great helpers and healers, psychiatrists have been and are still partly inclined to overlook the difference between what may be called the normal anxieties of the emotionally healthy and the neurotic or psychotic excess anxiety which should be subject to psychotherapy. For a long time, psychiatrists and psychotherapists have also overlooked the fact that anxiety has not only negative, disintegrative facets but also some positive, constructive ones. As we set out to clarify the philosophy of psychotherapy regarding neurotic and psychotic anxieties, we must keep these two aspects of anxiety clearly in mind.

Anxiety, as we know, shows in a great variety of ways. Subjectively it may be experienced as a most unpleasant interference with thinking processes and concentration, as a diffuse, vague, and frequently objectless feeling of apprehension or as a discomforting feeling of uncertainty and helplessness. As it arises in its milder forms, it may show objectively by a shift in tone of voice, and/or tempo of speech, by a change of

From *An Outline of Psychoanalysis*, edited by Clara Thompson, Milton Mazer, and Earl Witenberg. ("Modern Library.") New York: Random House, 1955. Reprinted here by permission of Grune & Stratton, for whom Dr. Fromm-Reichmann, at the time of her death, was preparing a book which would have included this paper.

posture, gesture, and motion, also by the anxious person's intellectual or emotional preoccupation or blocking of communication. In people who are even more anxious, anxiety manifests itself psychologically in more or less marked degrees of paralysis of thought and action. The well-known physical manifestations that may be caused by anxiety are symptoms of a hyperactive sympathetic system, such as change of turgor, perspiration, tremor, sensation of a lump in the throat, sinking abdominal sensations, diarrhea, vomiting, changes in pupillar reactions, in heart beat, pulse rate, and respiration. If anxiety-states become so severe that the anxiety-stricken person cannot handle them, mental symptoms and mental illness are the final outcome.

In the rare cases when anxiety is so severe that all these expressions of it and all defenses against it fail to bring relief, panic or terror may be the outcome. Panic, as defined by H. S. Sullivan, is an extreme concentration of attention and the direction of all available energy toward only one goal—escape, swift flight from internal dangers which are poorly envisaged; in the case of failure to escape, panic results in temporary disintegration of personality with random destructive tendencies against one's self and others. Also, according to Sullivan (29, 30), terror is anxiety of a cosmic quality in the face of a primitively conceived threat of danger. The terror-stricken person feels himself to be alone among deadly menaces, more or less blindly fighting for his survival against dreadful odds. Fortunately, terror and panic are short-lived. The organism produces quick defenses against the devastating influence which panic or terror of prolonged duration would exert. John Vassos' empathic pictorial work, *Phobia* (which, incidentally, is dedicated to H. S. Sullivan), should be mentioned here as an impressive contribution to the understanding of terror and panic (34).

In contrast to these various forms of anxiety, fear is a useful, rational kind of fright elicited by realistic external dangers. To be described presently, and in contrast to fear, are the dangers from within, which elicit anxiety.

What is anxiety in terms of its conceptions in dynamic psychiatry? Freud says in *The Problems of Anxiety* (9) that anxiety is felt by a person at the realization of formerly repressed inacceptable drives and wishes; his anxiety is with regard to loss of love and punishment, i.e., along the lines of Freud's libidinal concepts, castration-fear.

We need not go into the discussion of Freud's older explanation of anxiety as the result of repressed sexual desires (5) because he rejected it himself in *The Problems of Anxiety*.

Sullivan shares with Freud the concept of the anxiety-arousing power of inacceptable thoughts, feelings, drives, wishes, and actions. But in the framework of his interpersonal conceptions he sees these forbidden inner experiences as interpersonal ones, not as instinctual drives per se;

also the expected punishment is not seen as castration-fear. Rather, it is experienced by the anxious person as the anticipated disapproval, i.e., loss of love, by the significant people of his early life from whom he originally learned to discriminate between acceptable and inacceptable drives, attitudes, and actions. Later on, this fear of disapproval may be transferred from the original significant people who trained and educated the anxious person to their emotional successors. Guilt feelings, separately described by other authors (29, 30, 31, 32), are obviously implicit in Sullivan's conception of anxiety.

This disapproval by the significant people of one's early life, to which both Freud and Sullivan refer, is vital enough to account for severe anxieties because the infant and the young child are dependent upon the early important people for fulfilment of their basic needs. The infant's survival depends upon the loving care he is given by the mothering ones of his infancy.

Nearly all psychological concepts of anxiety have, in common with Freud and Sullivan, this one basic conception: that anxiety is tied up with the inner danger of inacceptable thoughts, feelings, wishes, or drives which elicit the expectation of loss of love and approval or of punishment. No matter how much these conceptions may differ in their explanatory details and regardless of whether or not this aspect of anxiety is explicitly mentioned in these conceptions, it is a viewpoint now commonly shared.

Let me quote a few outstanding representatives of various psychiatric schools of thinking. Rank (26) speaks of "separation anxiety," which is first experienced at birth and subsequently throughout life at all phases of personality development and individuation, from weaning, i.e., separation from mother's breast, to separation from one's fellow men by death.

Adler (1) uses his concept of inferiority feelings where other authors speak of anxiety. He asserts that these inferiority feelings can be overcome by people only in affirmation and strengthening of their social bonds with society, by enforcing the sense of belonging to a social group.

Horney (19) emphasizes the central significance of the interrelatedness between anxiety and hostility—anticipated in others and sensed in the anxious person himself; here again anxiety is seen as being tied up with the fear of disruption of one's interpersonal relationships.

Fromm, Berdyaev, Halmos, Kardiner, Riesman, and other social psychologists find the source of man's anxiety in his psychological isolation, his alienation from his own self and from his fellow men. They consider this the common fate of man in modern society, irrespective of his state of emotional health (3, 10, 18, 22, 27). A poetic version of this viewpoint may be found in Auden's *Age of Anxiety* (2).

Goldstein's conception of anxiety as being the subjective experience of a danger to existence in the face of failure (15, 16) may also imply anxiety regarding loss of love and recognition by those who recognize the anxious person's failure.

The same holds true for Rollo May's definition of anxiety as (23) "the apprehension set off by a threat to some value which the individual holds essential to his existence as a personality."[1] Again this concept implies the fear of losing interpersonal recognition or acceptance, since this could be tied up with the loss of essential values in the life of the individual. I will return later to the discussion of some other aspects of the conceptions of these authors. At this point I am primarily interested in demonstrating the ubiquitously implied acceptance of the concept that anxiety is connected with anticipated fear of punishment and disapproval, withdrawal of love, disruption of interpersonal relationships, isolation, or separation.

This conception of anxiety as the expression of the anticipated loss of love and approval, or separation, social isolation, or disruption of one's interpersonal relationships implies its close psychological affinity to loneliness. In fact, I believe that many of the emotional states to which psychiatrists refer as anxiety are actually states of loneliness or fear of loneliness.

Now I wish to return to the discussion of the psychodynamics of anxiety. According to Sullivan, the infant and child's need for love and approval and the anxiety connected with rejection and disapproval are utilized by the significant adults in handling the necessary early processes designed to train the infant and child for his interpersonal adjustment, his socialization and acculturalization. Out of this educative process evolves the part of human personality which Sullivan has called "self-system." This self-system operates in the service of people to obtain satisfaction without incurring too much anxiety. In the process of establishing the self-system, certain infantile trends must be barred from awareness, dissociated. If they break into awareness, anxiety will reappear because the structure of the self-system, the nature of which tends toward rigid maintenance of its protective status quo, is threatened with change. This defensiveness against change makes for the danger of personal rigidity, which in turn increases the potentialities for further anxiety (29, 30). This anxiety connected with change is eternally in conflict with man's general innate tendencies toward growth, toward the change which is implied, and particularly with the innate motivation of mental patients toward health. One of the great responsibilities of the psychotherapist is to help patients face and overcome this conflict constructively (12).

I would like to offer an additional explanatory concept about the fac-

1. Rollo May's book is most stimulating as a monograph in its own right but also as an excellent survey of the theories of anxiety. The *Proceedings of the Thirty-ninth Annual Meeting of the American Psychopathological Association, 1949*, ed. Hoch and Zubin (New York: Grune & Stratton, 1950), ought to be quoted as another useful compendium on the subject.

tors which make people expect punishment, disapproval, and loss of love. This idea has helped me to understand better than I did previously the psychological significance of the anxieties of people in general and of mental patients in particular. Let us ask again: What do people disapprove of most gravely in themselves, i.e., which trends in themselves do they expect will bring the most severe disapproval on the part of the significant people in their lives? Are there other significant causes for the anxiety-arousing anticipation of disapproval and isolation in addition to those we have quoted? Let me offer the following hypothetical answer.

It is a well-known psychological fact that a person may misvalue the significant people of his childhood so that his early interpersonal tie-ups remain unresolved. If these early patterns stand uncorrected, he will distort the images of various people whom he meets in the course of his life. He may or may not dimly sense that he does so, but he will not recognize the interpersonal misconceptions of early childhood as the root of the distortions in his present interpersonal relationships.

An adult who finds himself compulsively appraising other people inadequately, incorrectly evaluating their reactions, acting upon and responding to them in line with these misconceptions in terms of early patterns of living, may many times become semiaware of his erroneous judgment and behavior. However, he may feel inadequate and helpless in his dim wish or attempt to change and correct his judgment and his emotional reactions because he is unaware of their unconscious roots, the unmodified fixations to the patterns of interpersonal relationships which he acquired in his early years. This helplessness in the face of the need to change anachronistic, distorted patterns of interpersonal relationships meets with self-disapproval and discontent; it interferes with the innate tendency to self-realization; it produces deep insecurity in people and meets with the anticipated disapproval of others; thus it is the expression of anxiety, and it produces further anxiety. Goldstein could demonstrate this type of anxiety in his brain-injured patients. When they were faced with a simple task which they could not accomplish for reasons unknown to them, stemming from their neurological brain injury, they became the prey of an abject feeling of helplessness, of nothingness, or a "catastrophic reaction," as Goldstein has called it (15, 16).

The hypothesis is offered that mentally disturbed people frequently develop a "catastrophic-reaction" anxiety in response to their compulsively determined inability to change their distorted, immature patterns of interpersonal relationships. This task may be set by the demands of their own conscience or by the actual or assumed demands of their elders or friends. This helplessness in the presence of the need to envision and to relate one's self adequately to other people, i.e., in accordance with one's chronological age and one's psychological reality, without full awareness of its causes, is most frightening for more than one reason. It elicits a general feeling of helplessness and paralysis. It means that the person concerned is living in an unreal psychological world and that he feels he is in danger of pulling the people of his environment actually or in fantasy into the same threatening abyss of unreality. Being unable successfully to avail himself of the possibility of using new means of evaluating people and of relating himself meaningfully to them amounts to being blocked in the utilization of learning processes which serve growth and change. This absence of growth and change is tantamount to psychological stagnation and emotional sterility, i.e., psychological death (14). In other words, the repetition-compulsion to follow early patterns of interpersonal evaluation and relatedness and the inability to learn to replace them by new patterns deprive a person of the freedom to live and move about in the world of psychological reality which should be his, deprive him of the freedom for self-realization, and convey feelings of stagnation and sterility—hence the fear of psychological death, of Tillich's "not being" or Goldstein's "nothingness" (15, 16, 33).

By "self-realization, to repeat a definition I have previously given (12), I mean a person's use of his talents, skills, and powers to his satisfaction within the realm of his own freely established realistic set of values. Furthermore, I mean the uninhibited ability of patients to reach out for and to find fulfilment of their needs for satisfaction and security, insofar as these can be obtained without interfering with the laws and customs which protect the needs of their fellow men. Goldstein's "self-actualization," Fromm's "productive character," Whitehorn's "mature personality," and the "self-affirmation" of the existentialists are formulations of the same concept (10, 15, 35). In the classical psychoanalytic literature insufficient attention has been given to the concept of self-realization as a great source, if not the greatest source, of human fulfilment. Freud has referred to it in his teachings on secondary narcissism and ego-ideal formation (7, 8), but he has dealt more with the investigation of the origin of the phenomenon than with the elaboration on the psychological significance of the end-product, mature self-realization.

The lack of freedom for self-realization and the feeling of stagnation and "nothingness" that goes with it, this sense of psychological death, seems to me to be at the root of the anxiety of many persons. To repeat, they cling to infantile interpersonal patterns and as a result feel helpless without really knowing why. They are unable to grow emotionally, to develop or change. They are not able to think, feel, and act according to their chronological age. They live anachronously in a deadening emotional rut where they compulsively continue to distort their interpersonal images of new people whom they meet and to misvalue the interpersonal reactions and behavior of these people along the line of the conceptions gained in their unresolved interpersonal childhood contacts.

Example: A young woman, Anna, went to see her older friend and confidant, Mr. N., whom she trusted unequivocally. Anna asked him to contact certain significant persons in her family and explain to them some facts about her life which she felt would be of immeasurable value for them and for her in the general family picture. Mr. N. assured Anna of his complete willingness to do this, and when Anna left him, she was confident that Mr. N. would take care of the situation with understanding and skill. For valid rational reasons, which are beside the point of our discussion, Mr. N. later decided not to meet the members of the family for a talk along the lines suggested by Anna. He did not have an opportunity to discuss this with her. When Anna found out about it a few days later, she felt deep resentment against Mr. N. and developed a spell of severe anxiety. Why? She felt that her friend had not accepted her appraisal of the total situation or given it serious consideration. She also felt he had treated her as her parents had always done: to judge everything the little girl suggested or offered for consideration as not being worthy of serious thought on their part, since "little girls are too emotional." Anna realized, though, that her resentment against Mr. N., who she felt had betrayed her and had not taken her suggestion seriously, was somehow unfounded, and she sensed dimly that he might well have fallen down on their agreement for valid, rational reasons. However, she felt completely incapable of overcoming her resentment, and her severe spell of anxiety lasted for hours. The semiawareness she had about the irrationality of her anxiety and resentment did not help any until, by psychoanalytic investigation, she finally discovered the reasons of which she had been unaware. Then she recognized that her resentment was due to a distortion of the present situation between her and Mr. N., in the light of the unresolved interpersonal pattern of living with the parents of her childhood ("little girl"—"too emotional" —judgment and suggestions deserve no consideration).

Jurgen Ruesch's interesting new concept of anxiety, which he gained from observation and investigation of people under stress, fits into this context. He says that anxiety arises as a result of overstimulation which cannot be discharged by action (28). The anxious people who have been described are barred from discharging tension by action, from converting anxiety into euphoria, because they live in a state of "not-being," or "nothingness."

The anxiety-producing aspects of unresolved early tie-ups and involvements, of which people are only partially aware, receive additional reinforcement because so many of these anxiety-producing aspects are experienced as forbidden and elicit anxiety-connected guilt feelings. Love for the parent of the opposite sex and competitive hatred of the parent of the same sex should be mentioned here as the most outstanding example of such anxiety- and guilt-evoking psychological constellations.

The resolution of early tie-ups with one's parents, which I have implicitly recommended as a preventive against anxiety, should not be confused with manifestations of a child's outwardly breaking away from his parents. Children who succeed in breaking away from their parents early may experience increased anxiety, since this emerging independence of a child meets with a sense of loss on the part of the parents, hence frequently with their disapproval of the child.

The psychology of masturbation is illustrative of our last statement. There has been much discussion about the following question: Why are there so many children who have never been exposed to any warning against masturbation and so many adults who intellectually do not consider masturbation forbidden or dangerous and yet practically no people who masturbate without feeling guilty and anxious about it? How can we explain this fact? I believe that guilt-eliciting masturbatory fantasies are only partly, if at all, responsible. Many cases of masturbatory feelings of guilt and anxiety seem to be connected with the fact that masturbation represents a child's first act of independence from his parents or others who have raised and mothered him. He needs his elders for the fulfilment of all his basic needs: getting food and fresh air and for being kept clean and getting fresh clothes and bedding. Masturbation is the only pleasure he can obtain without their help. As such, it constitutes an act of breaking away from one's parents, for which the child feels guilty and anxious, regardless of the permissive or non-permissive attitude of the elders toward the act of masturbation per se.

It has been stated that practically no one in this culture gets ideally rid of his early interpersonal tie-ups and the resulting interpersonal problems. In other words, almost no one is entirely prepared to face the anxiety-provoking dangers of his present life, fully undistorted by interpersonal entanglements with the "ghosts of his past" and with full command of his adult emotional equipment. As Grinker puts it, in his research report (17) on "Anxiety and Psychosomatic Transactions": "The stimulus [which arouses anxiety] must be perceived in the light of inner expectation originating at an early and particularly helpless time in the organism's history, to be dangerous to its protective attachments and hence to his existence," i.e., to have the power to produce anxiety.

People's fear of nothingness, of helplessness in the face of "psychological death," postulated here as being a central cause of human anxiety, has a factual correlate in the practically universal experience of anxiety with regard to actual death. The fact that life ends with death remains to most people an inconceivable experience of ultimate psychobiological separation. To others, the fact that time and cause of death are unpredictable conveys a painful sense of ultimate powerlessness. This fear and anxiety of death gains reinforcement from the fact that it does not stand only for itself but is also an expression and a symbol of other unknown and unpredictable forces which govern human existence. "It is this fact of our being in a finite and limited time, the awareness of (our) mortality and uncertainty of the future," which renders us helpless and anxious, as Podolsky puts it (25). That is, people seem to feel the same helplessness and anxiety in the face of the phenomenon of actual death as they do in the face of the above-defined personal experience of "psychological death."

There are various ways in which people may try to counteract the anxiety and the narcissistic hurt inflicted on them when they are faced with the necessity of accepting the reality of death. The powerfulness of these defenses is a measuring rod for the intenseness of the anxiety which people try to fight off with them.

The religious concept of the Hereafter is the greatest attempt to counteract the inconceivable separation experience which is death.

The well-known phenomenon of guilt feelings after the death of a close person is, in my judgment, caused not only by the ambivalence toward the deceased but also and more so by people's anxiety about the uncertainty and unpredictability which go with the very nature of life and death. Feeling guilty about a death means assuming part of the responsibility. If we are partly responsible, the inconceivable, unpredictable character of death is mitigated; it is put into some more acceptable context with that which man can influence—or fails to influence—by virtue of his own skills and powers.

A more pathological way of counteracting the anxiety connected with death is used by certain emotionally disturbed people to whom its uncertainty is so anxiety-provoking and unbearable that they evade its acceptance, or at least find satisfaction in fantasying that they can evade it, by committing suicide. To these people, suicide means doing away with the unpredictability of the end of their lives, as if, by their own determination, they take the power of decision out of the hands of the Lord, of fate, or of nature, as their conceptions may be (36, 37).

These examples show that the defenses that people feel the need to erect against the anxieties connected with actual death are just as powerful as the symptoms with which mental patients try to protect themselves against the anxiety connected with "psychological death."

Some psychoanalysts may ask, at this point, how this concept of anxiety in the face of psychological and factual death ties up with the classical psychoanalytic concept of the death instinct. Freud postulated, in his metapsychological treatise, *Beyond the Pleasure Principle* (6), that man is born with aggressive and destructive impulses against himself and others. Man's death instinct, according to Freud, operates throughout his life as the expression of these self-destructive tendencies against himself.

Other psychoanalysts in writing about this topic have tried to prove the existence of the death instinct in terms of what, in their judgment, are self-destructive operations which we can observe in most people, such as their neglect in seeking medical help for obviously harmful pathological processes (24). I believe this seemingly self-destructive behavior can be better understood as the outcome of man's fear of death than as the response to his death instinct. He does not consult the doctor lest he be faced with a fatal prognosis of his ailment which might increase his fear of death.

I find myself in agreement with Sullivan, Fromm, and several other dynamic psychiatrists and psychoanalysts who do not find any evidence of primary inborn hostile and destructive tendencies in the human mind, but who deduce from their psychiatric experience that the rise of hostile and destructive tendencies is the outcome of and the response to the adversities of people's interpersonal experiences throughout their lives. Consequently, these authors do not see any evidence of the original existence of self-destructive tendencies, of a death instinct, as a given ubiquitous phenomenon (11, 29).

Irrespective of the controversial issue of Freud's concept of the death instinct, we agree with his conceptions that man must have some kind of inner awareness, or sense some kind of reflection of the changes of the organism which take place daily and hourly in the direction of its final dissolution and death. I believe that man's inner awareness of these changes of the organism on its gradual way from birth to death contributes to his fear of death and to his anxiety about the unknowns connected with the facts of death, rather than that these are an expression of his death instinct.

So much for the anxiety connected with what I have called "psychological death" and the anxiety connected with the psychological facts of actual death as a general human phenomenon. Our data corroborate our introductory statement about there being almost no one permanently free from anxiety. Yet healthy people learn to handle their anxieties without converting them into symptoms. They may even be able to turn them into assets, a topic on which I have elaborated elsewhere (13).

In the same context let me also quote Horney, who states that both types of anxiety—that of the mentally healthy and that of mentally disturbed people—render them helpless, and this helplessness in turn produces more anxiety, "secondary" anxiety. However, Horney says that anxiety in the face of actual death and other powers of nature must be accepted and does not call for the development of the defense mechanism and the hostility and destructiveness which people develop in response to other—neurotic or psychotic—forms of helplessness and anxiety (19). The contrary may even be true. Grinker corroborates this viewpoint when he states: "If anxiety is mild, it is stimulating and facilitates increased and efficient action or thought" (16).

As Fromm pointed out, anxiety in the face of the overwhelming and unpredictable powers of nature, which is the common fate of all of us, may be used as a motivation for increasing the common bonds between human beings.

Freud and also Adler have emphasized the viewpoint that human efforts to allay anxiety have led to the development of civilization. Jung and Adler also emphasize the positive powers of constructive defense which may be aroused in people for the sake of counteracting their anxiety (1, 6, 21).

The existentialists, including one of the outstanding psychiatrists among them, Binswanger, stress the constructive aspects of anxiety even more. They consider it the equivalent of the tension aroused in a person who is able to face the universe and the task which is set to men, to conquer the emanations of the universe by action (4, 35).

States of anxiety which are severe enough to call for expression and defense by mental symptoms, i.e., the states of excess anxiety which neurotic and psychotic patients suffer, are, of course, not constructive except when they are reduced to milder degrees.

It should not be overlooked, though, that the anxiety of mental patients under treatment can be psychotherapeutically utilized—as a signpost indicating underlying conflicts and as a challenge to solve them. This holds true for neurotic patients as well as for psychotics. In fact, it may be generally stated that mild degrees of anxiety, discomforting as they may be, can be useful danger signals to mentally healthy and to mentally disturbed people (9, 35).

Some readers may be surprised that I suggest psychotherapeutic intervention not only with excess anxiety in neurotic patients but also in psychotics. Clinical experience during the last twenty-five or thirty years has taught dynamic psychiatrists that both neurotic and psychotic excess anxieties can be successfully treated with psychoanalysis or psychoanalytically oriented dynamic psychotherapy. Time and space permitting, I could corroborate this statement with many examples from my own experience and that of many other psychiatrists who work with both types of patients. We cannot enter into a discussion of the psychotherapeutic techniques which dynamic psychiatrists use in the treatment of anxiety. If our initial statement, that anxiety is at the root of every mental disturbance, is correct, then it is also true that any discussion of psychotherapeutic methods in the treatment of neurotic and psychotic anxieties would amount to writing a paper on psychotherapy at large.

I will restrict myself, therefore, to the following brief comments: We have seen that people who suffer from anxiety are at best only semiaware of its causes. Therefore, the focal point of all psychotherapeutic guidance or treatment of anxiety states is to help the anxious person uncover and understand the unconscious reasons for his helplessness and anxiety. Beyond that, it follows from our distinction between mild degrees of anxiety and their predominantly constructive aspects and severe degrees of anxiety with their predominantly disjunctive aspects that the specific psychotherapeutic usefulness of dynamic psychiatrists in helping anxious patients encompasses three central therapeutic tasks. One therapeutic goal should be to guide people in understanding and then accepting and learning to live with and to utilize mild degrees of anxiety. In the case of more intensive states of anxiety, the psychotherapeutic goal should be to help people (patients), for preventive reasons, uncover, resolve, and integrate the causes of these anxieties, lest they lead up to an expression by mental symptoms which simultaneously are used as defenses against the awareness of these anxiety states. In cases where a person's anxiety is severe enough to express itself in mental symptomatology and mental illness, the psychotherapeutic goal should be to help the mental patient with the methods of intensive psychoanalytically oriented dynamic psychotherapy to gain insight into the emotional roots of his anxiety and of his symptomatology, to understand the psychodynamic linkage between anxiety and symptomatology, and to face, work through, and eventually vanquish his excess anxiety. Caution is indicated regarding the timing and the dosage of therapeutic intervention and enlightenment, lest a patient be made to face more dynamic insight into his anxiety and greater amounts of open anxiety than he can accept at a given time.

The discussion of the psychotherapeutic aspects of anxiety would be more than incomplete if its focus were not extended to the problem of anxiety in psychotherapists. If it is true that there is practically no one who is permanently free from anxiety, and/or none in whom anxiety cannot be temporarily aroused by all kinds of adverse experiences, then this fact, of course, holds true for psychotherapists as well. In their case, we are especially interested in the feelings of anxiety which may sometimes be brought forth in them by their patients.

A psychotherapist who does not know and integrate this fact, who dreams about his non-vulnerability to anxiety, be it aroused in his exchange with patients or other persons, a psychotherapist who dreams about "complete emotional security" as an unreal goal for his own inner life, cannot guide his mental patients to wholesome, constructive testing and evaluation of their anxieties and to a constructive adjustment to the facts and data of their internal and external reality. Awareness of his anxiety, not freedom from or denial of it, and sufficient emotional security to accept and handle it constitute the philosophical attitude toward anxiety to be expected of a competent, mature psychiatrist. Incidentally, there was a time when it was my belief that a well-analyzed psychotherapist should be altogether free from anxiety and emotional insecurity. As a matter of fact, my printed elaborations on such utopianism can still be read in my book *Principles of Intensive Psychotherapy* (12). To repeat, I now believe, or, better still, I know that a state of mind permanently free of anxiety is utopianism for the psychotherapist by the same token that it is for anyone else.

There are many pitfalls in the psychiatrist's interaction with patients and, for that matter, in the interaction of other people engaged in responsible interpersonal guidance of their fellow men, if they are not willing and able to accept the awareness of a certain amount of anxiety and emotional insecurity within themselves. Conversely, there is a great and constructive source of help for psychotherapeutic effectiveness in the psychiatrist's awareness and creative acceptance of his own anxieties whenever they are elicited. The therapist's anxiety is frequently indicative of emotional experiences in patients which arouse anxiety in him. Thus the psychiatrist's anxiety becomes an important divining rod for the discovery of many emotional experiences of patients which might otherwise remain undiscovered and hidden for a long time, as in the case of a psychiatrist who would not feel free to use his own anxiety as a guide to anxiety-provoking emotional experiences in patients.

A therapist's denial of his own anxieties may cause him to overlook the possibility of his contaminating patients with them, a danger which in extreme cases may be eliminated or corrected only by its free discussion between patient and doctor or, for that matter, between any other two participants in such an experience. Furthermore, in a therapist, denial of anxiety may arouse all kinds of defenses in him which will interfere with his therapeutic usefulness. That is, he may feel he must reassure himself against the onslaught of anxiety aroused in him by a patient by giving the patient uncalled-for reassurance. Or he may try to propitiate his patient by assuming, for his own defense, all types of roles in the therapeutic process (e.g., the "better" parent, the "great" doctor), instead of operating for the benefit of the patient. A psychotherapist (like any other person participating in an interpersonal exchange) is able to listen with unimpaired alertness, perceptiveness, and creative responsiveness, i.e., he is able to operate effectively, only to the extent to which there is no interference from defense against his own recognized anxiety.

At present, I am engaged, along with several colleagues at Chestnut Lodge, in a research project on the intuitive elements in the doctor's therapeutic approach to schizophrenics.* There we have ample opportunity to observe clearly the marked interference with free utilization of intuitive abilities stemming from our anxiety, with regard to our patients as well as with regard to our colleagues in the research group, as long as this anxiety operates unrecognized.

There is one more important psychotherapeutic issue which is in danger of being obscured in cases of psychiatrists' unrecognized anxiety. A therapist who fails to recognize and to accept his own anxieties will also fail to differentiate correctly the type and degree of pathological excess anxiety in mental patients, which is subject to treatment, and the general human experience of non-pathological anxieties which everyone may suffer and utilize as part of the business of living. To put the same thought differently: psychotherapists are not gods who can change man's fate,

---

* Published as "Intuitive Processes in the Psychotherapy of Schizophrenics" by Frieda Fromm-Reichmann, M. Adland, D. Burnham, H. Searles, and A. Szalita in *J. Am. Psychoanal. Assoc.*, III (1955), 5–88.

which includes, at times, being subjected to states of anxiety. In their role as individual psychiatrists, they cannot alter, except very slowly and imperceptibly, the structure of a culture and a society which may elicit anxiety in its members. However, psychiatrists can and should be useful in man's fight against his individual, irrational excess anxieties, and in encouraging people to accept and integrate constructively and without psychotherapeutic help the milder degrees of anxiety which we may loosely call "normal" anxiety.

Summary

Anxiety is seen as a universal emotional experience. The reader's attention is directed toward the realization that milder degrees of anxiety have both disintegrative and constructive aspects.

Severe degrees of anxiety are described as leading up to the development of mental illness, mental symptoms being simultaneously an expression of severe anxiety and a defense against it.

The existing genetic theories on anxiety are briefly reviewed, and the fear of anticipated disapproval, withdrawal of love, and separation from significant environmental figures is discussed as an etiological factor, the significance of which is recognized by most authors.

The hypothesis is offered that the genesis of anxiety may also be understood as a result of unresolved early emotional tie-ups with significant persons of one's early environment. People are stuck with these early interpersonal patterns and with their early interpersonal evaluation which remained uncorrected. These fixations, of which people are only partially aware, if at all, render them psychologically helpless, interfere with their ability to change, with their growth, maturation, and self-realization, and with their correct evaluation of their own and other peoples' interpersonal interactions. The result is "psychological death," which elicits anxiety. This anxiety is compared with the anxiety which is called forth in most people by factual death and similar phenomena which are beyond human control and therefore arouse helplessness and anxiety.

A distinction is proposed between psychotherapeutic guidance in cases of milder forms of anxiety and psychotherapeutic intervention in cases of severe forms of anxiety, which lead to neurotic or psychotic symptom formation and mental illness.

Finally, the anxieties which may be elicited in psychotherapists during the treatment situation are discussed in their constructive and disintegrative aspects.

References

1. ADLER, ALFRED. *The Neurotic Constitution.* Translated by BERNARD GLUECK. New York: Moffat, Yard & Co., 1917.
2. AUDEN, W. H. *The Age of Anxiety.* New York: Random House, 1946.
3. BERDYAEV, NICHOLAS. *Solitude and Society.* London, 1938.

4. BINSWANGER, LUDWIG. *Grundformen und Erkenntnis menschlichen Daseins.* Zurich: Max Niehaus Verlag, 1942.

5. FREUD, SIGMUND. *A General Introduction to Psychoanalysis.* New York: Liveright, 1935; Garden City Pub. Co., 1943.

6. ———. *Beyond the Pleasure Principle.* London: Hogarth Press, 1942.

7. ———. "On Narcissism: An Introduction." In *Collected Papers,* IV, 30–59. London: Hogarth Press, 1946.

8. ———. *The Ego and the Id.* London: Hogarth Press, 1935.

9. ———. *Problems of Anxiety.* New York: W. W. Norton & Co., 1936.

10. FROMM, ERICH. *Man for Himself.* New York: Rinehart, 1947.

11. ———. "Selfishness and Self-Love." *Psychiatry,* II (1939), 507–23.

12. FROMM-REICHMANN, FRIEDA. *Principles of Intensive Psychotherapy.* Chicago: University of Chicago Press, 1950.

13. ———. "Remarks on the Philosophy of Mental Disorders," *Psychiatry,* IX (1946), 293–308.

14. ———. "Psychoanalysis and Dynamic Psychotherapy: Similarities and Differences," *J. Am. Psychiat. Assoc.,* II (1954), 711–21.

15. GOLDSTEIN, KURT. *Human Nature in the Light of Psychopathology.* Cambridge: Harvard University Press, 1940.

16. ———. *The Organism.* New York: American Book Co., 1939.

17. GRINKER, ROY R. *Psychosomatic Research.* New York: W. W. Norton & Co., 1953.

18. HALMOS, PAUL. *Solitude and Privacy.* New York: Philosophical Library, 1953.

19. HORNEY, KAREN. *New Ways in Psychoanalysis.* New York: W. W. Norton & Co., 1939.

20. ———. *The Neurotic Personality of Our Time.* New York: W. W. Norton & Co., 1937.

21. JUNG, C. G. *Collected Papers on Analytical Psychology.* Translated by C. E. LONG; London: Baillière, Tindall & Cox, 1920.

22. KARDINER, ABRAM. *The Psychological Frontiers of Society.* New York: Columbia University Press, 1945.

23. MAY, ROLLO. *The Meaning of Anxiety.* New York: Ronald Press, 1951.

24. MENNINGER, KARL. *Man against Himself.* New York: Harcourt, Brace & Co., 1938.

25. PODOLSKY, E. F. "The Meaning of Anxiety," *Diseases of the Nervous System,* XIV (1953), 4.

26. RANK, OTTO. *Will Therapy and Truth and Reality.* New York: A. A. Knopf, 1945.

27. RIESMAN, DAVID. *The Lonely Crowd.* New Haven: Yale University Press, 1950.

28. RUESCH, JURGEN. "The Interpersonal Communication of Anxiety," *Symposium of Stress* (Washington, D.C.: Walter Reed Army Medical Center, 1953), pp. 154–64.

29. SULLIVAN, H. S. *Conceptions of Modern Psychiatry.* Washington, D.C.: William Alanson White Foundation, 1947; new ed., New York: W. W. Norton & Co., 1953.

30. ———. *The Interpersonal Theory of Psychiatry*. New York: W. W. Norton & Co., 1953.
31. ———. "The Meaning of Anxiety in Psychiatry and in Life," *Psychiatry*, XI (1948), 1–13.
32. ———. "The Theory of Anxiety and the Nature of Psychotherapy," *Psychiatry*, XII (1949), 3–12.
33. TILLICH, PAUL. *The Courage To Be*. New Haven: Yale University Press, 1952.
34. VASSOS, JOHN. *Phobia*. New York: Covici-Friede, 1931.
35. WEIGERT, EDITH. "Existentialism and Its Relation to Psychotherapy," *Psychiatry*, XII (1949), 399–412.
36. ZILBOORG, GREGORY. "Considerations on Suicide with Particular Reference to That of the Young," *Am. J. Orthopsychiat.* (1937).
37. ———. "Suicide among Civilized and Primitive Races," *Am. J. Psychiat.*, XCII (1936), 1347–69.

VI

Epilogue

EDITOR'S NOTE

At the time of her death Dr. Frieda Fromm-Reichmann had in mind the preparation of a paper on "Loneliness." In it she wished to present some conclusions she had come to during the course of her many years in psychiatric work.

A rough draft of her ideas was subsequently found in her desk. These thoughts, somewhat abbreviated but in the original sequence, are offered here as a last chapter of this book—like her life, ended but unfinished. The notes are more fully presented in a recent issue of *Psychiatry: Journal for the Study of Interpersonal Processes*, Vol. XXII, No. 1 (February, 1959).

In the version that follows, some quotations from the writings of others have been omitted along with certain fragmentary and repetitious passages characteristic of a first draft. Gaps in continuity remain and an occasional lack of transition between paragraphs, indicating the provisional order and incompleteness of the original. Nevertheless, her genuine concern with the topic, her own deep awareness of the devastating effects of loneliness, shine through like a beacon light.

D. M. B.

(23)

ON LONELINESS

I do not know for sure what inner forces have made me for years ponder about and struggle with the psychiatric problems of loneliness. There has been a strange fascination in thinking about it and subsequently trying to break through the aloneness of thinking about loneliness by attempting to communicate what I believe I have learned.

The writer who wishes to elaborate on the problems of loneliness is faced with a serious terminological handicap: Loneliness seems to be such a painful, frightening experience that people do practically everything to avoid it. This avoidance seems to include a strange reluctance on the part of psychiatrists to seek scientific clarification of the subject. Thus it has come about that loneliness belongs to the least satisfactorily conceptualized psychological phenomena; it is not even mentioned in most psychiatric textbooks. Very little is known among scientists about its genetics and psychodynamics, and various experiences which are descriptively and dynamically as different from one another as aloneness, isolation, loneliness in cultural groups, self-imposed aloneness, compulsory solitude, and real loneliness are all thrown into the one terminological basket of "loneliness."

In contrast to the disintegrative effect of the essential loneliness of mental patients, temporary states of self-induced solitude, which may be voluntarily and alternately sought and rejected, quite frequently turn out to be most constructive. Regarding the loneliness of the creative worker, we should also remember that nearly all works of creative originality are conceived in states of constructive aloneness. In fact, only the creative person who is not afraid of this constructive loneliness will have command over the productive emanations of his creative mind. Some of these people, "schizoid artistic personalities" in Karl Menninger's nomenclature, submit to us as products of their detachment from normal life "fragments of their own world—bits of dreams and visions and songs that we—out here—don't hear except as they translate them." In addition, an original, creative person may be lonely not only for the time of his involvement in creative processes but subsequently also because of them, since creations of genuine originality ordinarily antedate the ability of contemporaries to understand and/or to accept what the lonely creator has to offer.

However, to many of the "other-directed types" of our present culture, as Rollo May has observed, "loneliness is such an omnipotent and painful threat that they have little conception of the positive values of solitude, and are at times very frightened of the prospect of being alone."

This may even hold true, for example, in the case of the subjective feeling of aloneness of a person who has to stay in bed with a cold on a pleasant Sunday afternoon while the rest of the family is enjoying the outdoors. He may complain about loneliness and feel sorry for himself, but, needless to say, he is not "lonely"; he is just temporarily alone. Such little problems will therefore not be included in our discussion.

The same holds true, though on another level, for people who suffer from the sense of loss and of being left alone which is connected with mourning for a deceased person. Freud and Abraham have described the dynamics of the mourners who try to counteract this aloneness by incorporating the deceased beloved person. They have brought to our attention the fact that the process is descriptively verified by the development of likenesses to the lost loved ones in looks, personality, and activities. In other words, there is a power immanent in the human mind to fight the aloneness after loss of a beloved person by incorporation and identification.

Real loneliness, however, leads ultimately to the development of psychotic states. It renders people who suffer it emotionally paralyzed and helpless. These are the states of loneliness with which we wish to deal in this paper. To put it in Sullivan's words, they are "the exceedingly unpleasant and driving experiences connected with an inadequate discharge of the need for interpersonal intimacy" with which every human is threatened.

The infant thrives on living in intimate and tender closeness with the person who tends him and mothers him. In childhood the healthy youngster's longing for intimacy is, according to Sullivan, fulfilled by his participating in activities with others; in the juvenile era, by finding compeers and acceptance. As an adolescent, and in the years of growth and development thereafter, man feels the need for friendship and intimacy jointly with, or independently from, his sexual drive.

John C. Lilly reports on psychological experiments in isolation on very young animals. He found that the effect can be an almost completely irreversible lack of development of whole systems, "such as those necessary for the use of vision in accomplishing tasks put to the animal."

René Spitz demonstrated the fatal influence of lack of love and of loneliness on neglected infants, in what he called "anaclitic depression."

Anna Freud, in her lecture at the 1953 International Psychoanalytic meetings in London, described sensations of essential loneliness in children under the heading of "Losing and Being Lost."

Sullivan and Suttie have investigated what may happen if a person's infantile need for tenderness remains unsatisfied or if its satisfaction is prematurely interrupted. The child may resort to substitute satisfactions in fantasy, which he cannot share with others, i.e., he becomes a lonely child.

Robert Lindner has presented an impressive example of the fatal results of such faulty developments in his treatment history of Kirk Allen, the hero of "The Jet-propelled Couch," a "true psychoanalytic tale."

Lucy Sprague Mitchell offers an interesting discussion of the impact of loneliness in childhood in her "Two Lives," a "dual autobiography-biography." She contrasts the influence of her childhood loneliness with the affection, approval, and security her husband had as a child in his home. Mrs. Mitchell also realized the importance of the human need for friendship and intimacy and its importance for the development of a unified personality.

The lonely child's primary sense of isolation may subsequently be reinforced if, despite the pressures of socialization and acculturation, he does not sufficiently learn to discriminate between realistic phenomena and the products of his lively fantasy. He may then further withdraw into isolation in order to escape being laughed at or being punished for replacing reports of real events by fictitious narratives.

The process of the child's holding on to the uncorrected substitutive products of his early fantasy life and the social isolation connected with it can be avoided if the mothering one does not wean the infant from receiving her love before he is ready to try for the satisfaction of the modified needs for intimacy characteristic of his ensuing development phase. That is, we agree with Suttie's warning against the danger that separation from the direct tenderness and nurtural love relationship with the mother may outrun the child's ability for making substitutions. This is a rather serious threat to an infant and child in our age of taboo on tenderness among adults. If and when it happens, the roots of permanent aloneness and isolation, "love-shyness" (Suttie), and fear of intimacy and tenderness are planted in the child's mind, and the defensive reactions to separation may lead to psychopathological developments.

Karl Menninger described the milder states of loneliness in adults which result from this failure to handle infants and children—his "isolation types of personality."

More severe developments include the unconstructive desolate phases of isolation and real loneliness which are beyond the state of feeling sorry for oneself, *the states of mind in which the fact that there were people in one's past life is more or less forgotten and the hope that there may be interpersonal relationships in one's future life is out of the realm of expectation or imagination.*

This loneliness, in its quintessential form, is of a nature that is incommunicable by the one who suffers it. Nor, unlike other non-communicable emotional experiences, can it be shared via empathy. It may well be that the second person's empathic abilities are obstructed by the anxiety-arousing quality of the mere emanations of the first person's loneliness. I wonder whether this explains the fact that real loneliness defies description, even by a master of conceptualization like Sullivan.

People who are in the grips of severe degrees of loneliness cannot talk about it, and those who *were* there seldom do so either. Because of the extremely frightening and gruesome character of the experience, they try to dissociate the memories of the sense of loneliness, including their fear of it. This frightened secretiveness and lack of communication about their loneliness seem to increase the threat entailed in it for the lonely ones, even in retrospect: it produces the sad conviction that nobody else has experienced or ever will sense what they have experienced or what they have submerged.

Incidentally, there may be a secondary element in the perseverance of the loneliness of some psychotics. Because of their interpersonal detachment, some of them may be more keen, sensitive, and fearless as observers of the people in their environment than is the average, non-lonely, mentally healthy person. They may feel free to express themselves with many painful truths regarding others, things that would otherwise remain unobserved or suppressed by their healthy and gregarious fellow men. The case of the court jester is an example of what I have in mind. Persons outside the fool's paradise that is granted to the jester may be displeased if not frightened at hearing these unwelcome truths, and they may erect a psychological wall of ostracism and isolation around such psychotic "court jesters" as a means of protecting themselves.

Cervantes has given a poetic description of this mechanism in his novel *The Man of Glass*. He depicts there a psychotic man who suffers from the delusion that he is made of glass and who indiscriminately offers the pearls of his uncensured human wisdom to the people in his environment. They listen to him as long as they experience him as a psychological recluse who is isolated from them by virtue of his "craziness." In this setup they can laugh off the narcissistic hurts to which the wise psychotic man exposes them. As he recovers from his delusions, however, the public prevents him from getting back on his feet. The unwelcome truths of "the man of glass" are acceptable only so long as he lives in the psychological isolation of his psychosis. Since his truths have been accepted, the people around him prefer that he remain mentally sick or else that he remain isolated by virtue of their ostracism.

While all adults seem to be afraid of *real loneliness*, fear of *aloneness* and tolerance for it vary from person to person. I have seen, for example, people who got deeply frightened when facing the infinity of the desert with its connotations of loneliness, others who felt singularly peaceful and serene and pregnant with creative ideas when left alone with their "oceanic feelings" in the face of nature. I would like to digress here from the subject of real psychotogenic loneliness by asking the reasons for the deep-rooted fear or anxiety connected with aloneness and the threat of ensuing loneliness that is felt by one group of people and the fearless enjoyment of it felt by others. Why are so many people afraid of temporary aloneness or even such experiences as mere silence, which may—or may not!—connote potential aloneness?

The answer seems to be determined by the following facts: It appears that in our culture people can come to a valid self-orientation or even awareness of themselves only in terms of their actual overt relationships with others. "Every human being gets much of his sense of his own reality out of what others say to him, and think about him," as Rollo May puts it. While alone and isolated from other human beings, people feel threatened by the potential loss of their boundaries, of the ability to discriminate "between wakefulness and sleep—between the subjective self and the objective world around them." Valid as this general explanation for the rise of fear of aloneness may be, it leaves the significant question unanswered: Why is not this fear a ubiquitous phenomenon?

Generally speaking, I believe that the degree of a person's dependence on others for self-orientation, the degree of anxiety aroused in him by the threat of isolation from them, depends upon the vicissitudes of personal development. Whether or not individual variation in *tolerance for aloneness*—anticipated or actual—is related to the onset of *real loneliness*, we do not yet know. The answer might come from an intensive scrutiny of the developmental histories of the pathologically lonely ones. Unfortunately, it would be hard to conduct such investigations because of the lack of communication previously mentioned as one of the reasons for our actually knowing so little about the genetics and dynamics of real loneliness. As Zilboorg puts it, we do not yet know when being alone will lead to creative "social, artistic, philosophic or characterological performances" and when mental illness will be the outcome.

Sullivan characterizes the need for intimacy as belonging to the same group of basic needs as hunger, sleep, and sex. Anyone who has encountered persons who are under the influence of real loneliness understands why they will go to such lengths to avoid that degree of solitude which they classify as loneliness. They may even resort to anxiety-arousing experiences if it helps them escape loneliness, even though anxiety itself constitutes an emotional experience against which people fight, as a rule, with symptom-formation and every other defense at their command.

Sullivan was of the opinion, in fact, that psychiatrists must resign themselves to describing real loneliness in terms of people's defenses against it. Freud points his thinking about it in the same direction; he refers to loneliness and people's defenses against it in *Civilization and Its Discontents*.

As one of the drastic defensive maneuvers to which a person may resort when he feels threatened by loneliness, compulsive eating should be mentioned. As we learned from Hilda Bruch's research on obesity, these compulsive eaters try to counteract their loneliness with overeating, which serves at the same time as a means of getting even with the significant environmental people whom the threatened eater holds responsible for his loneliness.

One patient told me that her most endearing childhood memory was of sitting in the darkened living room of her childhood home and secretly eating stolen sweets. In her first therapeutic interview she encountered me with the statement: "And then you will take away my gut pains [from overeating], my trance states [her delusional states of retreat], and my food; and where will I be then [i.e., if I give up these defenses against loneliness]?"

Needless to say such symptom-formation does not hold true as long as a person is fully in the grip of true, severe loneliness, with its specific character of paralyzing hopelessness and unutterable futility. This "naked horror" (Binswanger) at its peak is beyond anxiety and tension: defense and remedy seem out of reach. Only as its all-engulfing intensity decreases may loneliness enter into fusion with anxiety. In the last analysis, anxiety and fear of real loneliness merge where they are an anticipation of the fear of the ultimate isolation and separation, of the inconceivable absolute loneliness which is death. Realizing all this, we understand why lonely persons are experienced by others as people with whom "something is vaguely wrong"—as though "some pariahed aura of untouchability or sickness hovered around them."

Binswanger comes nearest to a philosophical and psychiatric definition of loneliness when he speaks of it as "naked existence," "mere existence," and "naked horror" and when he characterizes lonely people as being "devoid of any interest in any goal." Tillich describes by implication people whom I would call "lonely" as those in whom "the essentially united experiences of the courage to be as oneself and the courage to be as a part" are split, hence "disintegrated in their isolation."

An example of severe loneliness comes from the previously mentioned schizophrenic patient who emerged from a severe state of schizophrenic depression. She asked to see me because she wished to tell me about the deep state of hopeless loneliness and subjective isolation which she had had to undergo during her psychotic episodes. Even though the patient was in fine command of the language and came with the intention of talking, she was just as unable to tell me about her loneliness in so many words as are other people who are engulfed in or have gone through a period of real psychotic loneliness. After several futile attempts, she finally burst out saying: "I don't know why people think of hell as a place where there is heat and where warm fires are burning. That is not hell. Hell is if you are frozen in isolation into a block of ice. That is where I have been."

Every now and then a creative mental patient succeeds in conveying his experience of essential loneliness artistically after having emerged from it. Mary Jane Ward succeeded in doing so in her novel *The Snake Pit.* The most impressive poetic document on loneliness from a mental patient of which I know has been written by Eithne Tabor, a schizophrenic patient at St. Elizabeths Hospital:

> And is there anyone at all?
> And is
> There anyone at all?
> I am knocking at the oaken door . . .
> And will it open
> Never now no more
> I am calling, calling to you—
> Don't you hear?
> And is there anyone
> Near?
> And does this empty silence have to be?
> And is there no one there at all
> To answer me?
> I do not know the road—
> I fear to fall
> And is there anyone
> at All?

The recovered catatonic woman patient, the poet on whose treatment history I commented in my paper on the philosophy of mental disorder* has told us about the genesis of psychotic loneliness in a poem, "The Disenchanted," which she dedicated to me. She warns me about the difficulties of helping her (and her fellow patients) to emerge from their states of loneliness:

> The demented hold love
> In the palm of the hand,
> And let it fall,
> And grind it in the sand.
> They return by darkest night
> To bury it again,
> And hide it forever
> From the sight of man.

* See Paper 1, p. 3—Ed.

In another poem, which she wrote after her recovery, under the title "Empty Lot," she depicts this loneliness symbolically:

> No one comes near here
> Morning or night.
> The desolate grasses
> Grow out of sight.
> Only a wild hare
> Strays, then is gone.
> The landlord is silence.
> The tenant is dawn.

All these poems have—seemingly coincidentally—one feature in common regarding their titles: they are not titled "Loneliness," but "Pain," "Empty Lot," "The Disenchanted." Is this because of the well-known general inclination of the word-conscious and word-suspicious schizophrenic to substitute direct communications and definitions by allusions, symbols, circumlocutions, etc.; or could it be that it is an unconscious expression of the poets' fear of loneliness, which is so great that even naming it is frightening? Remembering our insight that fear of loneliness is the common fate of the people of our Western culture, be they mentally healthy or disturbed, we wonder whether the choice of the titles of these poems is determined by this fear. So much for the artistic expression of loneliness by the people who were there, the psychotics.

There are two sources of verification for our assumption that real loneliness cannot be endured more than temporarily without leading to psychotic developments or that it occurs as an inherent part of mental illness. One stems from the people who develop psychoses in solitary confinement, the other from psychosis-like states following experimentally induced loneliness.

As to states of solitary confinement, we must differentiate between three groups: The first comprises voluntary confinement, such as may come about in the course of polar expeditions or in the lives of rangers who live at solitary outposts. This may be tolerated without serious emotional disturbances. Courtauld's report on "Living Alone under Polar Conditions" may be mentioned as representative to some degree. The second group consists of people who are, for example, subjected to seafaring isolation. Most of them suffer from symptoms of mental illness. Slocum, for example, as a solitary sailor, developed hallucinations of a "savior" type, a reflection of his inner convictions of survival. The third group comprises those who are subjected to solitary confinement in prisons and concentration camps. They are, of course, seriously threatened by psychotic developments, and they are frequently victims of mental illness.

Christopher Burney was able to write a report about his survival, without mental illness, of eighteen months' solitary confinement by the Germans during World War II, with all its physical and emotional humiliations, intensified by a near-starvation diet. On the few occasions when there was an opportunity for communication, he found that the muscles of his mouth had become stiff and unwilling and that the thoughts and questions he had wanted to express became ridiculous when he turned them into words. "Solitude," he says, "had so far weaned me from the habit of intercourse, even the thin intercourse of speculation, that I could no longer see any relationship with another person unless it were introduced gradually by a long overture of common trivialities." He describes the devices he developed systematically to counteract the danger of becoming mad. He disciplined himself to divide his lonesome days into fixed periods by spreading the eating of his scarce food over the whole day, despite the craving of his hungry stomach for immediacy. He did the floor of his cell, tried to estimate the size of the bed, table, and toilet seat, and manicured himself daily with a wooden splinter. He brought a snail into his cell, which was company of a sort and, as it were, an emissary from the world of real life.

The intensity of his efforts to remain adjusted in his solitary life may be measured by the fact that at the first opportunity to communicate he did not dare to talk lest he "show himself to be mad . . . if he opened his mouth." He constantly "had to check [his tongue] for fear of uttering some impossibility."

Ellam and Mudie, and Bernicot report similar experiences. "The inner life becomes so vivid and intense that it takes time to readjust to the life among other persons and to reestablish one's inner criteria," says John C. Lilly in his report about these people.

One more remark about Mr. Burney's experiences: I believe his unquestioned matter-of-fact belief in the spiritual validity of the political convictions which were the cause of his imprisonment may have worked as an additional factor which helped him survive his ordeal without becoming mentally sick. That makes his confinement more of a piece with the voluntary isolation of the people of our first group than, for example, with the imprisonment of delinquents who have neither the intelligent determination nor the devotion to a cause which helped Mr. Burney stay mentally sound, even though he was nearly the whole time deprived of the opportunity to work and to receive stimulation by reading. These are the two effective antidotes against the humiliating effects of solitary confinement and against the rise of distintegrating loneliness in the confined ones.

The last new important source of attaining further insight into the psychodynamics of loneliness has been offered by the very significant experimental work of Donald Hebb and his group at McGill University and that of John C. Lilly at the National Institute of Mental Health. They have brought about marked temporary impairment of emotional reactions, mental activities, and mental health by cutting down the scope of their subjects' physical contact with the outside world through experimental limitations of their perception and decreased variation in their sensory environment, i.e., by exposing their subjects to experimentally created states of physical and emotional isolation. The most striking result of these experiments was the occurrence of primarily visual, but also auditory, kinesthetic, and somesthetic, hallucinatory experiences. The subjects had insight into the objective unreality of these experiences, but they were neverthelss extremely vivid to them.

Most authors agree, explicitly or implicitly, with the definition of anxiety as "a response to the anticipated loss of love and approval by significant people in one's interpersonal environment." It is my impression that *loneliness* and fear of loneliness, on the one hand, and *anxiety*, on the other, are sometimes used interchangeably in our psychiatric thinking and in our clinical terminology. I would not be surprised if, after learning to differentiate the two dynamisms more sharply from each other, we would see that loneliness in its own right plays a much more significant role in the dynamics of mental disturbance than we have been ready to acknowledge so far. There is good reason for this hypothesis on the basis of my own experiences with patients and on the basis of many reports of my colleagues.

We cannot offer these considerations without wondering about the origin of this mix-up between anxiety and loneliness. Could it be that the mix-up was brought about originally by the fear of loneliness that psychiatrists share, of course, with their non-professional fellow men? Or is this supposition an oversimplification? Is there another reason for the tacit conspiracy among psychiatrists to accept unchallenged the conceptual merger between loneliness and anxiety? I believe the ever increasing insight of psychiatrists into the enormous psychodynamic significance of anxiety for the understanding of human psychology and psychopathology has brought about such a degree of preoccupation with this one universal emotional experience that it has limited our ability to study adequately other ubiquitous emotional experiments.

At this point I should like to add some psychotherapeutic remarks regarding my experience with lonely patients, some pertaining to the patient, some to the role of the psychotherapist. We have seen that most patients keep their loneliness hidden as a secret from others, many times even from themselves. "They go and see the doctor allegedly for physical treatment, actually because they are lonely," as Otto A. Will puts it in his report about a recorded psychotherapeutic interview. "Miss A. may talk about many things, but not of her most essential problem, her loneliness."

I think this great difficulty which patients have in accepting the awareness of being lonely, and, much more, in admitting it to the therapist in so many words, furnishes an explanation for the relief with which some lonely mental patients respond if the psychiatrist takes the initiative of opening the discussion about it, for example, by offering a sober statement to the effect that he knows about the patient's loneliness. Of course, I do not mean to say that such a statement can be offered to patients before they have overcome at least some fraction of their isolation. This may be accomplished by the doctor's mere presence without therapeutic pressure. The doctor should offer his presence to lonely patients, first in the spirit of expecting nothing but to be tolerated, then to be accepted simply as some person who is there. The possibility that psychotherapy may be able to do something about the patient's loneliness should, of course, not be verbalized at this point. To offer any such suggestion in the beginning of one's contact with an essentially lonely patient could lend itself only to one of two interpretations in the patient's mind: Either the psychotherapist does not know anything about the inextricable, uncanny quality of his loneliness, or he himself is afraid of it. The mere statements, however, that "we know" and "I am here," put in at the right time by implication or in so many words, may be accepted and may replace the patient's desolate experience of "nobody knows except me." I have tried this device with several patients and have been gratified by its results. It has helped to make an initial dent in their inner loneliness and isolation and has thus become a beneficial turning point in the course of their treatment.

The psychiatrist's specific personal problem in treating lonely patients seems to be that he has to watch for and recognize traces of his own existing loneliness, or fear of loneliness, lest it interfere with his fearless acceptance of manifestations of the patient's loneliness. This holds true, for example, in cases when the psychiatrist, hard as he may try, does not succeed in understanding the meaning of a psychotic communication. He may then feel excluded from a "we-experience" with his patients. Such an exclusion may well evoke in the doctor a sense of loneliness, or fear of loneliness, which makes him anxious.

Last but not least, a word about physical loneliness should be added to our discussion of emotional loneliness. The need, or at least the wish, to have at times physical contact is an all-human phenomenon, innate and consistent from the time when the human leaves the womb and is physically separated from his mother. Physical and emotional disturbances caused by consistent lack of physical contact have been repeatedly described. Among the people of the middle and upper social strata in our Western culture, physical loneliness has become a specific problem, since this culture is governed by so many obsessional taboos with regard to people's touching one another or having their physical privacy threatened in other ways.

Summary

To conclude and summarize, an attempt has been made in this paper to invite the interest of psychiatrists in investigating the psychodynamics of loneliness as a significant, universal emotional experience with far-reaching psychopathological ramifications. Developmental histories might be studied for certain trends specific to persons suffering from real loneliness.

Various types and degrees of loneliness, such as solitude, aloneness, isolation, and real loneliness should be differentiated, including the voluntary and involuntary, the temporary and lasting, types of loneliness.

A significant interrelatedness between loneliness and anxiety has been postulated, along with the need for further conceptual and clinical examination of loneliness in its own right and in its relatedness with anxiety.

I suspect that such scrutiny will reveal the essential role of real loneliness, as yet not fully recognized, in the genesis and understanding of the dynamics of mental disorders.

BIBLIOGRAPHY OF PAPERS WRITTEN IN GERMAN BY FRIEDA FROMM-REICHMANN

1914

"Ueber Pupillenstörungen bei Dementia Praecox" ("Changes in Pupillary Reactions in Dementia Praecox"), *Arch. f. Psychiat. u. Nervenkrankh.*, LIII, 302–21.

"Ueber die körperlichen Störungen bie der Dementia Praecox" ("Bodily Symptoms in Dementia Praecox") (with KURT GOLDSTEIN), *Neurol. Centralbl.*, XXXIII, 343–50.

1915

"Ueber Schussverletzungen peripherischer Nerven" ("Observations on Gunshot Peripheral Nerves"), *Deutsch. med. Wchnschr.*, XLI, 668–71.

1916

"Klinische Beobachtungen an Schussverletzungen peripherischer Nerven" ("Clinical Observations on Gunshot Peripheral Nerves"), *Arch. f. Psychiat. u. Nervenkrankh.*, LVI, 290–327.

"Ueber nervöse Folgezustände nach Granat-Explosionen" ("On Nervous Disturbances after Shell Shock") (with ERNST MEYER), *Arch. f. Psychiat. u. Nervenkrankh.*, LVI, 914–52.

"Beiträge zur Kasuistik und Symptomatologie der Kleinhirnerkrankungen" ("Cases and Symptomatology of Cerebellar Injuries") (with KURT GOLDSTEIN), *Arch. f. Psychiat. u. Nervenkrankh.*, LVI, 466–521.

1917

"Zur neurologischen Kasuistik der Kleinhirnverletzungen," ("Neurological Symptoms from Injuries of the Cerebellum"), *Arch. f. Psychiat. u. Nervenkrankh.*, LVII, 61–72.

"Zur praktischen Durchführung der ärztlichen und sozialen Fürsorgemassnahmen bei Hirnschussverletzten" ("Medical and Social Care of Gunshot Brain Injuries"), *Arch. f. Psychiat. u. Nervenkrankh.*, LVIII, 114–40.

"Ueber Fürsorge für Kopfschussverletzte" ("Social Care of the Brain-injured"), *Med. Klin.*, XIII, 10; *Berl. klin. Wchnschr.*, LIV, 699.

"Beitrag zur differentialdiagnostischen Bedeutung des Bárányschen Zeigeversuchs" ("Bárány's Fingerpointing Test") (with ARTHUR BLOHMKE), *Arch. f. Ohren- Nasen- u. Kehlkopfheilk.*, CI, 80–107.

1918

"Kasuistischer Beitrag zur Frage des Vorbeizeigens bei Stirnhirnläsionen" ("The Fingerpointing Test in Injuries of the Frontal Lobe") (with ARTHUR BLOHMKE), *Internat. Zentralbl. f. Ohrenheilk. u. Rhino-Laryngol.*, XVI, 42–50.

"Zur Uebungsbehandlung der Aphasien" ("On Re-education after Aphasia") with EDUARD REICHAU), *Arch. f. Psychiat. u. Nervenkrankh.*, LX, 1–36.

1919

"Ueber corticale Sensibilitätsstörungen, besonders am Kopfe" ("On Cortical Disturbances of the Sensibility, Especially of the Head") (with KURT GOLD-STEIN), *Ergebn. d. ges. Neurol. u. Psychiat.*, LIII, 49–79.

1920

"Ueber praktische und theoretische Ergebnisse aus den Erfahrungen an Hirn-schussverletzten" ("Experience with Brain-injured Soldiers in Practice and Theory") (with KURT GOLDSTEIN), *Ergebn. d. inn. Med. u. Kinderh.*, XVIII, 405–530.

1921

"Ueber Schnellheilung von Friedensneurosen" ("On Rapid Cures of Peace-time Neuroses") (with J. H. SCHULTZ), *Med. Klin.*, XVII, 380–84.

1922

"Aufgaben der Schwester bei der Pflege Nervenkranker" ("The Nurse, and the Care of Mental Patients"), *Die Schwester*, V, 162–66.

"Zur Psychopathologie des Asthma bronchiale" ("The Psychology of Bronchial Asthma") (with J. H. SCHULTZ), *Med. Klin.*, XVIII, 1090–92.

1923

"Trauma und Wirbelsäule" ("Trauma of the Spine"), *Monatschr. f. Unfall-heilk. u. Versicherungsmed.*, XXX, No. 7, 145–61.

"Zur Schilddrüsenbehandlung der Dercumschen Krankheit" ("The Treatment of Dercum's Disease with Thyroidin"), *Deutsch. med. Wchnschr.*, XLIX, 1018–19.

"Zur Soziologie der Neurosen" ("Social Factors in Neuroses"), *Jahresvers d. Deutsch. Ver. f. Psychiat.*, V, 20; IX, 21; also *Ztschr. f. d. ges. Neurol. u. Psychiat.*, LXXXIX, 60–67 (1924).

1924

"Ueber Psychoanalyse" ("On Psychoanalysis"), *Deutsch. med. Wchnschr.*, L, 758–61.

1927

"Das Jüdische Speiseritual" ("Jewish Food Ritual"), *Imago*, XIII, 235–46.

1929

"Zur psychoanalytischen Trieblehre" ("The Psychoanalytic Instinct Theory"), *Ztschr. f. psychoanal. Pädagogik*, III, 266–68.

1930

"Pädagogische Diskussionsbemerkungen zur psychoanalytischen Trieblehre" ("Pedagogical Implications of the Psychoanalytic Instinct Theory"), *Ztschr. f. psychoanal. Pädagogik*, IV, 38–44.

1931

"Zur Entstehungsgeschichte sozialer Minderwertigkeitsgefühle" ("On the History and Development of Social Inferiority Feelings"), *ibid.*, V, 19–29.

"Zur Bedeutung der Angehörigenaussagen in der Psychotherapie" ("The Evaluation of Statements of Relatives in Psychotherapy"), *Nervenarzt*, IV, 257–68.

"Kindliche Darmträgheit infolge falschen Erziehung" ("Infantile Constipation Caused by Improper Training"), *Ztschr. f. psychoanal. Pädagogik*, V, 460–64.

Indexes

AUTHOR INDEX

Hebb, D., 33, 333
Hill, L. B., 26, 50, 117, 123
Hinsie, L. E., 34 n., 163
Hippocrates, 66
Hoch, P., 35, 111, 228
Hoelderlin, 12
Hollos, J., 163
Horkheimer, M., 291
Horney, K., 30 n., 50, 53, 92, 93, 103, 110, 170, 308, 315
Hubbard, L. D., 228

Jackson, D., 28 n.
Jacobson, E., 234
Janet, P., 27
Jones, E., 33
Jung, C. G., 8, 27, 39, 161, 315

Kallman, F. J., 229 n.
Kardiner, A., 92, 308
Kasanin, J. S., 160
Katan, M., 26
Kempf, E. J., 26, 164
Klein, M., 97, 110, 236–41 passim, 244, 260, 295 n.
Knight, R. P., 34, 301
Kraepelin, E., v, 17, 226, 227, 228
Kretschmer, E., 229
Kris, E., vi, 109, 185
Kubie, L., 35, 103

LaForgue, R., 124 n., 163
Lampl-de Groot, J., 108
"Late Inmate at Gartnavel," 16, 17
Lenau, 12
Levine, M., 29, 39 n.
Lewin, B., 235, 254
Lewis, N. D. C., 228
Lewy, E., 305
Lidz, T., 35, 110, 172
Liébeault, A. A., 27
Lilly, J. C., 326, 333, 334
Lindner, R., 327
Loewenstein, R. M., vi, 109, 185
Loomis, E. A., 33

McLean, H., 52 n.
McQuown, N., 36 n.
Malinowski, B., 90, 293
Marx, K., 109, 110
Maskin, M., 55
Masserman, J., 28, 37
May, R., 111, 309, 309 n., 325–26, 329
Mead, M., 291
Menninger, K., 84, 117, 158, 298 n. 325, 327
Menninger, W., 158, 159
Mesmer, 27
Meyer, A., 18, 28, 30, 37

Mitchell, L. S., 327
More, 30, 31
Moreno, J. L., 26, 28, 31 n., 32, 33, 35
Morgan, L. H., 296
Mudie, 333
Mullahy, P., 90
Muncie, W., 28, 37
Murray, H. A., 301, 302, 303, 304

Nietzsche, F., 9, 36
Nijinsky, 14, 15

Paracelsus, 25, 26, 30
Payne, S. M., 167
Pinel, 26
Pious, W. L., 185
Podolsky, E. F., 313
Poe, E. A., 12
Porter, W. C., 61
Powdermaker, F., 179

Querido, A., 33

Rachlin, H. L., 228
Rado, S., 110, 111, 229, 232, 233, 240, 260
Rank, O., 110, 308
Redlick, F. C., 32
Reese, H. H., 33
Reich, W., 109, 185
Riese, W., 30
Riesman, D., 308
Riley, J. W., 284
Rioch, D. McK., 34, 221 n.
Rioch, M. J., 210 n.
Rogers, C., 35
Rosen, H., 28 n.
Rosen, J. N., 26, 162, 168, 171, 184, 185
Ruesch, J., 30, 111, 312

Saul, L., 30
Schilder, P., 17, 26, 171
Schopenhauer, A., 12
Schultz, I. H., v
Schumann, R., 13, 14
Schwartz, M. S., 33, 187, 202
Schwing, G., 197
Scott, W. C. M., 59
Searles, H., 35
Secheheye, M. A., 197, 203
Segal, H., 181 n.
Sharpe, E., 110
Silberer, H., 8, 9
Silverberg, W. V., 110, 163
Simmel, E., 84
Sivadon, P. D., 33
Slocum, I., 333
Smith, O. C., 221 n.
Spiegel, R., 190

AUTHOR INDEX

Spitz, R. A., 110, 236, 326
Stanton, A. H., 33, 187, 202, 221
Staveren, H., 221
Steinfeld, J., 18
Stekel, W., 286
Stone, L., 284
Storch, A., 160
Sullivan, H. S., 9, 18, 26, 28, 31, 32, 37, 38, 50, 51, 82, 90, 91, 92, 103, 106, 110, 117, 124, 159, 160, 161, 162, 164, 168, 170, 171, 185, 197, 198, 217 n., 228, 229, 237, 256, 258, 265, 307, 308, 309, 315, 326, 328, 329
Suttie, I. D., 326, 327
Szalita, A., 35

Tabor, E., 331
Tausk, V., 8
Tchaikovski, P., 12
Thompson, C., 118 n.
Tillich, P., x, 311, 330
Tosquelles, 33
Tower, S. S., 169, 221
Tuke, W., 27

Van Gogh, V., 12, 13
Vassos, J., 308
Vigotsky, L. S., 160
Vives, J. L., 30, 31

Ward, M. J., 331
Weigert, E. V., 119 n., 227 n.
Weininger, B., 171, 221 n.
Weiss, E., 27 n., 234
Wexler, M., 26
Weyer, J., 25, 30
Wheelwright, J., 39
Whitaker, C., 39
White, M. J., 189, 221 n.
White, W. A., 18, 143, 144 n., 159, 230
Whitehorn, J. C., 26, 28, 29, 34, 38, 39, 40, 103, 110, 311
Wilde, O., 12
Will, O. A., 36 n., 210 n., 334
Wolberg, L. R., 28

Ziferstein, I. F., 33, 35
Zilboorg, G., 31, 35, 235, 236, 329
Zubin, J., 111

SUBJECT INDEX

Academy of Psychoanalysis, ix

Acting out, 135–36, 168

Agoraphobia, 279–80

Ambivalence, 7, 199, 243–45, 277, 286–87, 299; *see also* Dependency-hostility conflict

Anthropology, 281, 293–94, 296–97, 304

Anxiety: bipolarity of, as symptom and defense, 6–8, 76, 119, 164, 170, 185–86, 189, 196–208, 254, 258, 260, 278–82, 306; childhood roots of, 92–93, 110–12, 170, 307–8, 309–10, 312; constructive aspects of, 40, 101–2, 104, 307, 315–16; about death, 313–15; *defined*, 92, 307, 334; dynamics of, 307–10; and guilt, 307–8, 312, 313; and loneliness, 308–9, 329–30, 334; manifestations of, in the brain-injured, 310, in mild forms, 306, in panic, 307; and masturbation, 313; normal, and psychotic, 198–99, 315–16, 319; in psychotherapist, 78–80, 317–19; self-realization, blocked by, 309–12; separation, 308; theories of, 170, 307–10, 312; therapy of, 140–41, 154–55, 316–17

Approval, disapproval, 92–93, 170, 307–8, 309–10

Assaultiveness, 19, 100–101, 139–41, 152, 154–55, 171, 173–74

Authority, 90, 198, 277, 281, 302–3; dependence upon, 256–57; and domination, 292, 298–99; in family structure, 90, 290–97, 303–4; of therapist, 70–73

Autonomic nervous system, 278–79, 284–85

Behavior; *see* Normal behavior

Boasting, 8

Castration complex, 295–96, 304

Catatonic state, 119, 129–30, 200–201, 211

Center for Advanced Study, Stanford, x

Change: possibility of, 102–4; resistance to, 309–11

Chicago Psychoanalytic Institute, 51 n., 97

Child development: as phases of interpersonal experience (Sullivan), 90–92, 106–7; as psychosexual phases (Freud), 89–90, 105, 107; related to forms of psychosis, 236–40, 243–45

Childhood experiences: of approval, disapproval, 92–93, 117; and creativity, 10–16; and ego development, 57–58, 198–200, 212,

236–40, 243–45; in etiology of mental illness, 92–93, 110–12, 117–18, 194, 198, 210–12, 222–24, 241–49, 286–87, 292–93, 297, 298–300, 307–8, 309–10, 326–27; and fantasy, 327; interpersonal relationships in, determined by culture, 90, 281, 290–97, 302–4, not necessarily sexual, 65, 90–91, 135, 281, 293–94, 295, 303, Oedipus constellation in, 64–65, 90, 92, 293, 300, 303, as pattern for later relationships, 64, 89, 310; love-deprivation in, 194, 198, 203, 210, 212, 292, 297–98, 326–27; repression of, 36, 108–9, 135, 210, 277–78; in toilet training, 85, 298–99, 301, 305

Closeness, ambivalence about, 153, 188, 199, 212, 243–45

Communication: of anxiety, 95 (*see also* Defense mechanisms); cryptic comments, 131–32, 212–15; forcing, 135–36; by free association, 95–96; non-verbal, 36, 129–30, 135–36, 168, 201, 202, 204, 205; of understanding, 124

Compulsion: eating, 330; hand-washing, 6; repetition, 310–12

Conscience, 49, 50, 51, 293

Conventionality: in manic-depressives, 104; in neurotics, 81–82; not a therapeutic aim, 22–23; in psychotics, 81–82, 104, 125; in schizophrenics, 175; in therapist, 81

Conversion symptoms, 53, 135, 278

Couch, 96, 133–34, 170

Countertransference, 31, 64, 65, 211, 215–17, 265–68; *defined*, 28

Creativity, 3, 4, 5, 10–16, 325

Cultural attitudes: in child-rearing, 90, 170, 281, 290–97, 302–4; and competition, 277; toward fear and anxiety, 59–60; on "maternal instinct," 294–97, 301; toward mental illness, 25–26, 31, 32; and migraine, 286–87; and unconscious drives, 49, 50

Dancing, 14–15

Death: defenses against fear of, 313–14; instinct, 50 n., 75, 236, 314–15

Defense mechanisms: as security operations, 95; *see also* Symptomatology

Defense mechanisms, types of: agoraphobia, 279–80; anger, 7–8; boasting, 8; catatonic stupor, 119, 129–30, 200–201, 211; compulsion, 6, 310–12, 330; conversion symp-

[346]

SUBJECT INDEX

toms, 53, 135, 278; cryptic comments, 131–32, 204–6; delusions, fantasy, and hallucinations, 102, 168, 198, 204, 327; elimination disturbances, 201–2, 278, 283, 285, 305; laughter, 130, 202; melancholia, 231, 280–82; migraine, 278–79, 283–89; negativism, 6, 179; obsession, 6–7, 250, 256, 258; projection, 202–3; psychosomatic symptoms, 51 n., 278–79; regression, 102, 162–63, 210; repression, 210, 277–78; self-belittling, 249–51; self-mutilation, 196–97, 198, 206; stereotypies, 129–32; sublimation, 11–16; withdrawal, 6, 11, 102, 161–63, 200–201, 280–82

Delusions, 102, 168, 198, 204

Dementia praecox, 26, 228

Dependency-hostility conflict, 198, 199, 211, 212, 258–62, 277, 292–93, 298–300; origin of, in childhood, 76–80, 92–93, 110–12, 117–18, 194, 198, 210, 212, 286–87, 297–300; symptomatology resulting from, 197, 198–208, 278–82, 250, 256, 258, 260

Depressions: anaclitic, 236, 326; common features of, 234–35; melancholic, 280–82; of mourning, 327; mourning and melancholia compared, 231; see also Manic-depressive psychosis

Doctor-patient collaboration, 50–52, 53, 64–65, 83–87, 126, 207–9; communication in, 124, 129–32, 204–6, 212–15; dependency in, 70–72, 83–85; disappointing, 118–22; establishing, 118, 135–36; interviews in, 141–43, 149–51; in manic-depressive psychosis, 251, 255, 260–65, 265–68, 270–72; physical contact in, 69–70; resistance to therapy in, 28, 38, 100, 195–96; review of case with patient, vii–viii, 217; in schizophrenia, 162, 164–66, 168, 171, 173, 178–80, 186–89, 191–92; sexual aspects of, 52, 67; successful, 83, 104, 143–44, 172–75; time elements in, 122–23, 150–52, 171; transference, 64–65, 107–8, 118–22, 206–7, 302; as a "we" experience, 103, 335

Dreams, 96, 205; compared with thoughts of psychotics, 8–9; of normals, 5; of psychotics, 9, 171–72, 184–85

Drives: Freudian conception of, 49–50; related to anxiety, 307–8; for self-achievement, 292–93

Dynamic psychiatry: and classical psychoanalysis, 49–54, 88–100, 105–12, 133–36; defined, 29; see also Psychoanalysis modified for psychotics

Ego development, vii, 57–58, 198–200, 212, 236–40, 243–45

Ego psychology, 108–9, 215

Elimination disturbances: in catatonic stupor, 201; and hostility, 201–2; in migraine, 278, 283, 285; related to toilet training, 305

Environment: effect of patient on, 187–88, 252; influence on child of, 31–33, 90, 170, 281, 304 (see also Childhood experiences)

Epilepsy, 279

Experimental neuroses: in animals, 28–29, 37, 326; drug-produced, 34; with isolation, 33, 333–34

Family structure: American, 291–92, 303–4; European, 290–91; in other cultures, 293–94, 296–97; in patriarchal and matriarchal societies, 90, 296–97, 304; in psychotic histories, 222–24, 241–49

Fear: agoraphobia, 279–80; and anxiety defined, 307; cultural attitude toward, 59–60; of hostility, 279–80; of recovery, 4; of rejection, 131, 211; in therapist, 73–74, 75, 76–78, 80–81, 317–19; in wartime, 59–60; see also Anxiety

Free association, 95–96, 134, 171

Group experience, in war, 59, 60

Group therapy, 32–33, 97, 145

Guilt, 211, 256–57, 281, 288, 307–8, 313, 314

Hallucination; see Delusion

Headache, 279; see also Migraine

Health, tendency toward, 5, 6–9, 102, 163

Hostility: in childhood, 198, 277, 293; and dependency (see Dependency-hostility conflict); fear of retaliation for, 279–80; in genesis of mental disorder, 58–59; physiological effects of, 278–79; repression of, 277–78; source in modern culture, 277; and symptomatology, 198–208; in wartime, 59

Hydrotherapy, 155

Hypnotherapy, 26–27, 28

Hypomania, 249, 254

Hysteria, 27; see also Conversion symptoms

Identification: child's, with non-aggressive parent, 302–3; in early development, 243–45; girl's, with mother, 295; in melancholics, 281; in primitive peoples, 281

Insight, 95, 194, 217

Instincts, 49–50, 294–97, 301, 308, 314–15

Intellectuality: and migraine, 287–88; and overinterpreting, 53

Intensive psychotherapy: defined, 18, 143; see Psychoanalytic psychotherapy

Intensive Psychotherapy, Principles of, ix, 317

Interpersonal relatedness, 6–8, 161, 329; and adjustment to reality, 51, 329; art and science of, 91–92; patterned on childhood relationships, 64, 89; at various ages, 90–92, 106, 243–45, 326, 327

Interpretation: "correct," 182–84; *defined*, 94–95, 166; direct, 95, 184–85; by patient, vii, 213; possibility of multiple, vii, 194, 204–6; technique of, 53, 134–35, 167–70, 180–82, 205, 212–15; timing of, 213, 215

Interview: couch in, 96, 133–34, 170; interrupted, 141–43; patient's refusal to attend, 149–50; setting for, 68–69, 84, 133–34; special, 142, 151; time elements of, 122–23, 150–52, 171

Intuition, 35, 318

Isolation: experiments in, 326, 333–34; of prisoners, 332–33; psychological, 308; tolerance for, 328–29; voluntary, 332; *see also* Loneliness

Laughter, hebephrenic, 202

Libido, 89–90; *defined*, 89

Loneliness, non-pathological forms of: aloneness, 326, 328–29; bereavement, 326; creative solitude, 325

Loneliness, as psychiatric problem: and anxiety, 329–30, 334; artistic expression of, 327, 328, 331, 332; in childhood, 326–27; communication of, 327–28, 333; defenses against, 329–30, 333; fear of, 325, 328, 332, 334; and ostracism, 325, 326–27, 328; psychotherapy of, 334–35

Love: maternal, 298–301, 303, 305, deprivation of, 194, 198, 203, 210, 212, 292, 297–98 (*see also* Childhood experiences); mature, 82; non-sexual, 303; of others, as measure of self-love, 7 (*see also* Self-respect); as "outcome of sexual attraction" (Freud), 90; as "state of relatedness" (Sullivan, Fromm), 91

Manic and/or depressive syndromes, 228, 236

Manic-depressive psychosis: anxiety in, 251; and attitudes toward authority, 256–57; classification of, 225–26, 228; compared to obsessive neurosis, 250, 256, 258; compared to schizophrenia, 104, 222–25, 244–45, 258–60; defenses in, 254, 258, 260; dependent-exploitive traits in, 249–52; doctor-patient relationship in, 251, 255, 260–65, 265–68, 270–72; dynamics of, 222–25; etiological factors in, 222–24, 229–30, 241–49; guilt feelings in, 256–57; hostility in, 252; interpersonal relatedness in, 249–52; oral character of, 227, 232, 258; psychoanalytic research on, 230–40; psychotherapy of, 104, 221, 229–30, 254, 255, 260–

72; stereotyped responses in, 224–25, 261–63, 274; suicide in, 235–36, 255–56, 270–71

Masturbation, 313

Maternal factors in mental illness, 197–98, 210, 292, 297–300

Maternal "instincts": American theories about, 294–95; Freudian concept of, 295; in other periods and cultures, 296–97, 301

Maternal "principle" (ideal parental attitude), 298–301, 305

Maternal role in family, 290–94, 296, 301, 303–4

Melancholia: etiology of, 280–81; and hostility, 281–82; and mourning, 231; suicidal impulses in, 281–82; symptoms of, 280

Mental illness: bipolarity of symptom and defense in, 6–9; cultural attitudes toward, 25–26, 31, 32; *defined*, 17; and mental health, 4, 5, 8–9, 31; postrecovery values of, 4, 5, 10, 23–24

Migraine: angioparetic variations of, 285; family background in, 286–88; and hostility, 278–79, 283–89; neuropathology of, 278–79, 284–85; symptoms of, 278, 279, 283–85; therapy of, 289

Mourning: and loneliness, 326; and melancholia, 231

Narcissism, 161–62, 210; *defined*, 19

Negativism, 6, 179

Neuroses: conventionality in, 81–82; defense mechanisms of, 3, 4, 6–9, 53; doctor-patient relationship in, 143, 152, 154; psychoanalysis of, 27, 30, 95–96, 133–36, 143, 150, 152, 154, 167, 184; and psychoses, compared, vii, 143, 150, 152, 154, 167, 184

Normal behavior: anxiety and, 198–99, 306, 307–8, 319; basic concepts of, 23, 27, 29, 32, 40, 88–92, 102; change and, 102–4; continuum from, to psychotic behavior, 4, 5, 8–9, 31; dependency-hostility conflict in, 212; psychogenic physical symptoms in, 278; and psychotic behavior, 167, 184, 198–99, 212

Obsession, 6–7, 250, 256, 258

Oedipus constellation, 64–65, 90, 92, 293, 300, 303; *defined*, 65

Panic, 170, 258, 307

Paranoia, 202–3

Parataxis, 38, 65, 95; *defined*, 65

Patient: anxiety in (*see* Defense mechanisms); dependency-hostility of, 76–80, 83–85, 118–21, 153, 188, 199, 212, 279–80; disturbed, 19, 78–79, 100–101, 139–41, 152, 154–55, 171, 173–74; needs of, 137–47;

problems of (*see* Childhood experiences; Guilt; Manic-depressive psychosis; Mental illness; Schizophrenia; Symptomatology) ; reassurance of, vii, 4, 78, 118, 120, 139–42, 203; self-respect of, 68, 78, 152; sensitivity, 139–42, 145, 152–53, 154, 164, 175; suspiciousness of, 19, 149–50, 213, 216; therapeutic values to, 4, 5, 10, 23–24, 103–4; in therapy (*see* Communication; Doctor-patient collaboration; Psychoanalytic hospital; Psychoanalytic psychotherapy; Transference)
Penis envy, 295–96, 304
Personality types, 30
Physical contact: as basic need, 335–36; in therapy, 69–70
Projection, 202–3
Psychoanalysis, 19, 28–31, 37–38, 49–54, 63–65, 88–91, 92, 97–98, 129, 133–36, 177, 198, 210, 292–96, 303–4; basic doctrines of, 105–9, 227–28; *defined*, 105
Psychoanalysis modified for psychotics: anxiety concept, 92–93, 110–12; child-development theory, 89–92, 105–7; doctor-patient relationship, 51–52, 64–65, 83–87, 107–8, 122–23, 126; drive theory, 49–50; interpretation, 53, 95, 108–9, 134–35, 167–70, 180–82, 205, 212–15; techniques, 53, 95–96, 133–36, 143 n., 160–62, 170, 175–78; types of patients, 53–54, 95–96, 109, 176–77
Psychoanalytic hospital: activities in, 143–44, 145, 148, 157; administrative therapist and psychoanalyst in, 143; assigning patients to doctors in, 143, 146; closed wards in, 141; group therapy in, 145; nurses in, 140 n., 145; patient in, disturbed, 139–41, 148–49, 152, 154–55, influenced by staff attitudes, 139–42; privileges of, 137–39; staff conferences in, 145–46; as "therapeutic community," 141–51
Psychoanalytic hospitals, examples of: Chestnut Lodge, vi, ix, 18, 146, 163, 180, 185, 189, 318; Dr. Boss's Hospital (Zurich), 163; Forest Sanitarium, 18, 163; The Haven, 18, 163; Menninger Clinic, 18, 163; St. Elizabeths, 164, 230, 331; Sheppard and Enoch Pratt, 164
Psychoanalytic psychotherapy: aims of, 18, 23, 37–40, 49, 82–83, 103, 194–96; basic concepts of, 26–31, 50–52, 93–94; choice of patients for, 53–54, 85–86, 97–98, 109, 176–77; emergency, 56–59; and interpretation of communications, 94–95, 167–70, 212–15 (*see also* Defense mechanisms; Repressed material) ; results of, 83, 103–4, 143–44, 172–75; techniques in, summarized, vii–viii, 50–53, 93–96, 133–36,

170, 175–78 (*see also* Doctor-patient collaboration)
Psychodrama, 28, 32–33
Psychogenic physical symptoms: gastrointestinal syndromes, 51 n.; in healthy persons, 278; migraine, 278–79
"Psychological death," 310–12
Psychosexual phases: in child development, 89–90, 105, 107, 162; and manic-depressives, 227, 232, 258; in regression, 162
Psychosomatics, 27, 30, 97
Psychotherapist: anxiety in, viii, 78–80, 101, 136, 174, 317–19; authority, use of, by, 70–73; conventionality in, 81; countertransference and, 2, 8, 31, 64, 65, 211, 215–17, 265–68; insecurity in, 73–81; intuition in, 35, 318; need-satisfaction of, 67–70, 84; personal psychoanalysis of, 52, 65, 86–87, 96, 102; personality requirements of, ability to listen, 65, 78–79, courage, 78–79, faith, 103–4, self-acceptance, 63, 73, 86–87, self-respect, 21, 72–73, 77; relationship to patient, impersonal empathy, 51–52, 203, indulgence, 203–4, liking, and disliking, 84–86, respect, 31, 73, 154; training of, 65–66; values of, personal, 82–84, 103, 136, professional, 103
Psychotherapy: brief, 54, 97; history of, 25–33; schools of thought in, 28, 33–34, 37–39, 52; as a science, 29, 31–33, 34–35, 35–37; *see also* Psychoanalytic psychotherapy

Reassurance, vii, 4, 78, 118, 120, 139–42, 203
Recovery: criteria for, 83; factors governing, 104; in schizophrenia, 172–75; spontaneous, 143, 144
Regression, vii, 102, 119, 161–63, 164–66, 173, 195, 198, 210, 280–82
Relatives, 32, 156–57
Repressed material, 94, 95, 135, 277–78
Resistance, 38, 103, 108–9, 195–96, 265; *defined*, 28

Satisfaction, 67–70, 84; *defined*, 66
Schizophrenia: anxiety in, 6–7, 102, 119, 164, 170, 185–86, 189, 195, 197, 198–208, 211, 258 (*see also* Anxiety) ; childhood experiences in etiology of, 161–62, 163–64, 170, 173, 189, 194, 198, 210, 212; communications in, and interpretation, 36, 53, 88, 94–96, 129–32, 160–61, 184–85, 194, 202, 205, 212–15; conventionality in, 103–4; defense symptoms in, 6–7, 102, 119, 129–32, 161–63, 198–208, 211, 280–82; doctor-patient relationship in, 162, 164–66, 168, 171, 173, 178–80, 186–89, 191–92, 212–15; dynamics of, 118–20, 163–64, 173–74, 178, 198, 203, 211, 212, 222–25; and manic-depressive

psychosis, compared, 221–25, 244–45, 258; psychotherapy of, vi–vii, 122–23, 133–36, 160–62, 175–78; recovery, 104, 172–75; regressive character of, vii, 102, 119, 161–63, 164–66, 173, 195, 198, 210, 280–82

Sedation, 56, 57, 60, 154–55

Self-acceptance, 63, 73, 86–87

Self-achievement, 292–93

Self-disapproval, 211, 281, 288, 310, 311

Self-mutilation, 196–97, 198, 206

Self-punishment, 256–57, 281, 288

Self-realization, 82, 83, 91, 310–11

Self-respect: loss of, in anxiety, 7–8; loss of, in psychoses, 68, 78, 152; and mature love, 82; and respect for others, 73; self-belittling, 249–51; in therapist, 21, 72–73, 77

"Self-system" (Sullivan), 309–10

Sex concepts, of children, 295–96, 300, 303, 304

Sex drives, 49–50

Sex-specific psychological traits, 296–97, 301 n.

Sexual attraction: child-parent, 300, 303; in therapeutic situation, 52, 67

Sexual capacity, 83

Sleep: "falling-asleep" state, 9; induced, 56, 57, 60, 154–55; in interview, 67–68; self-denial of, 281, 288

Stammering, 297

Stereotyped behavior, 129–30, 131–32, 224–25, 261–63, 274

Sublimation: defined, 11; famous examples of, 12–16

Suicide, 149, 235–36, 255–56, 270–71, 281–82, 314

Superego, 256, 293

Symptomatology, 6–9, 76, 102, 197, 198–208, 254, 258, 260, 278–82; see also Defense mechanisms

Toilet training, 85, 298–99, 301, 305

Transference, 30–31, 37, 64–65, 107–8, 118–22, 206–7, 260–65, 302; defined, 18, 28, 215

Trauma: childhood, 57–58; in infancy, 118; psychotherapy for, 56, 57–58, 59

Unconscious, the, 27, 29, 47, 88, 108–9, 129

"Victrola-record attitude," 134

Wartime psychotherapy, 55–62; role of therapist in, 60–62; theoretical basis of, 57–58, 61

Washington School of Psychiatry, ix, 180, 221, 227

"Weltanschauung," 82, 83

William A. White Foundation, 55

William A. White Institute, ix

Withdrawal, 6, 11, 102, 161–63, 200–201, 280–82

Working through, 30–31, 37, 95